Goodthink

The MIT Press's publishing mission benefits from the generosity of our donors, including Cindy and John Reed.

Goodthink

The New Science of Collective Intelligence

Damon Centola

The MIT Press
Cambridge, Massachusetts
London, England

The MIT Press
Massachusetts Institute of Technology
77 Massachusetts Avenue
Cambridge, MA 02139
mitpress.mit.edu

The MIT Press would like to thank the anonymous peer reviewers who provided comments on drafts of this book. The generous work of academic experts is essential for establishing the authority and quality of our publications. We acknowledge with gratitude the contributions of these otherwise uncredited readers.

This book was set in ITC Stone Serif Std and Trajan Pro by New Best-set Typesetters Ltd. Printed and bound in the United States of America.

Library of Congress Cataloging-in-Publication Data is available.

ISBN: 978-0-262-05468-3

10 9 8 7 6 5 4 3 2 1

EU Authorised Representative: Easy Access System Europe, Mustamäe tee 50, 10621 Tallinn, Estonia | Email: gpsr.requests@easproject.com

For Milan and Marcello
And in memory of mentors passed, Daniel Dennett and George Smith

No AI was used in the writing of this book, though plenty of CI was.

Contents

INTRODUCTION

For centuries, philosophers and social scientists have complained that social influence is the root of group madness. Even today, the belief that people are much smarter when they act alone, as solitary, reflective individuals than when they behave as members of interacting crowds holds enormous sway. There are lots of examples that support such a conviction—stock market bubbles, degrading political contests, the seemingly unstoppable spread of misinformation, the unraveling of urban neighborhoods into gang violence, and on and on.

However, the truth is just the opposite. The source of our greatest intelligence (the ability to solve complex problems, make accurate predictions, achieve coordinated behavior, and forge successful cooperation) is not our isolation from one another, nor the differences between our own beliefs and those of others. Rather, it is the very thing that has become the modern scapegoat for crowd madness: our ability to influence one another.

The ideal of independence—the idea that groups are smartest when everyone in the group makes their decisions independently—dates all the way back to the Enlightenment, and for over a century scientists have struggled to identify the right combination of individuals who, once all of their independent decisions are aggregated into a group decision, can produce the smartest collective choice. But, as I'll show you in the pages to come, it's a mistake to believe that the intelligence of groups boils down to who is in them. In fact, the secret to increasing the intelligence of collectives is to structure the networks between people to transform the crowd's wisdom into the wisdom of individuals—what I call *structural intelligence*.

Because I am a sociologist who studies the dynamics of social change, I have a unique perspective on all of this. In 2002, I began unraveling the mysteries of how ideas and behaviors spread across our personal networks. In the decades since, my team and I have worked to decipher how these vast channels of social influence affect changes in our intelligence. Now, thanks to scientific approaches leagues more sophisticated than were possible when I started, we have our first glimpse of the scientific principles governing collective intelligence.

Twenty years ago, this book would have been impossible to write. The science simply wasn't there yet. In fact, it is only in the last few years that some of these scientific puzzles, which have lasted for nearly a century, have finally been solved. These breakthroughs are due in large part to the unprecedented power of new computational methods, and the remarkable precision with which large-scale internet experiments reveal the real-time collective outcomes that emerge from thousands of people—voters, music fans, patients, financial investors, doctors, engineers, scientists—making real-time decisions.

Putting all of these findings together into a single picture is thrilling, but it requires humility; there are after all vast areas of human activity that still remain inscrutable to scientific theory. The undeniable excitement of this project comes from the fact that this new scientific picture is surprisingly effective for tackling many of the most immediate challenges that individuals, firms, and nations confront every day. As a result, we'll explore not only mathematical simulations and traditional theories of networks, but unexpected moments of cultural synchronization, surprising secrets behind the world's most innovative research centers, and the triumph of mutual understanding across political echo chambers. "Cracking the code" of such dynamics reveals how we can establish social networks that produce creativity and inspire collaborative outcomes.

Take the internet.

In the early 1990s, the launch of popular internet tools to accelerate global connectedness, like web browsers and chat rooms, invited us all to look to the horizon, enthralled by the breathtaking promise of unprecedented mass speech. It was a new form of informational transparency that was supposed to offer improved understanding across social divisions and give rise to universal access to accurate information.

In 1996, Judge Stewart Dalzell was one of the first federally appointed jurists to assess the First Amendment status of the internet. He wrote:

> It is no exaggeration to conclude that the Internet has achieved, and continues to achieve, the most participatory marketplace of mass speech that this country—and indeed the world—has yet seen. . . . Federalists and non-Federalists may debate the structure of their government nightly, but in newsgroups or chat rooms rather than in pamphlets. Modern-day Luthers still post their theses, but to electronic bulletin boards rather than the door of the Wittenberg Schlosskirche.

The dawn of the internet was indeed a heady time for scholars of society. But it appears that the predicted zenith of intellectual exchange (if it ever existed) is behind us now. Today, the dangers of social influence have become an accepted fact of modern life, so much so that the ill-fated trajectory of interacting collectives on the internet has become a banality for an entire generation. Even well-established scientific conclusions about global warming and tobacco risks (to take but two examples) appear subject to the capricious trajectories of the collective online mind. As we watch the arc of our collective intelligence descend back toward the Earth, an increasingly destructive result seems inevitable.

But it isn't.

Because in social networks intelligence has its own kind of gravity, which enables collectives to be pulled toward an improved understanding of the world, and of each other, without even realizing that they are moving. The collective structure of our social networks determines the trajectory of our individual choices. A change in structure can change a group's mood. It can alter people's collective beliefs. And it can significantly increase the intelligence of an entire population. What's amazing is that this can happen without actively removing disinformation or censoring public discourse. It happens just by letting people talk to one another in a structure that is designed to increase their collective intelligence.

It is important to remember that social networks are not necessarily digital. They have existed for as long as humans have been around. They include everyone we talk to, collaborate with, live near, and seek out. Our personal networks make up our social world. The science of social networks studies the web that binds our overlapping social worlds together—from neighbors living on the same street to strangers on different continents—and how changing patterns of interaction can increase intelligence and engagement among us.

The idea that social networks can affect collective intelligence is not new. Social networks have long been central to debates about how free societies succeed. In the mid-1800s, Alexis de Tocqueville and John Stuart Mill were outspoken admirers of the young democracy on the North American continent. In particular, they were fascinated by the sense of personal responsibility and integrity that pervaded citizens' accounts of their own civic duty. Tocqueville was especially enthralled by New England town meetings, which he believed illustrated a new breed of "public spirit" in which citizens felt accountable for the success of their government. Tocqueville judged this form of social responsibility to be historically unique—a spirit of democratic engagement that European democracies had not yet come to enjoy.

There is a blissful feeling of camaraderie that can emerge from these civic moments of public spirit. But a sense of civic responsibility alone is not enough. A vigorous public debate needs to be grounded in a functioning system of collective intelligence—for what good is a town meeting if everyone walks away with a renewed sense of civic pride yet having made a poor collective decision?

To be useful, the science of collective intelligence requires a way to resolve the ancient tension between what people feel and what people know. This is a problem that haunted James Madison, who was not among the town meeting faithful. In 1787, he declared:

> Pure democracy, by which I mean a society consisting of a small number of citizens, who assemble and administer the government in person, can admit of no cure for the mischiefs of faction. A common passion or interest will, in almost every case, be felt by a majority of the whole; and there is nothing to check the inducements to sacrifice the weaker party or an obnoxious individual.

This problem of the "tyranny of the majority" has long plagued champions of democracy. The danger hidden within the popular ideal of the "voice of the people" is that it silences not just the minority voices but also the best voices. Even Tocqueville lamented that majority rule "bases its claim to rule upon numbers, not upon rightness or excellence." For centuries, this concern has led authors to conclude that many (in fact most) of the citizens in a populace may not be well enough informed to serve as effective members of its electorate.

My findings offer a new take on this old problem. Knowledge should not be a prerequisite for political participation because, in the right structures, participation becomes the best source for enhancing people's knowledge. Uninformed citizens become informed citizens by virtue of properly structured civic engagement. In fact, my findings reveal that the extent of individual learning that takes place within a collective—that is, the extent of improvement in individual opinions—is often the best metric for the quality of the collective decision. As you will see, this conclusion can be put to work immediately in the places we inhabit the most—on the internet, in the neighborhoods where we live, and within the organizations where we work.

Across these settings, our daily lives are pervaded by four grand challenges of collective intelligence: choosing, creativity, coordination, and cooperation. For generations, the problem that has hamstrung the science of collective intelligence has been identifying the boundaries between these distinct challenges. The conflation of each with the other has produced thousands of scientific studies without any coherent understanding of how the findings fit together. Individually, each study is thoughtfully executed, but as a collective body of knowledge they are incoherent. As Copernicus famously protested, "[I]t is just like someone taking from various places hands, feet, a head, and other pieces, very well depicted. . . . [B]ut not for the representation of a single person . . . a monster rather than a man would be put together from them." This book offers a unifying perspective that carefully delineates these grand challenges and identifies new solutions to them.

These four grand challenges share a rare and valuable feature: In every case, the intelligence of both individuals and groups is objectively measurable. Once you see how each of these grand challenges works, you will see that together they offer us a larger picture that allows us to anticipate the consequences of each one for the other.

1. *The Grand Challenge of Choosing.* When independently making a choice, we are sometimes forced to do so without feedback about the quality of our guess, or about the quality of anyone else's guesses. Think

about guessing the future price of a well-known stock or estimating the impact of foreign aid on our economy. There is a lot of information out there, but it's hard to know which bits matter the most for forming an accurate estimate. Without knowledge of the accuracy of anyone's beliefs, an exchange of ideas may only result in the blind leading the blind.

2. *The Grand Challenge of Creativity.* Unlike the grand challenge of choosing, the grand challenge of creativity focuses on problems in which teams must work together to innovate and make novel discoveries. Researchers can test their ideas, gathering continual feedback about quality. But how much information should be shared among the researchers? Without any communication, siloed team members would be unable to learn from one another's mistakes and innovations. However, too much communication among team members might result in rapid convergence on a familiar solution, unintentionally limiting the exploration of unusual ideas that could lead to breakthrough discoveries.

3. *The Grand Challenge of Coordination.* There are some challenges for which the success of our individual choices is determined by how well we match our choices with everyone else's. (Oftentimes for social conventions, it may not even matter which behavior we match on, so long as we match.) Usually, we succeed so often that the grand challenge of coordination is invisible to us—for instance, when we walk down a busy hallway or choose what to wear to work. However, when conventions suddenly break down, as they did during the 2020 pandemic—when the simple act of standing in line for groceries suddenly became a mentally taxing and socially complex behavior—we quickly realize just how difficult and pervasive this grand challenge actually is.

4. *The Grand Challenge of Cooperation.* Perhaps the oldest puzzle of collective intelligence is how cooperation can succeed in a world where defection is rewarded with greater individual success. The best answer so far has come from the principle of reciprocity, which has proven to be a robust rule for sustaining cooperative societies. But what happens when we cannot rely on reputation, for instance, because our interactions are anonymous or because we are forced by necessity to trade with people we've never met before? How can we trust that they will give us a fair deal?

The first part of this book addresses the grand challenge of choosing. The next parts of the book unravel the grand challenge of coordination, followed by the grand challenge of cooperation, and, finally, the grand challenge of creativity. This analytical approach allows me to address an overlooked problem in the science of collective intelligence: the problem of *collective adaptation*—the source of the unintended consequences that arise whenever a structure that solves one grand challenge unintentionally creates new problems for other grand challenges. The greatest impediment, by far, to collective success is the failure to foresee the unintended consequences that inevitably emerge from well-intentioned solutions. This book shows how we can anticipate these unintended consequences, and what can be done to guide the adoption of intelligent decision structures within the ever-evolving landscape of social networks and grand challenges.

At a moment when we need structural intelligence more than ever, these discoveries could not be more essential. With that in mind, I urge you to embrace the first of our grand challenges, and choose to turn the page.

I

Choosing

1

Why We're Not as Smart as We Could Be—Yet

Telecom billionaire Donald Burns was sick of the fancy Bermuda-style homes lining the Florida waterfront. Burns was different, and he wanted his new house to reflect his Spartan motto of "lifestyle simplicity." Oddly, given the phrase, he wanted this new home to be twice the size of the other mansions along the elite Palm Beach coastline.

The Town of Palm Beach did not share Burns's vision, but Burns was up for a fight, so much so that his team of white-shoe lawyers dragged the municipality all the way to the Supreme Court of the United States. But, just as Burns was about to enjoy the sweet taste of simplicity (Palm Beach style), an unexpected voice from the past torpedoed his plans. It was none other than Founding Father James Madison.

The presiding factor governing the legality of Burns's maverick mansion was whether it was protected by the First Amendment (drafted by Madison in 1789). According to the law of the land, if the "structure's predominant purpose was to be communicative," it would be protected by Madison's famous defense of free speech. The Court ruled that the proposed residence was neither artistic nor expressive, and that a viewer of Burns's masterpiece was unlikely to understand it to be anything other than "a *really* big house."

We'll call that a win for the little guy. You go, James Madison.

In fact, James Madison shows up in a lot of Supreme Court cases. And not just him: Pretty much every major Supreme Court case that you know of, and dozens that you've never heard of, make unflinching reference to the ideas and opinions of the Founding Fathers and to their intellectual influences, such as John Locke.

It only takes a quick glance beneath the surface of our modern world to see that the big ideas from centuries past are still governing our lives. They circumscribe our freedoms, shape our understanding of ourselves, and guide our expectations for civic life. Yet how these classical ideas should be integrated into modern living is far from straightforward.

Unlike the natural sciences, where practice often leads to agreed-upon fact, many of the greatest contemporary debates in the social sciences reach back hundreds of years and remain ongoing. For a new synthesis to succeed—and to understand what the science of collective intelligence can offer for our lives today—we need to be able to see clearly the key assumptions about human behavior that laid the foundation for our current predicaments, and what they reveal about where we are going next.

As we explore this archaeology of ideas, I will show you pivotal moments in the development of collective intelligence that have led us to the global challenges of the present. You will quickly see that although we are at the forefront of a new science, our contemporary ideas are driven by the same fierce intellectual urgency that, just a few short centuries ago, led to the revolutionary overthrow of governments in America and France. For then as now, the science of collective intelligence is the science of freedom.

THE TERROR

In the autumn of 1793, terror was spreading through the streets of Paris. Four years had passed since the glory days when French citizens stormed the Bastille and claimed liberty for all. Back then, the Marquis de Condorcet had been celebrated as one of the great intellectual champions of the French Revolution. But once the campaign of Terror began, no one was safe. Thousands of French citizens were executed within a year, and many more were being hunted.

Hiding in his friend's basement in the 6th arrondissement, Condorcet listened to the screams of his countrymen as the vicious revolutionary government culled its citizens. Yet after living in secret for half a year, Condorcet's paranoia eventually dissipated, and in the spring of 1794 he abandoned his hideout. Within days, he was captured and killed.

But not before making his mark on history.

Today, Condorcet is regarded as perhaps the most influential political thinker of the modern era. The centerpiece of his contribution is a simple theorem on democracy. It proves when and how democratic rule by the masses can achieve collective intelligence for all. The irony of Condorcet's famous theorem was not lost on him. In his final days, he recorded his thoughts on the matter.

THE 51 PERCENT MIRACLE

Condorcet's recipe for intelligent democracy begins with the basic assumption that everyone is terrible at making good choices. If we are forced to choose between two candidates, a coin flip gives us a 50 percent chance of choosing the right answer. Condorcet's master stroke was to show that even if people individually have only a flimsy 51 percent chance of getting the right answer, a big group of those people put together has a much better chance of choosing the right answer than any individual in the group. And the bigger the group—that is, the more inclusive the democracy—the greater the chance that the popular choice will indeed be the right one.

Suppose there are ten people choosing between two candidates. Each person has a 51 percent likelihood of choosing the better option. A minimal majority of six voters has a 52 percent chance of choosing correctly. Not much better than one individual choosing alone. The collective vote is basically random.

Now let's open the vote to 1,000 people. Even though the individuals in this large group are not any better at choosing than the original ten people (every person still has 51 percent chance of guessing right), something magical happens in a large group. The likelihood of the collective vote choosing the right answer jumps from 52 percent to 73 percent.

How good can this get? Let's increase the number of people voting to 100,000 people, or one million people. A successful choice is almost guaranteed. In fact, in a large enough democracy, a group of individuals with almost no personal ability to choose the right option will collectively always make the right choice.

This isn't just a theory of democracy. It is *the* theory of democracy.

But there is a dark lining to this silvery cloud. It is the inescapable question of whether it is really such a good idea for uninformed masses to have equal influence in democratic elections. If some people are simply more informed than others about candidates, policies, world affairs, and the inner workings of the economy, shouldn't their opinions be given greater weight than those of the uninformed individuals who lack any knowledge of these things? The naïve democratic assumption is that they absolutely should. But that far from resolves the question. In every nascent democracy from the Americas to Asia, the question inevitably arises: Should poorly educated people be permitted to influence the course of national elections?

A clever extension of Condorcet's theorem reveals why uninformed voters not only can vote but *should* vote. This finding is often referred to as the *miracle of aggregation*. Unlike Condorcet's generous assumption that people have a 51 percent chance of getting the answer right, this approach assumes that almost everyone is uninformed, and thus has a 50 percent coin-flip chance of guessing correctly. Nevertheless, we may also assume that there will always be a small number of highly informed souls in any collective. Unlike the uninformed 90 percent of the population, the informed 10 percent are knowledgeable enough to know which option is the right choice.

At first glance, 90 percent random guesses versus 10 percent informed opinions does not sound like good odds for a successful democracy. For a small group, it's not. If ten people are voting, nine people will choose randomly and one will choose wisely. In such a small group, the informed individual has virtually no control over who will win. The collective choice is essentially random.

But here's the miracle.

Take a much larger democracy, with 100,000 people. Ninety thousand of these people are uninformed and will therefore vote randomly. This evens out to 45,000 votes for one candidate and 45,000 votes for the other. The remaining 10,000 votes are then cast by the informed citizens. The result? The better candidate wins by a margin of 55,000 to 45,000! This miracle only gets better with size. The larger the democracy, the more certain the outcome is. Even though larger democracies have more uninformed voters, they are nevertheless far more likely to make the right collective choice.

Here is the most interesting part. The success of democracy only works if we encourage *all* of the uninformed voters to vote. The more voters there are, the greater the chances that the random votes will cancel each other out, allowing the informed individuals to guide the collective choice. Very large masses of uninformed voters guarantee the intelligence of the outcome. That is the miracle of aggregation.

A 2,000-Year Grudge Match

The problem with the miracle of aggregation is that it very often fails us. To understand what goes wrong, we need to take a quick trip back in time to the original discovery of the intelligence of collectives.

Writing around 350 BCE, the ancient Greek philosopher Aristotle was among the earliest thinkers to appreciate that collectives might have a kind of intelligence that a single person does not. He knew this idea had big implications for society.

> The multitude, though not individually good men, yet when they come together may be better, not individually but collectively, than those who are so—just as public dinners to which many contribute are better than those supplied at one man's cost. For where there are many, each individual has some portion of virtue and wisdom, and when they have come together, just as the multitude becomes a single man with many feet and many hands and many senses, so also it becomes one personality as regards the moral and intellectual faculties. This is why the general public is a better judge of the works of music and those of the poets, because different men can judge a different part of the performance, and all of them all of it.

Aristotle offered an inspiringly democratic vision of collective intelligence. Because we all bring something unique to the table, together we are able to enjoy a shared feast that is far better than any portion of it that we might enjoy alone. This idea made an indelible mark on the Western imagination. In 1971, two millennia after Aristotle first penned this principle, Harvard University philosopher John Rawls mused:

> In everyday life the exchange of opinion with others checks our partiality and widens our perspective; we are made to see things from the standpoint of others and the limits of our vision are brought home to us. . . . Even representative legislators are limited in knowledge and the ability to reason. No one of them knows everything the others know, or can make all the same inferences that they can draw in concert.

It is a reassuring notion that humans can enjoy a form of collective harmony that makes us both more intelligent and more successful than our individual logic alone allows for. Aristotle analogizes this natural capacity for a more-than-the-sum-of-its-parts kind of collective intelligence to the collective harmony enjoyed by other social species, like bees and ants. Collective intelligence is, for Aristotle, part of the essential nature of all political animals.

But there is a big problem with Aristotle's view. It has echoed down through the ages and still confronts us today with the very real challenges that we face in national political debates. The problem is that people do not have much of an incentive to intelligently combine their respective views. Why not simply argue for the supremacy of their own beliefs rather than try to shoehorn their ideas into a shared perspective? Beyond that, even if people did have an incentive to combine their ideas, there is a technical challenge. How exactly should we combine the enormous diversity of views found among the multitude? What machinery ensures that people's diverse perspectives will complement one another to make a bountiful feast, rather than simply lead to an endless competition of all against all?

These concerns were brought to a head in 1651 by the British philosopher Thomas Hobbes, who responded to Aristotle's beatific vision of human collective intelligence with unprecedented skepticism:

> It is true, that certain living creatures, as Bees and Ants, live sociably one with another, (which are therefore by Aristotle numbered amongst Political creatures;) and yet have no other direction, than their particular judgments and appetites. . . . [T]herefore some man may perhaps desire to know, why Man-kind cannot do the same. . . . To which I answer . . . that men are continually in competition for Honor and Dignity, which these creatures are not . . . [and] these creatures, having not (as man) the use of reason, do not see, nor think they see any fault, in the administration of their common business: whereas amongst men, there are very many, that think themselves wiser, and abler to govern the Publique, better than the rest; and these strive to reforme and innovate, one this way, another that way; and thereby bring it in Distraction and Civill warre.

Hobbes cleverly upends Aristotle with the simple observation that the human capacity for reason, creativity, and ambition inevitably drives citizens to challenge one another for power. Unlike other political species, our uniquely human gifts lead us into an endless competition for advantage. The Enlightenment was in many ways a century-long attempt to answer Hobbes's challenge. But for Hobbes, the only way out of perpetual war is for people to subjugate themselves under the rule of a monarch with absolute power. In essence, Hobbes concedes that perhaps we should indeed do what the bees do, and place ourselves under the rule of a queen. Strikingly, in the chapters ahead you will find that this solution is not far from what has happened in the virtual world of social media.

Hobbes's stark view of human society is not what Condorcet had in mind. But neither did Condorcet share Aristotle's optimistic vision of organic harmony. For Condorcet, the proper working of society required adherence to strict rules. He believed in the mathematical principles that could reliably extract intelligence from ordinary collectives.

Condorcet promised no great banquet. He did not see collective intelligence as a harmonious experience of intellectual discovery. It was simply the proper tallying of votes. Intelligence came from the correctness of the collective choice, not the discovery of new options. For Condorcet, the only thing that was unknown was which of the options the people would choose.

Aristotle wanted something more. For him, the virtue of collective intelligence was that it allows groups to discover insights that could not be found by any individual alone. For Aristotle, the collective mind was special because it outpaced individual ability.

The problem with Aristotle's inspiring vision is that he does not give us the machinery to get there. Hobbes's response to Aristotle is to deny that any such machinery exists. In Hobbes's version of things, Aristotle's beautiful feast will inevitably deteriorate into a barnyard feeding trough.

Whatever the human potential for collective intelligence may be, we cannot make use of it unless we understand how a debate among peers could produce anything more than the simple victory of one side over another. To grasp the potential for collective intelligence, we need to know if there are any mechanisms that are capable of bringing forth new kinds of shared intelligence from a multitude of competing views.

Fortunately, if the Enlightenment was good for anything, it was good for mechanisms.

Rousseau's Idiot-Proof Recipe

Now I want to take you back to the Enlightenment, around 1760, a few decades before Condorcet's big breakthrough. We arrive at the countryside home of our hero, Jean-Jacques Rousseau.

Rousseau is the lynchpin in our story. His work takes us from the ancient harmony of collective intelligence to the modern logic of democratic society. His writings laid the foundation for the modern social scientific conception of collective intelligence, including several of the key principles underlying Condorcet's thinking. He also provided the key inspiration for the French and American Revolutions, which still guide much of our thinking today. Rousseau's pivotal role in these historical events comes from the fact that he was among the first thinkers to identify the exact machinery that would be needed to achieve collective intelligence from the masses.

The big idea at the center of it all is Rousseau's concept of the *general will*.

The general will is only found through the careful balancing out of the many sides from citizens' self-interested opinions, known as *particular wills*. Like Aristotle, Rousseau believed that collective intelligence is something greater than the sum of its individual parts. Rousseau's big leap forward was to claim that simply adding up people's opinions will not do anything more than reiterate people's private desires. By contrast, the general will could be discovered by balancing out overestimates and underestimates to reveal the collective truth that emerges from them.

Rousseau's balancing-out procedure offers a way to combine people's earnest, if inaccurate, views of the world to produce a novel collective view that is more accurate and insightful than any of the particular wills. This newly revealed collective intelligence is the general will.

Here is Rousseau's step-by-step recipe for how to achieve collective intelligence:

> If the populace held its deliberations (on the basis of adequate information) without the citizens communicating with one another, what emerged from all the little particular wills would always be the general will, and the decision would always be good.
>
> But when plots and deals lead to the formation of partial associations at the expense of the big association . . . the particular wills become less numerous and give a less general result.

> If the general will is to emerge clearly, it's important that there should be no partial society within the state, and that each citizen should think only his own thoughts . . . And if there are partial societies, it's best to have as many as possible and to prevent them from becoming unequal . . . These precautions are the only ones that can ensure that the general will is always enlightened and that the populace is never in error.

Rousseau concludes that it only takes three mechanistic principles to guarantee the collective intelligence of a multitude:

1. People are informed.
2. People think and choose independently.
3. A large fraction of the populace participates.

In short: information, independence, and inclusiveness.

The modern view of collective intelligence is by and large Rousseau's view, with an unexpected twist added by Condorcet.

One of Condorcet's core innovations was the discovery of a hidden relationship between information and inclusiveness—or, in Condorcet's terms, between information and size. A few pages ago, I showed you that each person only needs to be right about 51 percent of the time in order for a large democratic population to make good choices.

This appears to be a reassuring insight. If we allow for Condorcet's and Rousseau's minimal assumption about information (that is, individuals are informed enough to be accurate 51 percent of the time), then all it really takes for collective intelligence to succeed is independence and size.

That does not seem like a big ask, but . . .

Brace yourself—the other shoe is about to fall.

There is a second half to Condorcet's big theorem at the heart of democracy. It reveals a much less optimistic side of things. We already know that if people are able to guess correctly more than 50 percent of the time, then big collectives are basically guaranteed to succeed. But what happens if people are right *less than* 50 percent of the time? In that case, large multitudes will fail. And they will fail huge. In fact, the larger a collective is, the more certain it is that the popular choice will always be the wrong choice. Condorcet's insight cuts to the heart of the miracle of aggregation. If we cannot assume that most people are at least as good as a coin flip, then the small minority of informed citizens will always wind up being governed by the uninformed opinions of the majority.

Even if most people are right 49 percent of the time, large-group democracy fails. In this situation, a smaller group of elites is significantly more likely to choose a better answer than a large group of citizens. And the worse that people are, individually, at guessing the right answer (48 percent, 47 percent, and so on), the smaller the group that makes the ultimate choice should be.

From here, things go in a decidedly antidemocratic direction.

If people are consistently less accurate than a coin flip, the best outcome is derived from having a very small group of people, or perhaps even a single person, choose for the entire population. (You can see where this is going.)

If an uninformed electorate is even slightly biased toward making a bad choice, then a popular vote is guaranteed to lead everyone to ruin. In this all-too-common situation, less inclusive governments run by a small group of elites are smarter than big governments run by a democratic multitude. The smaller the number of voters, the better the collective outcome for everyone. We can easily arrive at a situation in which the most informed person for choosing between, say, electoral candidates also happens to be one of the candidates. So much for democracy.

Condorcet's pessimistic conclusion is a far cry from Aristotle's naturalistic vision of collective intelligence. For Condorcet, it is not about a beautiful feast. It's just about the numbers. Everything comes down to a 1 percent difference. If each of us is 1 percent better than a coin flip at guessing the right answer, massive democracy is always right. If each of us is 1 percent worse, massive democracy is guaranteed to get it wrong.

In that small margin hangs the fate of society. The bad news: It takes only a tiny bit of bad judgment to make things a lot worse. The good news: It takes very little improvement to makes things a lot better.

Hard Problems, Easy Problems, and Information Problems

Information is the knife edge that divides the promise of large-scale collective intelligence from the tyranny of the uninformed mob. From Condorcet's point of view, the only question that matters is whether the population is informed enough to be right more than 50 percent of the time. If so, then all we need are independence and size, and we are guaranteed to have a collective win. But if not, then we need to give up on Aristotle's beautiful idea of collective intelligence from the multitude.

A few years ago, some brave souls set out to measure people's chances of being right 51 percent of the time. Their strategy was to compare popular opinions on important policy topics to expert opinions on those topics. These widely discussed results proved to be a major blow to the idea of large-scale collective intelligence. In a poll conducted by *The Washington Post,* Americans were asked which of the following six budget categories were the two top areas of federal government spending in 1993: foreign aid, welfare, federal debt, defense, social security, or health. The most popular choice, selected by 41 percent of respondents, was foreign aid. In reality, the top two spending categories were social security (21.6 percent of the federal budget) and defense (20.7 percent). Foreign aid was the lowest of the six (just 1.2 percent).

This discrepancy between popular opinion and the actual facts is important because it directly impacts the kinds of policies that candidates can support during their campaigns. For instance, an incumbent candidate who suggests an increase in foreign aid as a thoughtful measure to stem the tide of international economic warfare may be voted out of office by constituents who incorrectly believe that most of their tax dollars are already going to foreign aid. A challenger candidate who promises to reduce spending on foreign aid may win the election on the strength of this promise even though such a policy would have very little impact on the federal budget and may inadvertently create new economic tensions abroad.

But the news is not all bad.

Here is another poll question given in 1993: "When your child reaches your age, do you expect them to have a higher or lower standard of living?" Everyone (experts and laypersons) agreed that their children's standard of living would be "about the same" as their own.

Only sometimes do people have enough information to pierce the 51 percent barrier. What does this portend for large-scale collective intelligence? Scholars of American democracy, like Mill and John Dewey, worked diligently to solve this problem over a century ago. They believed that the only solution was to educate the masses. Without superb educational institutions, collective intelligence would be unreliable, and democracy could not be trusted.

Today, scientists have come up with a new way of handling this challenge. To make sense of the inconsistent quality of popular knowledge, one strategy has been to divide the policy world into hard problems and easy problems. For easy problems, people are generally correct more than 50 percent of the time, so the multitude will be collectively wise. However, on hard problems, the opposite is true. People are typically below 50 percent, so the masses will inevitably get it wrong. On these problems, large-scale democracy leads to failure.

Unfortunately, this approach is not terribly optimistic. If we divide the world's problems into easy and hard, we are likely to find out that most of them are hard. Certainly, a problem like how to divvy up water rights in parched California is a hard one. But if we're honest, so is choosing a leader who will serve the common good. In fact, the greater the terrain surveyed, the more pervasive hard problems appear to be. For this reason, there is a growing body of scientific scholarship today that argues that citizens are, generally speaking, insufficiently informed to be effective participants in democratic decision-making.

This skepticism is not new. Doubts about the potential for collective intelligence among uninformed citizens was a concern well before the Enlightenment and endured through centuries of debate about democracy. Even before the French Revolution, Condorcet had misgivings about welcoming the unschooled masses into voting booths. But the Reign of Terror showed the world just how dangerous a government run by the people could be. Instead of a wise collective polity, the new French government devolved into violent score-settling and factional warfare. As the philosopher Thomas Hobbes had predicted, the only way to end the "war of all against all" was for the people to submit to the rule of an absolute monarch—a leviathan who could save the unruly and unsophisticated multitude from themselves.

THE TROUBLEMAKERS

With Condorcet's death in 1794, the end of the Enlightenment drew nigh. France's bold experiment in democracy quickly backslid into autocracy, just as Hobbes foretold. Only a few years after French citizens ran through the streets of Paris crying freedom, they bowed in reverence to the crowning of Napoleon Bonaparte. It was the rise of the French empire. A Romantic vision of European nationalism swept across the Continent. In stark contrast to the Enlightenment philosophers' obsession with the mechanistic principles of social order, a new zeitgeist of historical inevitability loomed over the estates of old Europe.

In England and on the Continent, the Industrial Revolution was in full swing. Unbridled new wealth was emerging, and its opponents were amassing. The brave new philosophy of Communism would soon embolden the working class.

Change was everywhere, and emotions were running high. The aristocracy grappled with these tectonic shifts in society by rekindling a long-held distrust of the multitude. A vigorous new skepticism about crowd intelligence took hold.

In 1841, the Scottish journalist Charles Mackay published his time-worn classic, *Extraordinary Popular Delusions and the Madness of Crowds*. His three-volume tome reported on historical patterns of market bubbles and crashes, social epidemics, and mass hysteria, attributing these collective eccentricities to the irrepressible irrationality of crowd behavior. In one of his more famous examples, Mackay gleefully details the remarkable explosion of tulip bulb prices in Holland, beginning in 1634—a phenomenon known ever after as "tulip mania."

This colorful story of Dutch exuberance abruptly ends in 1637 with the collapse of the tulip market and an ensuing economic depression. Although Mackay's journalistic account of market mania has been effectively debunked by recent economic historians, his narrative is nevertheless a sticky one. His stories offer a compelling and entertaining view of human collective behavior. So much so that his Victorian-era text is still used today by many scholars as an authoritative account of the challenges of achieving collective intelligence in free markets.

By the end of the nineteenth century, skepticism about collective intelligence among the masses was *de rigueur* among the intelligentsia. In 1890, the great French sociologist Gabriel Tarde defined crowd behavior as a novel species of criminal behavior.

> A mob is a strange phenomenon. It is a gathering of heterogenous elements, unknown to one another; but as soon as a spark of passion,

> having flashed out from one of these elements, electrifies this confused mass, there takes place a sort of sudden organization, a spontaneous generation. This incoherence becomes cohesion, this noise becomes a voice, and these thousands of men crowded together soon form but a single animal, a wild beast without a name which marches to its goal with an irresistible finality. The majority of these men had assembled out of pure curiosity, but the fever of some of them soon reached the minds of all, and in all of them there arose a delirium. The very man who had come running to oppose the murder of an innocent person is one of the first to be seized with the homicidal contagion, and moreover, it does not occur to him be astonished at this.

Going still further, in 1896 the French polymath Gustave Le Bon capped off the nineteenth century with perhaps the most memorable and long-lived jeremiad against crowd intelligence to date:

> The present epoch is one of these critical moments in which the thought of mankind is undergoing a process of transformation. . . . While all our ancient beliefs are tottering and disappearing, while the old pillars of society are giving way one by one, the power of the crowd is the only force that nothing menaces, and of which the prestige is continually on the increase. The age we are about to enter will in truth be the *Era of Crowds*. . . . The divine right of the masses is about to replace the divine right of kings.

Le Bon's text is dripping with aristocratic anxiety about the rising tide of democratic and Communist sympathies across Europe. His class-based rhetoric notwithstanding, there is one observation about which Le Bon was infamously not wrong: "An orator wishing to move a crowd must make an abusive use of violent affirmations. To exaggerate, to affirm, to resort to repetitions, and never to attempt to prove anything by reasoning, are methods of argument well known to speakers at public meetings."

Here Le Bon's study veers away from scientific description toward something more like a playbook for political manipulation. It is a playbook that was well-known to twentieth-century fascist leaders like Benito Mussolini and Adolf Hitler, who both owned dog-eared copies of Le Bon's text. The same methods of which Le Bon speaks are still used today by numerous politicians and pundits.

At the dawn of the twentieth century, these concerns about the unbridled power of the unruly crowd were top of mind for intellectuals and the aristocracy. Le Bon's critique of crowds was well-known and highly appreciated. Yet, surprisingly, it was against this backdrop of antidemocratic sentiment that the modern idea of collective intelligence found its greatest and most unlikely champion.

The Ox and the Aristocrat

The old chestnut about the ox and aristocrat is one of the weirdest and most beloved stories in the annals of collective intelligence. The story begins with a high-society English scientist named Francis Galton. In the 1860s, Galton's cousin, Charles Darwin, had won international fame for his theory of natural selection. Darwin of course did not dare to speculate about what his discoveries might imply for artificial selection among humans, but Galton did—making his reputation from his pioneering study of a pseudo-Darwinian pseudoscience called *eugenics*. Intellectually speaking, Galton's research program was as bad as it gets, and some scholars of the day deplored it. Yet for many members of the aristocracy, it set their minds at ease, freeing them from their rising fears about the growing power of the masses.

Eager to make a bigger name for himself among the British peerage, Galton set out to prove once and for all that democracy—that is, the rule of the uninformed crowd—was a fundamentally flawed idea. Amusing himself one afternoon at a country fair, he came across a carnival game in which peasants and farmworkers were attempting to guess the dressed weight of an ox. ("Dressed weight" is a euphemism for the total tonnage of meat, bone, and fat on a slaughtered animal's carcass.) "Surely," Galton would have reasoned, "a husbandry expert would be far more qualified to guess the exact weight of the slaughtered animal than a crowd of uneducated citizens." Galton collected the guesses of nearly 800 fairgoers, and then, once the animal's dressed weight was known, compared the guesses to the correct amount. Remarkably, the collective guess was within 1 percent of the true answer. In 1907, Galton published his result in the elite scientific journal *Nature*. It became an instant classic.

The story of Galton's heroic demonstration of the wisdom of the democratic crowd has been repeated thousands of times. Enough times, in fact, that despite Galton's intellectual indiscretions, history remembers him kindly. His narrow escape may well have come down to a single, self-reflective sentence in his 1907 paper: "The result is, I think, more creditable to the democratic judgment than might have been expected."

Galton's reluctant concession nicely sums up the prevailing view of collective intelligence throughout the twentieth century. Writing nearly one hundred years after Galton, *New Yorker* staff writer James Surowiecki (in his 2004 book *The Wisdom of Crowds*) recounts his own experience with collective intelligence by saying, "Even after I'd written an entire book about collective wisdom, there was still a part of me that instinctively questioned whether it would really work. This story is, I think, a testament to how uncanny—and counterintuitive—the wisdom of crowds really is."

History is littered with independent discoveries of the idea that the collective tendency of a group is more intelligent than the tendencies of its individual members. But the most surprising implication is not that crowds are wise, but that Rousseau and Condorcet were both wrong. They both argued information was essential for collective intelligence, but Galton showed that it actually wasn't. Citizens do not need to be expertly informed for their collective guesses to make expert-level judgments. In fact, each individual can be quite far below the 51 percent threshold, and yet, thanks to crowd size and independent deliberation, the collective judgment may nevertheless still be spot-on.

For a century, scientific consensus held fast to Galton's conclusion that independence and size alone are sufficient to secure collective intelligence. Yet, despite this consensus, the explanation for why this works as well as it does remained unclear until 2007.

THE DIVERSITY WEDGE

Scott Page is an amiable and energetic mathematician-cum-political scientist at the University of Michigan. He has enjoyed a fascinating career, including dabbling in a few colorful extracurricular projects like becoming a cowboy—a short-lived but truly fascinating side hustle. At his day job within the academy, Page has made a living by finding simple and elegant mathematical solutions to complicated political science problems. His early work on collective intelligence explored the labyrinth of team performance problems that arise in organizations, known as the grand challenge of creativity (which we will tackle in chapter 10). Page's work on creativity soon led him to explore new approaches to the grand challenge of choosing. Following in Galton's footsteps, Page wanted to uncover a mechanism that could explain why independence and size were sufficient for making intelligent collective choices. Just as in his early work on organizations, Page would once again use diversity as his North Star, but in a different way this time.

Suppose you and I are guessing the weight of an ox. My guess is +5 over the true value, and yours is –5 below the true value. Since we are both 5 points away from the true answer, our individual error, on average, is 5. But if you combine our guesses, as Rousseau and Galton had suggested, letting overestimates and underestimates cancel out, then our collective error is 0. The collective guess is significantly smarter than the average of our individual guesses. So far, so good.

Page used this simple observation to point out that the collective error can never be worse than the individual error. For example, if instead of me guessing +5 and you guessing –5, suppose I guess +5 and you guess +5. There is zero diversity in our answers. As before, our average individual error is 5. But now our average collective error is also 5. When there is zero diversity, we get the worst possible performance from our collective answer. It's just as bad as our individual answers.

But that's as bad as the collective answer gets. And that's good news since it means that the collective is never worse than the average individual. It's very easy for the collective guess to improve, even while individual guesses do not, as long as you introduce some diversity across individuals. If people's guesses go in different directions (I overestimate and you underestimate), then the collective error instantly drops below the average individual error.

Thus, the larger the group and the more independent everyone's thinking, the higher the odds of greater diversity—and the greater the diversity, the more likely it is that the collective guess will outperform the individual group members' guesses.

Page's work led to a blossoming of new scientific research on how to mathematically optimize the collective intelligence of crowds without requiring improvements in information. Each measure has its champions, but most researchers agree that under most conditions the central tendency of a collective (calculated in any number of ways) may be expected to outperform most or all of its members.

So, in theory, we should be able to take solace in the fact that the wisdom of the crowd problem has been all but solved—except for one thing: When you look at the world today, does it feel like we're surrounded by an abundance of collective intelligence? Do we see it in the stock market, in our national elections, or in our civic forums? Or, for that matter, in our virtual online spaces? Does it feel like our crowds are wise? There has been over a century of scientific progress on this question. So, why does the ground still feel shaky when we talk about the collective wisdom of uneducated voters?

The reason is independence.

From Rousseau and Condorcet down through Galton, Page, and the rest, nearly everyone agrees that independence is necessary for collectives to make intelligent choices. But what if people are not independent? What if people are influencing one another all the time? What if "the crowd" is exactly what Le Bon said it was—the real-life embodiment of nonindependence run amok?

Welcome to the real world.

The Independence Illusion

In 2006, University of Chicago law professor Cass Sunstein and his colleagues wanted to know what would happen if Americans were given the chance to talk with one another about key political issues prior to a national election. At the time, Colorado was a politically balanced swing state, a place where the strength of a candidate's platform can have the greatest impact on a presidential race. Sunstein and his colleagues gathered groups from the conservative city of Colorado Springs and from liberal Boulder. Participants in each group were asked to provide independent responses to three positions on current political topics. Then they were asked to deliberate publicly, sharing their opinions with one another. Finally, they were asked to give their final opinion on the matter.

These were the three positions:

1. Global warming is real and requires urgent action.
2. Affirmative action is a good idea.
3. Same-sex couples should enjoy the legal benefits of marriage.

These were all hot-button issues in 2006, and they remain so today.

The towns were initially divided. On a 1–10 scale, from "disagree very strongly" to "agree very strongly," the groups from Boulder scored very high, around 8.07 overall, showing strong support for each of the three positions. By contrast, the groups from Colorado Springs were against each position, scoring about 3.48 overall.

You might assume that when people from each town talked with their peers about their opinions, their beliefs would edge a bit closer to the middle of the road. In fact, the opposite happened. The Boulder group became even more extreme in their views, moving all the way up to 8.50 on the 10-point scale. The Colorado Springs groups moved in the opposite direction. Their opinions became more strongly against the positions, dropping all the way down to 2.26. When we compare ourselves to our peers, we inevitably, often unconsciously, move toward the members of our particular reference group. Comparing polarization across the two towns before and after their discussions, internal group deliberations created a 35 percent increase in ideological polarization between them.

This wasn't surprising. For several decades now, scientists have conceded that group deliberations tend to lead collectives toward increasingly extreme viewpoints. This extreme shift phenomenon can go in any direction. Some groups become excessively conservative (e.g., risk-averse), while others become excessively liberal (e.g., risk-seeking). Subtle biases within the group become amplified by group discussion, leading everyone to gravitate toward beliefs that are far more extreme and far less accurate than the crowd wisdom they started with. As people's beliefs converge within each group, group diversity is reduced and collective intelligence is lost. The most notable consequence is that the gap between the groups—their polarization—widens substantially. As consensus within groups increases, polarization between groups worsens.

Non-independence is, of course, an inescapable social and political reality. The ubiquity of social and political influences—family, acquaintances, neighbors, coworkers, to say nothing of print and broadcast journalism and of course social media—prevent any of us from enjoying the kind of independent reflection that earlier thinkers envisioned. Thus, all of the classical solutions to the grand challenge of choosing—from Rousseau to Condorcet to Galton, even down to our most recent and sophisticated algorithms for calculating crowd averages—fail when we try to provide a modern picture of how and why collective intelligence can actually work. If collectives are just large numbers of interacting people without independence or information, size doesn't make things better. In fact, Victorian-era suspicions about the unruly mob and the easily manipulated masses seem entirely warranted.

Cue the internet.

2

Crowd Madness in the Twenty-First Century

Shortly after I began working on the challenge of large-scale collective intelligence, a tech-industry whistleblower released tens of thousands of internal documents revealing exactly what becomes of collectives when independence and information are removed, and people are left only with size.

Once I show you what happened in this infamous tale of crowd madness, I will take you behind the scenes of my team's discovery of why networks can offer a surprisingly effective remedy.

Birds of a Feather

As the adage goes, birds of a feather flock together. But the larger and more diverse the social media universe becomes, the more likely that universe fragments into subgroups of people who have much more in common with one another than with anyone else.

On prominent social media sites, this tendency of people to flock in groups was particularly noticeable among teenage girls. By the millions, teenage girls broke off into social media microcosms, feeding off one another's beliefs and desires. The more enthusiastically people seek out others based on their own goals, talents, and traits, the more efficiently people's engagement pools can be narrowed to people who share those same goals, talents, and traits.

For teenage girls on social media, one of the main sources of usefulness and entertainment was dieting information. The result, however, became a tragic story of how a connected universe of unbounded size can easily evolve into a social trap that dismantles collective intelligence and undermines social and psychological well-being on a national scale.

The logic of how this happens is disturbingly simple: The more you interact with people like yourself, the more influenced you are by them. As your new friendships influence your interests and your sense of yourself, earlier acquaintances who now appear to be less similar to you are dropped from your social network, while new people with greater similarity to your new tastes and ideas are sought out.

This is where influencers come in. Influencers are people with a disproportionately greater number of social ties than the average user—sometimes exponentially so. That alone does not tell you whether they are actually influential, but the fact that they have so many connections means that they are in a very good position to surveil the social mood and tailor their messages to match it. Their extraordinary connectivity also means that they are easy to find. Once a person reaches a certain level of popularity, they become hubs in the social network, which means that their messages and posts are pushed by social media algorithms to become more easily discovered, making newcomer attachment more likely. Just by virtue of the simple rule of cumulative advantage (i.e., the rich get richer), the more popular a person is, the easier they are to find and attach to, and thus the more popular they are likely to become. The more ties someone has, the more ties they attract, inevitably increasing the popularity of these social hubs (sometimes referred to as *firehose networks*).

The whistleblower that I mentioned above had stolen documents that revealed in intimate detail how a platform's network algorithms can create a feedback loop between this social process of selection and influence and the psychological process of social comparison. As more people arrive to an online community, the middle of each group keeps shifting. Social comparison within these influencer communities favors movement toward extreme views, which the hubs can increasingly cultivate and market to their outsized followings. We can visually map this process. Networks often start out as egalitarian, in which people have relatively equal connectivity. In these social patterns (also called *fair-trade networks*), no one has a social advantage. Nobody has disproportionately more ties than anyone else. Everyone has equal power and can share their ideas with equal influence (see figure 2.1).

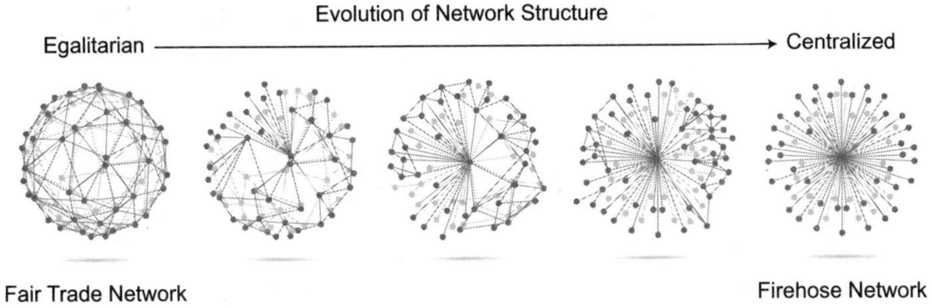

FIGURE 2.1
Evolution of network structure

But as time passes, their older, more personal connections evolve. As people latch onto highly connected influencers who provide validation for their new beliefs, online networks start to become centralized around influencer hubs. As networks become more centralized, the resulting firehose patterns enable influencers to efficiently disseminate a constant stream of messaging to their audience engaged in the scramble to keep up with their peers.

The big bombshell was not that this was happening, but that social media platforms were actively encouraging it. The stolen data released by Facebook's Frances Haugen, who leaked her company's internal reports (which also included damning information about Instagram, owned by the same parent company, Meta), was horrifying. Instagram was routinely pushing hundreds of thousands of teenage girls toward massively connected influencer networks centered around influencers with names like "skinny binge" and "apple core anorexia." From there, girls' norms and expectations only became more extreme—and potentially deadly. In fact, as social media members moved toward the center of their new social and informational networks, they were invited to connect to new users with even more extreme points of view.

This problem went far beyond teenage girls and the dangers of life-threatening body issues. It turned out that adults were just as susceptible. The same dynamics that led teenagers to harmful dieting behaviors also swept up millions of adults learning about conspiracy theories. Referencing Lewis Carroll's *Alice's Adventures in Wonderland*, the term *rabbit hole* was coined to refer to the chain of conspiratorial stories that sucked users into increasingly extreme worlds of online connections centered around conspiracy-theorist influencers. Just like teenage girls seeking out beauty advice, adult users became seduced by tales of government deceit and corporate cover-ups. The data revealed that it only takes a few iterations of the selection, influence, and comparison process for users to find themselves following influencers whose extreme beliefs they would have considered to be absurd and dangerous only a few months ago—but which now seem normal within their new online social circle.

THE GEOMETRY OF SOCIAL LIFE

There is a certain freedom that comes with firehose networks. A sea of anonymous ties means that you can say anything—or believe anything—without needing to worry about what your close friends and family will think about you. As a member of a firehose network, you are free from personal reputation—and free from familiar forms of social control found among friends and family. The downside of all this freedom is that social proof—that is, your reliance on independent contacts and external sources to confirm the credibility and legitimacy of new ideas—is set adrift. Down this rabbit hole, reliance on an outside reference point for evaluating the truth of what anyone is saying risks attack and exile. The consensus of the crowd invisibly becomes a new form of social control. As the influencer's network grows, the larger the gang waiting to attack dissenters.

While firehose networks may have been bad for facts and tolerance, they were good for Facebook. In 2018, the platform was struggling. Engagement—measured in terms of comments, reshares, and likes—was waning and company executives needed to reignite interest in the site. Their solution was a series of changes to the News Feed, which they hoped would amplify the spread of the most popular content farther across the Facebook community.

On its face, the strategy was a perfectly good one, and it worked: User engagement increased. The problem was that the material that people clicked and shared was highly inflammatory. Facebook's uptick in user participation came from hostility between users.

These implications were felt worldwide. An internal analysis of how political actors responded to the changing demands of Facebook's News

Feed concluded, "They have learnt that harsh attacks on their opponents net the highest engagement. They claim that they 'try not to,' but ultimately 'you use what works.'"

Nothing creates greater interest in sticking with the leader than the visceral fear of a shared enemy. Political parties in Poland and Central Europe soon complained that they were being forced to make increasingly negative, even hateful, political content in order to maintain a competitive presence in the Facebook News Feed. For the same reasons, Spanish officials reported a 43 percent jump in their use of insulting and threatening posts regarding the culture clash with Catalan separatists. Similar complaints came from government officials in India and Taiwan, who felt forced to change the tone of political content, making it more divisive and less accurate, in order to maintain their presence in the Facebook News Feed.

Just as Sunstein discovered, once a community's norms shift in the direction of increasing extremism, even the most reluctant actors are forced to move farther in that direction too. The race to keep up is actually a race to the bottom. Players are driven into a downward spiral of social comparison, which eventually draws everyone into the gravitational pull of firehose networks. As influencers stir up more controversy, more people flock to them, and everyone's ideas become more extreme. And, if you try to resist, and if your team stops using malicious adds and unseemly content, you quickly find yourself moving backward in the rankings. You have to keep running just to stay in the same place.

This downward spiral seems to be unending. From entertainment and health to news and politics—everyone is driven by the need to keep up and is faced with the inevitability of missing out or falling behind if they do not.

But there may be hope yet.

True and False Contagions

In 2018, my colleagues at MIT conducted an extraordinarily large and detailed examination of the accuracy of the messages that had spread across the prominent social media platform Twitter (now X), over the course of its inaugural decade (2006–2017). What kinds of stories were people sharing, and which ones spread faster and farther than the others?

The researchers analyzed a corpus of 4.5 million tweets and retweets (comprising approximately 126,000 unique stories). They divided the stories into true and false content based on reports from six independent fact-checking sites to confirm the veracity of each story.

The findings were unambiguous. The lies had it, hands down:

> Whereas the truth rarely diffused to more than 1000 people, the top 1% of false-news cascades routinely diffused to between 1000 and 100,000 people. . . . Falsehood reached more people at every depth of a cascade than the truth, meaning that many more people retweeted falsehood than they did the truth. The spread of falsehood was aided by its virality, meaning that falsehood did not simply spread through broadcast dynamics but rather through peer-to-peer diffusion characterized by a viral branching process.

In 2021, another team of researchers reanalyzed the data from this study and found that all of the results from the 2018 study could be reduced to a single variable: "the higher person-to-person infectiousness of the information."

Unlike true stories, which often get bogged down in the complicated details of real events, most false stories are outlandish and fun to spread. Their contagious appeal is their novelty, which means the more outlandish a story is, the more likely you are to repeat it after only hearing it once. You want to be out on the leading edge of fun gossip, not lagging behind.

It helps that false stories are designed to be easy to understand. They may be novel, but always in a familiar way, latching onto our baser assumptions about people and their motives. Even if these stories have lots of details, they do not require more than minimal mental effort to grasp. Moreover, lies have the distinct advantage that they can be tailored to match our fears, suspicions, and tastes. They can be molded to fit a particular social group's values and its prejudices.

Firehose networks are the perfect accelerant for highly contagious falsehoods, since a single influencer can propel a false story into the minds of hundreds of thousands of followers. However, their outsized impact disappears when it comes to spreading less infectious truths. This is primarily because true stories are often mired in the mundane details of the real world, which means that influencers must do much more work to convince their followers that they should pay attention. Not only that, but an influencer may soon lose their status as influencer if they try to advocate a view that everyone in their community actively dislikes, which is what happened in 2021 with the Centers for Disease Control's stunningly ineffective attempt to use celebrities like Dolly Parton and George W. Bush to encourage vaccination among reluctant conservatives. This potential for failure is something that every successful influencer is acutely aware of, and in the competition among influencers to grow their firehose networks faster than their competitors, there is a clear advantage to running as fast as they can with false stories that resonate, rather than taking the time to advocate for true ones that don't. As the French revolutionary Alexandre Ledru-Rollin is rumored to have said, "There go my people. I must find out where they are going so I can lead them." The more firehose networks there are, and the bigger they become, the more likely it is that falsehoods will dramatically outpace truths.

Take vaccines.

On April 13, 2021, the CDC paused the use of the Johnson & Johnson COVID vaccine because researchers had become concerned about the possibility that in some people the vaccine was causing dangerous blood clots. Scientists got to work analyzing data, and by April 23, the CDC had confirmed that the J&J vaccine was not responsible for the blood clots, and its rollout was permitted to continue.

This is a true news story that contains useful facts about the J&J vaccine and shows things working exactly the way that they are supposed to: The CDC researchers monitored vaccine side effects, just as they are supposed to do. They thought they might have found something dangerous, so they shut down production and distribution to take a closer look, just as they're supposed to do. After investigating, they found that there was no significant correlation between the vaccine and blood clots. With these findings, they gave the greenlight for production and distribution to start back up again, just as they're supposed to do.

In the end, it is a mundane story about an effective bureaucracy. It's a success story, but not the kind of fun and entertaining story that influencers are likely to share, particularly if they want to remain influencers.

There is, however, a way to *make* it fun, and that's by asking certain types of questions.

"What *really* happened at J&J?"

"Were some CDC officials trying to stop a harmful vaccine from being distributed but were silenced?"

"Is there a battle for control inside the CDC?"

In theory, these questions are not reckless if asked with the intent to provide a full, nuanced, and accurate answer. But, undoubtedly, they make good fodder for unscrupulous media personalities. In April 2021, cable news anchors transformed these inquiries into implicit accusations via leading questions to media guests. These kinds of tantalizing suspicions are dangerous enough, but they become even more dangerous in the hands of online influencers, where such wild speculations can be simply stated as facts: "Johnson & Johnson tried to stop the vaccine, but corrupt government officials forced them to release it again."

This is the kind of contagion that Facebook's News Feed algorithm was specifically designed to propagate.

The structure of firehose networks means that it only takes a small number of these influencers to infuse an entire social media platform with compelling, entertaining, and almost irresistible falsehoods. This is because firehose networks exist in concert with cohorts of others. If someone is a member of one, they are likely to also belong to another that overlaps in subject or content. A sports fan may belong to a group devoted to their favorite team but also to a group devoted to the entire league and to groups operated by the journalists who cover the teams and the sport in general. News about a player's injury can start on one of these firehose networks and spread rapidly to all of them.

Strikingly, the vast majority of misinformation about vaccines on popular social media sites (65 percent of the most-talked-about topics) comes from only a handful people. These people are not news anchors or broadcast professionals. They are firehoses. They are actors with outsized followings on social media.

The 2018 MIT study showed how such contagions can spread. But even more surprising is that the bigger the lie, the faster this happens. The more outlandish and unbelievable the falsehoods, the more likely they are to be propelled through firehose networks to achieve widespread social media success.

When all of these findings started coming to light, all I could think about is what would have happened if we had taken a different path with social media from the start.

From the beginning, social media encouraged the evolution of firehoses. But what if organizations had implemented networking rules and incentives that encouraged platforms to evolve into fair-trade networks instead of firehoses?

There were reasons to be skeptical. The world as it is today seems almost inevitable. It's easy to believe that changes in network structure would not make any appreciable difference. After all, regardless of the networks, social media would still be populated by the same people with the same appetites. Social consensus can be seductive precisely because it brings with it a growing sense of empathy among peers. Effortlessly, almost as if by design, the harmonious glow of group members' shared consciousness may in fact serve to obscure their eroding collective intelligence.

Infectious falsehoods will always be available and enticing. Regardless of whether social media was built around influencers or built to be egalitarian, the fate of life online might still be the same.

Perhaps.

But maybe changing network structure would change the kinds of ideas that spread most effectively. Perhaps it would improve the quality of the content that people consume and the quality of what they produce. Perhaps restructuring networks would allow them to take shape around the best ideas rather than the most influential personalities. Indeed, perhaps the principle of egalitarian structure is the very mechanism that Aristotle had been missing so many millennia ago.

The more I thought about it, in true Alice in Wonderland fashion, the curiouser and curiouser I became. Would giving more people more voice suddenly make the truth spread faster than lies? Would the lies suddenly stop spreading altogether? At the very least, I wondered whether there was a way to find out.

The Conspiracy Experiment

To find out what would happen, my team leads, Jingwen Zhang and Elaine Khoong, and I spent two years building a social media platform of our own, called Health Connect. We released it right in the middle of the pandemic, when hysteria about vaccination was at its peak. Between September 2021 and March 2022, we recruited 958 people from other social media sites to join our new platform. These members agreed to participate in a social media community in which they would discuss their beliefs about vaccines. But, unbeknownst to participants, we had created two versions of the platform.

In one version of the platform, participants were networked together in a centralized community that looked like a firehose, with one person at the center. This central person was the "influencer" for that community. (I'll tell you in a moment how I chose the influencer.)

In the other version of the platform, participants were networked together into an egalitarian community that looked like a fair-trade network. Everyone in the network had the same number of contacts as everyone else. Initially, there were no influencers because no one had disproportionate control over the flow of information.

In total, there were thirty-two independent communities—sixteen firehose communities and sixteen fair-trade communities. Each community had between thirty and forty people. This allowed us to watch the evolution of people's opinions across multiple independent (and otherwise identical) social media sites to see if there were predictable trends that emerged in each version of the platform.

Once all the participants had joined the site, we asked them: "According to the most recent data, for every 10 million people in the US vaccinated for COVID-19, how many experienced a severe allergic reaction (anaphylaxis) [answer between 0 and 10,000]?"

Then they were prompted to provide a response. They had a strong incentive to get the answer right—we paid them a handsome reward (up to $45) for guessing the correct answer, but no reward for getting it wrong.

After everyone answered the question, they participated in a network-wide chat, in which everyone in their community was encouraged to share their ideas and opinions. The conversations ranged from horror stories about vaccination, to rumors about zombies, to questions about job openings in the military. It was a live, free-flowing social media exchange.

Then we asked them the same question again.

But this time, we showed people the average responses of their network peers from the previous round. There was no demand that participants use this information, but after we provided it, we asked them to respond a second time, and then they could resume the free-flowing chat with their network community.

This same procedure (looking at the most recent responses and then providing your own) would happen one final time. This meant that by the end of the study, every participant had provided a sequence of three responses to the same question about vaccine safety and participated in three rounds of chatting with peers.

Were communities smarter at the beginning of the study or at the end?

At the beginning of the study, before people interacted, everyone's responses were independent. Therefore, the group response was wiser than the average individual response. Galton had told us that, and Page had shown why it works. Galton, Page, and Sunstein would all agree that the initial responses should be more accurate than the final responses.

Here is their prediction. After three rounds of interactions—people seeing other people's guesses and revising their responses accordingly—diversity of opinions would shrink. Group beliefs would migrate away from the wisdom of the crowd, toward an extreme collective belief that would make the crowd and everyone in it less intelligent.

That's a clear enough expectation.

An online version of Sunstein's Boulder versus Colorado Springs findings was, of course, worrisome, but not even close to how bad things actually are. What would happen if each community also had a disinformation agent intentionally trying to derail the intelligence of the group? On social media, this is exactly what we have, particularly on topics like vaccine safety, so we added a twist to our study: Every network had a secret person whose job it was to actively spread fake news, misleading gossip, and vastly inflated estimates about the dangers of vaccination. None of the participants knew that there was a member of their network who was not actually an experimental participant, but a part of my research team, whose goal was to derail collective intelligence by sowing fear and spreading lies—big lies.

In the firehose communities, the disinformation agent was in the influencer position, right in the middle of the network (see figure 2.2). In the fair-trade networks, all positions are equal, so the disinformation agent was positioned randomly. The black node in each network shows the location of the disinformation agent.

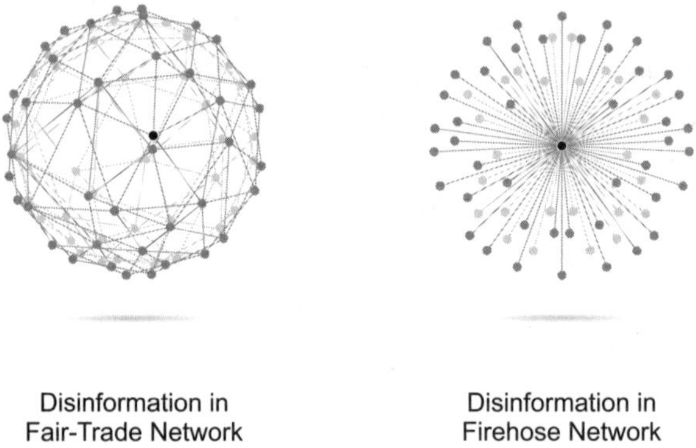

FIGURE 2.2
Disinformation in fair-trade and firehose networks

At the time of the study, the correct answer to the question about vaccine safety was that for every 10 million people vaccinated, thirty-five people had severe allergic (anaphylactic) reactions. Our disinformation agent told people that the true answer was 8,000, and she was not shy about it.

Every round, she entered the answer 8,000, and in every group conversation, she vehemently argued that vaccines were dangerous. Different members of our research team acted as disinformation agents in different communities, but to ensure that all thirty-two communities were subjected to the same extreme levels of disinformation, all followed the same script. They entered the same answer in every round in every network, and in every network they worried:

"i heard my friends having really bad reactions to it"

"what long term effects do you worry?"

"my friend got the blood clot, very rare but she got it"

"do you worry for yourself of any long term? I was thinking even just short term.."

"my kids' school is pushing on it"

"i hate that idea . . . especially for schools"

"especially for kids"

They offered anecdotal evidence:

"my mom got her arms swollen for a month"

"my friends had the heart problem and not getting a booster" "yes, i heard a lot of bad reactions"

And they defended their position:

"that's why i did put a big number"

"yeah, there are so many vaccines"

"i still saw a high average number"

"Like 8000?"

"I put in an even larger number"

"just feel like there is little reporting on this, so worried to underestimate it"

These messages preyed on people's fears about vaccines, fanning the flames of doubt. Our disinformation agents made the same inflammatory remarks, and asserted the same inflated estimate, in every trial. The only difference between the experimental groups was the structure of their social networks.

We hypothesized that the disinformation agent's position of influence at the center of the network would give them an outsized impact on people's beliefs. But we didn't know how big an impact they would actually have on people's estimates about vaccine safety.

As it turned out, the impact was enormous.

Average collective intelligence of the communities with a disinformation agent at their hub dropped by nearly half. Average group error increased by 48 percent (figure 2.3). Across all sixteen independent firehose communities, with hundreds of willing participants, the results were consistent and highly significant.

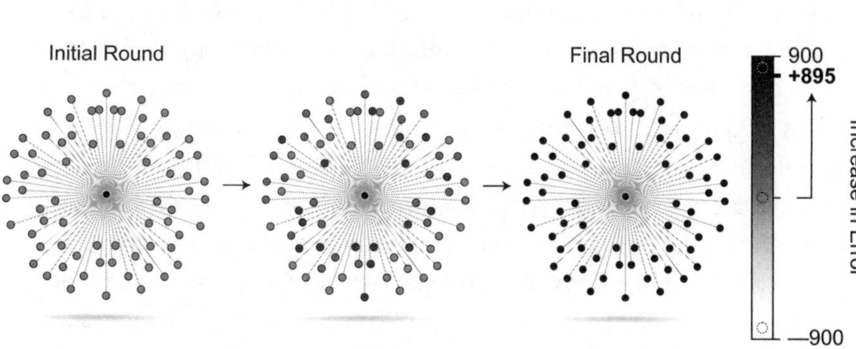

FIGURE 2.3
Increase in error in a firehose network

What possible difference could the network structure make? It could certainly slow down the spread of disinformation; after all, in the influencer networks, the disinformation agent had direct access to everyone. But in the fair-trade communities, while the disinformation agent was still there, pumping disinformation into the networks and attempting to incite fear and panic among her peers, she had direct access to fewer individuals.

I still worried that the fair-trade communities' collective intelligence would be compromised by the disinformation agent. But I hoped that things would not be as bad as they were in the firehose networks.

So we were stunned by what happened next.

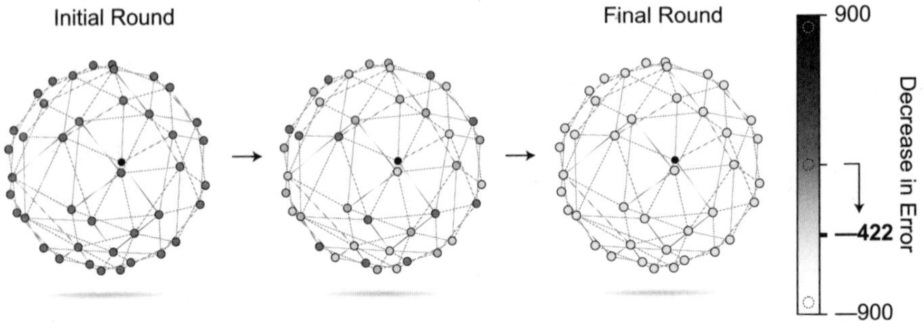

FIGURE 2.4
Decrease in error in a fair-trade network

In the final round, participants in the fair-trade communities had become significantly *more* accurate in their beliefs about vaccine safety than they were at the beginning of the study (figure 2.4). Collective intelligence had *increased*. And not just in one community, but across all of them.

Over sixteen replications of the fair-trade communities, egalitarian networks produced a 21 percent reduction in group error. These improvements in collective intelligence were large and highly significant. It was the exact opposite of what happened in the firehose networks. As a result of interacting within social media networks, crowds somehow became smarter.

Not only that, but individuals got smarter too. On average, the participants in the sixteen fair-trade communities became 24 percent more accurate in their individual estimates than they had been at the beginning.

Individuals got smarter, and crowds got wiser. All the while being subjected to a disinformation campaign.

This was a finding that Le Bon had not predicted. Nor Galton, for that matter. Nor Page, Rousseau, Condorcet, nor Sunstein. No one had.

In fact, it was supposed to be impossible for crowds to get smarter by interacting, let alone with crowds subjected to disinformation agents actively attempting to reduce the group's collective intelligence. So how is it possible?

I'll reveal that secret in a moment. But first, I want to show you the next finding, which is even more surprising. It was not only people's intelligence that was changed by the fair-trade networks but their emotions.

In the firehose networks, the emotions of participants were significantly elevated. In particular, expressions of anger (often using swear words) were significantly more common in the firehose networks than the fair-trade networks. Here things get very interesting. There was a direct connection between people's mood in their social media conversations and the trajectory of their community's collective intelligence. Conversations that were more emotional with more swear words were correlated with lower collective intelligence.

What is most striking about this finding is that participants were experimentally randomized to each network condition. If people had the good fortune to be put into the fair-trade networks, they had better conversations and improved understanding of vaccine safety, even though there was a disinformation agent in their community. If those same people had the bad fortune to be put into a firehose network, they were likely to experience more anger in their conversations and come away with a much poorer understanding of vaccine safety.

The latter sounds a lot like what happens on social media. But our experiment showed that the explanation for why social media is like this is not because of the people, nor the social influence among them. Nor is it solely because of disinformation agents. It is because of structure. The structure of our social media networks influences not only how we think but also how we feel.

The conspiracy experiment revealed that personal influences are not necessarily an unruly tumult of pressures that sabotage the purity of otherwise intelligent collectives. All of us are embedded in networks at our jobs, in our communities, and across our lives. But this embeddedness is not a curse. In fact, embeddedness is the only thing that can set us free.

GRAVITY'S RAINBOW

Let us go backward for a moment to understand another metric of group intelligence: relevancy. In 1974, American statistician Morris DeGroot wanted to understand what would happen if lots of people exchanged their opinions within a network. He discovered a result that has since been elaborated upon by hundreds of scholars, and forms the basic idea behind much of today's network science of collective intelligence. (So much so that the process of social learning in networks is sometimes referred to as "DeGroot learning.")

DeGroot found that people tend to adjust their answers based on the peers around them in a fairly predictable way, tending to move toward the average of their contacts, as each contact also simultaneously moves toward them. This collective averaging process has the inevitable conclusion of consensus, but not just any consensus: If everyone has, on average, equal influence, then the collective process leads to consensus on the group average.

Thus, if the influence process leads everyone to adjust their answers toward the middle, then eventually each person will be just as smart as the group. In 2003, the economist Peter DeMarzo and his team uncovered an important exception to DeGroot's findings. If some people have network positions that give them more power, then they can influence the trajectory of DeGroot learning in a way that leads the entire population away from the original group mean. DeMarzo's team referred to this phenomenon as "persuasion bias."

A few years later, in 2010, DeMarzo's results were significantly bolstered by Stanford University economists Matt Jackson and Ben Golub, who proved exactly how inequalities in network power can lead crowds astray (via the dynamics of persuasion bias). Their proofs showed how creating an equal distribution of network power (in essence eliminating persuasion bias) would lead everyone's opinions to balance out, resulting in an accurate consensus—just as DeGroot had originally predicted.

In our study, persuasion bias explains what happened in the centralized networks. A single person had disproportionate influence, which pulled the population toward an extreme view. This is consistent with Sunstein's findings among Colorado voters.

But in 2011, a group of Swiss scientists was interested in understanding whether this phenomenon of social influence leading groups astray could also happen without centralization. They gathered students from their university into groups of twelve and asked them to evaluate general knowledge questions, like "What is the length of Switzerland's border?" They asked the question five times. In the first round, everyone responded in isolation. In all subsequent rounds, students were divided into "social groups" and "independent control groups." In the social groups, students were allowed to see their fellow group members' responses from the previous round and to use this information when giving their next response. In the independent control groups, students continued the study in isolation, with no exposure to other participants' responses for four additional rounds, just like the first round.

The Swiss researchers' findings provided one of the major contemporary demonstrations of the problem of social influence for collective intelligence, even without centralization. In the independent groups, there were no changes in accuracy among students, nor were there any changes in students' confidence in their answers over the duration of the study. The diversity of responses in these group did not change over five rounds.

However, in the groups in which the students shared their opinions, diversity was all but eliminated. As participants converged on a shared opinion, they became more confident in their answer. Their collective answer was no better than when they started, but everyone had become much more confident in their conclusion.

In a thoughtful follow-up to the 2011 Swiss experiment, an Australian social scientist reanalyzed the experimental data. But this time he was looking exclusively at individual performance, rather than collective wisdom. The original Swiss study had shown that as individuals communicated with one another, diversity decreased and confidence increased. But the reanalysis of their data showed that something else was happening too. As individuals in the social groups influenced one another, they did not simply converge . . . they converged toward the right answer. The diversity of opinions in the social groups did indeed shrink. But rather than everyone being led astray by an extreme answer, the opposite happened. Group members were pulled from the extreme toward the middle. Everyone was converging on the wisdom of the crowd. This is exactly what DeGroot had predicted.

It also explains why the 2011 study found that group intelligence was not compromised. People who initially had low answers were influenced to guess a little higher, while people with high answers were persuaded to guess a little lower. A few individuals did get worse, but most improved. And overall the group's collective intelligence stayed the same.

How can we square the 2011 Swiss results, which conform to DeGroot's optimistic predictions, with Sunstein's fatalistic findings on social influence among voters and Page's proofs about the importance of diversity?

An obvious answer could be that DeGroot's prediction works when people don't care about the topic. No one cares about the length of Switzerland's border, so it makes sense that social interactions could lead everyone to converge on a wise answer, just like DeGroot had predicted. Not so for politics. Colorado voters care about public policies. Perhaps what Sunstein's experiment shows is that when people care about a topic, social interactions lead to greater extremism and reduced collective intelligence. If this were true, it would be a big problem since it would mean that the idea of network structures improving collective intelligence only works when no one cares about the topic.

Fortunately, as our conspiracy experiment showed, the obvious answer is wrong.

People care about vaccine safety. Emotions run high when people discuss this topic. Life and death decisions (to get vaccinated or not) are made based on these beliefs. Vaccination is a topic that matters. Yet we found that individuals and collectives could in fact get much smarter about vaccine safety by virtue of learning from one another in egalitarian networks. Indeed, they became far more intelligent than DeGroot had imagined.

Sunstein and DeGroot would have both agreed with the Swiss scientists and with DeMarzo. They would all predict that the unyielding influence of the disinformation agent would pull the egalitarian networks away from the wisdom of the crowd and toward collective error.

So how do we reconcile all of these different findings? The 2011 Swiss experiment, Sunstein's 2007 study of Colorado voters, and the

2024 Conspiracy experiment on social media all seem to offer different conclusions—which one is right? The solution to this puzzle comes from taking a fresh look at network structure.

Think of every person in a social network as having some amount of gravity. In networks with persuasion bias, a single person acts as a gravity well, pulling everyone toward them (figure 2.5). The population moves toward this central person regardless of truth.

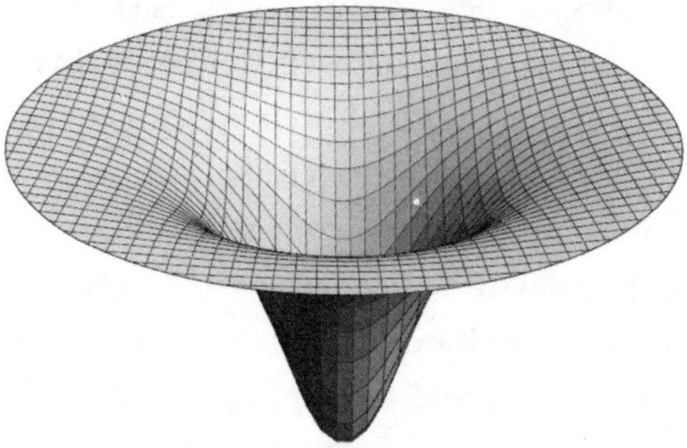

FIGURE 2.5
Gravity well in a centralized network

But in egalitarian networks, gravity wells emerge around the people who are most accurate (figure 2.6). As the conversation evolves, everyone moves toward the people with the most accurate opinions, and diversity in the network diminishes. The group converges, not toward the average answers, but toward the best answers. The most accurate people become focal points for the trajectory of the entire network, pulling the average intelligence of the group upward.

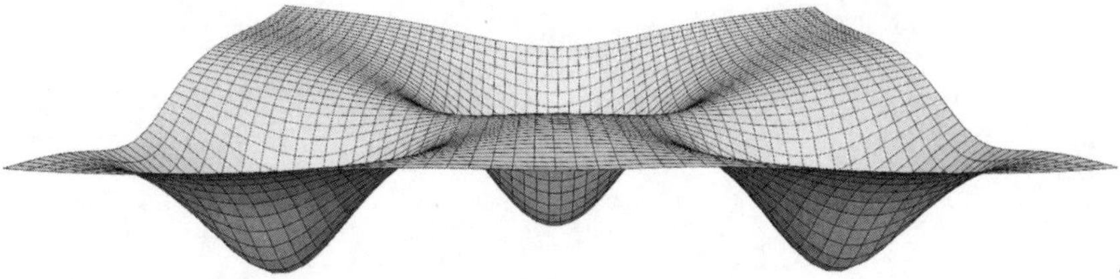

FIGURE 2.6
Emergent gravity wells in an egalitarian network

But why?

Because the most accurate people in the network revise their answers less, while the least accurate members of the network revise their answers more. Think about this for a moment. The result is a subtle, almost backward form of social influence. Instead of social influence happening in the familiar sense of people pushing their opinions toward everyone else, this kind of influence in egalitarian networks emerges simply by virtue of the people with the best answers letting everyone come to them. By standing their ground, and revising their answers less, these people become centers of gravity in the network. No one even notices it. Invisibly, the entire network gravitates toward the most accurate people, not because these people advertise their accuracy, but because, simply by holding steady, these people allow the network to move toward them.

How do people know who is the most accurate person in the network? How do those people who become centers of gravity in an egalitarian network know that they should be leading rather than following? And might egalitarian networks also be subject to persuasion bias, or even lead groups toward collective madness?

The answers to these questions come from following a remarkable trail of breadcrumbs left behind by one famous economist's surprising (and delicious) method for revealing the secrets behind market mania and market crashes.

3

Deciding How to Decide

It felt like the world was ending. It was almost like being caught in an earthquake . . . there's this incredible sense of disbelief.
—Economist at MCM Moneywatch on Black Monday

In the future, we will surely have even bigger such bubbles . . . and we will have to invent new names for them.
—Robert Schiller, Nobel Laureate in Economics

Can't put me finger on what lies in store, but I fear what's to happen, all happened before.
—Mary Poppins

The summer of 1987 was a good time to be an investor. The Dow Jones Industrial Average, which reports the average performance of thirty of the most prominent US stocks, such as Disney, 3M, Boeing, IBM, and Intel, had been rapidly climbing all year, increasing by over 40 percent between January and September. But in late September, warm summer winds began to carry the cool chill of autumn.

By early October, a backslide had begun. On Friday, October 16, the Dow closed lower than it had in weeks. On Saturday afternoon, James Baker, the secretary of the treasury, announced a plan to consider devaluing the dollar in response to a larger-than-expected US trade deficit. Something had changed—everyone could feel it. Even before the markets opened on Monday morning, the tension was palpable.

At the opening bell, prices went into a free fall. In just seven hours, the Dow lost more than 22 percent of its value. Nearly $2 trillion (in 1987

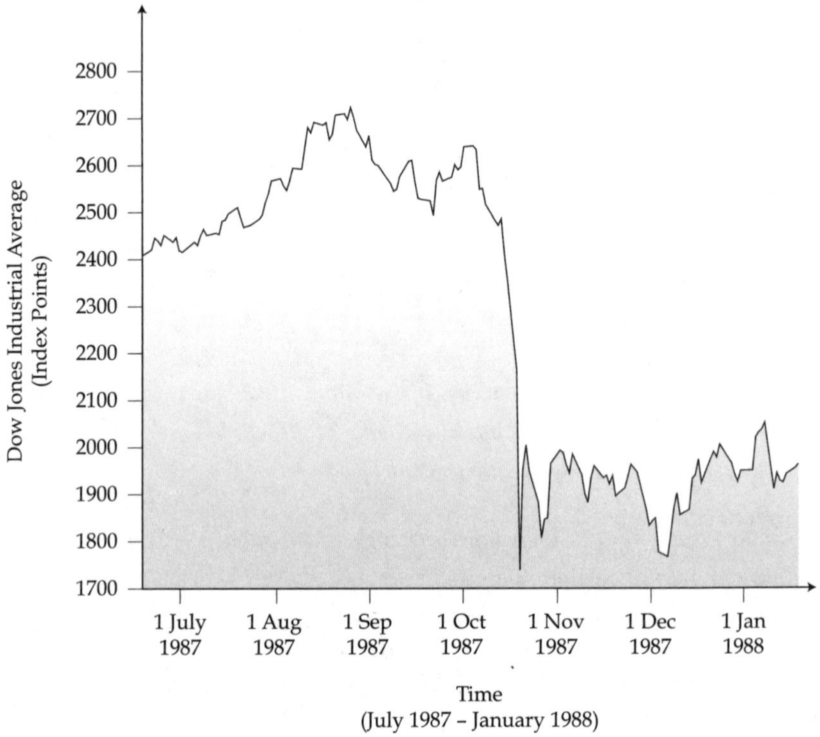

FIGURE 3.1
Black Monday 1987. Based on publicly available data provided through CC3.

dollars) had disappeared in just a few hours. Now known as Black Monday, it was the largest single-day drop in US history, almost double the size of the market crash in 1929 (figure 3.1).

This is the kind of phenomenon that Charles Mackay, writing nearly 150 years earlier, would have happily described as the "madness of crowds." Andrew Grove, then CEO of Intel Corporation, commented on the events of the day by noting, "It's a little like a theater where someone yells 'Fire!'" Even if it's not true, everyone panics and all is lost.

Anyone who studies markets knows that successful investors have ice water running through their veins. So how could so many serious professionals collectively make such dangerous and self-destructive financial decisions? These were the same investors whose confidence in the market had accounted for so much growth leading up to Black Monday. As far as explanations go, "everyone panicked" is something you only resort to when you think there is no science to be had. It suggests that there is no predictive model, and thus not much hope for finding a way to prevent future Black Mondays.

But there is hope, and remarkably, it comes from jelly beans.

Trillion-Dollar Jelly Beans

In June 1987, four months before Black Monday, the well-respected economist Jack Treynor published an unusual paper in the *Financial Analysts Journal*. Treynor's study challenged a popular view of collective intelligence in free markets, known as the *market efficiency hypothesis*, according to which market prices always reflect the true value of their underlying assets. If that's correct, a sudden collapse in value, like Black Monday, should not be possible. Treynor believed in market efficiency, but he did not believe the prevailing explanation for how it works (or how to prevent it from failing).

The standard view was that market efficiency comes from the shrewd efforts of smart investors (with near perfect information) tirelessly evaluating their portfolios. Unceasing scrutiny of market assets leads to continuous adjustments in pricing, which accurately reflect even the smallest shifts in the true value of the underlying assets.

Treynor didn't buy it.

Instead, he offered a very different explanation for collective intelligence in markets that takes us all the way back to Galton and the ox. According to Treynor, market efficiency "comes from the faulty opinions of a large number of investors who err independently." In other words, it's not smart individuals making precise adjustments that make markets intelligent but rather large numbers of inaccurate individuals making independent mistakes.

To make his point that independence and size were all it takes for markets to be smarter than any individual investor, Treynor asked a group of forty-nine independent "novices" (that is, students in an investment class at the University of Southern California) to guess the number of jelly beans in a jar. The jar held 810 delicious, brightly colored jelly beans.

The mean estimate of the group of independent students was 841—quite close. Only two students outperformed the collective guess. Then he ran the experiment again with another group of independent students. This time, the jar had 850 beans. Only one student out of a class of fifty-one outperformed the group average of 871.

Treynor wrote, "Apparently it doesn't take knowledge of beans, jars or packing factors for a group of students to make an accurate estimate of the number of beans in a jar. All it takes is independence."

Then, following in Gabriel Tarde's footsteps, Treynor prodded, "But what assurance do we have that investors' errors are really independent? Are errors *ever* independent across the population of investors? Who is to say whether GM or AT&T is correctly priced or mispriced?"

Treynor was ready to deliver his coup de grâce. He ran another experiment in which he polluted the clear waters of independence by providing his novice students with shared information that was intended to help improve their guesses. He told them to account for air space at the top of the jar. He noted that the jar was plastic rather than glass, which meant that the plastic jar had a thinner wall than a regular glass jar, and therefore had a greater capacity for holding jelly beans than a glass jar with the same dimensions. These technical tidbits were given to the novices as helpful facts for making predictions in their artificial economy of counting jelly beans. Of course, the real purpose of these facts was to stand in for the continuous stream of news and informational updates that inundate investors trying to gain an edge on the market.

What was the effect of giving all of the same new information to every member of the crowd? Collective error *increased* by 25 percent!

Of course, the real problem was not information. It was independence. The problem was that everyone in the class now had the *same* information. Diversity in their opinions dropped, and with it the collective intelligence of the whole. It was the same problem on Wall Street.

Information is the oxygen of the market. Consistent with the market efficiency hypothesis, professional investors race to gain a competitive edge by unearthing every morsel of relevant information they can find. They bathe themselves in the intoxicating nectar of rumors and opinions and gossipy news shared by everyone. Treynor realized that the more deeply investors breathe the same air, the more inevitably they are all led to share the same hazy dream. The frenzied search for advantage eliminates their independence from one another. The more information that is available, the more unintentionally coordinated everyone becomes. Collectively, unconsciously, they all steer together as a single body straight for the rocky shoals, unintentionally sabotaging the collective.

Four months after Treynor published this critique of market stability, Black Monday offered seismic evidence in support of his argument. Treynor's analysis particularly emphasized the dangers of broadcast communication, like Baker's Saturday-afternoon announcement. This kind of centralized messaging has the ability to synchronize large numbers of traders to make the same errors. But Treynor's implications went beyond just errors: Reducing independence among traders destabilizes free-market economies.

These revelations seem like terrible news for the network theory of structural intelligence, but I couldn't help but wonder—would changing the structure of traders' information networks impact their investing behavior? Is the problem with markets really that shared information eliminates independence among investors, or is the problem that the information sources are centralized? Could structural changes be made that would improve market stability? Could information-exchange networks instead improve collective stability and individual results? And, if so, could we find a better way to prevent Black Monday from happening again?

Intelligence Games

I was champing at the bit to test Treynor's jelly bean theory of collective intelligence. But to do this right, we were going to need many more than fifty participants, and we would need to go beyond jelly beans.

My graduate students Joshua Becker and Devon Brackbill designed a study in which they recruited 1,360 subjects and used nine different kinds of quiz questions. The experiment had a game-show quality to it. We even included a set of questions designed to be similar to the Showcase Showdown on the popular television game show *The Price Is Right*. The goal was to make this experiment fun enough that people would want to participate and make the incentives strong enough that participants would want to push themselves to get the answers right: They would get a cash reward for guessing the right answer, but no reward for guessing poorly.

We set up the experiment just like the vaccine study. Participants were randomly assigned to network conditions. But this time, there was no disinformation agent. The networks were entirely composed of live subjects.

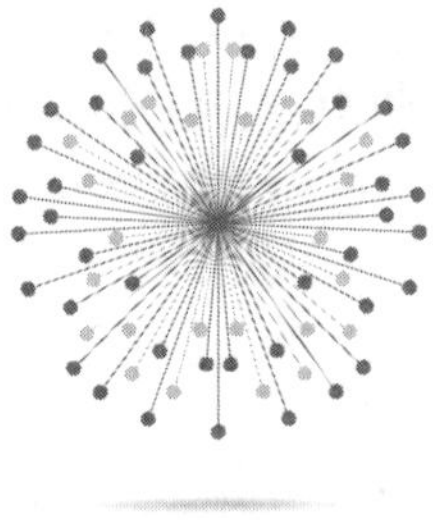

Centralized Firehose Network

FIGURE 3.2
Experimental condition 1

In each replication of the Intelligence Game, there was a centralized firehose network (figure 3.2) and an egalitarian fair-trade network (figure 3.3). Each one contained forty people.

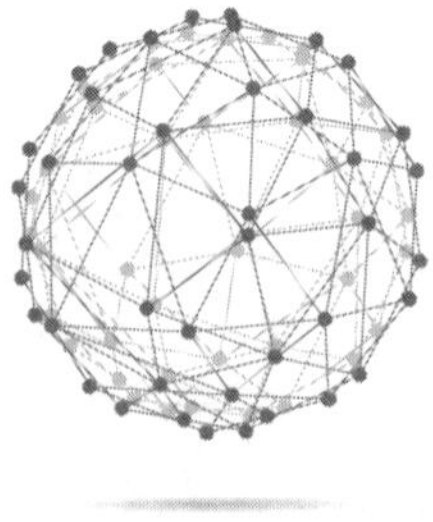

Egalitarian Free Trade Network

FIGURE 3.3
Experimental condition 2

There was also a third condition in each trial—the control condition. The control group was just like Galton's study: a group of isolated individuals making their guesses independently, for whom we could calculate the average wisdom of the crowd (figure 3.4).

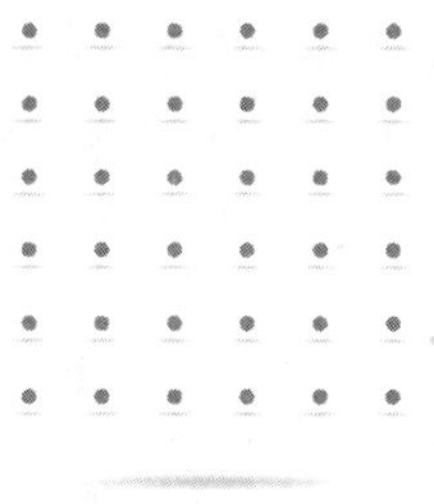

FIGURE 3.4
Control condition

But why do we need a control condition? Why can't we just compare the centralized network to the egalitarian network, like we did with the vaccine study?

The answer is placebo effects.

A PLACEBO EFFECT FOR INTELLIGENCE

In medical drug trials, at least three different patient conditions may be needed to test a single medication. In one group, sick patients receive a dose of the drug. A second group of equally sick patients receives no treatment. The first group is the treatment group, and the second group is the control group.

But the crucial test of a drug's effectiveness is not just whether the first group improves more than the second group. It is also whether the first group outperforms a third group. In the third group, patients receive sugar pills that look like the drug but have no therapeutic value. The third group is the placebo control.

The third group is needed because of an English physician named John Haygarth. In 1799, Haygarth found that simply telling people that they were being given a medical treatment could be just as medically beneficial as giving them an actual treatment. Haygarth's study was the first systematic account of a placebo response, in which patients would improve from fake treatments. In 1955, after the accumulation of over a century of similar cases studies, the American physician Henry Beecher published a celebrated article titled "The Powerful Placebo." Beecher forcefully argued that there is an established (yet still inexplicable) psychosomatic effect of placebos in medicine, where *psychosomatic* means "mind over body," in which the therapeutic response of placebo groups may be significantly better than groups of patients who are untreated. Beecher emphasized the importance of placebo controls in medical drug trials.

Today, there is still no consensus among medical scientists about whether placebo effects actually exist. In social science, however, the placebo effect cannot be avoided. It often takes the form of researchers' unintended influence over their results. In the 1920s and 1930s, for instance, a series of studies were conducted at the Hawthorne Works factories outside of Chicago to see whether industrial lighting (low light versus high light) affected worker productivity. Significant improvements in workers' performance were found during the study, but those effects disappeared after the study was concluded. In a subsequent analysis of these results in 1953, John R. P. French identified the "Hawthorne effect." It turned out that it was not the change in the lighting that improved worker performance but the presence of the researchers who were studying them. The Hawthorne effect reveals that the mere presence of researchers studying group performance can directly impact group performance.

Could this kind of placebo effect also impact the study of collective intelligence? Might improvements in groups' performance be explained by virtue of their awareness that they were being studied?

In the jelly-bean experiment, for instance, just as in the vaccine study, participants were given three rounds to provide responses to the intelligence question. First, they provided independent answers, just like Galton's and Treynor's first round, showing the classic wisdom of the crowd: Everyone responds independently, and the group average always outperforms the average individual.

In round two, however, people could see their peers' responses. Once there is this exchange of opinions, people's judgments are no longer independent. The same thing happens in round three. Our question was whether the social influence from subsequent rounds would improve collective intelligence or undermine it. In the vaccine study, we found that network structure mattered—in egalitarian networks, and only those networks, social influence made groups smarter.

Though we were looking at similar network structures as we had in our conspiracy experiment, the removal of the disinformation agent and the addition of a placebo group added different twists to the study. We wanted to find out if improvements in group intelligence could also be explained by a sort of placebo effect that naturally resulted from asking people to respond to a single question repeatedly without intentional interference. The independent control group was a lot like taking the SAT or MCAT. Does independently reflecting on your answer two times before providing your final response help you improve your score?

After everyone's final answers were collected, we pooled people's independent responses into groups of forty, just like the networks. We could then use Galton's method of averages to see if there were any changes in collective intelligence in the placebo condition from the first round to the final round, and compare this to any changes that we found in the networks.

THE JELLY-BEAN TRIALS

In total, we conducted thirteen experimental trials of the jelly-bean study. There were thirteen egalitarian fair-trade networks, thirteen centralized firehose networks, and eight placebo control groups. Because everyone in the placebo controls was independent, we required fewer replications to achieve the same statistical power.

In six of the thirteen trials, we asked participants to answer four different count questions (figure 3.5), such as: How many pennies in this pile? How many jelly beans in this jar? How many calories in this meal? And so on.

FIGURE 3.5
Collective intelligence questions

Take calories.

How many calories do you think are in this cheesesteak sandwich? Even people from Philadelphia need to ponder this one for a moment. What's your guess?

You may be surprised that the correct answer is seven hundred and five.

In the other seven trials, we asked participants to answer five different percentage questions, such as what fraction of people in a picture are wearing hats? What fraction of the dots in a picture are blue? What fraction of people in a picture have black umbrellas? And so on.

In independent control (placebo) groups, not much changed: While every participant had the same amount of time to revise their answers as in the networks, few made any significant revisions to their initial responses. Overall, diversity of responses stayed about the same, with a small 3 percent decrease from the first round to the last round. Correspondingly, there was a 3 percent improvement in the accuracy of individuals' responses—some individuals' overestimates came down, and some individuals' underestimates came up. But consistent with previous conclusions, the wisdom of the crowd did not change. There was no movement in the mean or median of the collective response.

But in the networks, everything changed. In centralized networks, that change, for better or for worse, depended on who was in the central "influencer" position—because people were randomly assigned to their network locations, the effect of the person in the influencer position on collective intelligence was a crap shoot.

If the centrally placed influencer was more accurate than the wisdom of the crowd (like the one or two hyper-accurate people found in Treynor's jelly-bean experiments who outperformed the group average), they improved the accuracy of the entire group.

The second way that centralized networks could improve collective intelligence is more common but less reliable. If the person in the center is less accurate than the group, but they are wrong in the opposite direction from everyone else, then their individual error can cancel out a lot of group error. This works because, as Galton and Page showed, by definition, the wisdom of the crowd is more accurate than the average individual. So, unless the rare savant takes the center spot (as above), the central individual will be less accurate than the crowd—but that does not necessarily mean that central actor will lead the group astray.

The key issue is bias. Does the central person's error show the same bias as the rest of the group? If so, this influencer will increase the group bias and reduce collective intelligence. But if the central person errs in the opposite direction from the group, then despite being wrong, their outsized influence counterbalances group error. In that case, the central actor can unintentionally pull the entire population back toward the correct answer, leading to a significant increase in the group's collective accuracy (and a significant reduction in group bias).

Both kinds of beneficial centralization emerged in our study—sometimes the highly accurate savants found their way to the central position, and sometimes individuals with incredibly inaccurate (but also highly deviant) responses found their way into the center. But because the deviants' inaccurate responses were wrong in the *opposite direction* from the group bias (that is, the central person overestimated wildly, while everyone else in the community underestimated), centralized networks accidently corrected group bias and increased collective intelligence.

Across all of the experimental trials in which these "lucky" influencers helped to improve crowd intelligence, the group mean improved by an average of 43 percent and the group median typically improved by 48 percent—a massive difference from the placebo group. That all sounds pretty good: Centralized networks can luck into making crowds smarter. But, before putting on our party hats and claiming victory, let's take a look at what happened the rest of the time. Over 60 percent of the time, centralized networks got unlucky in their choice of influencer. This is because most people share the same bias as the rest of population. So, most often, if someone finds their way to the center, they will tend to have the same biased views as everyone else, which reinforce the beliefs held in common in the community. That's fine if the problem is easy, since group bias probably leads in the right direction. But if the problem is hard, then centralization runs into problems. When the response of the central actor amplifies the group bias, and the group is generally wrong, then social learning in centralized networks consistently reduces the wisdom of the crowd. In the majority of centralized networks, on average the accuracy of the group mean decreased by 19 percent and the accuracy of the median decreased by 32 percent.

The biggest concern when it comes to centralized influencer networks is what happens when the group faces different kinds of questions. In this case, the real problem with influencers is that once a person has the status and power to sustain an outsized number of network ties, they remain influential even when the topic of conversation wanders far from their expertise. This happens to all of us, online and offline, and it is an inevitable consequence of the power of persuasion bias. Among the influencers in our study, there was no correlation between their accuracy on one question and another question. The same influencer who pulled the crowd toward the right answer in one instance would then pull the crowd in the wrong direction in another. This is often an insurmountable challenge for communities structured as firehose networks.

Egalitarian networks offer a way out.

In our jelly-bean trials, egalitarian networks consistently made everyone smarter. As people influenced one another, there was on average a 43 percent reduction in diversity from the first round to the final round. This reduction in diversity led to a 23 percent increase in individual accuracy. People were converging not toward the wisdom of the crowd found in round one but beyond it.

In egalitarian networks, collective intelligence consistently increased over all three rounds. The accuracy of the group median improved by 12 percent, and the accuracy of the group mean improved by 10 percent. These are large improvements that significantly outpace the wisdom of the crowd, and they happened as a result of people freely exchanging information.

So why did Jack Treynor find that giving people shared information lowered their collective intelligence, but we found that letting people share information increased collective intelligence? The answer is that the way Treynor introduced information was centralized. His information about the jars forced all of the participants to consider the same particular features of the jelly-bean problem without any regard for whether this way of thinking would be helpful or harmful. That kind of centralized information was doing the same thing that a centralized network was doing in our experiment: forcing everyone toward convergence on a single idea that was not based on the most insightful individuals but rather governed by an external influence.

In a centralized network, that external feature is network position. A particular individual is influential based on their structural position without any regard for accuracy. Treynor's information experiment did a similar thing. It forced everyone to be guided by the same information irrespective of whether that information was actually helpful for improving their judgment.

Forcing a population to pay attention to one particular information source (such as a senior government official) or one particular influencer (such as a popular TV pundit) will often lead them to underperform as a collective. This is because the power of the influencer is insensitive to information quality.

In egalitarian networks, just as in the firehose networks, the most accurate individual changed from question to question. But unlike the firehose networks, this change did not derail collective intelligence. Instead, the people who were most accurate on a particular question became the most influential people in the entire network. These individuals acted as centers of gravity that pulled everyone toward a better answer. When the group was faced with a new question, new people emerged to lead the group to a better answer.

It cannot be known ahead of time who the most accurate people will be for a particular problem. This makes it challenging to decide who should lead the group when a new challenge arises. In egalitarian networks, this problem is solved because the *unmoved mover* emerges based on their ability to address the problem. Social power is fluid. When the problem changes, so does the center of influence. The egalitarian network empowers the most accurate individuals to lead the group, regardless of who they are.

How did the egalitarian networks know how to do this? And what does it tell us about how to choose leaders who will increase our collective intelligence?

Unmoved Movers

Since all of our findings on egalitarian networks are explained by the fact that accurate people tend to stick with their answers, figuring this out is important. Because everyone has equal influence in an egalitarian network, those who stay put become the centers of gravity for the entire network. They are the unmoved movers who pull everyone else toward them.

This seemingly minor individual tendency has big implications for collective intelligence. If accurate people stick with their answers while less accurate people typically move toward their peers' answers, the collective drifts toward the most accurate people. This collective shift in belief is precisely how egalitarian networks improved the accuracy of people's opinions about vaccine safety. It is also how our participants became more accurate in counting jelly beans, and in winning the Showcase Showdown. This collective movement is the reason why intelligence increases in egalitarian networks.

Surprisingly, people behave exactly the same way in firehose networks as they do in fair-trade networks. In both networks, accurate people revise less, and inaccurate people revise more. But these individual tendencies have very different effects on collective intelligence in fair-trade networks versus firehose networks because of the structural power of the influencer.

Another surprising result from our study of jelly beans is about group size. Classical work on crowd wisdom (by Galton and Treynor) shows that bigger groups have greater collective intelligence. But this assumes that everyone is independent. Collective intelligence comes from an accurate approximation of the group mean. The larger the group, the more accurate that approximation is.

But things change when you take learning dynamics into account. When centers of gravity emerge, they lead people away from the mean. The structural intelligence that emerges in small egalitarian networks can outperform the mean approximation from even a vast collection of placebo-controlled responses.

But the group can't be too small either.

In the last chapter, I told you about the 2011 Swiss research that concluded social influence "undermined" the wisdom of the crowd. What they really meant was that confidence increased while collective intelligence stayed the same. But the follow-up study showed that in fact individuals improved in those networks. Yet no one found the results that we uncovered, that the average intelligence of the entire collective improved. Why not?

The answer is group size. The networks they used were too small. They used groups of twelve students, and they connected everyone together in a massive ball instead of having a locally connected fair-trade structure.

There was not enough initial diversity in the group to allow different opinions to pull the population in new directions. Over several thousand computational trials, we found that it takes groups of about thirty people to regularly see significant improvements in collective intelligence. Once groups get up to forty people, collective improvements are almost certain to be found. Above that, it's just icing on the cake.

I was trying to understand why these results had not been discovered before. Then I remembered that Jack Treynor had only run his jelly-bean experiment on each crowd of students once. When he identified those one or two people who outperformed the crowd, he had no way of knowing if those people were smart or if they were lucky. In a centralized network, the answer to that question matters a lot. If a person is accurate on one question, before you put them into the position of power you want to know if they were smart or lucky—because once a person has the power of the influencer, they will control the population regardless of whether they are right or wrong.

But in an egalitarian structure, whoever does the best job on a question becomes the center of gravity for the network and pulls everyone toward a greater level of intelligence. In egalitarian networks, the important thing is not the person but the quality of the person's responses.

INTELLIGENT INEQUALITY

DeGroot's assumption about people's behavior had been that each individual's likelihood of revising their answer is random across the population. The chances of a person sticking with their first answer or moving to a new answer would be, on average, the same for everyone. Economists refer to this as the assumption that people's chances of moving are "identically and independently distributed" across the population. That means that every person is equally likely to be a mover or a stayer.

One of our main discoveries was that this famous principle wasn't true for the wisdom of crowds. People's likelihood of sticking with their original answer or moving to follow their peers was not random—in fact, it was predictable.

People who were more accurate were more likely to stick, while people who were less accurate were more likely to move. At first, that makes sense. If I'm accurate on the first round, of course I do not move. But this is one of those scientific facts that becomes less obvious when you start looking at it more closely.

At first, you think, "Of course accurate people do not move. Why would they?" But we also know that the same person can be more accurate on some questions and less accurate on others, so the reason why accurate people do not move is not that they are more willful or have stronger personalities but that they seem to have a better sense of when they are wrong (so will be more flexible), and when they are right (when they will be less so).

That still seems to make sense. But it gets slightly more complicated when people lack any preexisting knowledge of which answer is likely to be correct (like guessing the number of jelly beans in a jar). In such cases, and without any informational feedback among participants about the quality of their guesses or about the quality of anyone else's guesses, people have no way of knowing how accurate or inaccurate they are relative to anyone else. Nevertheless, we find that when people are wrong, they tend to move to follow their neighbors, and when they are right, they tend to stick to their guns.

Even when we take into account the distance between a person's initial guess and the average guess of their neighborhood (a small version of the wisdom of the crowd), people who were wrong tended to move more, and people who were right tended to stick with their original answer, regardless of how close it was to their neighbors' guesses.

The most intuitive explanation for why people who are accurate stick with their original response is because they feel more confident that they're correct. Similarly, when people are less accurate, they probably feel less confident in their answer. To test this, we can simply ask people how confident they feel about their answers.

But it turns out that there is generally no correlation between confidence and accuracy. In the cases where a significant correlation is uncovered, it is usually negative: The people who report being most confident in their answer are often the least accurate. Similarly, the people who have the most accurate answers typically report feeling the least confident about them.

Now we have a genuine scientific puzzle. The people who are most accurate, and act the most confident by sticking with their answer, report being the least confident. But if they aren't confident, why are they sticking with their answers? Even more striking is the fact that this pattern was consistently found across networks in which people were asked multiple questions. That means that people were intuitively adjusting their choices to stay instead of move based on actual accuracy, even as their confidence was changing in an unrelated way. How is this possible?

The (Un)Confidence Paradox

Years before our jelly-bean experiment, and also in the years after, dozens of studies have tried to identify the connection between people's self-reported confidence in their answers and their accuracy. The only consistent insight is that self-reported confidence is not a reliable way of guiding collectives toward greater intelligence, particularly when we face hard problems. In fact, most of the time the most useful thing about self-reported confidence is that it tells us who *not* to follow.

In 2015, two Spanish scientists tried to unravel the confidence puzzle by re-reanalyzing the data from the 2011 Swiss study. (As you can see, that data has been subject to a lot of analyses.) Instead of focusing exclusively on learning and collective intelligence, the Spaniards focused on confidence. They found that three times out of a hundred, a person's "self-weight"—that is, their inclination to stick to their own answer rather than change their response to follow their peers—is explained by their self-reported confidence. The rest of the time (i.e., 97 percent of the time), self-reported confidence does not predict whether people will stick with their answers. The magnitude of these figures was surprising even to veteran researchers.

The second part of the analysis was even more surprising. Self-reported confidence fails to predict not only self-weight but accuracy as well. When you put these together, you come out with the plain result that self-reported confidence does not predict anything—the same results that we found in our jelly-bean study. Self-weight predicts accuracy. But confidence does not.

One way to make practical use of these discoveries would be to try to find the most accurate people by measuring individuals with a high self-weight, and then put them into leadership positions. But even if you could identify such people early on, self-weight varies from question to question. Indeed, you wind up back where you started, trying to let the network find the right person each time the group faces a new problem.

Back in 2012, a few years before the Spanish findings were published, Israeli psychologist Asher Koriat conducted an interesting study that put the confidence question in a new and helpful light. Two years before, in 2010, a group of British psychologists had argued that two heads are better than one for the grand challenge of choosing—but only when people share their self-reported confidence with one another. They found that in such cases confidence *was* in fact correlated with accuracy. In fact, simply by allowing people to reveal information about their confidence when they shared their answers, groups of two were reliably able to select the better choice (by following the more confident individual) each time.

But then Koriat took a closer look at the results and decided to run some experiments of his own. Just as the British researchers had claimed, two heads could indeed be better than one when both followed the more confident member of the pair. But there was a catch: This was only true for easy questions. Confidence was a good indicator of accuracy when the problem was easy enough that most people knew the right answer. This is because your confidence in your answer tends to be based on whether your opinion reflects popular consensus.

But since confidence is based on agreement with popular opinion, everything goes off the rails when the problem is hard. By definition, when a problem is hard, popular opinion tends to get the answer wrong. In that case, people who are right stand against the consensus view.

There are some striking implications for Koriat's conclusion.

First, this means that whenever confidence is a good indicator of accuracy, it doesn't much matter who the leader is because the problem is easy and the correct answer is already the popular view.

Second, when the problem is hard, this is when the leader really matters, and confidence is exactly the wrong thing to look for, because the person who reports low confidence in their answer is the person who will lead the collective to the most intelligent solution.

Third, when it comes to hard problems, although the most accurate people will report low confidence in their answer, they will privately stick to their guns. They know it goes against the crowd, but they will not abandon their "better" judgment.

In most situations, people must advertise their confidence in order to gain a leadership role their community. But not in egalitarian networks. In these information structures, the people who quietly but resolutely maintain their views become the unmoved movers for the network. When dealing with hard problems, these people don't seek to take credit for going against the herd, nor do they recruit others to follow them. Rather, they quietly hold onto their view, even though they suspect that the majority view may be right. And without anyone ever noticing, these individuals invisibly raise the intelligence of the entire collective.

Now recall Sunstein's Colorado study, in which social interactions drove people to adopt extreme opinions. As they became more extreme, they also became more confident. The troubling conclusion is that the more confident groups become about the consensus they have reached, the more likely it is that collective beliefs have become more extreme and less intelligent.

These revelations are not reassuring. If feelings of confidence are not reliable signs of group intelligence, what is?

SOLVING THE CONFIDENCE PROBLEM

Condorcet was more correct than he knew. When it comes to easy questions, for which the majority of people choose correctly, majority rule is the best way to go. But for hard questions, for which most people would choose wrong, Condorcet showed that the most intelligent way to choose would be to allow a small group of elites, or even a single person, to choose for everyone. This is because when a problem is hard, most people will get the answer wrong, and will do so with aplomb. The majority of people will not just walk off a cliff—they will gallop over it with enthusiasm.

Structural intelligence shows that the way to solve Condorcet's problem is to break his cardinal law of independence. In an egalitarian information structure, people do not follow the most confident individual.

Quite the contrary: By eliminating self-reported confidence from the collective calculus and replacing it with authentic self-weight, an egalitarian structure empowers the accurate few—whether they are elites or not—to guide the group toward intelligent collective decisions on hard problems.

Modern critics of inclusive democracy stand on Condorcet's shoulders. They argue that the majority of voters are uninformed and biased, and will therefore make the wrong choices. In these situations, critics of democratic inclusiveness nominate elites to take over. That sounds plausible at first. The idea is that smart, educated, confident, and serious people should take over when problems are too complicated for the majority to decide effectively.

While the elite solution sounds good at first, the more you think about it, the worse it becomes. Several decades before the Swiss study, in 1972, the psychologist Irving Janis had reached a similar conclusion. He identified the phenomenon of groupthink, which was similar to the one described by the Swiss scientists. Except that Janis's version was far more dangerous. His conclusion was based not on experiments but on a careful study of the White House. Analyzing hundreds of documents from White House senior staff meetings during the Kennedy and Johnson administrations, Janis found that camaraderie and loyalty among Ivy League–trained elites was responsible for corrupting the decision-making powers of some of the best minds in American government—leading the world's most powerful nation into a series of foreign policy fiascos. As Janis explained:

> Kennedy's groupthinkers believed that Premier Fidel Castro's air force was so ineffectual that obsolete B-26s could knock it out completely. . . . They also believed that Castro's army was so weak that a small Cuban-exile brigade could establish a well-protected beachhead. . . . In addition, they believed that Castro was not smart enough to put down any possible internal uprisings in support of exiles. They were wrong on all three assumptions.

Janis borrowed *groupthink* from the sociologist William H. Whyte, who coined the term as an allusion to George Orwell's famous term "doublethink," from his novel *1984*, which he used to capture the maddening cognitive dissonance that citizens were forced to endure under Stalin's rule. Janis's phrasing cleverly pinpointed a Cold War irony: American policymakers were floundering in their fight against communism by falling into the very same trap that the Communists had set for their own subjects. Top American minds were devolving into Orwellian consensus-driven crowds.

Janis argued that close-knit groups easily coalesce into a consensus view. As group members become more comfortable with one another, they can become excessively, even recklessly, confident in their conclusions. Consensus itself becomes both a source of inflated confidence and an anchor on intelligence. Just like the Swiss scientists in 2011, Janis concluded that social influence can actively undermine collective intelligence, even among the brightest minds.

Treynor's additional insight from his jelly-bean experiments was that elites are all privy to the same narrow pool of privileged information. Consequently, they will all reason in similar ways. By virtue of elites attending the same elite schools, reading the same elite journals, and socializing in the same elite circles, they tend to share the same errors of judgment. They also tend not to notice these errors because of the confidence that comes with this kind of informational consensus.

So Condorcet was right about hard problems—only a small number of people are suited to find the best solution. But Janis and Treynor showed that these rare individuals need not be elites. The problem with elites is not where they are educated, nor that they have achieved positions of status and influence. The problem arises when this hard-earned individual intelligence is hemmed in by deference to a centralized model of informational consensus, where nuance and detail take a back seat to authority and conformity. When this happens, the structural machinery of power can trap even the best minds in a failure mode of unwarranted confidence. As one political commentator sharply remarked, "All I know is, we got into Vietnam courtesy of the Beltway Chapter of the Harvard Alumni Association." Without the right structures, elites, no matter how well-intentioned, will rarely be able to escape the failure mode of confidence . . . because elites are elites.

So how do we decide what to do when we are faced with a hard problem? How do we find that small number of rare individuals who can lead the collective to a better solution? The answer is to let structure decide for us. The right structure guides populations toward the best leaders. Indeed, the challenge of hard problems is what structural intelligence was born to solve. We can even say that hard problems are the only situations for which structural intelligence is required. It solves the confidence conundrum because in the right structure, authentic self-weight has greater pull than outward self-confidence. In an egalitarian structure, centers of gravity emerge around those individuals who can pull the population away from group bias and toward more intelligent solutions. Most importantly, once the problem is solved, the network seamlessly adapts by shifting the locus of power to find new leaders who are best suited to guide the collective through the next problems they face. Power is fluid. Influence is transient. Intelligence is enduring.

4

Herd Immunity for Your Brain

Long before Serendipity 3 introduced its world-famous $1,000 sundae, it was already a favorite hot spot for movie stars and celebrities. Jackie Onassis once asked the owner of the trendy New York City restaurant if she could buy the secret recipe for his signature fan-favorite dessert, Frrozen Hot Chocolate. He said it was not for sale.

Serendipity 3 has a long list of pricey desserts. It's enough to make a $22 slice of cheesecake seem positively frugal. And that's precisely the idea: If you put absurdly expensive items on the menu, they anchor people's expectations. It makes dessert prices in the low hundreds seem reasonable by comparison. Most importantly, it significantly increases sales of Serendipity 3's $22 slice of cheesecake.

And that's just for desserts. Serendipity 3 didn't really cash in on the anchoring effect until they figured out a way to quadruple sales of their $18 cheeseburger. How did they do it? They added a new menu item that won them a spot in the *Guinness Book of World Records*. At $69, Serendipity 3's record-winning foot-long hot dog (2006 World Record, "Most Expensive Hotdog in the World") was not expected to sell. Neither was the $1,000 sundae, for that matter. These items were on the menu to set pricing anchors for the other dishes. The most expensive items were always listed as the first items on each page. They set expectations for everything below. This simple trick worked surprisingly well: As soon as Serendipity 3 introduced the $69 hot dog, sales of the $18 cheeseburger skyrocketed.

Anchoring effects have had an enormous impact on the field of marketing—and they made Serendipity 3 a lot of money. But they also challenge one of the fundamental principles of economics, which is that people use all of the information available to them to make welfare-maximizing choices. That means that a person's decision about whether or not to buy an $18 hamburger should be based on market expectations about the going price for hamburgers. The existence of a $69 hot dog is irrelevant. Or it should be, anyway.

Anchoring effects throw a big wrench into the machinery of modern economics. Suddenly, all kinds of irrelevant things—like $1,000 sundaes—can affect normal people's consumer decisions. They can even affect professional traders' investment decisions. This discovery helped to jump-start an entire field of economic research called behavioral economics. In this field, economists are interested in how people actually make decisions, rather than in how they ought to make decisions.

In the 1970s, psychologist Daniel Kahneman began his groundbreaking work with economist Amos Tversky uncovering a host of cognitive biases, like anchoring, that affect how real people solve economic problems. Kahneman and Tversky's experiments boldly reminded everyone that the idea of rationality was not a law of economic behavior but rather a hypothesis about human reasoning. The economics community applauded these findings so loudly that Kahneman was awarded the 2002 Nobel Prize in Economics. The field of economics would never be the same.

Kahneman and Tversky were studying cognitive biases, not group behavior, but the idea is similar to Treynor's findings on jelly beans: If you give lots of people the same anchors, then everyone will make the same errors in judgment. Treynor showed that centralized information was a bad idea since it forced everyone toward a homogenized view of the market, which would inevitably lead to bubbles and crashes. In Mackay's interpretation, this would appear like the madness of crowds. But in the field of behavioral economics, this kind of collective error could be seen not as madness but as the result of predictable features of human reasoning.

Once we know how anchoring bias works, are we able to use our science to outsmart our own biases? Unfortunately, knowing about anchoring bias does not make you immune to it. In this respect, social science is like physics. Knowing how gravity works does not make you immune to falling. Knowing about anchoring bias does not change how you reason.

But that does not mean that we are helpless. Once scholars know how human reasoning works, it should be possible to design choice settings (and even social structures) with this knowledge in mind. Could embedding people into intelligent networks help them to outsmart their own biases?

The only way to know for sure was to try it and find out.

THIS IS YOUR BRAIN ON CROWDS

My student Calvin Isch and I designed an anchoring bias study by using one of the questions from the jelly-bean experiment. We showed participants a picture of a massive stack of pennies and asked them to guess how many coins there were. But this time, we began the study with Kahneman and Tversky's method for triggering anchoring bias. In the low-anchor group, we asked participants, "Is the number of pennies higher or lower than 118?"

It worked.

The median guess of the population without an anchor was 185, but with the anchor the median guess dropped down to 141. The correct answer was 246. The anchor was effective for pulling most people away from the correct answer. This is often talked about as a *harmful anchor.*

We also wondered what would happen if we gave people a high anchor, and asked participants in this anchor group, "Is the number of pennies in this pile higher or lower than 353?"

Once again the anchor worked perfectly, with the median guess in this group increasing from 185 to 200. The value of the anchor itself was incorrect, but its effect was to pull the population toward a more accurate answer.

This is similar to how influencers improved people's answers in the jelly-bean experiment: If the influencer was wrong, but they were wrong in the right direction, they could pull the entire population toward the correct answer. Here we called this a *helpful anchor.*

Digging deeper, we then divided the harmful anchor group and the helpful anchor group, giving each a control condition and a network condition. In the first round, everyone answered independently. In the control groups, everyone continued to answer independently in two additional rounds. In the egalitarian networks, in rounds two and three subjects could see their network neighbors' previous round responses before giving their answers. The result was a horse race for intelligence between the egalitarian network and the placebo control condition for each of the anchors.

The dominant prediction for the harmful anchor groups—let's call it the Sunstein prediction—was that social influence would exacerbate bias, leading the harmful anchor networks further from the true answer, as compared to the harmful anchor control groups.

But the opposite happened.

In the egalitarian networks, the entire group started to disentangle their collective beliefs from their anchoring bias. Both collectively and individually, networked populations exhibited a self-correcting march away from their own anchor and back toward truth.

Structural intelligence worked for harmful anchors and helpful anchors. For helpful anchors, egalitarian networks led to an amplification of the anchor, which seems like it's the opposite of what happened for harmful anchors. But in both cases, the network populations moved toward the truth—people adjusted their responses away from the harmful anchor and further toward the helpful anchor. The overall effect for both kinds of anchor was increasing collective intelligence in egalitarian networks.

The explanation for how this happened is exactly the same as it was for the jelly-bean experiment. It turned out this same mechanism of collective learning also works in populations that are subjected to anchoring bias, because people who are biased in the right direction tend to stick with their bias, and people who are biased in the wrong direction tend to move away from it.

We replicated this entire study eight times in total, studying 1,600 people, divided into thirty-two groups. Across all of these replications, we consistently found the same results every time: In egalitarian networks, populations recovered from harmful anchors and amplified helpful anchors. Structural intelligence offers a robust solution to anchoring bias. In fact, the best antidote to the predictable irrationality of individuals subject to anchoring bias is the surprising rationality that emerges from a networked crowd.

Here's our response to the $69 hot dog. Next time you go out to eat, bring a collective with you to help decide what to order. Individually, each of us is susceptible to the anchoring effects of a $69 hot dog, but collectively we tend to agree on what's a reasonable price for a hamburger. And if we're in a hot-dog mood, a group is much more likely to collectively mobilize to find one for $3 from a food cart instead.

CONFIDENCE IN OTHERS

Structural intelligence in the grand challenge of choosing always comes back to one basic question: How do accurate people know that they should stick with their answers? Even when people are subject to anchoring bias, they somehow figure out who should stick and who should move. How does it happen?

While our experiments had shown that confidence is not the answer, we still found that hard to believe. How can confidence *not* explain it?

So we took a new approach. In the anchoring experiment, we asked everyone to provide their self-reported confidence in their own answers, just as people had done in past studies. Then we also asked them to report their confidence in their peers' answers.

This second question was the key. The responses to the first question were exactly what past studies would predict: There was no correlation between people's self-reported confidence in their own answers and their actual accuracy. This was true in the first round and in the last round. Just as expected, confidence did not predict accuracy.

But then, when we examined people's confidence in other people's accuracy, we found something. People who had more confidence in other people were significantly more accurate in the first round and in the last round. Accuracy came down to confidence in others.

This discovery presented us with a puzzle. We know that people who are more accurate in the initial round tend to stick with their answers, even if they expect that others are likely to be more accurate. So why would they report being more confident in others when they are the same people who resist social influence the most?

It's because self-reported confidence does not measure accuracy; it measures consensus. People's confidence corresponds to how well their beliefs match up with everyone else's. If their beliefs match the consensus, then they are confident in themselves. If they don't, then they are confident in others. Interestingly, it is this latter case, in which a person knows their views differ from everyone else's, that they are most likely to be among the best people to lead the collective through a hard problem.

The first thing we know about this kind of person who reports having greater confidence in others than in themselves is that they are unlikely to be an influencer. They are unlikely to try to hold court over popular opinion. They are unlikely to take center stage or cultivate thousands of network ties. As a result, their private knowledge is unlikely to benefit anyone, particularly in a setting in which status, power, and connectedness dominate collective beliefs (as they do almost everywhere). The ability of these capable individuals to contribute to the collective's intelligence—and their potential to solve Condorcet's puzzle of democracy—does not come about through independent voting. Rather, the solution that invigorates collective wisdom is to embed the population into a structure that invisibly gives these people greater influence by virtue of their greater self-weight. Even though these people would not ask for this power, an egalitarian structure brings the population under the influence of the people who are best suited to lead them.

In an intelligent structure, these individuals' steadfast conviction brings the crowd back to reason when it has inadvertently gone astray. The heroes of the network simply stand their ground, and the crowd is drawn to them by the force of their gravity until collective belief aligns with wisdom. When the next challenge arises, these heroes step aside and allow new heroes to emerge within diverse parts of the network. As the need arises, each individual's intelligence is given rule over the collective, as guided by the adaptive intelligence of an egalitarian structure.

The heroes that emerge in egalitarian networks may be called upon (from every part of the population) to lead the collective to victory over a hard problem, which would have stumped almost everyone. When the heroes' work is done, they recede back into the crowd. The next time a challenge arises and the crowd is led astray, the former heroes may be led astray with them. But the network finds new heroes who emerge and act as ballast for the population, pulling everyone back toward the right path. In an intelligent structure, leadership continuously adapts to the needs of the occasion, each time allowing those heroes to emerge who are best suited to lead a population toward greater intelligence.

So how does this work in real life? Say, in an actual political debate, in which each of us must come to a decision and cast our ballot? How does collective intelligence emerge—and how do we know when we've made a smart group choice?

To answer these questions, I'm going to take you to the wilds of northern Alaska where we will see how this plays out during a referendum on immigration in one small American town.

5

When Echo Chambers Are Smart

Meet Ben Tyrer, the American everyman. Ben is a twenty-seven-year-old do-it-yourselfer from Homer, Alaska. He works as a janitor at the local Kenai Peninsula College. Ben is married and has a two-year-old daughter. He's not a particularly political person. In fact, he avoids the news if he can. He's the kind of guy who posts dad jokes on his Facebook page: "What comes after Colin Firth? Colin Thecond."

But in 2016, Ben's quiet apolitical life was upended by a contentious referendum over immigration that turned his small Alaskan town into a hotbed of partisan controversy.

Homer's Crisis

Homer, Alaska, is at the literal end of the road. If you drive north from California, up through Washington and into Canada, and then keep going, after a few days you will reach the tip of the Kenai Peninsula, about 200 miles southwest of Anchorage. The peninsula eventually narrows into the Homer spit, a seventy-five-foot-wide boulevard of shops and homes that extends for several miles into the iceberg-filled Kachemak Bay. The town of Homer runs down the spit, dead-ending onto a chilly beachhead surrounded by breathtaking Alaskan fjords.

Homer is an all-American town. The main activities are fishing and hunting. And—wetsuit absolutely required—surfing. Ironically, its all-Americanness is the reason why the town ultimately came undone.

In 2016, after the election of President Trump, the town council proposed a resolution that included language like this: "Whereas a new administration is in power in Washington, D.C., without a popular mandate, whereas during his campaign, President Donald Trump made statements offensive and harmful to the rights of women, immigrants, religious, racial, and ethnic minorities . . ." It went on like this for a while and then ended with a resounding punch line: Homer would be officially pronounced a safe and welcoming place for all US immigrants, legal and illegal.

This resolution was not a legally binding piece of legislation. It was not a law. It was not even an ordinance. In fact, it had no legal or municipal force whatsoever. It was simply a statement of principle that was intended to reflect the feelings of the people of Homer. Immigration was not a practical concern for residents of Homer. But the resolution nevertheless had teeth, at least emotionally. It was the principle that mattered. And to the people of Homer, it mattered a lot.

But it didn't reflect everyone's feelings. There are a lot of Trump supporters in Homer. These citizens have never met an immigrant, nor are they likely to ever meet one. But they supported Trump and Trump's policies. They loved the idea of building a wall to keep out Mexicans. Even though Mexico was over 6,000 miles away and on the other side of three contiguous national borders.

When the proposed resolution was publicly announced, civic life in Homer quickly unraveled. A miasma of fear and loathing hung over the town council meeting that week, which was convened to hear all sides prior to the referendum.

One resident expressed a widely held sentiment: "You bring in illegals, OK, by definition, they're criminals. OK, they live in the underworld. They don't have a stake in the game as we do. About the first time somebody gets raped or killed, I hope they come straight after the Homer City Council and sue the City to the point of bankruptcy. If you make this a magnet for that type of people, then, you know, shame on you."

No one was hit harder by the controversy than Ben Tyrer.

Ben took his civic responsibility seriously. He did not want to jump to any conclusions. He approached the referendum like he approached most things: by doing research. A few years earlier, Ben had built his family's house by himself based entirely on how-to manuals and helpful guidance he found online.

Ben, adept at sorting and gathering information, felt confident he could piece together the immigration issue and come to a responsible decision. But the more he researched, the more anxious he felt.

During the week prior to the town referendum, Ben was careful to balance right-leaning and left-leaning news sources. He obsessively consumed everything from *The New York Times* to *Breitbart*, attempting to build a coherent picture of the risks and benefits of immigration. His Google searches included questions about how many immigrants had come into the US that year, and about the immigrant situation in Europe. One statistic in particular stuck with Ben. It concerned something he found in *Breitbart* about rising criminal activity in Europe following increased immigration in 2014. The report began, "A massive migrant crime wave is surging across Germany," citing a 135-page study by the German Ministry of the Interior, claiming that Germany recorded roughly 402,000 crimes by migrants in 2015, a huge uptick in overall criminal activity from the previous year.

Ben struggled to internalize this information. As he recounted, "My brain is telling me to at least be cautious, to really keep an eye on this—to keep an eye on them. And then there's my heart that says, these are people, too. I mean, if the shoe was on the other foot, if the United States was a third world, war torn country, I would do whatever it took to get my family out of here, legally or illegally."

In order to ensure that he made his decision without peer pressure, Ben didn't talk about his research with others, instead using his time to read and think more deeply (just as Rousseau would have advised). Ben's wife noted, "It was an intense week." They had gone through several stressful life events together—having a child and building their own home. But, it seemed to her, nothing came close to the immigration vote in Homer.

On the night of the vote, there was a final town council meeting. Ben gave an impassioned speech about the importance of understanding immigration and its nuanced implications for all Americans, and then he cast his vote—against the resolution.

All the votes were counted. The resolution had been defeated.

"Believe it or not, it kind of changed my worldview," said Ben. "I have this part of me that I want everyone to get along . . . And the fact that I was making a decision to kind of crack down on a group of people really tore me up, bad. It's just kind of sad, really." But his vote had been cast, and he—and many others in Homer—was glad that the battle was over.

Then some new information came to light.

BBC reporter Damien McGuinness had been covering Germany for a decade and was asked to comment on the events unfolding in Homer—and, in particular, on the story of Ben Tyrer. Damien was impressed by Ben's diligence and was familiar with the German report, which he had read cover to cover, even though, as he put it, "you know, it's a slog."

Then McGuinness dropped a bomb. "The 400,000 figure is actually including the crime of crossing the border as an asylum seeker. Now by definition, that can only be committed by migrants, and in fact, is how most refugees, by legitimately accepted international law, actually apply for asylum." When you took away the crime of illegally crossing the border, the crime rate in Germany in 2015 was unchanged from 2014. Now, remember the lead for the *Breitbart* article, which Ben had found so convincing, was "a massive migrant crime wave is surging across Germany." McGuinness's revelation put things in a different light.

"Wow," said Ben, considering his vote. After a contemplative moment, he confessed, "I mean, not through lack of trying. But, I think I was wrong."

Of Heroes and Scapegoats

We all feel like Ben sometimes. Amid mounting, often contradictory, news and information, it takes Herculean effort to claw yourself to the top of the mountain of detritus and see which choice represents a clear and responsible decision. In such cases, a common heuristic is to focus on just a few facts, or even just a single fact that we believe is the most salient and consequential piece of information. This single fact can give us confidence and resolve, even when making a complex political decision.

For Ben, this singular fact was the number of immigrant crimes reported in the *Breitbart* article. But each person can choose their own salient facts and figures, which then become anchors in their thinking.

Ben endured the tug of war between his innate intuitions and the information he encountered, while locked into a lonesome revision process, trying to think his way out of his own biases. He was stuck in the control condition, and what the control condition in our experiments has taught us is this: Try as he might, Ben's solitary reflection could not help him to escape his bias. But what if we could give Ben the chance to share his ideas with other people—give him a chance to evaluate the facts together with his peers? Would that have helped him to make a better political choice?

Today, the problems of worsening partisan extremism and increasing ideological and affective polarization among voters are the most talked-about problems in national and international politics. This is precisely what Cass Sunstein found in Colorado. Well-intentioned citizens were driven toward more polarized views just by virtue of their interactions with like-minded minded peers.

The biggest scapegoat by far in these conversations is the political echo chamber. Echo chambers are political communities and parties in which people talk exclusively with peers who share similar political views. The Colorado groups that Sunstein studied would be considered echo chambers, as would the vast majority of online communities in which people self-select into discussion groups with others who already share similar political beliefs.

Echo chambers are not a new phenomenon, but the internet has intensified their creation and impact. Today, many scholars and pundits argue that the common-sense solution to partisan extremism in US politics is simply to disrupt these echo chambers by forcing everyone into a larger, more inclusive national conversation, on- and offline.

It's not that people haven't tried.

In 2018, my team published a study showing that exposing Democrats and Republicans to one another's views on contentious topics, such as climate change, can successfully lead bipartisan groups toward greater mutual understanding. Not only that, we also found that both groups reached far greater levels of factual accuracy in their beliefs about climate trends. Over 90 percent of members in both parties learned to make accurate predictions. But, as encouraging as these findings were, we also found important limitations when individuals were exposed to "partisan primes," like pictures of party logos or graphics showing party leaders. Partisan primes don't just cause bipartisan networks to fail; they cause them to backfire, leading both groups to retreat further into their ideological camps. And because people are almost constantly exposed to partisan primes (on social media, in print media, in broadcast media), forcing people to interact across partisan boundaries can actually lead them to adopt beliefs that are far more extreme and inaccurate than those they started with.

That's the first problem with the common-sense solution. The second problem is practicality.

Bipartisan networks are a lot like therapy—there's no point in going unless you want to be there. Unless people actually want their discussion networks to be more politically integrated, requiring their networks to be more bipartisan is a hard solution to enforce. People's tendency to seek out others who think like us is one of the few ironclad facts of social life, to say nothing of political life. Given this, the solution to partisan bias is not to stop people from flocking together but to control the potentially harmful consequences of these associations.

James Madison already nailed this point in 1787, when he declared, "The latent causes of faction are thus sown in the nature of man. . . . The *causes* of faction cannot be removed . . . relief is only to be sought in the means of controlling its *effects*."

Could structural intelligence control the effects of factions? Could political echo chambers be structured to increase party members' collective intelligence?

There was only one way to find out.

We're Not in Colorado Anymore

In 2019, I partnered with Joshua Becker (whom you may remember from the jelly-bean experiment) and a political scientist from George Washington University, Ethan Porter, to design a new experiment, in which Republicans and Democrats were randomized into four homogeneous groups: two Democrat groups (one echo chamber and one placebo control group) and two Republican groups (one echo chamber and one placebo control group). Each group contained thirty-five people. In each echo chamber, participants were embedded into a politically homogeneous egalitarian network, while in the control group members were kept in isolation from one another.

Just like the previous studies, there were three rounds for each question. In the first, all participants responded independently. In the placebo control groups, rounds two and three were the same as round one. By contrast, in the echo chamber networks, members could see the responses of their network neighbors in rounds two and three. Participants were rewarded based on the accuracy of their final responses. If they performed poorly, they received no payment.

To ensure the ecological validity of our experimental design, we included partisan primes in our study. To make things challenging, we used the same partisan primes from our 2018 study.

The trap was set, now we were ready to see what would happen. We asked participants in each condition: "In 2007, it was estimated that 6.9 million unauthorized immigrants from Mexico lived in the United States. How much did this number change by 2016, before President Trump was elected?"

Just as you would expect, initial responses were biased by party ideology. Democrats' responses were much lower and more accurate than those of Republicans. We expected that. What we did not expect is what happened in the control conditions.

In previous experiments, the control groups did not show much change from the initial round to the final round. However, this time, control group members started to become more extreme in their views simply through independent reflection. In particular, Republicans' answers started moving farther away from the correct answer as they were prompted to reconsider their responses. By the final round of the study, the control groups were approaching a significantly greater level of polarization than they had shown in the initial round.

In this respect, our control groups resembled Sunstein's voters in Colorado. We were seeing a similar trend to the one Sunstein found, but the people in our control groups were not talking to one another. Sunstein had argued that his Colorado voters became more extreme in their views because they were talking to one another in political echo chambers. But perhaps social influence was not to blame. Given enough rounds of reflection, perhaps Colorado voters would have become just as extreme in their opinions simply by virtue of considering the same questions repeatedly, even if they didn't talk with each other.

This is what happened during the referendum in Homer. Simply by reflecting on the question, people who were initially biased against immigration were becoming even more extreme in their views. The only difference in the experiment was that we were seeing this tendency emerge right before our eyes.

We then watched something far less expected happen in the echo chambers.

In the egalitarian networks, we watched as the Republican echo chamber moved in the opposite direction—that is, toward greater accuracy—from the Republican control groups. By the third round, members of the Republican echo chamber had revised their collective beliefs to become significantly more similar to the Democrats. In fact, the Republican and Democrat egalitarian echo chambers had actually started to converge, with polarization between the echo chambers decreasing, and both groups becoming more accurate.

There is only one thing to do when you find results this surprising: You try again.

This time, we randomly assigned a new batch of Democrats and Republicans to egalitarian echo chamber networks and control groups. Then we asked them a different question: "For every dollar the federal government spent in fiscal year 2016, about how much went to the Department of Defense (US Military)?"

This time it was the Democrats who were biased: Their initial responses were higher and less accurate than those of Republicans. But, once again, egalitarian echo chambers had a positive effect: Democrats revised their collective beliefs to become more similar to the Republicans', and in both echo chambers, overall polarization decreased and overall accuracy increased.

We tried again, using newly recruited groups of Democrats and Republicans, and posed two more questions.

The first asked, "How much did the unemployment rate in the United States change from the beginning to the end of Democratic President Barack Obama's term in office?"

The second asked, "About how many US soldiers were killed in Iraq between the invasion in 2003 and the withdrawal of troops in December 2011?"

The results were the same, and continued to be so as we tried further variations and expansions. In total, we recruited over a thousand participants to this study. We conducted two dozen echo chamber replications and over half a dozen control group replications. Over all of these replicated trials, collective intelligence decreased nominally in the control groups. Groups of solitary individuals finished with slightly lower collective intelligence than when they started. By contrast, for both political parties, egalitarian echo chamber networks consistently improved intelligence and reduced polarization, showing a 31 percent increase in collective intelligence across all questions from round one to round three. Even more striking, polarization between the echo chamber networks decreased by a stunning 46 percent over three rounds. By contrast, control groups became slightly more polarized. Contrary to expectations, it turns out that independent reflection can actually exacerbate our biases, while social influence can help to correct them.

The results for echo chambers suggest a remarkable opportunity for collective intelligence in politics. So why don't we see this kind of intelligence on social media? In fact, why do we consistently see the opposite?

The answer is centralization. What do you think would happen if the people in our study were embedded into centralized echo chambers rather than egalitarian echo chambers? To find out, we used our experimental data to simulate what would have happened if the networks in our echo chambers had been centralized.

The results help to explain why social media is as polarized at it is. In the best-case scenario, these networks can slightly improve with regard to accuracy, but they tend not to reduce polarization, since that only happens if the person in the center opposes their own group's political bias. The more common case is that the person in the center shares the group bias. The more extreme the central person's opinion is, the less intelligent and more polarized the groups become as a result of social interaction.

We saw a similar thing happen in the vaccine study. Centralization turns intelligent people, capable of great feats of social learning, into increasingly biased individuals in increasingly polarized crowds. The fault lies not with our natural tendency to form affiliations with like-minded souls. Rather, it comes from allowing our like-minded affiliations to be co-opted by centralized power.

A Smarter Way to Decide

In light of our discoveries, there is something really sad about Ben's story.

It is not just that he voted no, and then regretted it. It is that he was right on the cusp of voting yes. But he couldn't find a way to express the nuance and complexity of his private thinking in his act of public choice.

Binary votes have this effect. It is what economists call a *discrete choice*. It means that instead of estimating the likelihood that a proposal will succeed, you are forced to simply vote yes or no.

Discrete choices sweep clean the effort and care that we invest into our political decisions. They have a totalizing effect, transforming our thoughtful, nuanced, and all-too-human evaluations into stoic up-or-down judgments. Like Ben, many of us believe that the sincerity and diligence of our political evaluations will earn us a fairer and safer world. But the ultimate expression of our sophisticated political beliefs is too often winnowed down into the savorless act of voting. Our uncanny human capacity to see many sides of an issue, even beyond our own interest, is flattened into a wholly unremarkable guess: a yea or nay.

Condorcet showed us that the margin between a collective success and collective error is a mere 1 percent difference in people's ability to discriminate between true and false. Sincere people like Ben, who care about the results and work remarkably hard to uncover the right choice, may nevertheless get it wrong.

Perhaps the saddest truth is this: Even if Ben had happened to get the answer right, he still would have felt like he was guessing. When the complexity of the modern world is transformed into a discrete choice, it is not easy for anyone to get it right, regardless of how much research they do. It's a coin flip either way.

There is another option, however.

Take Galton. He asked people to provide an estimate of an ox's weight rather than asking them to vote on whether the ox was worth buying or not. We took a similar approach in the vaccine study. Instead of asking people if vaccines are safe, we asked them to estimate the number of people who suffered severe reactions. This estimate was a proxy for their beliefs about vaccine safety.

Treynor did a similar thing to study the stock market. Rather than focusing on investors' decisions to buy or sell a stock, he was interested in how they determined a stock's value. This allowed him to use estimates of jelly bean counts as a proxy for market behavior.

In our own jelly-bean study, we used the same approach. Rather than asking participants to make discrete choices, we asked them to estimate candy counts, calorie counts, and Showcase Showdown values. Instead of asking participants to vote on whether immigration levels were too high or too low, we asked them to estimate the actual immigration numbers. This is the same approach we used to study partisan beliefs about military spending and unemployment levels.

When the question is continuous, guesses can be averaged to find collective wisdom in the crowd. Even if the result is only approximate, it may still contribute to the intelligence of the collective. But, while being close counts in horseshoes and hand grenades—and (it turns out) for hunches—it doesn't count for voting.

This is why Condorcet emphasized the importance of information. When choices are discrete, individual responses only contribute to collective intelligence if people actually choose the correct answer. Successful democracy depends on getting people above the 51 percent mark. But this is also the very same reason why critics have used Condorcet's voting theorem to leverage a skeptical view of democracy—because even a citizen like Ben Tyrer, who worked so hard to inform himself about the truth of immigration, can still wind up casting his vote incorrectly.

Galton's approach offers unexpected hope for citizens like Ben. Remember Galton's explanation for why his study of an ox's weight offered favorable evidence for democracy: "The average competitor was probably as well fitted for making a just estimate of the dressed weight of the ox, as an average voter is of judging the merits of most political issues on which he votes."

Galton was not studying votes. He was studying estimates.

What if, instead of a yes-or-no vote, Ben Tyrer had been asked, "If the resolution passes, what will be the percent change in the crime rate in Homer, Alaska?"

Going a step further, what if Ben had been given a chance to discuss this question with his peers? What would his final estimate have been? Would considering the problem this way have changed the outcome of the referendum?

The citizens in Homer did in fact have a public meeting to exchange ideas. But the exchange focused on votes. Everyone expressed their opinions about why the resolution should be approved or defeated.

It is hard to believe that changing the topic of the town meeting from discussing a vote to discussing an estimate would make much of a difference for the outcome. Yet there are facts in Ben's case that shed some light on this.

We know that the *Breitbart* report that Ben relied upon offered misleading information about immigration and crime rates. We also know that this misinformation was instrumental in Ben's decision to vote against the referendum. Could an exchange of ideas about the crime rate have corrected this misinformation? We have already seen that it worked for vaccine beliefs and for beliefs about immigration rates. What might have happened if Homer's citizens were prompted to share their intelligent, sincere, and imprecise beliefs about crime rates with one another? Would the collective process be more intelligent than having them argue for or against the resolution? Might they have collectively learned something that would have led them to a different decision?

My students Doug Guilbeault and Joshua Becker took these questions seriously—so seriously, in fact, that they decided to find out.

NETWORK LIE DETECTORS

Nine hundred subjects were recruited to participate in an online fact-checking study, in which they were shown news stories and asked to determine whether they were true or false. Participants were randomized between two experimental conditions. In one condition. people were given a binary choice ("Is the content of the news story true, yes or no?"). In the other condition, participants were asked to respond with an estimate ("What is the likelihood that this news story is true, from 0 to 100?"). In all conditions, participants were randomly embedded in egalitarian opinion-sharing networks.

As in all previous studies, the experiment had three rounds. In round one, everyone provided their independent opinion. Then, in rounds two and three participants could see the average opinion of their network neighbors. In the binary-choice condition, participants were shown the percentage of peers who chose each option in the previous round. For instance, "Is the content of this news story true? 62 percent of your peers answered 'No' and 38 percent answered 'Yes.'" In the estimate condition, participants were shown the average estimates of their peers in the network. For instance, "One a scale of 0 to 100, how likely is it that the content of this new story is true? The average answer of your peers is 38 percent."

Everyone evaluated four news stories, two true and two false.

Here are some of the stories that were used:

(1) Published article:
"Pediatricians' association admits HPV vaccine causes ovarian failure."

(2) Highly forwarded Twitter post:
"Passenger mistakes math for terrorist notes, gets professor kicked off flight."

(3) Highly forwarded Facebook post:
"Hundreds of birds dead during 5G experiment in The Hague, The Netherlands"

(4) Published article:
"Nazi salutes in Baraboo High School prom photo spark outrage online, district investigation."

Can you guess which are true and which are false?

Now, instead, try to estimate the likelihood that each one is true.

At the start of the experiment, most participants had no idea which stories were true and which were false. Across both conditions, participants had equivalent rates of guessing correctly. Given that, it does not seem likely that having people exchanging estimates rather than having them exchange votes would make any difference at all in people's ability to distinguish true stories from false ones.

But it did.

Networks in which people shared their yes/no votes about whether the stories were true or false showed no significant improvements over the course of the study. In the final round, participants were no better at distinguishing true stories from false stories than they were at the start. This is what you might expect.

However, in the networks in which people shared their estimates about the likelihood of the stories being true, there was a remarkable improvement. Over the course of three rounds, there was a 20 percent increase in the number of groups that could distinguish true stories from false stories. By the end of the study, 60 percent of the groups in which people used estimates could distinguish true stories from false stories.

Asking citizens to provide estimates rather than votes is a small change to the structure of how people evaluate critical decisions, but it can have a big impact on a group's ability to make better collective choices.

In the fact-checking experiment, these effects were particularly striking for news stories relating to terrorism. By the end of the study, in groups sharing estimates, there was a 60 percent improvement in the participants' likelihood of identifying true and false news stories. By contrast, in groups sharing votes, there were no improvements in the likelihood of evaluating stories correctly. Even more striking, when it came to identifying the truth of general news stories, like "5G towers killing birds," the groups sharing binary votes once again showed no improvements in their ability to determine the truth of the story. In the groups sharing estimates, 100 percent of groups were ultimately able to determine the truth of the story. (It's false.) That is indeed a network lie detector.

Remarkably, these collective learning dynamics improved the belief accuracy of Democrats, Republicans, and Independents. In fact, the more accurate the networks became, the less polarized they became. At the beginning of the study, Democrats and Republicans showed significant differences in their choices of which news content to trust. In the networks in which people voted, polarization increased. By the end of the study, Democrats and Republicans were further apart in their overall evaluations of which news stories could be trusted.

By contrast, in networks in which people shared estimates, polarization between Democrats and Republicans was eliminated. As their polarization decreased, their accuracy increased. Not only did Democrats and

Republicans come to a shared understanding about which content to trust, but their understanding matched the actual truthfulness of the news articles. Across party lines, people had become more aligned and more sophisticated in their ability to make judgments about the trustworthiness of social media content.

SCHOOLS OF PUBLIC SPIRIT

In the 1920s, the American philosopher John Dewey announced, "All valuable as well as new ideas begin with minorities, . . . [even] a minority of one." Civic discussions ensure that the "opportunity be given to that idea to spread and to become the possession of the multitude." For Dewey, the value of democracy goes beyond the vote itself; it is embodied in the process of learning that takes place prior to the vote. Society is made intelligent by the affordances of civic life that enable peers to be educated by one another about their interests and ideas.

That's certainly what we saw in the echo-chamber experiment and the fact-checking experiment. But perhaps we might go even further, with the value of collective political participation stretching beyond the intelligence of the collective decision. What if, as Tocqueville intimated, political participation is not just a source of collective intelligence but also the wellspring of our feelings of civic responsibility and mutual respect?

SMOKERS WELCOME

Could our findings on structural intelligence offer a new hope for creating this kind of civic virtue among the citizens in Homer? To find out, Doug Guilbeault and I designed a new study that was similar to the echo-chamber experiment. But this time, instead of squaring off Democrats versus Republicans, we used a different pairing of groups—ones that historically have shown an equally impressive lack of empathy for one another: smokers versus nonsmokers. Also, this time, instead of sorting people into homophilous echo chambers, we let everyone exchange opinions in mixed-composition networks.

We constructed four experimental groups. For the control groups, one contained forty isolated smokers and the other had forty isolated nonsmokers. There was one anonymous network, and one in which people could see their peers' status as smokers or nonsmokers; each network had twenty smokers and twenty nonsmokers integrated into an egalitarian structure. In the anonymous network, participants had no information about their peers. But, in the information network, every participant had a label "smoker" or "nonsmoker," so their network contacts could see which group they belonged to.

We asked everyone a pointed question about the risks of smoking: "How many people (in millions) are predicted to die from tobacco use in developed countries in 2030?"

As in all previous studies, the experiment had three rounds. In round one, everyone provided their independent opinion. In the networks, in rounds two and three participants could see the average opinion of their network neighbors before providing their responses. In the placebo control groups, participants responded in isolation for all three rounds.

We conducted ten independent replications of this experimental design. In total, there were 1,600 people in the study. There were some interesting findings. As we expected, participants in egalitarian networks improved significantly, while participants in the control groups did not. Although we predicted this result based on our earlier findings, it was still nice to see. In both networks, smokers and nonsmokers became significantly more accurate in their ability to identify smoking risks.

But there were also a couple of surprises. First, the network groups in which participants showed the greatest improvement in accuracy were not the anonymous networks but those in which participants could see their peers' status as a smoker or nonsmoker. When smokers and nonsmokers knew they were talking to each other, their learning about smoking risks was much more effective. These improvements were equally large for both smokers and nonsmokers.

The biggest surprise, however, was the change in people's feelings about one another. After the study was concluded, we asked everyone to give their opinion (from "strongly agree" to "strongly disagree") on the following statement: "Some say that smokers are more likely to misinterpret health information about tobacco than nonsmokers."

As you would expect, smokers and nonsmokers parted company on this question. Smokers strongly disagreed, while nonsmokers strongly agreed. But here's the interesting part—this discordance only happened in the control groups and the anonymous networks. In the networks with smoking status revealed, something unexpected happened. In these networks, the smokers and nonsmokers came to appreciate one another's points of view. In fact, in the networks with smoking status revealed, smokers and nonsmokers gave statistically identical responses to the opinion question.

What happened in those networks?

Even though the topic of discussion was contentious for both groups, both sides nevertheless learned from one another. By virtue of group members interacting and exchanging ideas, they came to appreciate one another's views. In particular, nonsmokers came to value and respect the opinions of smokers on the topic of smoking risks.

These findings offer a new perspective on why egalitarian networks work as well as they do to improve collective intelligence. Structural intelligence can lead people to respect one another's opinions. It can even change how people feel about one another.

These results offer a model of civic engagement in which people learn not only about the facts but also about one another and, in that sense, about themselves. These beneficial effects are likely not felt or seen by the individuals participating in a collective choice process, since nobody can divine the effects of the large networks they're in when they're in them. But these effects are nonetheless reflected in the quality of people's final judgments and in their feelings about one another afterward.

The Unforced Force

German philosopher Jürgen Habermas refers to "the unforced force of the better argument" as the mechanism that drives group deliberation toward an intelligent consensus. Our experiments show that if deliberation takes place within an egalitarian structure, such that no individual or idea is given precedence, and no ideas or individuals are artificially culled from the pool to which the community has access, then the exchange of ideas will indeed arrive at the best idea—with one big caveat.

Habermas requires an "ideal speech situation"—a setting in which the exchange of ideas is governed by rationality and equality. Here we relax the rationality assumption but strictly enforce equality—not just in the architecture of the network but also in terms of individual privacy. In our networks, any information about individuals that might reveal differences in status, rank, wealth, or power is explicitly protected. This approach ensures that every individual's opinion is given as much weight as everyone else's. Even in cases where participants' political identities are shown, or smoking behavior is revealed, differences in rank or status are not. In that sense, these egalitarian networks embody a particular version of an ideal speech situation—one in which equality is persistently enforced. But the fact that these structures reflect a philosophical ideal does not mean that they are idealized or impractical. In fact, quite the opposite.

Making It Real

The practical implications of these findings encourage us to rethink our expectations for political life on social media. Could putting people into structured networks on the internet really lead to increased intelligence within political parties or produce new forms of mutual understanding across them? A few pages ago, I told you about our 2018 study on cross-party networks. The findings there suggested that these lofty goals could only be achieved under pristine scientific conditions: They required completely integrated bipartisan networks and the complete elimination of partisan primes (political identifiers, partisan graphics, and party logos) that activate feelings of party loyalty.

Such pristine conditions aren't anything like the real world. In fact, once participants left our study, they probably immersed themselves back into homophilous political settings where partisan priming saturated the political discourse. You have to ask: What good are these scientific results when real-world political settings are so different from the experimental conditions?

Our study of echo chambers offers a surprising answer. There we found the uncanny result that when two harmful real-world factors—homophilous echo chamber and partisan priming—were put together, instead of making polarization and misunderstanding worse, this combination was beneficial. Two toxic ingredients produced a vital new synthesis that was not only beneficial but practical.

It's a lot like table salt, which is made by combining two lethal elements, sodium and chlorine. But when you put them together you get sodium chloride, which is an essential ingredient of life; in fact, we would quickly die without it.

We found a similar thing here.

In egalitarian structures, the apparently toxic combination of homophilous echo chambers and partisan priming does not destroy collective intelligence—it accelerates it. Without anyone in the network even realizing it, tribal loyalties become a vehicle for increased in-group learning on both sides, leading to diminished cross-group polarization and greater collective intelligence. For years, we have been convinced that tribal loyalties and homophily are responsible for increased enmity and misunderstanding across party lines. This observation isn't wrong; it's just incomplete. These harmful outcomes certainly happen, but only because people are in the wrong structures—centralized ones.

Once structure is taken into account, the seemingly worst features of the political world, which are impossible to eliminate from natural political settings—faction and loyalty—unexpectedly lead to improvements in belief accuracy within groups and the alignment of understanding across groups. The key to making all of this work, of course, is having a network structure that catalyzes these positive effects. In the next chapter, I will show how we went about implementing these structures in real-world settings.

6

The Myth of the Rational Doctor

At least once in our lives, each of us will be given a wrong diagnosis by our doctor. For many of us, this will happen more than once.

In 2015, the National Academies of Science, Engineering, and Medicine released a shocking report revealing that every year, roughly half a million US citizens suffer serious injury or death due to medical misdiagnosis and incorrect treatment. Estimating that 10–15 percent of all diagnoses in the US are incorrect, the report concluded that "improving diagnosis requires teamwork and good communication among the entire health care team."

That sounds nice, but what does it mean? It means that everyone knows that better communication networks are needed to improve healthcare. But no one knows what they will look like in practice or how they will actually function to reduce medical errors.

I wanted to change all of that.

Time and Money

A popular view of medicine is that if doctors just had enough time to reflect on their patients' cases, they would always get the answers right. Another popular idea is that doctors simply need greater financial incentives to do their jobs carefully.

In the early 2000s, new policies were deployed by many insurers to provide doctors with incentives for successfully completing a patient checklist. In some cases, your doctor receives a payment from your insurance company for completing this checklist after your visit is over. Another policy, which you already know about, is the co-pay that your insurance company charges you each time you visit your doctor. This co-pay is a fine that is designed to keep you away from the doctor's office. It's a practical deterrent to prevent hypochondriacs from clogging up your doctor's waiting room, so your doctor will have more time to give proper care to the seriously ill patients. The belief that motivates both of these policies is that medical errors are a problem of individual incentives. If you just give doctors enough time and money, they will not make mistakes.

The problem is that diagnostic errors and mistakes don't really work like that. They are typically not isolated incidents of tired or unmotivated doctors making careless errors. More often, they are the result of unconscious tendencies that doctors have. Not the tendency of a single doctor but of an entire medical community. Within hospitals and healthcare systems, doctors follow accepted clinical practices. These practices are confirmed and supported by their network of peers. If clinicians within a hospital system are making certain medical errors, chances are that other doctors in that community are making those same mistakes too.

I spend a fair amount of time talking to my colleagues in the Perelman School of Medicine at the University of Pennsylvania. I routinely give grand rounds lectures to the physicians there, so during one visit I asked some of my colleagues what they thought about the idea of using networks to reduce medical errors. Some thought it was a great idea and subsequently worked with me to implement a study there. But others said that structural intelligence would not work for them. They already knew the medical facts—what difference would it make to see other people's opinions?

The Hospital of the University of Pennsylvania is one of the top healthcare systems in the world. I had no doubt that the doctors there did indeed know all the relevant facts in their fields of medicine. But the purpose of structural intelligence in medicine is not to teach doctors new facts. Rather, it is to change the way that they interpret the facts that they already know. Structural intelligence is an unconscious solution for an unconscious problem. If it worked like I hoped it would, the doctors would not notice anything at all—but their patients would.

The Unconscious Solution

The most important part of reducing diagnostic errors and treatment mistakes is to understand how doctors think.

Doctors make discrete choices. They decide whether to admit you to the hospital or send you home. They decide whether to recommend further testing or immediate surgery. They decide whether to refer you to a specialist or keep you on your current treatment.

These discrete choices are a lot like voting. Each treatment option is a one-or-the-other decision. However, beneath the surface of doctors' treatment decisions, something different is happening. Although doctors typically talk, and sometimes even think, in terms of discrete choices, there is nevertheless an estimation process taking place in the background. Typically, it is a risk assessment like the one shown in figure 6.1.

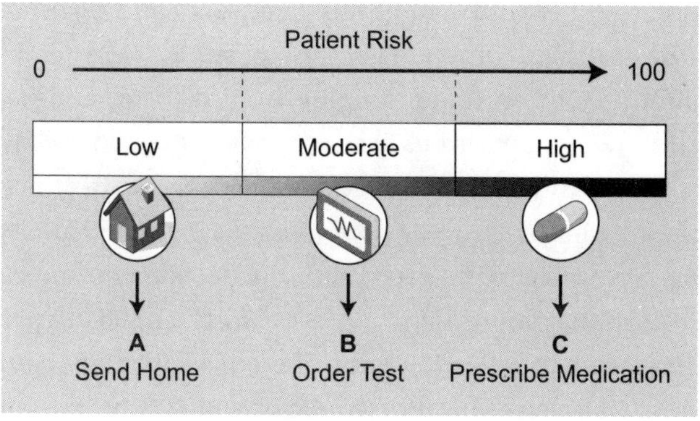

FIGURE 6.1
Patient risk and clinical decision-making process

Should, for example, a patient with cardiac chest pain be admitted to the emergency department for observation, yes or no? The answer depends upon the answer to the question "What is this patient's likelihood of having an adverse cardiac event in the next thirty days?" Should a patient with a cough get a chest X-ray, yes or no? The answer depends on the answer to the question "What is the likelihood that this patient has pneumonia?" Should an elderly patient receive at-home care for assistance with activities of daily living, yes or no? The answer depends on the answer to the question "What is this patient's risk of having a fall in the next thirty days?"

Sometimes doctors are aware of how these estimates factor into their treatment decisions, but oftentimes they are not. What would happen if we made clinicians' unconscious estimation process into a conscious part of their deliberation about which treatment to give a patient? That alone might not do anything. But what if we had clinicians discuss these estimates within peer networks? Would it affect the quality of their treatment decisions? Would it improve the quality of patient care? I wanted to find out.

EXPERIMENTING ON DOCTORS

My team of social scientists and physicians from the University of Pennsylvania and the University of California, San Francisco began by recruiting 3,360 clinicians from all across the United States. The doctors were then randomized between two groups, networks and placebo controls. To make the study as comprehensive as possible, we assembled seven distinct clinical cases on topics ranging from diabetes and heart attack to back pain and geriatric care. Each case was designed to have a clear, correct diagnosis and an established, evidence-based treatment recommendation. We randomized our pool of clinicians across all seven cases: 480 doctors were assigned to each clinical case, constituting eight egalitarian information-sharing networks with forty clinicians per network and four independent reflection control groups with forty clinicians per group. Across all seven clinical cases, we observed fifty-six experimental networks and twenty-eight control groups. It was the largest controlled-network study of doctors' decision-making ever conducted.

In every trial, we asked clinicians to answer two questions about the case. First, clinicians were asked to provide their diagnostic estimate regarding the patient's risk of having an adverse medical event. Second, they were asked to make a specific treatment recommendation for the patient (i.e., a discrete choice). For instance, after the clinician reads the patient's case and looks at any supplementary figures or charts, a typical first question would be "What is this patient's estimated lifetime risk of developing atherosclerotic cardiovascular disease?" The second question would then be "Would you recommend a moderate intensity statin for this patient, yes or no?" Every clinician in every trial was given the same two-question format, tailored to the details of each clinical case.

Just like previous studies, doctors were given three rounds to evaluate the case. They were asked the same two questions in every round. Across all experimental conditions, clinicians' responses in the first round were independent. This allowed us to evaluate all participants' initial levels of error. All clinicians were rewarded for participation based on the quality of their responses in the final round. If they assigned the patient the correct treatment, they could win up to $40. If they didn't, they would receive no payment.

Everyone in the study was anonymous to their peers. This was particularly important for this study because clinicians are sensitive to status and rank within the healthcare system. An important advantage of an anonymous egalitarian network is that leadership in the network (based on clinicians' self-weight) can change continuously, enabling a much greater diversity of voices to influence the collective perspective. Outside the context of our study, medical networks tend to be hierarchical, with the most senior people at the center of the network, and these high-status actors powerfully guide the flow of influence.

In the network condition, in rounds two and three clinicians could see their network peers' *diagnostic* estimates from the previous round. But they could not see their peer's *treatment* decisions. Here's where this experiment went beyond previous research on doctors' decisions. Doctors could see their peers' risk estimates regarding the patient but could not see each other's treatment recommendations, nor could they discuss them. Our theory was that this would unconsciously influence doctors to think differently about their clinical treatment decisions.

We did not need to wait long to find out if the egalitarian structure made a difference: Diagnostic accuracy doubled in the networks as compared to independent control groups. These improvements were most striking among the doctors who were the worst-performing from the first round; their improvements in accuracy were 10 percent greater in networks.

But what did that mean for doctors' actual treatment decisions? Overall, the proportion of clinicians who switched from the wrong treatment to making the correct clinical choice in the final round jumped from 13 percent in the control condition to 30 percent in the collective intelligence networks. Nearly one-third of doctors who initially made the wrong choice switched to make the right choice as a result of being in egalitarian information-sharing networks. The doctors whose initial diagnostic estimates were the farthest from the correct response—the "worst" doctors for our purposes—became 28 percent more accurate in networks. The resulting impact on decision-making was palpable: 19 percent of the initially worst-performing clinicians ultimately switched to make the right choice. By comparison, in the control group only 3 percent of the initially bottom-performing doctors ultimately switched to the right choice. Given the size of our study, that works out to be hundreds of doctors switching from bad decisions to good medicine simply from five minutes of sharing diagnostic estimates with one another in an egalitarian network.

This is one of the most powerful insights of structural intelligence for medicine. The network of doctors performed just like our previous network studies: The most accurate doctors became centers of gravity for the others. Peer influences within egalitarian networks did not average out the doctors' performance (allowing the worst to improve but causing the best to perform worse); rather, these networks created an upward movement across all clinicians' performance, increasing the collective intelligence of the entire medical community.

These findings were a big step forward. Yet anyone who knows about healthcare knows that the problem of misdiagnosis is just the tip of the iceberg. Once we had begun to address the problem of medical errors, it became apparent that the real challenge for improving medicine is not just to increase the quality of clinical care but to increase it for everyone equally.

Ask most any woman about her experience with the American healthcare system, and you will likely hear stories of maltreatment in the form of dismissal, undertreatment, or incorrect diagnosis. Add racial bias to the mix, and a woman's likelihood of being mistreated in medicine is even worse.

In the largest study of its kind to date, a 2020 analysis of more than three million US patients' hospital admissions between 2012 and 2017 found that adults who are Black or from other underrepresented racial or ethnic groups received up to 10 percent fewer early treatments for heart problems than white patients. Medical bias according to race and gender is so powerful that even megastars like Serena Williams have nearly died from it.

So, what can we do about bias that is unconscious, pervasive, and threatens the lives of millions of Americans? Institutions (including medical schools and hospitals) have responded to the problem with implicit bias training—the use of cognitive techniques to make people aware of their internalized assumptions about race and gender. But the data show that it doesn't work. Even when training sessions make clinicians sufficiently self-aware to score better on standardized tests for bias awareness, subsequent clinical records still show persistent disparities in patient treatment. Being taught directly about one's own internalized assumptions unfortunately doesn't seem to alter behavior. Could structural intelligence offer a solution?

THE UNCONSCIOUS SOLUTION TO THE IMPLICIT PROBLEM

To find out, we ran another medical study, this time with 840 clinicians recruited from across the United States. Clinicians were first randomized to be either in a control condition, in which they would evaluate the clinical case independently without any peer information, or a structured peer network, in which they could see other clinicians' responses. Within each condition, clinicians were then randomized to see either a white male patient or a Black female patient. In both cases, the patient presented with symptoms of cardiac chest pain via a short, standardized video (in which an actor portrayed the patient), and the doctor was given the patient's recent EKG chart. There were no clinically relevant differences between the white male patient and the Black female patient. Both patients were the same age, had identical clinical histories, and presented with the same chest pain symptoms and EKGs. (The actors in the videos wore identical clothing and spoke in similar style and cadence.) The correct diagnostic estimate and the correct treatment decision were identical for both patients. The only differences between the patients were the clinically irrelevant factors of race and gender.

The study proceeded as in the previous study of structural intelligence in medicine, with clinicians first providing a risk estimate for the patient, and then a treatment recommendation.

In clinicians' initial responses, the Black female patient was on average three times as likely as the white male patient to be sent home rather than admitted for proper treatment. Many of us have read statistics like this before, but I assure you it is quite a different thing altogether to see this happen in an experiment where there were absolutely no other factors that might be used to explain disparity in care by race and gender. The patients were clinically identical, without any differences in income, living conditions, family history, diet, or environmental factors (like air pollution). And the correct clinical answer was clear-cut for both patients. The fact that both patients did not get the same treatment left no other explanation than that there was an unmistakable bias in doctors' healthcare decisions.

Many studies have provided scientific evidence for treatment bias by race and gender. But previous studies had not distinguished between the diagnostic estimate and the treatment decision. By uncovering the relationship between doctors' unconscious estimates and their actual treatment decisions, we discovered something new and completely unexpected: Clinicians' diagnostic accuracy was identical for both patients! Why, then, were their treatment recommendations so different?

Here is where the theory of structural intelligence offers useful scientific guidance. A few pages ago, I showed you how diagnostic assessments translate into treatment decisions: A patient with a low diagnostic risk assessment is likely to receive a less urgent treatment recommendation, while a patient receiving a higher risk estimate triggers a more urgent treatment decision, and so on.

It seems cut and dry. But there are gray areas.

Suppose the white male patient and Black female patient receive the same risk estimate, which lies in the gray-shaded area between low risk and moderate risk (figure 6.2). Because the gray area lies between treatment options of either (a) sending the patient home with a one-week follow-up, or (b) admitting the patient for immediate monitoring, implicit bias is able to creep in. The diagnostic estimate itself is largely unconscious, so the translation of the estimate into a treatment decision can be guided by many implicit factors that fall outside a doctor's immediate awareness. Stereotypes, biases, and normative culture within the clinical community can invisibly nudge a doctor's clinical decision. The reason that implicit bias is hard to detect, and even harder to fix, is that for any patient in the gray area, both treatment decisions are defensible. What is not defensible, however—which is what we found—is a systematic disparity in the treatment recommendations across patients.

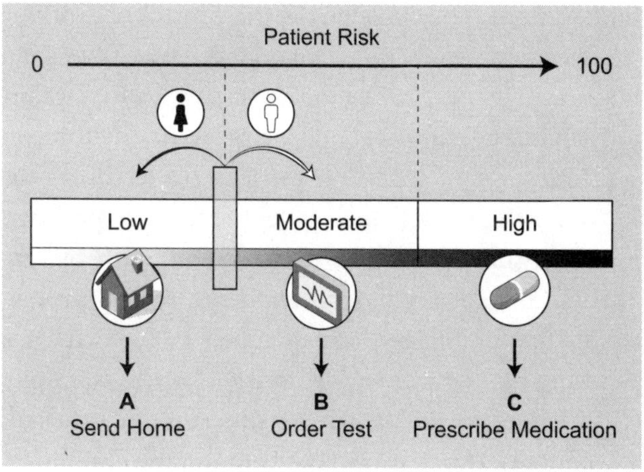

FIGURE 6.2
Implicit bias in clinical decision-making

But now that we know how this works, we can also see how to fix it.

Structurally intelligent networks are able to improve clinicians' treatment decisions by increasing the accuracy of their diagnostic risk estimates, effectively moving them out of the gray area. And with an improved risk assessment, implicit factors like stereotypes and biases play less of a role in clinicians' decisions. Improving the accuracy of the risk assessment makes the correct clinical decision undeniable.

The effects of peer information exchange in egalitarian networks were stunning. By the final round, clinicians in the network condition were averaging over 90 percent accuracy in their clinical risk estimates. Consistent with our hypotheses, these improvements were nearly identical for both patients. Simultaneously, treatment disparities between patients disappeared. The rate at which the Black female patient was sent home plummeted, and the rate at which she was admitted for care skyrocketed. By the final round, both patients were receiving proper care at the same rate—which translated into a disproportionate benefit to the Black female patient from improved diagnostic accuracy, because she had initially been given the wrong treatment at a much higher rate.

Egalitarian networks significantly outperformed the control conditions, but it's still possible that even without learning in egalitarian networks, there might be some nonzero benefit to independent reflection.

Alas, there was not. The clinicians in the control networks were given the same amount of time and the same financial incentives, and yet there was no significant change in healthcare disparities by race and gender. And not only that. The control condition showed something completely unexpected: Independent reflection actually made things significantly worse, not just for the Black female patient, but for all patients.

It's natural to assume that bias is exhibited primarily by turning away certain patients from getting proper treatment (which it often is). However, unlike the first physician study in which we focused exclusively on clinicians making the right or wrong decision, when examining implicit bias we also looked at the rates at which clinicians undertreated and overtreated their patients. Here the contrast between the egalitarian networks and the control conditions showed a remarkably different trend. For both the white male patient and the Black female patient, egalitarian networks produced a movement away from extreme medical recommendations. Unsafe undertreatment decreased for both patients, while the rate of correct care increased. We also found that the rate of overtreatment (in the form of recommending unnecessary surgery) decreased significantly for both patients. By contrast, the control groups for both patients showed a significant movement toward more urgent treatment, with a small number of doctors switching from unsafe undertreatment to the correct treatment. However, these small changes were the same for the Black female patient and white male patient, thereby preserving the overall disparity in care. More surprisingly, doctors in both control groups also significantly increased the rate at which patients were recommended for unnecessary surgery. This was true for both the white male patient and the Black female patient. Not only did independent reflection not help to alleviate disparities in care, but it was also responsible for significant increases in the rate of recommendations for unnecessary surgery for all patients.

The Structural Intelligence Moon Shot

The discovery of structural intelligence in medicine invites vital new questions about the potential for changing how medicine is practiced. The most obvious questions are the practical ones. However, you may be surprised to find out that the clinical routines for applying structural intelligence to medicine are easy to learn. Not only that, but the necessary time-management solutions already exist, as do the right physician incentives. Clearly, there are clinical situations for which the structural solution would not work, like emergency departments and trauma centers. How do we know in which clinical settings the structural solution works, and in which ones it does not? Ironically, the hard work that needs to be done to make the structural moon shot succeed is not clinical, or technological, or even administrative. It's philosophical.

Are we willing to believe that physicians are smarter collectively than individually? Are we willing to believe that doctors are social decision-makers rather than rational ones? These things are hard to see when you're in the doctor's office. But they are easy to see when you look at the data. The philosophical question is whether we are willing to allow the data to change our minds about medicine. Are we finally willing to change our expectations about the practice of medicine and the training of healthcare workers? Are we willing to let go of the familiar norms and power structures that may have once made sense but which have inadvertently allowed medical errors and health disparities to endure long after these problems have been identified?

E-CONSULTS

You probably don't know it, but your doctor may already use electronic consultation tools to discuss your healthcare problems with other clinicians.

In 2017, a primary-care physician was reviewing her patient's request for a medication refill. The patient, "Elsa," had been suffering chronic back pain since 2012. The doctor had prescribed opioids for pain relief in 2012 but had been unsuccessful at transitioning the patient from opioid medication to methadone. In 2017, the patient repeatedly violated her narcotic agreement contract. She requested refills early, failed to submit for urine drug screening, and tested positive for illegal substances. The physician no longer felt comfortable prescribing opioids for the patient. However, the patient (unsurprisingly) reacted negatively to the suggestion of a reduction in dosage.

Unsure what to do next, the primary-care physician posted an e-consults message to a specialist in addiction treatment. The message outlined the patient's history, the clinician's concerns, and their question about the best options for next steps.

The e-consults specialist replied with a modest bit of clinical advice: "Regardless if an opioid is prescribed or not, she should access a free naloxone kit from her pharmacy in case of overdose." But the main goal of the e-consults physician's response was not to give medical advice, but to help the primary-care physician feel more confident about their clinical decision to refuse opioids to the patient: "You cannot continue the status quo, because in your judgement it is not safe or effective. She is free to disagree, but her disagreement need not change your judgment."

Dr. Alfred Atanda is a pediatric orthopedic surgeon and e-consults specialist at Nemours Children's Hospital in Wilmington, Delaware, where he is chief of the sports medicine center and chief of clinician well-being for the hospital. In July 2023, he was invited to present to the American Medical Association on the use of e-consults. He said, "Imagine if patients can stay in their medical home in their primary communities, have somebody on the ground floor with them but infuse my knowledge and my advice and expertise to where it needs to go."

Atanda noted that if he receives an X-ray or a written summary of a clinical problem, he is able to provide an opinion or guidance to the requesting physician within a day or two.

> The [primary care physicians] in these situations are often very well-versed in the problem, but they just need a little bit more reassurance, a little bit of guidance. They may not be totally comfortable with just sending someone to therapy or getting an MRI, so it's very, very convenient and streamlined to just get my knowledge to where it needs to go rather than just sending the patient to see me for a nonoperative problem that can be really handled well and appropriately by the original physician.

The e-consults system is built to share the burden of medical decision-making across multiple actors and multiple institutions. It's a great start, but it comes with some real risks.

If a large number of clinicians put in e-consults requests to a prominent specialist like Atanda, his influence will grow throughout the medical community. And as we've seen with other firehose networks, as smart and dedicated as Atanda is, small errors in his judgment can become big errors when they are broadcast and reinforced throughout a centralized information architecture. The consults that Atanda offers may indeed build confidence among the large number of clinicians who are requesting advice. But as we saw earlier, we should be wary of confidence because confidence tends to come from agreeing with the consensus view rather than accuracy. If a clinician receives a reassuring message about the treatment they want to prescribe, this may indeed be helpful, but it is not in any way a litmus test for the quality of that medical decision. As our experiments showed, when a problem is hard—as it is likely to be when an e-consults query is made—the consensus view is not necessarily going be the correct view. This is the kind of situation where two heads are not necessarily better than one. But in an egalitarian structure, many heads can be.

You already know the solution. Suppose the goal of the e-consults was not, as Atanda suggested, for one clinician to "infuse [his] knowledge and . . . advice and expertise" into other hospitals and medical communities. Instead, what if the goal of e-consults was to extract the untapped collective intelligence found across many different medical systems? What if the goal of e-consults was to provide not an exchange of reassurance from an expert but an infrastructure for medical collective intelligence that actively sources new medical knowledge from diverse members of the medical community, from junior residents to section chiefs, allowing the network to guide the community toward increasing clinical intelligence and treatment equity throughout the country?

In our experiments, we drew thousands of clinicians from across the nation to participate with no guarantee of any reward. The time required to elicit collective intelligence from the medical network was about ten minutes. That's about half the amount of time that Atanda spends writing his clinical responses to e-consults requests. For structural intelligence, the response format is more streamlined. Clinicians in the network need only present their diagnostic assessment and treatment recommendations. It's more like a medical board exam than a chat forum. Yet these streamlined interactions consistently extract collective medical judgments that significantly outperform the clinical judgments of independent clinicians.

But perhaps the real promise of structural intelligence is its potential for teaching clinical trainees—residents and fellows—to look at their professional networks horizontally rather than vertically, by looking outside the standard models of top-down leadership and discovering how the insights of their equals and even subordinates may help to deepen their own clinical acumen. Clinical implementations of technologies that structure clinicians' information-exchange channels offer a surprisingly large range of opportunities for improving clinical collective intelligence, including for senior clinicians to stay current on changing clinical guidelines; for improving junior clinicians' cultural awareness about varying patient needs across different medical settings; for keeping clinicians of all ranks up to date on changing medical norms regarding how to best serve the needs of underserved communities; and so on.

Egalitarian networks like the ones used in our studies are easy to create. We did it with an app in Apple's App Store (which we built exclusively for this study on a shoestring budget) and a $40 incentive for doctors to get the answers right. Already today, several online communities exist to support clinical decisions using digital technologies. But until now, the missing piece was understanding how the information structure within those digital medical communities affected the quality of the advice they gave. Now we finally know that too—and because we do, we finally have the ability to make medicine a whole lot smarter for everyone.

II

Coordination: Convention and Quality

7

Syncing Up Without Trying

What's in a name? A rose by any other name would smell as sweet.
—*William Shakespeare,* Romeo and Juliet

The Lord said, "As one people speaking the same language [. . .] nothing will be impossible for them. Come, let us go down and confuse their language so they will not understand each other."
—*Genesis 11:5–6*

Here's a fun test.

What do you call flying insects that light up at night?

What's the word for a sugary carbonated beverage?

How do you address a group of people that you're inviting for dinner?

Your answers will depend on where you are from.

I grew up near Philadelphia, so it is obvious to me that the bioluminescent beetles flying around in the summertime are lightning bugs. But when I moved out to California I was surprised to find that California does not have lightning bugs. Out there, they have fireflies.

It gets a little more complicated with the tasty beverage formerly known as Coca-Cola. In Philadelphia, we call that "soda." There is also soda in California. But just a few hours west of Philadelphia, on the other side of the Allegheny Mountains, you need to order "pop," or else you're likely to get a root beer float. If you go down south to Louisiana, "pop" and "soda" will both fail you. You need to order "coke," regardless of the brand you want, and then specify the desired variety (Sprite, A&W Root Beer, and so forth). Or, if you're in Georgia, you have to ask for "cocola."

Road-tripping around the US, you get pretty familiar with these changing regional dialects. What is amazing about them is not that they formed in the first place, but that they have persisted for so long. Several generations ago, the Allegheny Mountains would have been a natural dividing line between cultures. It makes sense that such a formidable physical barrier would divide the state of Pennsylvania in half, making Western Pennsylvania more culturally and linguistically aligned with the Midwest than with the East. But it's striking that in our age of massively connected communications, these differences in how people speak, and what they understand words to mean, have not evaporated into a global monoculture. In fact, if you compare the pre–social media linguistic map of the US in 2002 with the one from 2015, regional linguistic boundaries are basically the same (figure 7.1). If anything, they've gotten sharper.

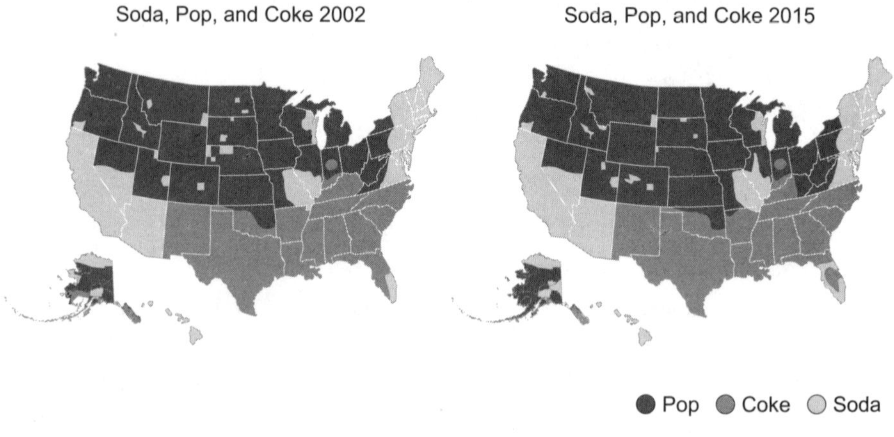

FIGURE 7.1
Soda, pop, and coke 2002 vs. 2015; adapted from data and visualizations developed by Alan McConchie.

Americans from the North (a.k.a. Yankees) invite "you guys" to come over for dinner, while Southerners invite "y'all." This simple distinction gets tricky for people who live on the cultural boundary that divides the North from the South, where the linguistic back and forth from continual exposure to both Northerners and Southerners can become so frustrating that it leads to the spontaneous creation regional neologisms.

Take the cultural DMZ known as New Jersey. People from Jersey invite "youse" to dinner or, you know, to go "down the shore." It gets even more specialized west of the Alleghenies, where in a magical land called Pittsburgh my personal favorite term, "yinz," emerged. (I've never actually heard anyone say "yinz," but I'm told that yinz live just a few hours away.)

Most of the time these regional dialects don't result in major failures of communication. When failures do happen (like the unfortunate Philadelphian who orders a soda in Pittsburgh), they stand out because of how rare they are. Most of the time, even internationally, we do not have much trouble figuring out what people and signs mean, regardless of where we travel. The fact that people have learned to coordinate effectively with one another across so many different physical regions, cultural boundaries, diverse histories, and starkly dissimilar lived experiences is stunning. Collective intelligence in language is so pervasive that it is hard to fully appreciate how impressive it is. We are surprised when it fails us because it's a form of collective intelligence that we enjoy without realizing it. In fact, it happens when we're not even trying to be smart in the first place.

Spontaneous Synchronization

Take baby names.

In the late 1960s, the name Ashley was hardly on the radar of Americans with new babies. It was ranked below more than 1,000 names on the Social Security Administration's list of popular baby names. But by the mid-1980s, Ashley had emerged from nowhere to become the ninth most popular baby name in America. A decade later, in 1990, a similar thing was about to happen to Aiden, which was ranked a lowly 324th on America's list of popular baby names. But by 1998, the name became a favorite, soaring into the top twenty for five years.

Generation after generation of parents trying to choose unique names for their children inevitably find themselves coordinating on the same baby names as everyone else. If you ask any expectant parent what names they are considering, they will share with you elaborate family histories and detailed cultural mythologies. But they are in for a surprise. Despite all of their efforts, once their child gets to preschool, they will inevitably discover that there are other children who have the same name. How did that happen?

This kind of unintended cultural synchronization happens far more often than you think. And it's not just with baby names.

Take spam.

If I tell you that I'm getting "too much spam," you know exactly what I mean, and that it has nothing to do with the hoarding of canned meat products. But why do you know?

The true history of how "spam" became widely used as a euphemism for mass-marketed junk email is lost in the mists of time. Some people attribute it to a 1970s television sketch by the British comedy troupe Monty Python. In the sketch, a waitress rattles off the menu items, including "spam, spam, spam, and spam; spam, spam, and spam." Then some Vikings appear and enthusiastically *sing* the word for no reason. So that's weird. And memorable.

From there, this history of how spam gets associated with email gets pretty murky. A Microsoft website (circa 2023) builds on the Monty Python idea to explain: "Their chants in the sketch became so loud and repetitive that they muted any other conversations. Eventually, this sketch became synonymous with annoying messages, and 'spam mail' was born."

Yet it is an explanation in which the key element of the explanation is a restatement of the problem; it still doesn't tell us how the expression became popular. There is some archaeological evidence that adds further nuance to the story of spam. Early documents show that some IT workers in the 1990s used the term internally to refer to electronically broadcast messages. From there, we can create a rough timeline that shows the term popping up intermittently. Spam shows up in an early Usenet community called news.admin.policy in March 1993 (when a bug in the Usenet code accidentally caused an admin post to trigger hundreds of cycles of replies and reposts from the admin account). The term then shows up again in January 1994. This was the first time that "spam" was used to refer an intentional spamming: a blanketing of Usenet groups with the message "Global Alert for All: Jesus is Coming Soon." He wasn't, but "spam" was. Within just a few years, "spam" became a household term, yet there is no clear explanation for how it became so widely used across so many different parts of society.

THE GOOGLE CONUNDRUM

A few years ago I was giving a lecture on this puzzle of spontaneous conventions to an applied mathematics group at the University of California, Los Angeles. All of the attendees were tech-savvy researchers. When I raised the question about the origins of spam, a confident colleague raised his hand and responded, "It's because Google uses the term 'spam' for its junk mail folder."

Right.

And how exactly did that happen?

Certainly, the Google explanation makes intuitive sense. Why do we all use a weird term? Because a big, public-facing organization adopted it, and then everyone else followed. It's simple and it's obvious. And it's wrong. The Google team used "spam" for one of its Gmail folders because the term was already so widely used that everyone knew what it meant. Which brings us back to a restatement of the original problem: How did the term "spam" become so widely adopted that millions of potential Gmail customers already knew about it? It's almost impossible to uncover the true origins of this coordination process when convenient explanations like "Gmail uses it" eclipse everything else. For that matter, it's just as hard to figure out the true causes of failed synchronization, which appear just as mysteriously.

Take linguistic boundaries.

The most common explanation for persistent cultural borders is to suggest that these divisions in language exist because of people's attachment to their cultural identity and regional history. But let's imagine a world in which regional terminology did not start off being culturally meaningful (once, perhaps, there was a time when no one cared whether you said "soda" or "pop"). But then give it a while. After these terms start to take hold, they may start to feel culturally meaningful, particularly when the boundaries between groups that use each term start to become persistent features of the social landscape. It doesn't matter why they are persistent; the simple fact of enduring linguistic differences encourages us to attribute greater value to those differences. The mere fact of their survival may suggest that they demarcate meaningful cultural boundaries.

Or not. All of our feelings notwithstanding, the evolution of language could just be a random process of cultural drift, being driven by tiny accidents of history and arbitrary features of the world (like the Allegheny Mountains).

Either way, how would we ever know?

Ideally, to study why spontaneous synchronization emerges in some settings while enduring cultural divides persist in others, we need to be able to play the tape of history many times, watching it over and over to see what makes these differing patterns emerge in some cases but not in others. If we could do that, then we could pinpoint the differences and make predictions about when collective intelligence will succeed and when it will fail. We might even be able to control the trajectory of coordination altogether.

But, of course, we can't rewind history. So where do we begin to study the origins of society?

THE STATE OF NATURE

Many Enlightenment philosophers, Rousseau chief among them, worried that humanity had been corrupted by civilized society, obscuring the truth of who and what we really are. To try to determine our true, authentic potential, early social contract philosophers such as Thomas Hobbes and John Locke had pioneered an ingenious conceptual tool called the "state of nature," an imaginary world in which fully conscious humans live in the wild, before society has taken hold. This is a hypothetical history that lives outside of any direct empirical access. In such a world, before society exists, how do people learn to communicate with one another? How do people agree on principles of fairness and responsibility? How does government come into existence? How do civic institutions emerge at all? Starting from the state of nature, how is society even possible?

I was fascinated by this idea, not only as a philosophical springboard but as a sociological tool. I wanted to see if I could build a state of nature that I could use empirically, as a way to explore how language and meaning, and even collective intelligence, could come into existence starting from nothing.

I wasn't the only one to think of this. Since the 1980s, researchers have been building experimental worlds in which two people are tasked with making up new languages to solve unusual coordination tasks, such as working together to navigate an elaborate maze. Sometimes these experiments used four people, sometimes even up to six or ten people, but they didn't get much bigger than that, as there were some insurmountable obstacles to studying how large groups of people might converge on inventing a new language from scratch. For one thing, only so many people could fit into a laboratory. Even more challenging, the more people who were added, the longer the experiment would take. In the end, it was impractical to study how collective intelligence might emerge with a group that was larger than about ten people—and even that was an impressive feat.

This was disheartening. My findings showed that the language dynamics that govern the behavior of large populations, with tens of thousands of people, work very differently than they do for four people. In fact, for language dynamics, populations need to be larger than about twenty people to reproduce the collective dynamics found in very large populations. That seems like bad news for any hope of studying the state of nature.

But there was some good news from my findings too. Because the critical point is at the population size of twenty, that means that if I could study populations that were just slightly larger, say twenty-four people, that would ensure that the dynamics I found would accurately capture what happens at much larger scales, even with millions of people.

Twenty-four is much more plausible than a million. Still, even twenty-four can be a big ask if we're trying to study something as free-flowing as the state of nature. What would I need to be able to create a state of nature that would allow me to observe the large-scale dynamics of collective intelligence in language coordination? The answer to these questions came, quite unexpectedly, from a physicist.

THE NAMING GAME

In 2011, the physicist Albert-László Barabási invited me to give a lecture at his research center at Northeastern University. I took the opportunity to share some of my early thoughts on these ideas about language and collective intelligence. I concluded by inviting the audience to share their suggestions about how I might go about studying social and linguistic conventions in a state of nature. Just as I was finishing, a curious Italian postdoctoral fellow ran up to the podium and introduced himself. Before I could say anything, he blurted out, "I know how to study the state of nature!"

Before I met Andrea Baronchelli, he and his PhD advisor, Vittorio Loreto, had worked for several years on an innovative model of language formation that they called the *naming game*. It was a way to study how large populations, starting from nothing, could collectively coordinate in the creation of shared linguistic conventions.

The naming game has some interesting properties. First, actors can invent their own names, and there are no limits on the number of names that each person can suggest. Even a small population can come up with hundreds of different names. Second, each name has the same value—as economists say, each name has the same payoff. In the technical language of game theory, this kind of coordination problem is called a *convention*, which means that it does not matter which name you and I coordinate on, so long as we agree on something. The naming game offers an explanation for how linguistic conventions can emerge from a state of nature.

It only took about half an hour of discussion for Andrea and me to realize that there was a big idea here. The very next week, he came over to my office at MIT, and we started to build the online naming game that would become our prototype for the state of nature.

This is how it works.

Everyone sees an object, say, a bottle of sugary carbonated water. People are then randomly matched into pairs. In each pair, both members simultaneously offer a name for it. If they match—that is, I say "soda" and you say "soda"—then we both receive a payment for successfully coordinating. However, if both members of a pair fail to match—that is, one says "soda" and the other says "pop"—then they both have some of their money taken away. That's right—both lose money if they fail to coordinate. So everyone has a big incentive to figure out how to coordinate with every new partner. If not, and if they keep failing, then all the money won on earlier rounds would disappear.

Once a round is over, both members of a pair get to see what their partner said and whether they succeeded or failed. Then a new round begins. Each is matched with a new partner, and the whole thing starts again.

Throughout the game, the same object persists in every round. The challenge is not about recognizing the soda bottle. It is about trying to figure out what each new person you encounter is going to call it. It is the challenge of inventing a shared language in the state of nature.

What would you do?

In the first round, do you guess "soda" or "pop"? Suppose you start by suggesting "soda," but your partner says "pop." You both failed to coordinate in round one. You both just lost a quarter. You now have –$.25, but there are fifty rounds to go, and lots of time to make it back. What do you do in round two? You just learned "pop" from your first partner, but they also learned "soda" from you. Your next partner will be a new person. Should you stick with "soda" or try "pop"?

Suppose in the second round you again fail again. You try "pop" this time, but your partner says "cola." Now you have even more options to consider. And you're down –$.50. What do you say on round three?

With a large group of people and new naming options emerging on each round, it seems impossible for any collective intelligence to emerge—and that's for a simple problem. Coordinating on terms for a soft drink is easy because there are only so many options to choose from. But what if we take a harder example, for which there are an infinite number of options? What if we use baby names? The options for baby names are boundless.

What's the likelihood that a large group of strangers interacting in a state of nature on the internet could ever converge on a name that would enable everyone to coordinate with everyone else? The litmus test for cultural success is when a person meets a total stranger for the first time, and they both coordinate effortlessly. That's when you know that a population has created a cultural norm.

This is the challenge we gave ourselves.

We ran a version of the naming game experiment in which we showed everyone a picture of a person. As with the bottle of soda, we used the same picture in every round, for all fifty rounds. Participants were rewarded $.50 for each round in which they successfully coordinated with a partner, and penalized $.25 for each round in which they failed to coordinate. The challenge was to see whether individuals trying to coordinate with partners one at a time would ever converge on a single name that was used by everyone. This was made harder by the fact that people could only see what their partners did on each round, with no information about what the population as a whole was doing. However, in their individual exchanges people could type whatever they wanted to. Some people tried to outsmart the experiment by typing "Copy me: use Simone." Others tried typing descriptions, like "Beautiful Girl" and "Blue Eyes" instead of names in the hope they would lead the other person to shared ground. One person even typed in forty lines of programming code in the hopes of creating a fast-learning name generator, but nobody coordinated on that either. Still others acted bizarrely, but everyone stayed in the game, round after round, despite their failed efforts. One person just typed "Phil" for fifty rounds straight. It's hard to understand why this person—whom I've taken to calling "Phil"—wouldn't just drop out of the experiment, but they never did; they just diligently repeated their response, losing more money on every round. Evidently, there's some kind of value that a person can get from participating in a coordination game, even if they never coordinate. What kind of utility is this? My team and I dubbed it *troll utility*.

With all these sorts of characters in the game, solving the grand challenge of coordination seemed like a long shot. Indeed, for the goal of achieving collective intelligence, the naming game in general seems like a pretty bleak universe. But then again, such is the state of nature, with so many people, with so many different ideas, and the feeling that the more people you interact with, the harder it becomes to figure out what to expect from the next person.

The answer to what happens next in our state of nature would depend, once again, on structure.

SPEED-TESTING COLLECTIVE INTELLIGENCE

We were interested in two different kinds of egalitarian networks. The first was geographical, like a residential neighborhood, and the second was spread out in all directions, like the internet. In both networks, everyone had an equal number of connections as everyone else, and there were no differences in network power between people. That meant there was no structural advantage to any particular spot in either network since no location was more influential than any other. That made sense because at the start we were not interested in power—we were interested in speed.

The key difference between the geographic network and the internet network is the overall number of ties (figure 7.2). In the geographic network, people have ties to their neighbors on the right and left, with some shared ties to neighbors across the street. For a new name to spread by word of mouth around the neighborhood, it must travel from neighbor to neighbor, block to block, until it reaches everyone.

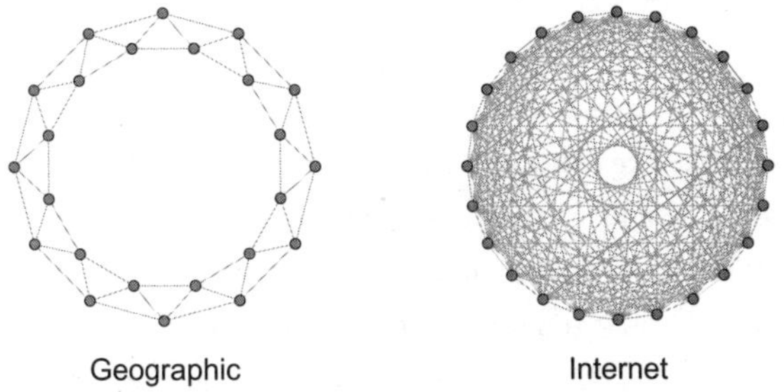

FIGURE 7.2
Geographic network (left) and internet network (right)

Not so in the internet network, where we assume that every person in the community has network ties to everyone else. This is a dense, fully connected network. That means that a new piece of information does not need to spread block by block through each neighborhood to reach me. At any time, I can chat directly with any other person in the network, and because I can talk to everyone, I can find out what each person is thinking and feeling.

Although both the geographic network and the internet network share an egalitarian power structure, they are very different when it comes to speed. In the geographic state of nature, people would repeatedly interact with the same four people in their immediate neighborhood. This meant that while they would be paired with a randomly selected neighbor, round after round, potential partners would be greatly limited by available ties—the selection of a partner might be random, but it was always going to be one their four neighbors. By contrast, in the internet network, each round of people could be randomly paired with another person from anywhere in the network. The internet network was clearly much faster than the geographic network for spreading new information. But which state of nature was more likely to lead to greater collective intelligence when it comes to creating a convention?

In the geographic state of nature, people began to coordinate with one another almost immediately. Within just a few rounds, neighbors agreed on a shared name for the person in the photo. As a consensus grew, people's scores increased, and they began to rapidly accrue wealth. Putting people in suburban neighborhoods really does accelerate the rate of conformity with social conventions.

But there was a problem with all of this neighborly getting along. It only worked on each block. Across blocks, clear differences in norms started to emerge. It quickly became almost impossible for people on the borders between blocks to figure out what was expected of them.

Within just a few rounds, the state of nature produced the same sorts of regional boundaries that we see for "soda" versus "pop." Except here, there were no cultural or historical differences between regions, nor even any knowledge of the network geography at all. For no apparent reason, there were suddenly incompatible differences in the conventions being used across different neighborhoods. Yet the very boundaries that defined each of the neighborhoods were themselves entirely emergent. Still, once they emerged, they became oddly entrenched.

For instance, a few neighbors in one part of the network agreed on the name Elise, while others in a nearby neighborhood converged on the name Rachel (figure 7.3). What happened to the people on the border between these neighborhoods, who were interacting with some people who say Rachel and others say Elise? If the members of the Rachel neighborhood were unwavering in their use of the term Rachel, their neighbors to the right and left would begin to give in. Eventually, Elise would disappear, and the Rachel neighborhood would expand. However, in some cases the frustration caused by going back and forth trying to figure out what their neighbor will expect led people in these boundary regions to spontaneously invent a new option. Caught between Elise on one side and Rachel on the other, a player might suggest a compromise, "Relise." It was reminiscent of people in Philadelphia, trapped between "you guys" to the north and "youse" to the south and east, inventing the colloquialism "youse guys" as their own creative solution to the local coordination problem.

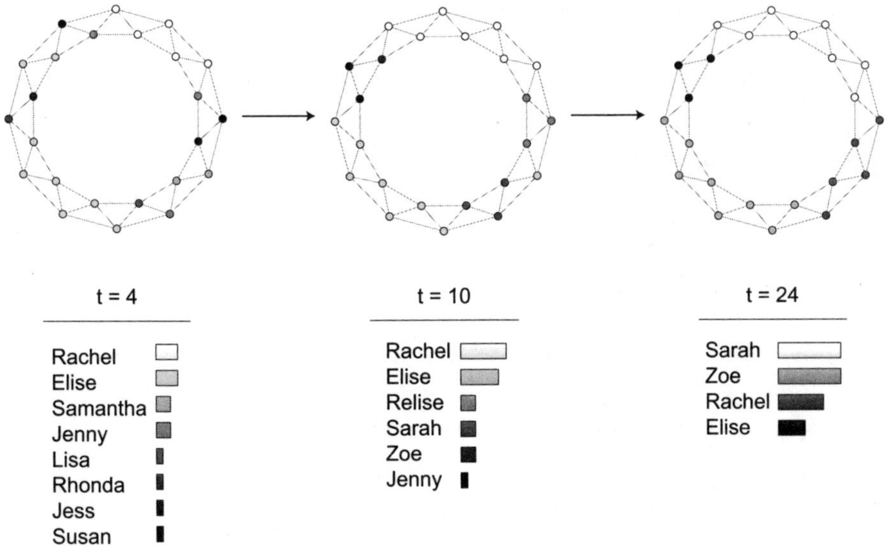

FIGURE 7.3
Coordination in a geographic network

Sometimes people on linguistic boundaries between different regions do not try to coordinate with anyone. They simply invent their own norms. Like people in Pittsburgh. They live on the boundary between "you guys" and "y'all." In Pittsburgh, they invented "yinz." It works for them. Now they are just waiting for everyone else to catch on, as were the advocates for "Relise."

This also happened in our experimental state of nature. While "Relise" might be offered up as a way to bridge the gap, its originality (and potential clunkiness) might prompt people caught between "Elise" and "Rachel" to quite unexpectedly suggest something like "Sarah." Most of the time, these Sarah novelties would disappear just as quickly as they emerged.

The growth in popularity of a name like "Rachel" could indicate that network-wide collective intelligence was emerging. Perhaps much of the entire network would coordinate on "Rachel" in the same way that "you guys" started spreading from New England toward the Midwest. (Today, it even appears to be gaining ground in the South.)

But then again, although "Elise" and "Rachel" seemed to be entrenched, that "Sarah" innovation might begin to spread to the Elise neighborhoods and win converts inside the Rachel camp. Soon, the two neighborhoods supporting "Elise" and "Rachel" might evolve into a large block of supporters for "Sarah" and a small remaining group of "Rachel" supporters. Those on the border between the two remaining options might try to coordinate, but they would eventually give in to one side, and the block of "Sarah" supporters would further grow, leaving "Rachel" to teeter on the brink of extinction but still holding on within pockets.

Over the course of linguistic evolution in the state of nature, many small neighborhoods would emerge using different names (Samantha, Jenny, Elise, Lisa, Rachel, Rhonda, Jess, and so on), but they would eventually merge into large blocks of Elise vs. Sarah neighborhoods.

In the state of nature, these emergent regional boundaries were powerful and could persist for millions of rounds. Nevertheless, there were perpetual skirmishes along the border areas. In a moment, the "Sarah" block could suddenly lose ground as the border people started taking a shine to "Zoe." But just as quickly, pushback from the "Sarah" neighborhoods could result in the border groups switching back to "Sarah" and taking a few of the "Rachel" neighborhoods with them. It is a perennial tug of war.

Competing name blocks are surprisingly resilient. Even if 99 percent of world was saying "y'all," large-scale coordination can still unravel. If the remaining 1 percent push back with "you guys," the people on the border neighborhoods may waver and switch back to "you guys" too. The entire population can repeatedly go from the brink of universal convergence all the way back to sizable blocks competing between "you guys," "y'all," and "yinz."

All of this is due to the structural dynamics of geographic networks. When people's interactions are structured by neighborhoods, cultural entrenchment takes hold, making it very difficult to achieve network-wide coordination. This happens with only twenty-four people and gets more entrenched as the numbers rise. The larger the world is, the more options people create, the more that locally limited network ties produce greater and more robust numbers of diverse blocks. No wonder "soda" and "pop" have stuck around for so long.

THE INTERNET SAVES THE DAY

In the internet state of nature, the story was exactly the opposite. At the beginning, no one could coordinate. Each round, strangers were plucked from the population to interact with one another. One player would say "Gina" while another would offer "Simone." On the next round, both players would meet new partners and try again. One would hear "Bethany" from their new partner, and the other would get "Arianne." Then they would both be whisked off to try again with two new strangers. Coordination seemed impossible.

After a few rounds in the internet state of nature, everyone had lost money, and most players were deep in the red. It was enough to convince you that while the geographic state of nature is no picnic, it's a whole lot better than the internet state of the world.

And then something magical would happen: Two lucky players spontaneously suggest the same name—say, "Jessica." After possibly many rounds of failing to coordinate, both players are thrilled to have found a match. They are unlikely to let it go, figuring that by now the size of Team Jessica has at least doubled (because each member of the pair had likely heard "Jessica" during a previous round, which is why they both suggested it). On their next round, with new neighbors, the same players both say "Jessica" again. Even if it doesn't work, they stick with it again and again.

Because initially the internet state of nature is much more challenging than the geographic one, people do not try so hard to make every match work. If, however, they find something that works, they tend to stick with that response, round after round, failure after failure.

Ironically, it is people's stubbornness that winds up jump-staring successful network-wide synchronization on shared linguistic conventions, which defines collective intelligence.

Once committed to "Jessica," it only takes a few rounds for that loyalty to pay off (figure 7.4). Having heard "Jessica" from at least one other person, other people start trying it out. This trend increases the odds that a player using "Jessica" meets someone else who has heard "Jessica" and decides to try it on their next round. By round ten, when two strangers meet for the first time, they both intuitively know that "Jessica" is the best bet—and it is.

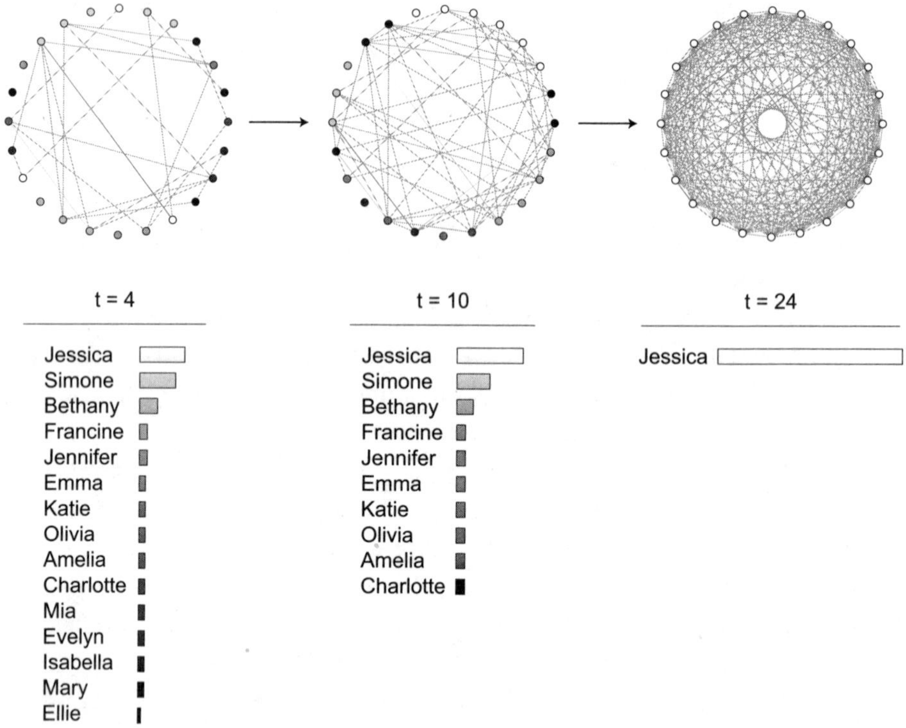

FIGURE 7.4
Coordination in an internet network

While the geographic network only had twenty-four people, it failed to achieve a shared convention. The internet network succeeded fairly quickly with twenty-four people. What would happen if we doubled the group size? We already knew what the model predicted. But we wanted to see it for ourselves.

We ran another experiment and found that forty-eight converged just as fast as a group half its size. So we doubled it again, this time with ninety-six people in the internet state of nature. In the first two rounds, an enormous number of different names were suggested, but just like before, a small spark of coordination triggered a cascade of norm change. Within just a few rounds, the entire ninety-six-person network achieved complete success. In fact, it happened just as fast with ninety-six people as with the initial two dozen. Each player had only interacted with a very small fraction of the entire population, yet after just a few minutes global collective intelligence had been achieved.

Speed and Power in Coordination

As I showed you in Part I, increasing the centralization of a network can be highly effective for achieving rapid alignment, since everyone is forced to interact with a central person. When it comes to coordination, this inequity in power forces the collective to rapidly snap into agreement on a single behavioral norm. The effectiveness of centralized networks is particularly appreciated by communities under the threat of attack. When attack is imminent and communities need to rapidly coordinate their actions, one of the most common structural strategies is to rally around the leader. It's quick, it's efficient, and it's effective.

This doesn't mean that centralization always produces beneficial results—we've seen firsthand how socially corrosive and dangerous it can be—but the dynamics of coordination are indisputable. So long as the goal is to arrive at a shared convention—in which all options are equal—then centralization is a highly effective structural solution for the grand challenge of coordination However, when the quality of the collective choice matters, then centralization can once again become a liability.

When Coordination Goes Bad

Ralph Waldo Emerson offered an inspiring view of collective intelligence in free markets: "I trust a good deal to common fame. If a man has good corn or wood, or boards, or pigs, to sell, or can make better chairs or knives, crucibles or church organs, than anybody else, you will find a broad, hard-beaten road to his house, though it be in the woods." More colloquially, "If you build a better mousetrap, the world will beat a path to your door."

It is inspiring. Unfortunately, it is also wrong. Take the keyboard on my computer. I'm typing these words on an awkward QWERTY keyboard, which is the standard keyboard that we all use today, instead of the much more efficient Dvorak keyboard, which was designed to improve human comfort and efficiency while typing. The same thing happened with VHS and Betamax videotapes; Betamax was clearly the better option, but VHS took hold of the central spot in the coordination networks and never looked back. Even when the stakes were very high, networks overpowered quality within US military contracts for nuclear reactors. The light-water variety won out because of their early foothold in military decision-making networks. All the while, heavy-water reactors were widely agreed upon as the safer and more efficient technology.

The dustbins of economic history are littered with examples of these market inefficiencies, in which the best products are driven to extinction by inferior competitors. This can happen when an inferior option gains an early position of power in the networks of influence and coordination.

But how do bad ideas take hold in the first place? In the state of nature, if we can collectively choose any option we want, why would any of us choose to coordinate on a bad one? Starting with so many different options to choose between, and given our ability to invent new options at any time, how can it happen that almost all of us choose the poorer option?

This is a hard question to answer for the same reason that it was hard to understand why "spam" became widely used. Once a convention exists, it is almost impossible to look back into the mists of time to divine its original path to dominance. But what if we could watch both good and bad options take shape across multiple cultural histories? If we return to the state of nature, perhaps we can understand why bad choices take hold even when many better options abound.

8

Why Bad Ideas Sometimes Win

Fair is foul, and foul is fair.
—*William Shakespeare,* Macbeth

J. K. Rowling is one of the most successful authors of all time. Her first seven books sold over 600 million copies, making her significantly wealthier than the king of England.

Back in 1993, however, she was just a young single mother who dreamed of being a writer. In the early 1990s, you could find Rowling sitting in a Scottish café, her infant at her side as she worked on the manuscript for her first book. As the years went by, she was forced to rely on government subsidies to support her small family. Five years after she began writing, her manuscript was finally ready to send out to potential publishers.

Her first book, *Harry Potter and the Philosopher's Stone,* was rejected. And then rejected again. And again. Not just by one or two publishers but a total of twelve publishers who offered gentle, and sometimes not so gentle, dismissals. Finally, on lucky try number thirteen, her book was accepted for publication by Bloomsbury press. Her advance was only $4,000.

If you've read that first Harry Potter book, you know within pages that you're in the hands of an absolute master storyteller. So why didn't the top professionals at the top publishing houses recognize what they had in their hands? You may be surprised to learn that this kind of failure of intelligence among the industry elite, and the subsequent rescue of great products by the intelligence of the masses, is not the exception but the rule.

To take another example, many years ago there was a novice writer named Ted, who desperately wanted to become a household name in children's fiction. He enthusiastically took his first manuscript to every publisher he could think of—twenty-seven in total—hoping to find at least one who would see its value. But for all his efforts, his only reward was twenty-seven letters of rejection. After that final letter, Ted walked the streets of Manhattan, then headed home to burn his manuscript. Trudging along Madison Avenue, Ted bumped into an old friend who had just joined the staff at Vanguard Press. Hearing Ted's story, his friend rushed Ted up to his office, where he convinced his colleagues to take a chance on the book. Ted got a contract that very day. After publishing that first book, he went on to write a new generation of children's books, some of which you may have read, like *The Cat in the Hat, How the Grinch Stole Christmas, Horton Hears a Who!, Oh, the Places You'll Go!,* and many, many others. Ted's penname, as you've likely guessed, was Dr. Seuss.

It also happens in the sciences. In the 1970s, a young graduate student submitted his bold new theory of social networks to a prominent sociological journal, *American Sociological Review*. His submission was roundly rejected. He wondered whether he should destroy his paper and start over, but instead he simply changed a few words and resubmitted it, this time to the *American Journal of Sociology*, which accepted his paper. Within a year, this article had become well-known across sociology. Within ten years, it had become celebrated as a watershed study in the field of social networks. Forty years on, this once-rejected article had become widely regarded as one of the most influential sociological contributions of the twentieth century, impacting disciplines from cultural anthropology to statistical physics. The scholar's name is Mark Granovetter and the article is "The Strength of Weak Ties," and today his paper is the most-cited research article in the entire field of sociology.

CUMULATIVE ADVANTAGE

There is a well-known scientific explanation for how these unlikely (yet surprisingly common) success stories are possible. It is called the theory of *cumulative advantage*. This theory offers a compelling account of why cultural superstars continually emerge despite industry elites' inability to anticipate them.

The clever wrinkle offered by this theory is that all of these big winners are not what they appear to be. They are not success stories. In fact, this theory suggests that most of the big cultural successes that you know of are actually massive failures of collective intelligence.

In cultural markets, consumers often use each other's choices to make inferences about the quality and value of cultural products. Many times we pay more attention to each other's choices than to the quality of the product itself. As the famous economist John Maynard Keynes once put it, markets are beauty pageants in which all the judges spend their time trying to determine who the other judges will vote for, while no one considers the contestants themselves. In cultural markets, this means that if a product gains an arbitrary early bump in popularity, new consumers will typically flock to it. When this happens, popularity can quickly outpace quality. Even the mere perception of a product's popularity can result in herds of consumers rushing to it, thereby growing a mediocre product into a huge cultural success.

According to the theory of cumulative advantage, the failure of collective intelligence here is not on the part of industry elites failing to recognize high-quality cultural artifacts. Quite the opposite. The failure is on the part of the consumers, who collectively reinforce the cultural success of unexceptional products, eclipsing any potential of finding the truly great innovations. On this account, massive inequality and massive lack of intelligence in cultural markets happen blamelessly. Inferior products win big all the time, but it's no one's fault. In the end, it is just a matter of luck.

In the early 2000s, the stark realities of this new form of cultural nihilism presented a serious challenge not only to social scientists but to the general idea of cultural progress. It suggested that every outcome in a cultural market is equally valid since every winner is equally undeserving. The expectation that outsized cultural success would be based upon the quality and merit of cultural products was an illusion. Regardless of who wins, the victor only wins big because of the feckless combination of arbitrary advantages and social feedback. Apparently, success in cultural markets really is nothing more than a beauty contest.

Around 2004, this dismal state of affairs drove one of my friends in graduate school, Matt Salganik, to dedicate his entire PhD dissertation at Columbia University to figuring out whether or not this theory of cultural success was actually true. Was success in cultural markets really reducible to cumulative advantage? Were the time-honored principles of quality and merit just anachronistic myths, without any real power to create success in the modern world?

It was an important project to undertake. But to do it, Matt would need a way to overcome the history problem.

Do you remember the history problem that got in the way of understanding why "spam" took off and "yinz" didn't? It's the same with any cultural success story. There is always an easy explanation that clouds the actual story of how any cultural product successfully navigated the stormy seas from obscurity to fame. For instance, if it were possible to observe two different versions of the world, you could find out whether *Harry Potter* always wins in both because it is just that good, or whether *Harry Potter* might take off in one world but be an also-ran in another world where a different author's book would become the world's best-selling novel (assuming both books had the same publisher, same promotion efforts, etc.). If that happened, it would tell us that *Harry Potter*'s big cultural success really is just a matter of luck. And it would finally provide social scientists with a way of knowing whether *Harry Potter*, and the rest of the big cultural successes out there—from Beanie Babies to Britney Spears—really deserve the success that they have earned or are all just big accidents of history.

The Music Experiment

Matt loved music.

Early on in graduate school, he maintained an exhaustive list of the best lyrics from contemporary rap songs. Given Matt's love of music, studying the popularity of songs was a natural way for him to investigate the dynamics of success in a cultural marketplace. His idea was to build a website where you could download music and use it to study how songs become popular.

Matt took full advantage of being in graduate school in New York City to look around for new music that he could use in his study. After about a year of gathering songs and getting artists to sign agreements to allow him to use their music in his study, he was ready to build his downloading site.

At the time, it was revolutionary. It was an entire music-downloading product—called Musiclab—akin to early pirating sites like Napster (but of course Matt had permissions to share the songs), in which people could browse music, listen to samples, and download everything for free. Matt's ingenious twist was that the entire thing was designed as an experiment in cumulative advantage.

He partnered with a teen news and media site, Bolt.com, and got them to advertise a link to his music-downloading site on their front page. For months, he had a steady stream of teenagers coming to his website and downloading as many songs as they liked, all for free. Of course, unknown to those teenagers, there were actually nine different versions of the site—nine different "worlds"—and each person was randomly assigned to only one of them.

Each world had the same forty-eight songs to choose from, and the site would keep track in real time of how many people downloaded each song so you could see their popularity based on other people's past downloads.

This was a different setup from the naming game. In the naming game, participants interacted in an evolving ecosystem so they could exchange ideas and influence one another (even changing their minds multiple times as they went back and forth in real time). In Musiclab, participants came through one at a time. They would listen to songs, download them, and then leave. As each new person arrived, the site kept a cumulative tally of which songs were downloaded that was visible to everyone who came next. It was just like a *Billboard* chart.

Over the course of two months, a constant stream of about 7,000 people were randomized across all nine worlds. Overall, each *Billboard* world got about 700 teens making music selections. After a few months of this, some songs were much more popular than others, and some were rarely, if ever, downloaded. The big question, of course, was whether the same songs got popular in each world or whether it was random. It was like asking if Britney Spears became a big star in every world, revealing her undeniable appeal, or whether she won big in one world largely by accident, and not in any of the others.

One of the nine worlds was the placebo control condition. This was a world (with approximately 1,400 subjects) in which people could download songs from the website, but there was no information about which songs other people were downloading—no charts or visible metrics of any kind. With no information about song popularity, there was no potential for cumulative advantage. The control condition offered a true account of each song's appeal since downloads were purely based on the songs themselves and not any social information about how many other people liked them. This design was an ingenious way of getting at the elusive concept of *quality*. Although no one can say for sure which songs were higher quality than others, the control condition could establish a baseline reference point for what might be called a song's *relative appeal*—its overall ranking in the control condition.

Each world was completely independent, so each one offered its own *Billboard* of top hits. Outside of the control group, people were provided with the same list of songs, along with a running tally of how often each song had been downloaded. To make the experiment a fair test of the emergence of collective intelligence in cultural markets, Matt had to make sure that all of the songs used in the study were unknown, so popularity could be attributed to the social learning in the site rather than, for instance, external promotions or tours that were happening in the city. It also meant that subjects' access to these songs came (almost) exclusively through the experimental music-downloading site. One of the bands included was Parker Theory, and its song was "She Said"; another band was Moral Hazard, and its song was "Waste of My Life." You probably have not heard of any of them, and that was the idea.

In the control condition, even though people did not have information about each other's music downloads, some songs nevertheless became more popular than others, but no song became much, much more popular than the rest. Just as the theory predicted, that only happens when there is social feedback. Notwithstanding, there was one song that became the most downloaded song in the entire control condition site: Parker Theory's "She Said."

The independent control condition enabled Matt and his colleagues to say that if it was possible to discover the inherent appeal of a song, then the control condition would be a good way to reveal it. Based on this definition, "She Said" established a baseline for the relative quality of the songs.

Now the question was what would happen across the eight worlds. Would big winners emerge? Would social feedback cause random songs—or even "poor quality" songs—to become big winners? Remarkably, the eight social worlds did not look very different from the control condition. The most popular song was not absurdly famous. In fact, it was only a bit more popular than in the control condition. Moreover, it was the same song: "She Said."

Matt's team was so surprised by these findings that they wanted to try again. This time, they tried to make it more likely that the dynamics of cumulative advantage could overwhelm the objective appeal of the song, so this time in the social information worlds they put all the songs into an ordered ranking, from the top of the page all the way to the bottom, based on how frequently the song was downloaded. The ranked song list was longer than the screen, so to find the less popular songs, users would need to scroll down to see the bottom of the rankings.

This design amplified the power of the top spot in the list. Once a leader emerged, it was clicked on more frequently, and it quickly became a big winner, growing much more successful than the lower-ranked songs in the list. These results seemed more like the kind of runaway success that we see in the real world.

But here's the unexpected twist. The big winner in almost all of the eight social feedback worlds was once again "She Said"! In fact, in every world, "She Said" was among the top three most successful songs. The main difference between the control condition site and the *Billboard* sites was that the latter were more likely to make big winners, but the songs that it made into big winners were actually the same songs.

These findings offer a surprising discovery about cumulative advantage. As the theory of cumulative advantage predicted, social information did indeed change the margins of success. A cultural product that might enjoy only modest success above its peers in the control condition can be transformed from a moderately successful winner into a huge cultural star in the social information groups. Just by allowing people to learn from one another, social feedback actually amplified the collective intelligence of the audiences, leading many more people to choose the "best" song. This was completely contrary to the theory of cumulative advantage.

But that discovery was not the end. It was just the beginning.

Even more than Matt loves music, Matt loves methods. He is a true-blue methodologist and an outspoken advocate for transparency in science. Months before the findings from his Musiclab study were published, he was already preparing his data so they could be easily reanalyzed by other scientists. Every detail of the Musiclab study was published online, enabling other scholars to use his remarkable experiment to explore new questions about popularity in cultural markets. Which is exactly what they did.

Another friend of mine from graduate school, Arnout van de Rijt, was fascinated by Matt's study. Poring over Matt's data, he discovered that there was a shift in music-downloading behavior when you compared the first few weeks of the study to the last few weeks. It turned out that the jumbled ranking of songs during the early days of the *Billboard* worlds were just transitory—they were temporary periods of disorder that would soon be corrected. The Billboards quickly began reordering themselves to resemble the rankings found in the independent control condition. By the end of the study, the statistical differences between the song rankings in the *Billboard* worlds and the rankings in the control condition—from the most popular songs all the way down to the least—had practically disappeared, with most worlds already converging on the same big winner: "She Said." Far from social feedback undermining collective intelligence in cultural markets, it was in fact an amazingly efficient method for exponentially increasing the most appealing song's popularity. Matt had chosen Parker Theory for his study because they were undeniably obscure. Yet no matter which history you started with, cumulative advantage led to the same remarkable feat of collective intelligence every time.

THE (UN)POPULARITY PUZZLE

Matt and his colleagues had one more test in mind: This time they would run the same music-downloading experiment as before, but they would artificially conceal the true preferences of the population. In each of these *Billboard* worlds, Matt's team falsely indicated that "She Said" was the *least* preferred song, manipulating the chart to show the song all the way down at number forty-eight. Going one step further, they took the least liked song, Post Break Tragedy's "Florence," which was number forty-eight in reality, and placed it up in the number-one ranking spot. Matt's team repeated this deception for every song.

For instance, they moved the second most popular song, Simply Waiting's "Went with the Count," down in the rankings to number forty-seven. Correspondingly, they moved the second least popular song, Deep Enough to Die's "For the Sky," to spot number two. And so on for all of the songs in the list.

Were people fooled? Was Matt's deceptive reordering of the rankings able to scuttle the intelligence of the music-loving crowd?

Not even a little bit. Collective intelligence was stunningly resilient.

Despite the fact that "She Said" was displayed at the bottom of the charts, with the least number of downloads, through the dynamics of cumulative advantage collective intelligence triumphed once again (figure 8.1). Parker Theory's song was like a buoyant object being forced underwater. The social learning that had originally pushed it to number one kicked in almost immediately. Once the experimenter's hand was removed and the charts started to reflect people's actual choices, "She Said" shot up the rankings. The more people who found it, the more it was downloaded. Within a very short time, in all of the *Billboard* worlds, it was back on its way to number one.

The simple truth is that no one had predicted that collective intelligence would be so resilient. The dynamics of cumulative advantage were not amplifying the *Billboard* rankings—which is what everyone predicted. They were correcting them.

And not just for the number-one song. Arnout's analysis showed that the number-two song was also on its way back up the rankings, quickly jumping from its starting position in spot forty-seven back up to spot eleven in one world, and spot eight in another world by the time the study was over. In fact, all of the best songs were buoyant. By the end of the study, song three was already bubbling back up, as was song four.

There is a surprising amount of intelligence in the process of social feedback. Matt made multiple attempts to trick the population of music lovers into making collective mistakes in choosing different big winners.

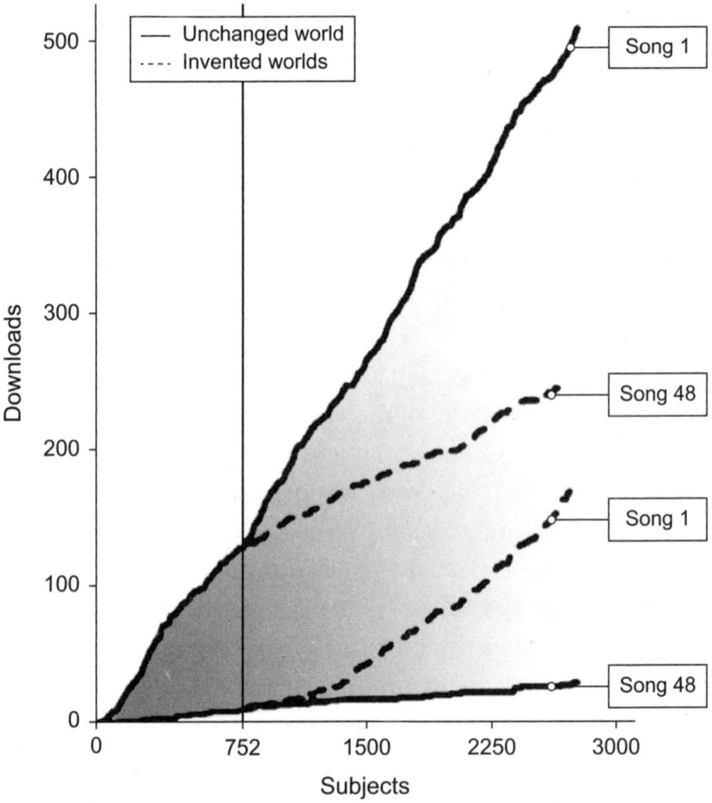

FIGURE 8.1
Musiclab rank-reversal experiment, adapted from Matt Salganik and Duncan Watts, "Leading the Herd Astray: An Experimental Study of Self-Fulfilling Prophecies in an Artificial Cultural Market," *Social Psychology Quarterly* 71, no. 4 (2008).

But every time, the collective dynamics of social learning enabled the population to rediscover the highest "quality" song. Every time, the population found its way back toward convergence on the best choice.

Far from the cultural nihilism of classic theories of cumulative advantage, these findings revealed a strikingly optimistic view of cultural markets. Given time and unconstrained social feedback, the cultural products that are successful are not random but in fact deserve to be successful.

We've all seen that the dustbins of social and economic history are filled with examples of inferior products succeeding in cultural markets.

Bad songs, films, and books sometimes win great popular acclaim. Matt's experiments showed us that the cause of these failures of collective intelligence is not cumulative advantage itself—which can actually be very smart—but rather the structure of the informational ecology in which cumulative advantage takes place. We know that social feedback can lead to surprising collective intelligence. But that's only when all of the cultural options remain equally available.

Matt's team could easily have created exactly the kind of undeserved success that cumulative advantage scholars have worried about for generations. All they had to do was let some songs die off.

The real mistake in Emerson's optimistic viewpoint was not his confidence in the crowd's capacity for intelligence but his mischaracterization of the structure of the informational ecology. Emerson assumed, as did Matt, that all options continue to remain available regardless of how popular they are. But that's not what happens in real cultural markets. In the competitive social world—in music, in politics, and in science—the least popular options are culled.

Options die off. And that causes all the problems.

As some songs rapidly grow in popularity, others are squeezed out of the spotlight. Any song that gains popularity faces continual threat from new music entering the marketplace. Every song must grow its audience or die.

But being squeezed is different from being suffocated. The more options that die off, the more attention accrues to a small number of winners. The faster this happens, the easier it is for good options, which may take slightly longer to catch on, to be prematurely culled from the marketplace. If Matt had booted "She Said" when the song was low in the charts, then Parker Theory would have quickly vanished from sight, never to return.

Fair Is Smart (and Smart Is Fair)

A few chapters ago, you saw how the egalitarian structure of the information and influence networks could secure collective intelligence for the populace. But even if the social influence network is perfectly egalitarian, the centralization of the informational ecology around a small number of lesser options can nevertheless lead to convergence on an inferior option. Despite structural equity within the information-sharing network, structural inequity in the informational ecology can have the same potentially hazardous result.

Matt's *Billboard* worlds were certainly hierarchical, but they were not Darwinian, with only the fittest surviving. In the music-downloading experiment, an option that was not initially popular could still be discovered later on. This is precisely what happened in the rank-reversal experiments. Even though the most appealing song was at the bottom, it could still be discovered and downloaded just as easily as if it were at the top.

In real cultural markets, however, powerful interests can artificially tip the scales of popularity, giving weighty advantages to some competitors over others. When cultural options face extinction, the effects of these pressures are not benign. Cultural products that do not keep up are quickly discarded. Even short-lived inequities in attention can be the difference between life and death. A small disadvantage early on can have big consequences for the survival of cultural products.

We saw this exact thing happen in the last chapter. In the naming game, internet-style network structures led to the rapid extinction of hundreds of options and the universal convergence on a single winner. There, all options were equal, so one option was as good as any other. It did not matter which convention they chose, so long as everyone agreed.

But what happens if there is one option that is better than the others?

In a fair world in which all options are equally available, collectives will consistently discover the best option. The Musiclab experiment showed that the most appealing cultural items can easily find success in an internet network in which everyone has equal influence and all options can be discovered.

Everything changes in a world in which solutions are quickly driven to extinction. Cultural items that do not receive early support can easily lose their footing, and once they no longer have an opportunity to be discovered, they disappear. Only the options that remain active within the cultural marketplace can win.

Restricting access to options is perhaps the most muscular use of power in a cultural market. The artificial culling of options is tantamount to the attenuation of collective intelligence. Particularly if membership in the marketplace of cultural ideas and products requires the ornaments of power—such as time, money, status, and social capital—then inequities in resources can indeed control a population's ability to arrive at the best cultural options.

In today's technologically evolving cultural marketplace, a lot of new work is needed to explore the intelligence of contemporary aggregation systems—such as Yelp, Spotify, Reddit, and TikTok, to name just a few—which are continuously shaping our engagement with a vast number of cultural products. Do these platforms help to amplify the best options, or do they force centralization around an inferior few? Do page rankings or upvoting and downvoting systems accelerate collective learning, or do they undermine it? Which forms of aggregation (such as lists, likes, and recommendations) limit the availability of the best cultural options and which ones amplify them? These are pressing topics for a new generation of research on collective intelligence.

In the real world, Parker Theory remains virtually unknown, its Instagram account with fewer than 150 followers and its Spotify monthly leadership below 1,000. Part of the problem in the real world is that there are many more than forty-eight songs. If Matt had used 500 songs (or even forty-nine songs) instead, perhaps "She Said" would have ended up as an also-ran.

One thing we know for sure is that time is the ally of intelligence. So long as all options are equally available, early users' explorations will eventually aggregate into useful signals for subsequent users.

The problem for collective intelligence is not cumulative advantage itself but rather the structure of the informational ecology in which cumulative advantage operates. Intelligent cultural markets require a basic principle of fairness. Knowing this, what can we do to help ensure that this principle of fairness is preserved so that collective discovery of ideas and innovations can succeed even when the inventory of options is inevitably constrained? We'll turn to that next.

III

Cooperation and Creativity

9

Why Nice Guys Finish First

On a rainy August morning in 2011, Rick Ruzzamenti's kidney was traveling eastbound on a red-eye from Los Angeles to Newark. Rick was resting comfortably in a hospital bed in Riverside, California, when his kidney was hurried to Saint Barnabas Medical Center in Livingston, New Jersey, where it was sewn into the belly of a sixty-six-year-old man.

The beneficiary of Rick's generosity had a thirty-four-year-old niece who happened to work as a nurse. She had wanted to donate her kidney to her uncle, but could not because she had type A blood, while he had type O. Although she could not help her uncle directly, she bartered for Rick's kidney by offering hers to Brooke Kitzman of Madison, Wisconsin. Brooke was able to receive the nurse's kidney because her ex-boyfriend, David Madosh, donated his kidney to Pittsburgh resident Janna Daniels. Then, in exchange for David's kidney, Janna's husband sent his kidney to Mustafa Parks, a San Diego resident and young father of two.

On and on it went.

When it comes to organ transplants, the challenge of saving lives has little to do with medicine. Kidney removals and insertions are routine procedures. The real challenge is the science of exchange networks.

It is remarkably hard to match donors with recipients even among members of the same family. Most organs will not work for most people. Organ transplants are a complex matching problem that arises from the enormous amount of genetic variation within the human species. This basic fact of biology is one of the major stumbling blocks for designing an efficient system of organ donation.

This matching problem gets exponentially harder when you go from two people to four people. It becomes an even harder mathematics problem when you go from four people to eight people, and as the numbers increase, it becomes almost intractable to identify the exact sequence of crisscrossing pairs that more challenging will match donors with compatible recipients. It becomes even less tractable to imagine doing this when you realize that the series of donor–patient pairs that are needed to link a donated kidney in California to an end recipient in Chicago can be dozens of steps long.

Rick's August 15th kidney donation was particularly special in this regard because it put into motion the longest, most life-saving chain of exchanges of kidney transplants in medical history. Several months and dozens of people later, on a chilly December morning, a final donated kidney, this one from Sherry Gluchowski in Southern California, arrived at the Loyola Marymount Medical Center in Chicago, where it saved the life of forty-five-year-old Donald C. Terry Jr.

In 2014, 4,072 people died while waiting for a kidney transplant that never arrived. Most people on the transplant list are waiting for a life-saving gift from a recently deceased organ donor. But the uncertainty of that eventuality, combined with the challenges of compatibility, make it a very dangerous waiting game. Donations from live donors offer a radically different opportunity to save lives. In fact, with so many people in the world, it may be possible to save everyone on the waitlist, if only a compatible donor can be found for everyone.

Between August and December 2011, sixty lives were saved as a result of a single chain of kidney donations. All because Rick Ruzzamenti overheard a conversation about kidney donations in his yoga class and wanted to do some good.

Structural Intelligence in Exchange

One of the key scientists who figured out the structural principles that made these life-saving networks possible is the economist Alvin Roth. For Roth, discovering this chain of kidney donations began as a theoretical problem in the science of exchange networks: Was it possible to design a structure that would enable dozens of complete strangers to trust one another enough to put their life-saving organs onto planes traveling around the country, in the hopes that a few days or weeks later a corresponding organ would miraculously arrive to save their loved one? This kind of exchange network can only function if people are able to trust that every step in the chain will work. For an economist, that means that every person must have the right incentives to donate as promised. The exchange structure must guarantee that every new person in the chain will create additional benefits for others further down the line. It is what is called a "complex" problem. It is so complex, in fact, that Roth (together with famed mathematical economist Lloyd Shapley) won the 2012 Nobel Prize in Economics for the discovery of how these exchange networks can be reliably designed to enable this live-saving form of collective intelligence to succeed.

The interesting idea behind Roth's solution is that kidneys are a lot like dorm rooms: In a market without money, the way to find good matches is to uncover small groups of the people who can trade with each other. After each small group completes a round of trades, you move on to the next group, and so on. A clever model (called the top trading cycle) shows that if you let a few students trade dorm rooms, then remove those people and their rooms from the pool of potential trades and start over again with those who are left, the process will ultimately cycle down to a final state in which the resulting matches are always better than the ones you started with. With a few tweaks, the same basic logic can be applied to kidney matching. Though with kidneys, the real complication comes from the perishable and personal nature of what's being exchanged.

WHY MONEY WON'T WORK

It is illegal to buy organs in the US. (In fact, it is illegal in every country in the world, except for Iran.) This legislation is rooted in a moral principle of fairness: People who are rich enough to buy organs should not be allowed to live while poor people who cannot afford them suffer and die. As a result, organ donation is based on medical priority and biological compatibility, not on individual wealth; when it comes to kidneys, there is no formal market since kidneys cannot legally be priced.

When it comes to matching, in the easiest case it takes just two couples to make a successful match. For instance, if I want to donate my kidney to my wife but our blood types are incompatible, I might call around and discover that we have neighbors who are in the same situation. Luckily, my neighbor Lucy is compatible to donate a kidney for my wife. As it turns out, Lucy needs a kidney for her husband, Tom, but is in a similar situation since she and her husband have incompatible blood types. Luckily, I am compatible with Tom. So I can donate my kidney to her husband, and she can donate to my wife. Lucy and I both give up our kidneys, swapping them to our respective spouses. Everyone lives happily ever after.

Things gets more complicated if Lucy is donor-compatible with my wife, but I am not donor-compatible with her husband. Now I need to hunt around to find a medical database in which there is a compatible donor for Tom. Once that's accomplished, I need to hope that I can donate my kidney to that donor's family so that they will donate to Lucy's family. But that's just the beginning. If I'm lucky enough to find this matching couple in the database, then I need to get everyone to agree on a timetable for how this is going work, including removal surgeries, flights, insertion surgeries, and logistical contingencies. This is way harder than it seems. For instance, if Tom's donor dies in a kidney-destroying car accident before Lucy's kidney is removed, Tom is left without a donor. For Lucy, her kidney is her only resource for saving her husband, so she's got to hold onto it until she can find a suitable exchange for him. Understandably, Lucy will almost certainly renege on her agreement to donate to my wife and will instead immediately start looking around for other options for her husband. And that's just for three couples. As the numbers climb, the complexity of the exchange increases.

The fact that this kind of problem cannot be solved with money makes it a special challenge for modern medicine. We cannot rely on market economics to simply match buyers with sellers. Instead, we need to find the perfect exchange structure that makes it possible for everyone to trust everyone else. The only way to do this is to ensure that everyone has something to gain from keeping the complete sequence of exchanges intact.

In itself, this life-saving system of fair exchange is a remarkable feat of collective intelligence. But what is even more remarkable is that people choose to follow through without needing any overarching external system of punishment to enforce it. No law mandates that Lucy must donate a kidney if Tom's donor cannot provide one, whether because there's no longer a kidney to donate or the donor simply changes their mind. How do so many people with such different backgrounds and resources all agree to cooperate in a system of fair exchange, particularly when the stakes are so high?

Roth's groundbreaking solution to kidney exchange reveals an important limitation to cooperation in society. Rick Ruzzamenti's altruistic act, as remarkable as it was, may not have saved anyone's life if not for the networks that made it possible. For Rick's individual act of generosity to have that kind of impact, it required a structure that connected everyone together in a way that maximized their collective good. Otherwise, Rick's act of kindness might have had very little impact on anyone.

Roth solved the first part of this problem: how to find suitable partners for kidney exchanges. But what happens when we move beyond kidneys and dorm rooms? For the vast number of other exchange relations in society, from itinerant farmers looking for steady work, to families looking for affordable housing, finding exchange partners is only the first problem. Agreeing on fair terms of exchange is the second.

What guarantees that exchanges will be fair rather than exploitative? The best way to see how fairness can emerge to become a stable feature of society—even when life and death are on the line—is to go all the way back to the state of nature.

FAIRNESS IN THE STATE OF NATURE

I introduced you to the state of nature a couple of chapters ago, the thought experiment in which we imagine how it is possible for social principles such as fairness to come into existence and become widely adopted. In the state of nature, people have not yet learned the norms of society. They have not observed their parents and grandparents getting along with their peers, nor have they earned social rewards for becoming good members of their tribe. In the hypothetical state of nature, everyone is wild. They can do whatever serves their self-interest the most.

This is a particularly harsh world to imagine. It is perhaps the worst version of our own world, a world red in tooth and claw, in which every choice is shaped by the drive for survival and profit. Yet, even from these rough beginnings, fairness can emerge. Whether or not it succeeds depends on the structure of people's networks, which can either drive the population toward cooperation or away from it.

Imagine two people sitting at the negotiating table. They can make a fair trade, which we can call a 50–50 split of resources. Something like: I'll give you a kidney that your spouse needs, if you give me a kidney that my spouse needs. But there may be some people who are greedier. They may, for instance, demand two kidneys—one from the spouse and one from a sibling—in exchange for only one. A desperate husband may reluctantly agree to this inequity if he believes it is the only exchange that will save his wife. We will call this arrangement a 70–30 split of resources, in which one side gets much more than the other.

In the end, there are only two exchange options that are meaningful: fairness and inequality. Do people wind up with fair 50–50 splits or with an inequitable 70–30 division (or some similarly disproportionate arrangement)? This may seem like a harsh world to imagine, but it has emerged many times in history. In sharecropping communities, for instance, landlords and tenant farmers must come to an agreement regarding a proper division of the harvest between them. In some agricultural communities in India, landlords and farmers agreed to unequal 70–30 splits, in which the tenant farmers who worked the land would get only 30 percent of the harvest, while the landowners would get 70 percent. Once an agreement like this is struck, it is hard to escape the established norm, even for future generations of farmers. Some economic theorists argue that this inequity is a natural arrangement because landlords and tenant farmers are not equally situated. The excess risk faced by the landlord, in addition to the asymmetry in power between the landlord and tenant farmers, suggests that a 50–50 split would not necessarily emerge. Nevertheless, there are many documented farming communities in comparable regions of India (with the same soil conditions, rainfall, etc.) that are similar in every way to the other farms, which arrived at even 50–50 splits between landlords and sharecroppers. What explains these patterns of fairness? They apparently emerged all by themselves, and once established, the expectation of fairness endured for generations. This happened not just in India but in the US as well. Norms of equitable distribution show up repeatedly across many successful communities, establishing stable expectations for fairness in exchange. Yet their origins can be hard to determine, particularly given the natural expectation that power inequality will result in resource inequity.

Nobody wants an inequitable division of resources to emerge within the world of organ donations. But it could. What if healthier people believe that their organs are worth more than unhealthy people's organs? What if smaller families believe that their organs are worth more than those from larger families? Any number of inequities can emerge in exchange networks, particularly when people are negotiating their own contracts.

Sometimes laws may help us. But laws are based on customs and customary beliefs about what is just and what is fair. In the state of nature, just like in international exchange, there are no laws. What ensures that the agreed-upon customs that emerge in these markets will be fair? The answer, once again, is structure.

Previously, we've seen that coordination in geographic networks slowed down the dynamics of collective intelligence while internet networks dramatically accelerated it. It's the *opposite* for fairness: For the grand challenge of cooperation, geographic networks are much *more* efficient than internet networks for achieving collective intelligence.

Why is this so?

In geographic networks, people interact repeatedly with the same small number of peers. In *clustered* geographic networks, those peers also interact with one another. Clustering is a key feature of geographic networks that is particularly important for successful cooperation. As shown in figure 9.1, it happens when there are triangles in the social network—so that the people you know also know one another. Clustering is important because it creates reputation effects—even among strangers. In a simple version of the state of nature, people are anonymous. Everyone attempts to come to an exchange agreement with their partners, but they have no idea who their partners are or what to expect from them next time. In more sophisticated versions of the state of nature, however, people remember whom they have interacted with. This convenience allows reputations to form in the network. If the network is large enough, a person can develop a reputation as an unfair player who demands 70 percent all the time, and others will soon stop trying to trade with them. The unfair parties will quickly lose trading partners while the fair ones will quickly learn to trade with one another. These reputation effects are famously referred to as the shadow of the future. The shadow of the future forces people to interact fairly with others for fear of future reprisals if they do not.

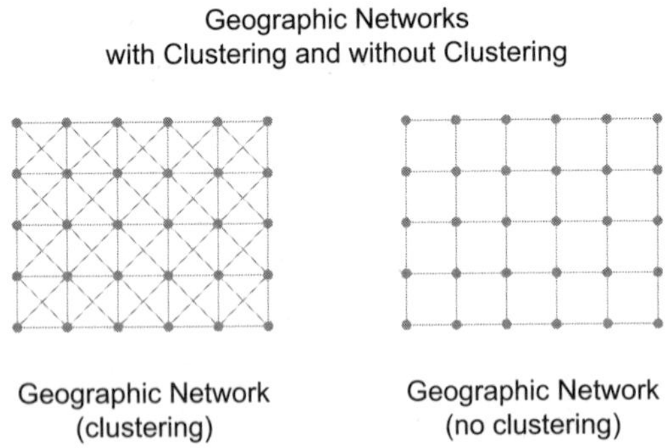

FIGURE 9.1
Geographic networks with (left) and without (right) clustering

But when interacting with strangers, people may lie about their identity or assume multiple different identities in different interactions. There is in fact a degree of anonymity in the kidney exchange networks in order to protect people's privacy. That way, if someone backs out or suffers some other change in life circumstance that prevents them from going through with the exchange, they are immune from being publicly castigated or privately harassed. However, this means we cannot rely on reputation effects to secure cooperation—strangers remain strangers. So why does the system work? How does cooperation emerge without relying on people's personal reputations to ensure that everyone observes the norm of fairness?

This question becomes a real problem when the state of nature has an internet structure. Suppose there is a player who asks for 50 percent but has the misfortune to interact repeatedly with other players who demand 70 percent. After several rounds of play, the fair player may feel compelled to accept 30 percent since they have not found any better options. In an anonymous world of strangers, the calculus of survival dominates the morality of outrage. After enough interactions, 70–30 just appears to be the norm. This is just like the inequitable sharecropping arrangements, in which the population of "players" becomes divided between people who exploit needy partners and those who have had the bad luck to only make exchanges with exploiters.

Things go a surprisingly different way in a clustered geographic state of nature. Even if players are anonymous, they are still forced to interact with a small number of neighbors. If two connected people happen to both choose 70, they will repeatedly fail to reach any agreement. If one of them offers 60, the other may reciprocate with 60, but still no deal will arrive. Eventually, if one of them finally offers 50, the other is likely to ultimately agree to 50. Now if these two neighbors offer one another 50, everyone else they are connected to may start to expect that offer too. These exchange partners may now go through the same series of negotiations, beginning from 70 until they also arrive at 50. From there, there is nowhere else to go since 50–30 makes no sense and 50–70 leads to a failed negotiation (as does 50–65, 50–60, 50–55, etc.).

Here is a quick illustration of how rapidly fairness can outcompete exploitation in a clustered geographic structure. Suppose that the exploiters in figure 9.2 demand 60 percent of the yield (represented as 6), while the exploited accept 40 percent (4), and the fair-dealers ask for a 50–50 split (5). Each player tries to trade with all eight of their network neighbors (above, below, on both sides, and on all diagonals). After all the trades

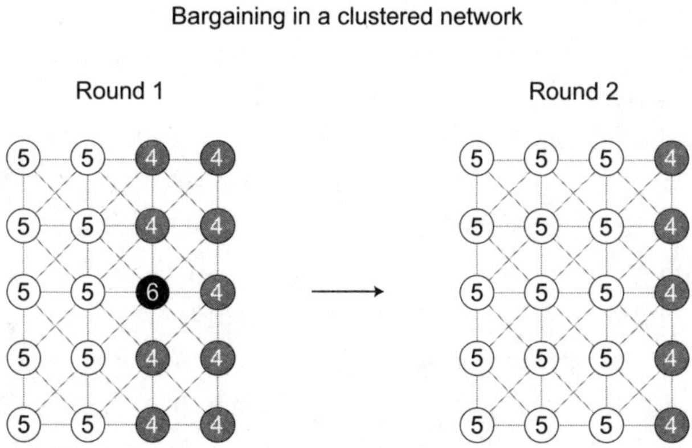

FIGURE 9.2
Two rounds of bargaining in a clustered network. Adapted from Jason Alexander and Brian Skyrms, "Bargaining with Neighbors: Is Justice Contagious?," *Journal of Philosophy* 96, no. 11 (1999): 588–598.

are done, players see how each of their neighbors has fared overall, and then they copy the strategy of their most successful neighbor. A player who encounters a successful exploiter will quickly change their strategy to become an exploiter too. It seems like exploitation would thrive. That can happen in an internet network with random interactions. But you'll see why a clustered lattice structure quickly snuffs out exploitation, leading everyone toward fair dealing.

In figure 9.2, each of the fair-dealing players (asking for 5) gets the requested 5 points from their fair-dealing neighbors. The exploited players (requesting only 4) each get 4 points from all eight of their neighbors for a total of 32 points. Finally, the exploiter (demanding 6) gets 6 points from each exploited player and 0 points from each fair player, just as each fair-dealing player also get 0 points from their attempts to trade with the exploiters. The end result from the initial round (round 1) is that the fair-dealing players who are neighbors with the exploiter each get 35 points (that is, they get 5 points from each fair dealer and from each exploited player, but 0 points from the exploiter). By contrast, the exploiter comes away with only 30 points (getting 6 points from each exploited player, but 0 points from each fair dealer). The exploiter quickly realizes that they can do better with a fair-dealing strategy than by trying to exploit the fair-dealers. In their next round, they switch to fair-dealing. Similarly, several of the exploited players also see how well the fair dealers have done. Now that they are no longer forced to contend with an exploiter, they also choose fair dealing. Very soon (by round 2), all of the neighbors of the fair dealers have become fair dealers too.

Fairness takes over so quickly because it is the only strategy that does well against itself. A clustered geographic network forces everyone who copies their neighbor's strategy to keep interacting with people who use the same strategy as themselves. It does not take long for both the exploiters and the exploited alike to realize that their best option in such a setting is to become fair dealers, just like everyone else around them.

Once fairness takes hold of a neighborhood, it quickly spreads to nearby neighborhoods. The initial group of fair players makes efficient use of a clustered geographic network to increase their numbers. By contrast, in an internet structure, as long as there are people who demand 60 and can find others to interact with who will accept 40, inequity can persist for generations. But a change in the network structure changes everything. Enduring systems of inequity break down almost immediately when people are forced to interact with neighbors, even anonymously. In clustered exchange architectures, even long-standing exploiters soon find they have no one to exploit, and they are quickly forced to accept 50–50, just like everyone else.

Henceforth, it is very hard for a few rogue individuals to try to invade the network: If anyone demands an unfair payoff, they will simply fail to strike a bargain with people who are used to always getting a 50–50 split with their neighbors.

In a clustered geographic structure, even if some people somehow manage to come to a complex pattern of unequal splits, it only takes a couple of players asking for 50–50 splits for the entire system of inequity to erode.

This principle of fairness extends across a vast number of settings in which people can achieve more together than they can alone. Whether it is a life-saving kidney exchange, community-strengthening division of neighborhood duties, or a marriage-saving exchange of household chores, the ability of equals to achieve intelligent cooperative arrangements often depends upon networks that support expectations of fairness between them.

The political scientist Robert Axelrod famously asked, "When should a person cooperate?" Axelrod's answer was that a person should cooperate when cooperation is reciprocated. But network structure can have a big impact on this potential. As Axelrod put it, "Whether players trust each other or not is less important in the long run than whether the conditions are ripe for them to build a stable pattern of cooperation with each other." Clustered geographic networks not only help to grow cooperation, they also keep cooperative groups stable by protecting them from being invaded by defectors.

Internet structures do the opposite. They vastly improve the reach of each person across the network, exposing them to many more people. But in doing so they make everyone far more vulnerable to exploitation from strangers. Without shared peers to enforce 50–50 splits, individuals interacting with distant exploitive strangers can easily become entrenched in 70–30 splits that persist indefinitely.

Clustered geographic structures create natural safeguards against exploitation. Repeated interactions within networks of peers who consistently interact with one another limits the ability of actors to make unfair demands of their exchange partners. The intelligence of these structures is that they reinforce and stabilize the value of fair exchanges among all parties, preventing individuals from unilaterally deviating. Once the idea of fairness enters these networks, it spreads rapidly to everyone, establishing a structural foundation for intelligent cooperation throughout the community.

After groups figure out how to cooperate, the next challenge is to optimize people's cooperative efforts to achieve group excellence. Good intentions are useful, but the willingness to work together does not tell us much about whether groups will be successful—to say nothing of whether they will be innovative. What can structural intelligence tell us about how to increase a group's ability to work together creatively to discover game-changing new ideas in science, technology, and the arts?

A lot, actually—and we'll turn to that next.

10

Courting Serendipity

If a building doesn't encourage collaboration, you'll lose the magic of serendipity.

—Steve Jobs on the design of Pixar headquarters

There is an old joke in Boston. If you go to Harvard, you can't count, and if you go to MIT, you can't spell.

One of the first things you find out when you join MIT is that it's not entirely a joke. MIT is indeed all about the numbers. If you ask an MIT student what their major is, they will tell you "Course 6" if they are a computer science major or "Course 15" if their major is management. The core MIT majors (or courses) are typically in the 1–10 grouping. Course 1 is civil and environmental engineering. Course 2 is mechanical engineering. Course 3 is materials science and engineering. You get the idea. Near the bottom of the list is Course 21—humanities (all of them).

This numbering system is even more interesting when it comes to the buildings. At the center of campus is Building 10, a.k.a. the Great Dome. This is the building you see on the MIT logo. Buildings 1–8 are organized in a symmetrical pattern around Building 10. Building 7 contains the entrance to the Infinite Corridor, which runs from Massachusetts Avenue along the east–west axis of the campus.

But by far the most famous MIT building of them all—the Rudolph the Red-Nosed Reindeer of the MIT campus—was Building 20. Building 20 was a ramshackle structure. It was originally built as a temporary home for the radiation laboratory during World War II. The Rad Lab, as it was called, housed the development of radar technology, which was instrumental in winning the war. As one physicist put it, "There are two prominent shrines of the triumph of science during the war: One is the desert installation at Los Alamos, N.M., where the atomic bomb was born; the other is the plywood building where radar was invented." Building 20 stood right in the middle of MIT's campus. It was valuable real estate, so according to its charter Building 20 had been scheduled for demolition immediately after the war. But for over half a century this demolition order was constantly being postponed.

In the late 1940s, with an influx of new students on the GI Bill, MIT's research facilities faced a housing shortage. Building 20 (a.k.a. the Plywood Palace) became the overflow unit for students and faculty from across the campus—acoustics, astronomy, architecture, biology, computing, physics, philosophy, linguistics, and many other fields found their homes there. It was a chaotic amalgamation of wildcards and hackers cohabitating without any organizational logic. The only thing they had in common was their shared joy of pushing the Rad Lab to its physical limits. Since it was scheduled for demolition anyway, occupants could rip down walls, drill holes, run cables, and rearrange the building as they saw fit to satisfy their scientific curiosity.

For nearly six decades, the Rad Lab remained standing. From its inception, it was never once in compliance with Cambridge city fire code, but no one dared tear down the old ruin. Because Building 20 had taken on another name: the Magical Incubator. Quite accidentally, MIT's Building 20 had become home to some of the twentieth century's greatest inventions.

Building 20 was the site of the world's first anechoic chamber (the rooms with all the fuzzy pyramids on the walls that prevent sound from echoing). Building 20's roof, covered in tar and stones, saw the invention of microwave astronomy. The dankest, darkest hole in the entire place was the Linguistics Department office assigned to Noam Chomsky. Largely because Chomsky's office was so unpleasant, he was forced to wander the halls, where he struck up conversations with researchers in biology, computer science, and psychology—fields that would later become relevant for his revolutionary theory of universal grammar. As Chomsky put it, "It was a fantastic environment. It looked like it was going to fall apart. But it was extremely interactive."

Down the hallway from Chomsky's office, Harold Edgerton's Strobe Lab pioneered the development of modern high-speed photography. Around the corner, members of MIT's Tech Model Railroad Club invented one of the first video games (*Spacewar!*) and helped to originate what would later be called hacker culture. Just a few steps away along another dank corridor, in a tiny office space, the first gravitational-wave detector was designed and prototyped, for which Building 20 researcher Rainer Weiss received the Nobel Prize in Physics.

Given this collage of talents and tastes along each hallway, it's no wonder that Building 20's room-numbering system was even more inscrutable than the rest of MIT's campus. In Building 20, B wing led into A wing, followed by E, D, and C wings. The building's undesigned design led to unpredictable and remarkably generative encounters between scientists trying to find one another's offices. While Amar Bose was squirreled away there working on his dissertation in engineering, he idly navigated himself down to the acoustics lab. He became so interested in their ideas that he combined them with his own research, leading to the founding of the Bose Corporation.

It is uncommon for a scientist in any field to try to measure up to the standards of another discipline. At top universities, peer reference groups are almost always based on the senior faculty within a department. The psychological forces of social comparison empower more successful peers in a department to shape junior researchers' sensibilities regarding what kind of scientific challenges are "good problems" and what kinds of discoveries qualify as important innovations.

But something different was happening in Building 20. There, researchers were surrounded by a disruptive mix of intellectual styles and forms of discovery. This novel setup was not simply encouraging the borrowing of techniques from one field and applying them to another. Rather, it inspired a creative synthesis of different approaches to scientific research. There were very different logics of scientific discovery between the fields of acoustics and physics, and even more so between the fields of physics and linguistics. But Building 20 had them all working together.

The term of art that is used to describe the unexpected wellspring of collaborative genius that percolated through Building 20 is *serendipity*—that is, the unexpected stream of innovations and discoveries that are catalyzed by having the right combination of thinkers placed into the right circumstances together. Although Building 20 is gone, the legend of its unprecedented capacity for serendipity lives on. Decades after its demolition, the directors of the world's leading university research centers and corporate R&D facilities still ask: "What made Building 20 so successful, and how can we reproduce it?"

Courting Serendipity

The temptation that most of us have when trying to reverse engineer the success of Building 20 is to attribute its success to the people who worked there. There is no doubt that they were all geniuses (though some might not have said that about each other!). But then again, the MIT campus has lots of geniuses. Knowing this, MIT has put vast sums of money into building office structures and research facilities that are designed to maximize the collective intelligence of its scientists. And not just MIT; the goal of any research campus is to provide facilities that inspire collaboration, innovation, and discovery, catalyzing the kinds of unexpected breakthroughs that can define a generation. Yet no single building, at MIT or anywhere else, has ever managed to cultivate the creative synergies found in the old Rad Lab. From the perspective of sheer innovation impact per annum, Building 20 is among the most successful structures in American history.

Since even before the razing of Building 20 in 1998, billions of dollars were spent trying to recreate the structural intelligence that epitomized MIT's Magical Incubator. Many places have tried, and some have come close.

The main campus of the Santa Fe Institute is nestled in the Sangre de Cristo Mountains just above the city of Santa Fe, New Mexico. When you first walk into the vast adobe structure, it can feel a bit like traveling back in time. It has ceramic floors, stone walls, massive wooden doors, and pristine views of the peaks and deserts of the Jemez Mountains. There are rocking chairs and throw rugs on the rustic stone terraces. It is also a stunning leap forward into the future. The interior floor-to-ceiling windows that support the massive, half-acre structure are adorned with daily scribblings of equations, scientific diagrams, and lunch orders. You walk past alcoves with state-of-the-art machines running some of the most advanced computational models of protein folding, quantum computing, and cultural evolution that the world has to offer.

To mimic the adobe style of construction (which prevents high-rise architectures), the institute is a sprawling one-story network of research pods, intermingled among lazy open spaces. The hallways stretch out in every direction, each winding arm filled with offices. At points along each hallway, the corridors open up into lounge-like foyers. Deep sofas, soft pillows, and massive whiteboards are comfortably strewn about. These spacious lounges are bathed in sunlight. Eventually, the wandering trails all lead back through a central feature of the structure, the kitchen/volleyball atrium, through which everyone must pass to get anywhere in the building. The inevitable result is designed serendipity.

The walk from your office to the bathroom might be about fifty feet, but it can take a good two hours to get there and back. The physical space invites you to stroll, lounge, gaze, sigh, chat, scribble equations, have tea, stroll some more, chat again, and then jot down several new ideas for collaborations. By the time you make it back to your office, your brain is teeming.

The Thing Called Diversity

One unmistakable ingredient for cultivating serendipity is a physical space that encourages people from different disciplines to bump into one another. The greater the variety of disciplines and approaches that people bring into a space, the more potential there is for unlikely synergies to emerge.

Earlier, I told you about Scott Page and his work on the grand challenge of choosing, and his conclusion that more diverse crowds are associated with more accurate collective judgments. Page called that result the *diversity prediction theorem*. It explains why Galton's approach to the wisdom of crowds works as well as it does. Yet that theorem depended upon everyone being independent. Once social networks enter the picture, you can easily find situations in which social interactions that reduce crowd diversity also increase crowd intelligence.

What does this mean for the grand challenge of creativity? When Page and his colleague Lu Hong began thinking about teams, they did not have to assume that people were independent. On teams, people can learn from one another and solve problems together. But how do you go about building an innovative team so that those problems can be better solved?

Suppose you're an administrator at MIT trying to put together a crack scientific team to work on the challenge of reducing carbon emissions. Would it be better to design a team with all the best thinkers in the field, or would it be better to create a diverse team with thinkers from lots of different fields (regardless of their individual accolades)?

Most of us would say the same thing: Get the best people! But Hong and Page found that not to be true. Their discovery was aptly named "diversity trumps ability." Hong and Page found that when you have a group of people trying to devise a novel solution to a complex problem, your team will find a better, more innovative solution if there are many different kinds of thinkers on the team, rather than simply the best thinkers.

This conclusion is surprising at first, but it makes good sense once you see how it works. The problem with building a team around the best thinkers in a field is that these researchers will tend to approach complex problems in the same way. This is particularly true if the best thinkers all have similar pedigrees, if they all read the same elite journals, and if they all work at the top universities. If they have all had similar training and access to similar information, they will all tend to think alike. Which means that they will all tend to make the same assumptions. And the same mistakes.

Take the Nobel Prize in Economics. For generations, this award was given to theoreticians who showed new ways of using rational choice theory to understand the economy and society. But no one ever stopped to ask whether the basic assumption of rationality was true. Everyone just assumed. It wasn't until psychologists and sociologists started making inroads into economic theory that there was a tectonic shift in thinking. Within a few years, the Nobel Prize in Economics started going to scholars outside of economics. These discoveries have had incredible real-world implications for the application of economic theory to public policies, such as "nudging" strategies in public health and organizational designs based on "satisficing" rather than optimizing.

Jack Treynor's jelly-bean experiments offered a similar revelation. Treynor concluded that the problem with the best people in finance is that they all tended to be hyper-invested in gathering the same information.

As a result, the best people all looked at their decision-making challenges in exactly the same way, which led them all to make the same mistakes. Surprisingly, Treynor found that groups of less sophisticated and more diverse decision-makers were far less prone to making these kinds of consequential collective errors.

Shared expertise *is* the problem. Collaborations among experts in the same field tend not to produce novel discoveries and unorthodox solutions. Rather, they tend to reinforce conformity with commonly accepted approaches.

For innovation, diversity is key, as was seen with the oddball alchemy of Building 20. But there is a second part of the story that is much more important and much less obvious: not the *who* but the *how* of innovative teams. That's because cultivating serendipity is not just about the new intellectual resources that you give to teams. It's also about the ones that you take away.

LESS IS DIFFERENT

One mistake that many organizations make when trying to recreate Building 20 is to assume that its success came from giving researchers a multitude of new and different interactions to supplement their regular ones. But the success of Building 20 was not based on increasing the number of network connections that people had across campus. Collaborations in Building 20 tended to be much more geographically constrained based on interactions within the building.

You already saw that for the grand challenge of coordination, a geographic network maintained diversity while the internet structure led to rapid convergence. Yet, in the grand challenge of cooperation, you saw that the geographic structure accelerated cooperation while an internet structure undermined it. Putting these findings together reveals one of the structural secrets of the Magical Incubator.

Building 20 created an exchange network that sustained the kind of diversity that you typically only get from an extraordinarily expansive network of contacts. Researchers were embedded within a geographic network that provided continual, reinforcing interactions from peers following different scientific norms. It was an environment that provided repeated engagement with diverse ways of thinking. These diverse yet structurally clustered interactions created a novel multidisciplinary environment for scientific discovery. Building 20 sustained both cultural diversity and collaborative cooperation—a rare and powerful combination. This means that residents' wellsprings of inspiration, as well as their reference points for scientific success, and even their sources of social reinforcement, were all rooted in the uncanny universe of Building 20.

The inhabitants believed that an integral part of Building 20's success was the fact that its architecture was *not* vertical. The long hallways of the Plywood Palace, many argued, were much more collaborative than stairwells and elevators. As residents of Building 20's replacement, the Stata Center, soon complained, impromptu conversations struck up in the elevator tend to end in the lobby.

In the late 1970s, MIT scientist Tom Allen became famous for identifying the exact mathematical structure of these "hallway effects" on scientific collaborations. Allen found that among researchers in both academia and industry, communication and collaboration were much higher if people had nearby offices on the same hallway, with a rapid drop-off in the likelihood of collaboration the farther offices were from one another (figure 10.1).

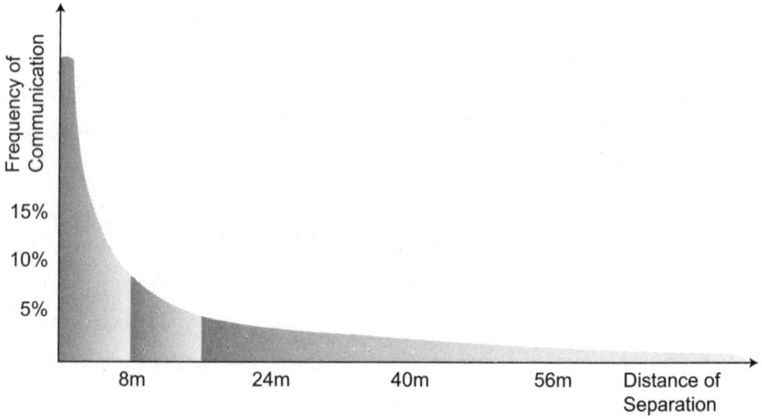

FIGURE 10.1
The "Allen curve" of exponential decay. Adapted from Tom Allen, *Managing the Flow of Technology* (MIT Press, 1977).

One obvious explanation for this effect of physical distance is that disciplinary departments might be organized by hallway. In that case, the people next to you are also, by design, the people who work on similar things as you. But Building 20 showed something different. It really didn't matter who those people were, or what their focus was. Regardless of the topics that people are working on, the geographic constraints of hallway interactions were still the main factor driving communication and collaboration.

Just like the Santa Fe Institute, Building 20's building materials themselves were partially responsible for the intelligence of the structure, since the Plywood Palace would likely collapse if it were much taller than three stories. According to Allen, this "undesigned design" produced more impromptu collaborations than would have happened if those same residents were housed in a high-rise structure.

This kind of peer learning environment—today we would call it an *incubator*—cultivates a species of cooperative thinking that is not just better—it is *different*. It has the potential to reorient researchers' expectations as to which discoveries count as "good science." In doing so, it can reshape their aspirations.

Building 20 gave its researchers a diverse network of scientific contacts, but it also limited their exposure to more mainstream influences that might reinforce standard institutional expectations, including departmental segregation and insularity. Building 20 was not just a research facility, it was a culture of open, free, unconstrained exploration made up of people who, despite their specific expertise, shared a reflexive curiosity. The two forces of diversity and cooperation are often in tension with one another; one easily collapses under the weight of the other. But a structure that can cultivate this tension and yet sustain both forces can catalyze unprecedented innovation. That was Building 20.

The challenge today for organizations interested in recreating the genius of the Plywood Palace is that it involves doing something that almost no administrator would be willing to do—limiting the networks of their researchers.

$300 Million More

The story of what happened next with Building 20 has become Boston legend. At the turn of the millennium, with a generous donation from

Bill Gates, MIT razed the beloved but dilapidated structure and replaced it with the eye-catching $300 million Stata Center (designed by the world-renowned architect Frank Gehry). The contrast could not have been more stark. With avant-garde afunctional pipes, portals, and beams sticking out in all directions, it was the antithesis of the rudimentary do-it-yourself functionalism of its predecessor. Perhaps most dissonant of all, it was called not by number but by name. That said it all.

Building 20 The Stata Center

FIGURE 10.2
Building 20 (left) and the Stata Center (right).

Inside, the Stata Center was designed to resemble an orangutan village (or "monkeys in the treetops"). The cavernous entrance sits under a vaulted, multistory ceiling, with panels of glass in the sky that reveal desks and offices, located at odd angles, in nonobvious directions from the lobby. It is not clear how to get there from here, which was the idea: The design of the Stata Center was intended to mimic the uncertainty and DIY quirkiness of Building 20's corridors (figure 10.2). But the shiny, new and attention-grabbing foyer certainly does not give the impression of being the kind of space that invites an impromptu rewiring of its circuitry.

What the Stata Center has going for it is transparency. Everyone can see everyone else. Stacked sequences of pane-glass office walls create a vast, multi-floor kaleidoscope of researchers at work. It is a multilevel, interactive forest for scientists, offering the promise of unparalleled opportunities for collective discovery.

The Stata Center proponents emphasize that it goes far beyond the old-fashioned logic of linear (two-dimensional) office space by creating novel hallway experiences that inspire vertical, horizontal, and diagonal integration. It's a three-dimensional conception of an office environment that is designed to inspire interactions above, below, and adjacent.

Today, the spatial geography of innovation remains a topic of great interest for the physical design of research facilities around the world. Compared to the two-dimensional geography of Building 20, what does the strange new design of the Stata Center herald for the future of scientific collaborations? And for the rate of scientific innovation? Perhaps Building 20's top spot along the Allen curve is something that cannot be replicated by monkeys in the treetops.

Simple and Complex Problems

The critical issue for determining the best organizational structure for creative problem-solving is knowing whether the problem itself is simple or complex. The complexity of the problem that researchers face determines the kinds of structures that will optimize their creativity.

When it comes to the grand challenge of creativity for complex problems, the goal is not simply to zero in on the right answer. (The right number of jelly beans, for example.) Rather, it's to discover a brand-new kind of solution that no one has yet dreamed of. For complex problems, researchers typically rely on collaborative learning, as their peers are likely to have lots of information that they lack, combined with enough individual freedom to be able to creatively explore uncharted terrain, perhaps even stumbling onto solutions that no one has thought of before.

This is why complex problem-solving is a trillion-dollar challenge that impacts everyone from rocket scientists to marketing gurus. Compared to the grand challenge of choosing, one upside of the challenge of creativity is that researchers working on complex problems have the advantage of being able to receive feedback on the quality of their solutions in real time. However, the downside is that more complex problems have many more possible solutions to explore, with vastly greater numbers of potential interactions among them. When a problem is complex, you cannot just follow the trail from a good solution to a great one; a promising initial start may lead to a dead end. The siren song of complex problem-solving is the tempting early discovery of a good solution that will never be great.

For organizations attempting to build the most creative and innovative teams to stare down this trillion-dollar challenge, the best networking strategy appears to be obvious: Cast your networks wide and try to accelerate the learning curve by providing your researchers with expansive access to the broadest possible collection of peers with whom to exchange ideas. It sounds compelling, but the unexpected serendipity found in Building 20 suggests something very different.

Experimenting on Scientists

I was fascinated by the idea that scientific creativity could be increased by changing the structure of researchers' networks—and in particular by *limiting* their reach. The practical question for any such investigation was how to study scientific innovation in a way that could be replicated. How could we evaluate whether changing the structure of scientists' collaboration networks—from an internet collaboration structure to a geographic collaboration structure—would directly impact researchers' potential for scientific discovery?

My graduate student, Devon Brackbill, came up with an ingenious solution: a series of scientific competitions. We would recruit data scientists from around the world, and then put them onto teams trying to solve complex data science problems. The best solutions would receive cash prizes, and the worst ones would get nothing. The money wasn't the issue, though. It was the pride. The cash prizes were more like trophies than payments, giving the winning teams bragging rights.

We recruited 194 data scientists from universities and corporate research centers across the world and randomly assigned them to be on two types of teams (figure 10.3). Members of the first set of teams were connected to one another using networks with a geographic "hallway" structure, in which people only had contact with a few peers to their right and to their left. These were the "Building 20" teams, where members could see the solutions that their immediate neighbors were using, but they could not see the strategies or solutions being explored by the other members of their team.

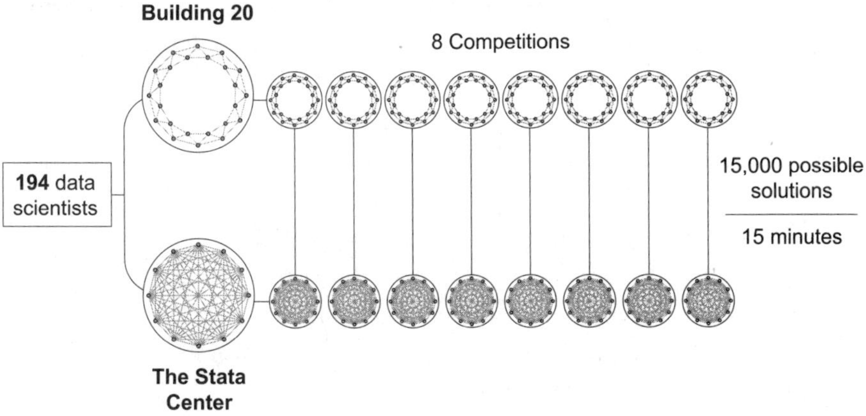

Figure 10.3
8 competitions; Building 20 versus the Stata Center

The other set of teams were the "Stata Center" teams. Here members were connected to one another via an internet structure, so they could see the solutions being used by everyone else on their team. To give the Stata Center teams the greatest chance of finding the optimal solution, the leading solutions were highlighted on a real-time leaderboard showing the team members with the best solutions, which everyone on the team could see.

Which teams would discover the most innovative solutions—the Building 20 teams or the Stata Center teams?

We started the contest by giving each of the teams a massive dataset containing the publicly available performance records of Fortune 500 firms. Contestants were given a suite of statistical modeling tools, and then asked to discover the best predictive model for a company's sales performance. One company sold sneakers. What were the key factors that predict shoe sales in the US? Is it price? Is it style? Is it celebrity endorsements? Or it is some unknown combination of factors? Another company sold beer. What determines beer sales? Is it advertising? Is it flavor? It is alcohol content, regional targeting, brewing process, or carbonation levels? Or is it a combination of them?

We had eight unique challenges in total. Each challenge had over 15,000 potential solutions. But there was only one optimal solution for each.

The final twist in our experiment was that every team only had fifteen minutes to find the best solution, so once the contest started, it was a mad race for discovery. Contestants were continually deciding whether to strike out on their own, but with the time pressure on, the temptation for researchers to follow the solutions used by their better-performing peers was intense.

We ran eight competitions in total. Each paired a unique Building 20 team against a unique Stata Center team trying to solve the same challenge. After conducting these eight independently replicated competitions, we had enough data to directly compare the overall performance of the Building 20 teams versus the Stata Center teams.

The structural intelligence of Building 20 was immediately apparent. In all eight competitions, the Building 20 teams (with a geographic structure) outperformed every single Stata Center team. Not only that, but while the Stata Center teams never found the optimal solution in any of the eight competitions, half of the time (in four out of eight competitions) the Building 20 team found the best possible solution to the complex problem within the fifteen-minute limit.

I admit that it was hard even for me to believe that the best way to build collaboration networks for complex problem-solving is to limit the reach of each team member. Wouldn't it make much more sense to give everyone more access to everyone else's good ideas?

The reason why not is that the alchemy of creativity takes time.

When it comes to the creative process of complex problem-solving, there are lots of false starts. With too much information flow, a good early idea can quickly become a golden anchor that prevents teams from discovering much better innovations later on. Finding the most innovative solutions often requires the kind of unorthodox thinking that can only survive if researchers are protected from coordinating on other researchers' ideas early on.

The reason internet structures are good for simple problems but unhelpful for complex problems is because simple solutions are highly contagious; they travel very effectively across narrow bridges, spreading rapidly throughout highly connected networks. For simple problems, speeding up the spread of intuitive solutions facilitates rapid coordination on a good idea.

But this is also why geographic networks are surprisingly effective structures for stimulating innovation on complex problems. These structures succeed because they slow down the spread of information. This enables them to sustain enough intellectual diversity to prevent researchers from converging around one idea too quickly. These structures balance this informational diversity with enough overlapping contact between neighboring researchers to sustain cooperative collaboration and enable effective knowledge transfer. The result is an emergent synthesis that arises from researchers' diverse explorations. A geographic structure protects uncommon ideas from the normalizing influences of the broader network, leading researchers to achieve exceptional heights of intellectual discovery. Just like Building 20.

The Secret Garden

The power of this principle has not gone unnoticed.

Stanford University's Center for Advanced Study in the Behavioral Sciences is one of the premier intellectual research centers in the United States. It was built in the 1950s upon the premise of designed serendipity.

The Center sits in a wooded grove high above the Stanford campus, nestled within a terraced high-desert garden and hidden behind a shaded thicket of juniper trees and hummingbird plantings. Unless you're looking for the Center, you're unlikely to stumble across it—and that's the idea. With its 1950s Bay Area architecture, dark wood walls and massive windows, the Center has managed to keep its distinctive old-world charm and a healthy air of intellectual independence from the Silicon Valley sprawl just a few miles away.

Each year, the Center's directorship curates a list of scholars who they believe would make an interesting and diverse collection of minds. Specialties include law, philosophy, sociology, political science, economics, education, literary studies, anthropology, psychology, and many other fields of expertise, ranging from entrepreneurs to the president of Latvia. There are no defining characteristics of a Center fellow, other than that they are interested in exploring the kinds of chance intellectual encounters that might arise from a year in residence on Stanford's secluded hilltop.

The least expected thing about the Center is the remarkable structural intelligence of its design, which subtly shapes the networks of the Center's residents to create an environment for inspired serendipity. Just a few minutes down the hill lies the Stanford campus, with its collection of National Academy of Sciences members, Nobel laureates, and White House appointees. Many of the Center's past directors were themselves members of the Stanford faculty. Under any other circumstances, there would naturally be a high volume of foot traffic from the campus to the Center. But here's where structure takes precedence. The trek from Stanford's campus to the Center is only a ten-minute hike, but it is not a particularly convenient one. It requires crossing Junipero Serra Boulevard—which, while not as imposing as the Allegheny Mountains of Pennsylvania, presents a physical barrier nonetheless. Then you need to head up past the Stanford golf course, past the old NBER building, and wind your way all the way up to the Center's entrance (just shy of the astronomy observatory). It's not just the Center's physical seclusion that's at work. Minimal protocols (like name tags for visitors) create subtle structural barriers, which over time invisibly guide the network-formation process among the fellows in residence. Even without explicit institutional rules, these features of the social space shepherd each year's group of fellows into a clustered and diverse social structure that supports intellectual exploration—just like the physical geography of the Center itself.

The scholars' offices are arranged in a longhouse pattern of concatenated cedar bungalows. The rooms run along the hilltop's ridge, suspended above the treetops below. A single rickety balcony runs along the bungalows' exterior, encouraging scholars to browse past their colleagues' floor-to-ceiling windows, occasionally peeking in to chat or to extend an invitation for drinks. Just like Building 20—the magic of the Center isn't magic, it's structure.

And the testament to the Center's success is its success—a library's worth of famous books and research papers that have emerged from serendipitous encounters there. The Center is an intellectual reprieve from the urgency of pursuing academic productivity at all costs, or else being left behind. It is a structure that offers softer ground and a slower pace, which readies curious minds for the uncanny potential of serendipity.

Smaller Is Smarter

Back home in university offices, the most pressing questions about scientific innovation come down to a matter of size. Are bigger teams needed to produce greater insights? James Evans is a sociologist at the University of Chicago who has spent the last twenty years searching for the answers to this question. In one of the most extensive studies of scientific innovation ever conducted, Evans and his team examined more than 65 million scientific articles published over the last sixty years. The goal was to see whether there is any relationship between the size of scientific teams and their capacity for innovation.

There is. Larger teams produce routine science. They bring insights that fit within the current scientific paradigm. They extend existing models and elaborate accepted theories.

Smaller teams are different. They are responsible for most of the big scientific breakthroughs. Nobel Prizes, paradigm-shifting discoveries, and the pioneering of new disciplinary fields all tend to come from small scientific teams.

Remarkably, team size also predicts disruption. The likelihood that a study will disrupt assumptions of mainstream science tends to drop off around a team size of five. For teams larger than five, there is a lower likelihood of producing something truly innovative. These results are similar across the sciences, but there is some variation by specialty. Disruption in biology and physics tends to drop off sharply above a team size of two. In my own research lab, I found that a half dozen was the magic number. With fewer than five, the exciting sparks of synergy among colleagues became less common. But when the lab grew too big (at one point we had fifteen people), I ended up having to take a leadership role on every project to keep things on track. Things kept moving, but I noticed that we were overlooking many of the smaller breadcrumbs that you really need to follow if you want to uncover big new scientific insights. Once that happened, I shifted gears and brought it back down to six, which is where we have stayed consistently productive. Surprisingly, Evans and his team found almost exactly the same thing. In the social sciences, the capacity for disruption tends to hold steady until the team size gets above six, after which the likelihood of true innovation drops off precipitously.

Remarkably, Evans's findings are the same even when taking into account the performance of well-known individual scientists. Everyone knows that some people are more creative than others. But it turns out that when you put creative people onto larger teams, their work is significantly less creative, and therefore much less likely to produce a major breakthrough. Put those same people on smaller teams, and a scientific revolution becomes much more likely. Surprisingly, small teams owe some of their creativity to their adherence to the "soft science" model of intellectual progress (as opposed to the "hard science" model of big laboratories often found in physics). Small teams elicit discoveries that end up having more historical impact, while larger teams tend hew closely to current conventions and immediate problems.

As Evans and his team of three put it, "Small teams disrupt science and technology by exploring and amplifying promising ideas from older and less popular work. Large teams develop recent successes by solving acknowledged problems and refining common designs." Simply put, smaller teams make bigger discoveries.

OK, but why? What is the explanation for the creativity of smaller teams and the stark drop-off in innovation that emerges from increasing team size? The answer is *flatness*.

The defining feature of innovative teams is that they are egalitarian in structure. In a word, they are flat: Everyone has equal power. Peers collaborate as equals, each one investing effort into multiple parts of the project, and everyone sharing credit for the discovery. Differences of rank and status fall away. Researchers prioritize the collaborative process of discovery over the recognition of status.

By contrast, hierarchical teams have a clear leadership structure, with a clear division of labor according to seniority and specialization. Each person works on their own part of the project, rarely venturing out of their lane, with the most senior person on the organizational chart at the hub, coordinating everyone else's efforts. If activities become too decentralized on a large team, a project can too easily meander in new directions that are not part of the research plan or the funding proposal that supports it. Someone needs to have the entire plan in mind.

That is the beauty of a small team. Because small teams are nimble, they can delve into unexpected anomalies, less constrained by the dictates of a specific grant or proposal. Even when they are following a proposal, small teams can adjust their course based on the insights of a single team member. In our experimental data science competitions, for instance, we found that if we put a creative scientist on a small egalitarian team, they were likely to produce a much more innovative solution than if they were placed onto a larger, centralized team. Regardless of how good the central person is—and they are always quite good—the structure of a large team limits the team's potential.

But large teams still have their place. In fact, many of the greatest feats of engineering have come from this kind of centrally coordinated effort. Following the United States' declaration of war against Japan in 1941, federal administrators pushed for the initiation of the Manhattan Project, a vast engineering enterprise dedicated to the development of an atomic weapon. The wisdom at the time was compartmentalization—decentralized, independent research facilities, each working to solve their piece of the puzzle. This structural strategy was designed to prevent any individuals from having enough intelligence about US advances in nuclear weaponry to leak the designs to foreign powers. However, due to the urgency of the task, and the need for a massively coordinated scientific effort, the demands of the moment inevitably led to the centralization of power. Under the guidance of J. Robert Oppenheimer, the coordinated enterprise, begun in 1942, rapidly succeeded in producing the world's first atomic weapon.

A similar plan of centralized leadership took hold of the National Aeronautics and Space Administration in the 1960s. Beginning in 1963, NASA's Apollo program was originally spread across the decentralized offices of the Manned Spacecraft Center in Houston, Texas, the Marshall Space Flight Center in Huntsville, Alabama, and the Launch Operations Center in Merritt Island, Florida. But the enormous technical challenges of coordinating a vast number of logistical and engineering efforts, along with the unprecedented urgency of the race against the Soviet Union for dominance over space, ultimately led to centralized control over all of the offices under the directorship of George Mueller from his headquarters in Washington, DC. The result was an unrivaled achievement in aerospace engineering. Within six years, an American astronaut stepped foot on the Moon and returned safely home.

Each of these engineering efforts succeeded with remarkable speed by coordinating vast numbers of talented individuals, each with a single-minded focus of achieving their collective goal. However, the intelligence of centralization has significant limitations. There is an appreciable difference between the kind of centralized structural intelligence that was necessary for the breakneck pursuit of engineering success at Los Alamos versus the form of egalitarian structural intelligence that cultivated generations of serendipitous discoveries at Stanford's Center for Advanced Study, to say nothing of MIT's Building 20.

These engineering successes were not paradigm-shifting scientific insights but rather examples of precisely what Evans found to be the bailiwick of large teams: faithfully and rigorously applying scientific knowledge to extend the current paradigm. By contrast, the greatest discoveries in the history of science—from the heliocentric universe to the structure of the atom—have not come from centrally directed large teams. Rather, they came from egalitarian explorations among small groups of diverse scientists. They came from scientists who were willing to work as equals to venture beyond the boundaries of convention.

As one Building 20 scientists recalls, "I believe that the role of Building 20 as an incubator is really the right word, because people got together and shared ideas and words without really worrying about who you were or where you came from." Building 20 was an egalitarian enterprise through and through. The scientist smiled fondly. "And I think that's the secret."

*

With all of the grand challenges now behind us, part IV turns to the practical and ethical questions that arise from these scientific findings.

*

IV

Collective Adaptation

11

Upending Social Engineering

Science is wonderful at destroying metaphysical answers, but incapable of providing substitute ones. Science takes away foundations without providing a replacement. Whether we want to be there or not, science has put us in a position of having to live without foundations.
—Hilary Putnam

On July 5, 1687, Isaac Newton published the *Principia Mathematica*. A towering treatise, it put the entire history of human scientific endeavor onto a new footing by explaining that the forces that govern everyday objects on Earth, like cannonballs and clocks, are the same forces that control the movement of the Moon around the Earth, and the Earth around the Sun. Everything from the food on our table to the stars in the sky is invisibly pushed and pulled by a single immutable force—gravity. Across the nations of Europe, there was a moment of earnest, awestruck appreciation, followed by a sudden, energized awakening. Now that "nature" was solved, it was time to solve society. It was the dawn of the Enlightenment.

But applying Newton's new science to society was tricky: If everything everywhere is governed by a single immutable force—underwritten by clear laws of cause and effect—where does that leave humanity? It was not until 1814 that the French polymath Pierre-Simon Laplace definitively articulated the nagging problem that had been lingering in the background for over a century.

> We may regard the present state of the universe as the effect of its past and the cause of its future. An intellect which at a certain moment would know all forces that set nature in motion, and all positions

> of all items of which nature is composed, if this intellect were also vast enough to submit these data to analysis, it would embrace in a single formula the movements of the greatest bodies of the universe and those of the tiniest atom; for such an intellect nothing would be uncertain and the future just like the past could be present before its eyes.

Quite simply, if everything that exists only exists because it is part of a long, causal sequence of events governed by a singular, unceasing force of nature, then everything that was, is, and will be is already determined. And if we live in a universe predicated on an interminable sequence of cause and effect, then how can a person be accountable for their behavior? Is anyone ever responsible for what they do?

When these questions are taken seriously, theological and philosophical concerns quickly give way to practical and legal ones. It is one thing for an individual to soulfully contemplate their own free will, either accepting or denying it. But for society, free will is an absolute necessity. To live together, we must see the actions of ourselves and others not as the gravitational tumble of inert objects but as the intentional efforts of capable souls. We must believe that we are accountable for ourselves in front of an audience of others who are similarly accountable. Our social existence depends upon our justified feelings of resentment when we are wronged and our feelings of gratitude when we are honored.

Still, the forward march of science has irrevocably altered our understanding of our own free will. By the end of the Enlightenment, science was becoming not only the arbiter of moral accountability but also the putative remedy for moral deficiency by offering interventions that could guide behavior in the "right" direction.

In 1835, the Belgian astronomer Adolphe Quetelet devised a breathtakingly influential program of social reform, which he called "social physics." In astronomy, measurements of heavenly bodies consistently exhibit natural variation (errors of excess and deficiency). The great mathematician Carl Gauss showed that the average of these errors approximated the correct value. Quetelet thought he could apply this big idea to society in a way that would liberate humankind from its flaws. And while there's a lot of variation in the human population—height, weight, "intelligence," etc.—Quetelet argued that if you could measure multitudes of people and then take the average, you would find the "correct" value. (Or, in his pre-Darwinian conception of things, the "ideal" value.) As he put it:

> Everything differing from the Average Man's proportions and condition, would constitute deformity and disease. . . . Everything found dissimilar, not only as regarded proportion or form, but as exceeding observed limit, would constitute a Monstrosity. . . . If an individual at any given epoch of society possessed all the qualities of the Average Man he would represent all that is great, good or beautiful.

Quetelet's social physics animated the machine of nineteenth- and twentieth-century American public policy. Across the country, corporations, the military, schools, sports teams, and other institutions endorsed and tried to cultivate the statistical ideal of the perfect person. This ideal is still remarkably influential in today's public policies, even when the proposed standards have been shown to be misleading. (One of Quetelet's statistical concoctions, body mass index, or BMI, is still the commonly recognized metric for determining a healthy bodyweight, and the contemporary policy agenda of stemming America's obesity "epidemic" is itself the legacy of Quetelet's social physics.)

The ideal of a free and healthy person—the "normal" individual who has complete autonomy—became the established reference point for capable, responsible, and moral people.

Quetelet's scientific paradigm for human perfection lasted for over a century. Then, one sunny California day at Stanford's Center for Advanced Study in the Behavioral Sciences, these long-standing scientific assumptions about human freedom and rationality were suddenly and irrevocably upended.

Starting from a small list of curious anomalies, such as anchoring bias and availability bias, discussions among three affiliates of the 1977–1978 fellowship class (economist Richard Thaler, psychologist Daniel Kahneman, and cognitive psychologist and mathematician Amos Tversky) soon mushroomed into a sweeping challenge to the age-old model of human perfection. The average person, it turned out, was not so free after all.

Nudging Away from Freedom

Kahneman, Tversky, and Thaler's groundbreaking work on cognitive biases was soon followed by the work of other scholars, like Dan Ariely and Cass Sunstein, who argued in new ways that there are fundamental flaws in the conventional models of how normal people reason. Experiment after experiment reinforced that our hardwired cognitive design fundamentally biases thinking toward making bad decisions (for instance, about finance, education, or health—to say nothing of long-horizon issues such as climate change) on an alarmingly frequent basis. Indeed, the people who do the best when it comes to making these decisions (i.e., *Homo economicus*) are not, in the everyday sense, normal.

Given this, a new approach to public policy was invented. Rather than trying to convince everyone's biased brain to conform to the rational ideal, social planners would instead build systems that took advantage of the fact that most people are actually quite poor decision-makers in everyday settings. These new policies would be designed to trick people's faulty brains into unconsciously making good choices without anyone ever realizing it.

A little while ago, we discussed the challenges of organ donation. Among the nations of the world, Americans have historically been poor judges of the societal benefits of such generosity (when applied posthumously). They often neglect to select the "organ donor" box on their driver's license applications. However, behavioral economics shows us that in these situations of uncertainty, people tend to accept whatever default option is presented to them. Thus, if the government were to change the driver's license form so the assumed choice was organ donation, so someone had to opt out of being an organ donor, then the vast majority of American drivers would suddenly become organ donors. People would still be free, in the sense that they could always deselect the organ donor box. However, the theory of cognitive biases says that most people won't, and will instead go with the default option.

The striking thing about this approach to public policy is that it promises to deliver a significant health benefit to society without needing to expend much effort to convince anyone to change their beliefs or their behaviors. A simple change to the design of the form would do it for them, and society would be much better off as a result.

This radical strategy is referred to as "nudging." Richard Thaler and Cass Sunstein offer a parable to explain how it works. Suppose I want to eat healthy food, but the cafeteria at my work has positioned the french fries in a choice location—the first item seen, displayed right at eye level. This convenient and attention-grabbing placement, combined with my hunger, will likely cause me to put them on my tray. But if the same cafeteria instead placed carrot sticks in that convenient, attention-grabbing location, I would probably wind up grabbing carrot sticks instead, particularly if I'm not paying much attention. In a fairly real sense, my choice of whether to eat carrot sticks or french fries is not entirely my own but is determined by the position of the food items in the cafeteria.

If you accept Sunstein and Thaler's example, it is easy to concede that there is no neutral way of building a cafeteria, or anything else for that matter. No matter what arrangement we choose, the structure of that arrangement will inevitably have some impact on the choices people make. This kind of evolutionary determinism doesn't mean that people are incapable of making decisions for themselves. Rather, it means that in a busy world with lots of influences and distractions, we have predictable tendencies that can only be overcome with a great deal of mental effort. (Which is why dieting is hard work.)

After the idea of nudging was introduced in 2008, it immediately took off. Around the world, firms, states, and nations welcomed with open arms this new, empirically grounded view of human potential. Within a decade, governments across Europe enacted nudging policies (for everything from organ donation to household energy consumption), which ushered in a sophisticated new era of enlightened public policy.

It only took a few years, however, for stories of nudging programs failing spectacularly (and even backfiring) to emerge. In Holland, for instance, federal legislation that implemented the default opt-in for organ donation forms resulted in an 80 percent *increase* in the number of citizens actively opting out. (It turns out that not everyone glosses over the fine print, and not everyone likes the feeling of their hand being forced.) Other studies uncovered boomerang effects, in which well-intentioned nudges accidentally pushed people in the wrong direction. For instance, a popular nudging strategy to lower household energy consumption was to provide homeowners with information about their neighbors' energy consumption. Unfortunately, it turned out that this policy inadvertently increased homeowners' energy usage rather than lowering it whenever they were informed that they were performing better than the norm.

But the problem with nudges goes much deeper than running the shower too long or forgetting to turn off all the lights at bedtime. If the nudging approach to public policy convinces governments that human minds are woefully ill-equipped for the complexities of the modern world, we may soon find ourselves subject to public policies that are deployed with the singular goal of saving us from ourselves. Our choice of behavior would be outsourced to the designers of a Potemkin existence, escorting oblivious citizens into the best of all possible worlds. The better angels of our natures would be sacrificed on the altar of absolution for our demons.

In any system of public policy, there must be mandates. Ultimately, someone needs to decide which public policy goals governments, states, and firms will pursue. But who—and how? The track record of governments does not inspire faith in the morality or efficacy of dictatorial administrations. And if policymakers themselves are subject to all of these same cognitive inadequacies as every other citizen, why do we trust their policy goals? How do we know that the nudges they implement—even if they work as intended—are nudging us in the right direction?

Nudging cannot provide an answer. But structure does.

An Unexpected Answer

At the beginning of this book, I told you about our study of social media users' changing beliefs about vaccine safety, with some structures leading collectives to much more accurate conclusions, and other structures leading them to converge on dangerously incorrect beliefs. In these studies, there was nothing guiding people to find the right answer. Quite the opposite: The only information that was programmatically entered into the communities was false information from a disinformation agent.

Every community began with a heavy bias toward overestimating the dangers of vaccination. Yet egalitarian communities somehow emerged better off than when they started, and they did this all by themselves. These social media users did not need to be told what to do or how to think. There were no nudges in those networks. Nor were there public health officials or community moderators telling people what to believe.

It was simply that citizens were embedded within an egalitarian structure that enabled them to collectively correct their own biases and work together to discover a better understanding of vaccine safety.

Every network exists within a context that can influence its dynamics. At the height of the COVID-19 pandemic in 2021, public health agencies were desperate to increase vaccination rates among reluctant populations. Among US conservatives, there were well-known suspicions about vaccines, which were nourished by a torrent of conspiracy theories. But perhaps more striking was the low level of trust in US public health agencies within the African American community, resulting in dangerously low levels of vaccination and surprisingly high levels of acceptance of disinformation about vaccine safety.

African Americans had good reasons to be skeptical. A few chapters ago, you saw how the legacy of racial bias still permeates American medicine, leading to continued mistreatment and undertreatment of Black patients. One of the most well-publicized cases began in the 1930s, when the US Centers for Disease Control and Prevention initiated an "experiment" that lasted for forty years, in which African American farmers in Tuskegee, Alabama, who had syphilis were given placebos rather than medical treatments, enabling physicians to observe the long-term health effects of the disease. None of the participants in the Tuskegee study were ever informed that they had syphilis.

White Americans, including many of those trying to encourage vaccination, had little idea just how powerful the legacy of Tuskegee—combined with a long list of other medical abuses—was within the Black community. (For instance, the forced sterilization of African American women in Southern health clinics continued through the 1980s. And in 2016, a study of American medical students and residents revealed that many believed African American patients experience less pain than white patients, and therefore require less clinical care for pain management.)

Knowing this, should we be shocked that in a 2022 survey about vaccine hesitancy among African American residents of Boston the most common reason for not getting vaccinated was lack of trust in American healthcare? As one interviewee put it:

> So not just the Tuskegee experiment; not just Flint, Michigan because those folks got no clean water, not just New Orleans ninth ward who's

> still dealing with Hurricane Katrina, like these things have not been addressed. And so, here we are again, you want to add, you know, "oh, black and brown communities, you guys need to get the vaccine." You haven't addressed the harm from years ago!

From this perspective, it is easy to understand why medical advice from family, friends, neighbors, and local clergy—not to mention from influential African Americans on the internet—would be far more trusted than recommendations from the CDC. For this, education is not a magic bullet. Studies have found no consistent relationship between education level and vaccine acceptance in the African American community; in fact, the more educated citizens are, the more aware they are of the long and shocking history of their mistreatment by medical experts—and the more suspicious they are of mainstream public health services. This dynamic of mistrust goes beyond any particular cultural group: When citizens become more culturally informed about past administrations' attempted manipulations and mistakes, it often serves only to increase their susceptibility to disinformation.

Here is where nudges are supposed to come to the rescue. When rational arguments do not work, nudges take care of things by doing an end run around deliberative thinking—simply tricking biased brains into making the right decision (even when rational brains would not). These nudging strategies are premised on the idea that populations should be manipulated into complying with public health recommendations even if they don't want to follow them—that is, that African Americans shouldn't read the fine print like the Dutch did with organ donation, but in this case, it is the fine print of history. The problem with this approach is not necessarily that it will fail to achieve its goals, nor even that it overlooks all of the legitimate sources of vaccine hesitancy. Rather, the problem is that this approach is shortsighted. It fails to see the potential for long-term backfire effects from policies that force citizens' compliance without engaging their reasoning. This worry clings to any successful nudging program in which citizens may feel that they've been tricked or coerced. Rather than resolving citizens' long-standing resistance to a policy goal, nudging can exacerbate resistance by causing mistrust is to grow—and then to emerge with even greater force when the next urgent policy initiative is rolled out.

This concern extends beyond the African American community, and even beyond America, to every cultural group and community around the world. In almost every context, examples can be found where compliance with the latest scientific and medical advice may not always be the smartest choice. (There have been many times when subsequent research has led to a clinical or pharmaceutical U-turn, as in parents using tinctures of baby oil and iodine as tanning lotion, or subjecting their children to X-ray therapy for acne, only to find out later that it significantly increases the risk of skin cancer.) But even when scientific advances are effective (as they often are) for improving public welfare—and perhaps especially then—the goal of public policy should not be to force compliance, given the risk of recoil, but to bring citizens into direct conversation with the latest evidence so that they might engage with it, challenge it, and understand it in a subtle and nuanced way—and then make better decisions because of it.

BUILDING FREEDOM THROUGH STRUCTURE

During the early days of any crisis, timely steps must be taken, and the right structures can help. For instance, within clustered geographic networks in residential communities, and among networks of local churchgoers, reinforcing support from friends and neighbors can effectively increase cooperative engagement with a vaccination drive. But a successful drive for vaccination is not the end of intelligent public policy; it is the beginning. While clustered social networks among churchgoers can make a difference in the short term, comprehensive change that lasts beyond the moment of crisis requires a social infrastructure that can support enduring civic inquiry, which stimulates sustained community engagement in the intelligent evaluation of public policy practices and the issues that motivate them.

This may sound more like an aspirational dream than a practical reality, but in fact, as you will see in the next chapter, it has already happened—and, just like Building 20, the structures that formed, and the collective intelligence they produced, emerged entirely by themselves. And while we cannot hope to eliminate entirely disinformation and conspiracy theories from civic discussion forums, the important point here is that we don't have to. Inaccurate, misleading, and even downright fantastical content is bound to appear. Bizarre ideas will inevitably have their moment in the spotlight. But the ultimate effect of this content is determined by structure. When it comes to the challenge of making good policy decisions, intelligent networks effectively activate peer learning, leading everyone toward a more accurate, more subtle, and more engaged understanding of the issues—an understanding in which all parties become much more capable of making intelligent decisions for their own future—and also become much more invested in implementing those intelligent solutions, having come to them themselves.

Why Freedom and Intelligence Matter

By the time she was seventeen, Gakirah Barnes was one of the most lethal assassins in Chicago. At the age of fourteen, she joined the previously all-male Fly Boys Gang, a splinter group of the South Side's well-known Gangster Disciples crew. Between 2011 and 2014, between her freshman year and senior year of high school, Gakirah was purported to have shot twenty rival gang members. She became known as the "teen queen of Chicago's gangland."

She never made it to eighteen. In April of Gakirah's senior year, King Von, a rapper and member of rival gang the Black Disciples, shot her nine times in the chest, jaw, and neck. The wounds were fatal. The murder was seen as revenge for Gakirah's own killing of a Black Disciples member three years earlier.

Gakirah stands apart from other high-profile youthful killers in US history by the fact that she kept a detailed social media record of it all. Her thoughts, feelings, loyalties, and vendetta targets were fearlessly and compulsively shared online. The details of her darkening worldview and her evolving social loyalties and rivalries—which spread block by block across Chicago's South Side—were laid bare for the world to see. In hundreds of Twitter posts, she posed with guns and made threats. But in the days before her own murder, she posted about her friend Raason Shaw, who had recently been killed by a police officer, revealing her own heartbreak and a level of vulnerability that fit awkwardly with her stone-cold reputation.

In the weeks leading up to Gakirah's murder on April 11, 2014, her thoughts turned to loneliness. Her isolation was palpable, and the realities of death at an early age were already a regular topic of conversation. Grief over the loss of friends alongside brazen promises of revenge consumed her mental and emotional life. Hundreds of Gakirah's messages—including her last one showing her location and taunting her killers to find her—tell the story of her journey from the realities of a South Side childhood to the horrors of teen infamy.

Who do we blame for the wanton violence among the children of Chicago's South Side? Do we blame Gakirah? Do we blame society? Where is free will now?

There is a new approach to solving this ancient problem. It begins, and ultimately ends, with the structure of our networks. But the key to solving this riddle is not the networks themselves but rather in how we get from here to there.

12

Things Fall Apart—And That's Progress

We are like sailors who on the open sea must reconstruct their ship but are never able to start afresh from the bottom. Where a beam is taken away a new one must at once be put there, and for this the rest of the ship is used as support. In this way, by using the old beams and driftwood the ship can be shaped entirely anew, but only by gradual reconstruction.
—*Otto Neurath*

The networks around us need not be a prison. In fact, they hold the potential for achieving our greatest freedom. This is the guiding principle of structural intelligence: to create structures that catalyze new freedoms and enable collectives to learn together and discover the best policies for their collective future.

Society Didn't Do It—Networks Did

When Northwestern University sociologist Andrew Papachristos first looked at the data from Chicago, he saw something that others had overlooked. Everyone knows that violent crime is more prevalent in some neighborhoods than others. Lots of established statistics reinforce common stereotypes telling which social groups are most susceptible. Papachristos, too, had been taught these things as a graduate student at the University of Chicago. But starting out as a young scholar, he brought a new computational approach to the problem. Poring over the data late at night in his Hyde Park apartment, he struggled to understand why some individuals with risk factors relevant to gun violence (demography, economic indicators, etc.) nevertheless had radically different trajectories than others who had those same risk factors. Statistically, these individuals looked identical. Yet some people managed to avoid the cycle of violence and retaliation, while others, like Gakirah Barnes, were ineluctably drawn into it. But if the difference wasn't their individual risk factors, then what could it be?

It was their networks.

Gang violence is surprisingly personal: People who shoot and get shot almost always know one another. The data are unavoidably clear on this point: It's not just neighborhoods and territorial boundaries that lead to violence—it's the real person-to-person networks that tell the story of who will get shot next and who is likely to get shot after that, and whether the terrible cascade is likely to keep going.

In the summer of 2020, over the course of three weekends from June 18 through July 5, there were 416 shootings in Chicago. It was one of the most concentrated periods of gun violence in recent American history. In a rapid response to the outbreak of violence, Papachristos and his team hurried to identify the network pattern of shootings within each community. Their report provided police and outreach workers with a snapshot of the trajectory of gun violence in the city, including who was likely to be a subsequent victim of that violence and who would be likely to pick up the baton and become a future perpetrator.

This map of Chicago's neighborhoods shows the community-by-community clustering of gun violence (figure 12.1). This is the sort of presentation that city officials have used for decades to help police and outreach workers identify the most dangerous and troubled communities. Each dot on the map represented a shooting victim, and while there were clear neighborhood patterns, that didn't help with the crucial task at hand, which was to stop the killing. This wasn't a small town where police could keep an eye on everyone 24/7, and the neighborhoods where people seemed most at risk were dense with large housing projects and multifamily dwellings.

But when the local networks (in which ties were based on people who had been arrested together) were overlain on these acts of violence across the neighborhoods—that is, shootings that occurred miles away

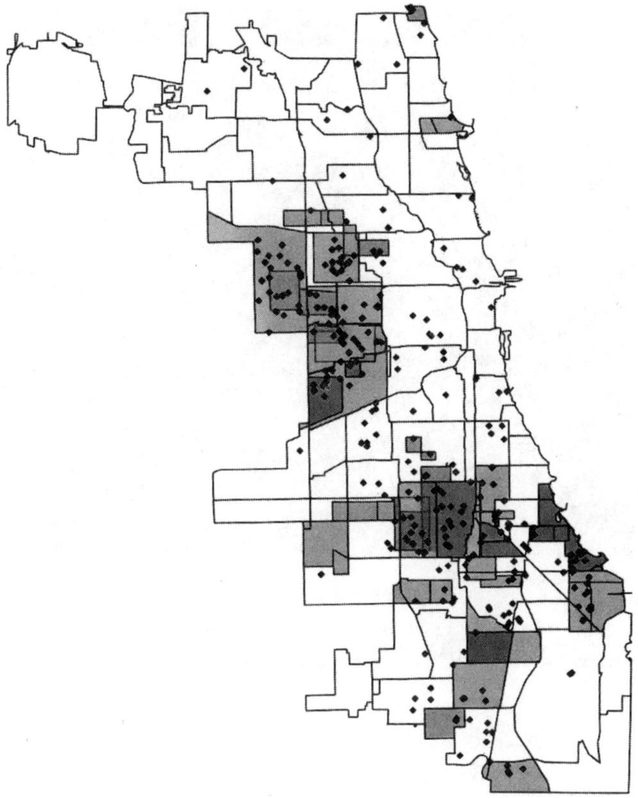

FIGURE 12.1
Shootings by location over two weeks in 2020. Adapted from Northwestern University IPR, Rapid Research Report (January 8, 2021).

from each other—something new was revealed (figure 12.2). In this network, the white nodes show gunshot victims during the same two-week period in 2020. The black nodes correspond to gunshot victims in the years prior. Gray nodes show connected individuals without a history of gun violence.

By themselves, the white nodes do not tell a story. They are interspersed apparently randomly throughout the network. However, when past gun violence victims, shown in black, are included, a previously undetected path is revealed: a long series of relationships among gunshot victims, from one to the next, that leads across the network. In nearly every case, the gunshot victims from the summer of 2020 were either

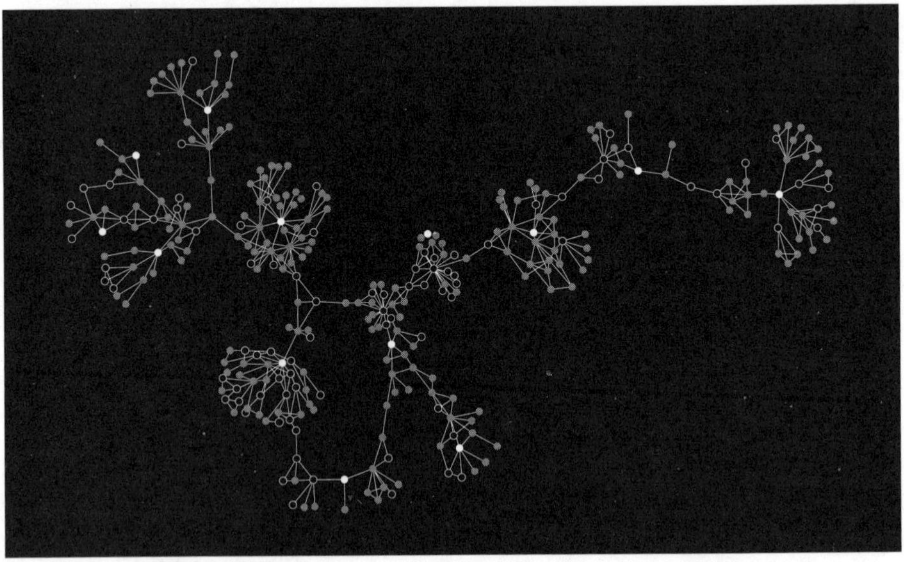

FIGURE 12.2
Network of gun violence preceding shootings over two weeks in 2020. Adapted from Northwestern University IPR, *Rapid Research Report* (January 8, 2021).

directly connected to a previous gunshot victim or were one step away, connected by an intermediary.

Those connections reveal not only a horrific past but the potential for a dreadful future. That's because the gray nodes situated between white nodes and black nodes indicate an imminent risk for gun violence. These individuals, regardless of where they happen to live, are the most susceptible to becoming the next victims in the contagion of neighborhood shootings.

People are tied to their networks through a chain of social cause and effect, of grief and retaliation. A person's tie to gunshot victims, even from many years earlier, is the strongest predictor of who will be shot next, and simply moving from one neighborhood to another will not solve the problem. Of course, if you decide to move far, far away—say Homer, Alaska—you might evade Windy City violence, but you also have to sacrifice all of the things that come from the tight connections with family, friends, and the larger community that you've left behind. And even from thousands of miles distant, it is almost impossible for individuals to completely extricate themselves from their social networks. The people we know influence us, even when we are not directly interacting with them, as we've seen with Gakirah and hundreds like her. Our community networks follow us online, and our online ties follow us home to where we live. Friends of friends of friends keep us engaged in the push and pull of life within our communities, past and present, in person or via Wi-Fi. And when it comes to violence, the shadows can be very long: Six years after shooting Gakirah, King Von himself was also murdered at gunpoint, thousands of miles from Chicago, in Atlanta, adding yet another white node to the network.

COLLECTIVE EFFICACY

Communities within Chicago vary widely in their cohesiveness—which is defined by the clustered geographic structure of the networks that bind the members of a neighborhood to one another. Cohesiveness, in this respect, mirrors the structural principles supporting the emergence of cooperation that you saw a few chapters ago. In cohesive communities, neighbors throw block parties, exchange favors, and ask each other for personal advice. These are the "borrow a cup of sugar" neighborhoods. Without realizing it, the people who live within these social networks experience agency within their community. They act when action is needed, compelled to intervene when trouble starts.

In academic circles, the study of how people and neighborhoods achieve this sort of self-determination is called "collective efficacy." Do people in a community take on self-assigned duties to monitor spontaneous play groups among children? Do neighbors intervene to prevent students from truancy and street-corner loitering? Do citizens step into the public space to confront persons exploiting or disturbing the common areas? It all boils down to individual community members' willingness to intervene when things start to go awry. These questions surface residents' feelings of moral responsibility for keeping their neighborhood safe, but the explanation for why people feel compelled to take on these duties—spontaneously, as the need arises—is rooted in the cohesiveness of the network structure of their neighborhood.

This is hard to see from a conventional sociological approach. Residents are the same demographically and economically in communities where active engagement does not happen. Yet in those neighborhoods, people will not intervene if children are truant. They will not break up a fight. And they will not confront someone vandalizing the public space. These are the communities in which gun violence escalates and residents are helpless to stop it.

Neighborhoods with low collective efficacy, like Gakirah's Woodlawn, have low residential stability. Frequent arrivals and departures create a feeling of constant churn. As people come and go, ties wither and neighborhood cohesiveness evaporates. The more movement there is, the fewer neighbors there are who are invested in their local networks. With greater mobility in and out of the community, the likelihood of gun violence among the children there increases dramatically.

It makes sense that residential stability is deeply correlated with collective efficacy. People who live together get to know one another. They come to have friends in common and learn very quickly who will help them out in a jam. People watch one another's children without ever being asked. They have greater incentives to clean up neighborhood parks and are more concerned with the conditions of vacant lots. Moral agency emerges through the simple, everyday influences of the social networks in which people are embedded. The greater the residential stability in a community, the more cohesive the neighborhood networks are, and the more likely it is that people will find themselves individually stepping forward to intervene when intervention is needed.

The philosopher Bernard Williams famously argued that ethical duty is based on personal attachments rather than objective principles. According to Williams, people have stronger ethical responsibilities to protect and intervene on behalf of those whom they know and love than they do for strangers. There are many nuances to this idea, but one striking parallel with the findings on collective efficacy is that in cohesive networks that create bonds of cooperation and solidarity within neighborhoods, residents' personal experiences with one another may engender a heightened sense of ethical obligation when it comes to caring for their neighborhood. From this point of view, feelings of personal integrity emanate from the structure of social relations. Evidence from Chicago's urban neighborhoods suggests that cohesive networks of neighborly interactions may sustain the kinds of strong personal bonds from which moral sentiments are born.

These implications for moral agency extend well beyond the neighborhood context. Take firms, for instance. In a society that often romanticizes hierarchical organization and competition as a means to efficiency, collectivist organization (in which responsibility falls equally on everyone) appears to be an invitation for poor performance. When everyone shares equally in the rewards, individual free-riding seems inevitable. But the truth is often the opposite. Though it looks irrational according to classical models of strategic behavior, employees of collectivist organizations exhibit surprisingly strong professional commitments to their organization's successes. Employees' high performance in collectivist firms cannot be explained by an economic model based on financial incentives. Instead, it is explained by employees' commitments to their organization's goals and to their colleagues who support it—by their sense of personal agency and responsibility for the success of their enterprise. In these collectives, an egalitarian reward structure is not a disincentive to perform; rather, it is the basis of employees' investment in their peers' improved capacity. As American sociologist Joyce Rothschild-Whitt reported, the entrepreneurial spirit of selfless "commitment to the cause" permeates every kind of collectivist organization, from neighborhood watch groups, to community health clinics, to activist newspapers and local law centers:

> At the Free Clinic, for instance, all full-time staff members were paid equally, no matter what skills or experience they brought to the clinic. At the Law Collective and Alternative Newspaper, pay levels were set "to each according to his need." Here salaries took account of dependents and other special circumstances contributing to need, but explicitly excluded considerations of the worth of the individual to the organization.

It's not a big step to think of communities as organizations, nor to think of organizations as communities. The sense of shared responsibility that emerges in collectivist organizations is similar to the collective efficacy that springs from cohesive neighborhoods. In both cases, the structure of relationships among a community of peers shapes community members' commitment to one another's success.

THE CHANGE DILEMMA

Collective efficacy within neighborhoods brings significant advantages to a community beyond its immediate cohesion. Neighbors who enjoy greater stability in their local networks have a greater capacity to pull resources from city and state offices. Long-term residents of a community learn how to gain influence in local politics and may even play a substantial role in the election of city officials. The resulting resources that residents are able to secure for their community can allow them to make greater investments in their children's future. Safer playgrounds and better teachers encourage more reciprocal investment among residents, creating greater accountability among parents. With investment comes returns. Children who are raised in neighborhoods with greater collective efficacy experience far lower exposure to gun violence and much greater potential for economic mobility. Their possibilities for work and college life outside the community dramatically increase. Children fulfill their parents' dreams. And with that comes change.

These happy benefits of generational success inevitably alter the structure of the neighborhoods that made these successes possible. As the next generation moves away to begin lucrative jobs and build families in more affluent areas, the networks within a community become more dispersed. Individuals building their lives elsewhere understandably invest less in their old neighborhoods. They cultivate friendships and neighborhood ties in their new communities, and, if they can, they may also move their parents to join them. With such relocations, vacancies increase, which invite the entry of transient residents who have less communal investment in the neighborhood. Neighborhoods with greater collective efficacy may be able to resist the economic influences of gentrification, diminishing the entrance of those unable or unwilling to maintain community standards. Typically, however, the ensuing cycle further erodes the cohesive structure of the neighborhood networks, reducing collective efficacy and diminishing moral agency. With this change comes an increasing trend toward gun violence among the youth. As the renowned urban sociologist William Julius Wilson put it,

> The basic thesis is not that ghetto culture went unchecked following the removal of higher-income families in the inner city, but that

> the removal of these families made it more difficult to sustain the basic institutions in the inner city. . . . As basic institutions declined, the social organization of inner-city neighborhoods (defined here to include a sense of community, positive neighborhood identification and explicit norms and sanctions against aberrant behavior) likewise declined.

Changes in residential stability invite predatory crime and interpersonal violence. The result is increasing gun violence among children, along with increasing susceptibility to the invading forces of economic development, both of which make neighborhoods more vulnerable to the economic forces of dislocation.

You will not be surprised to learn that it isn't just neighborhoods that can suffer these unintended consequences of evolutionary change. Firms, universities, and entire nations are subject to unanticipated failures of collective intelligence as a direct result of earlier structural successes. A policy that brilliantly solves one grand challenge of collective intelligence may itself be the source of the problem when it comes to confronting another grand challenge. Even more subtly, the structural intelligence that solves one grand challenge may result in new and unanticipated collective adaptations that create new grand challenges.

UNINTENDED CONSEQUENCES

Earlier I noted that comprehensive change that lasts beyond moments of crisis requires a social infrastructure that can support intelligent civic routines and ongoing community engagement. But when the grand challenges facing a community change, so do the structural principles of collective intelligence that ensure success.

For solving complex problems—such as making effective climate policy, cooperating on urban development plans, or cultivating novel scientific and literary innovations—collective intelligence emerges from clustered egalitarian structures, which slow down the rate of convergence and invite the potential for many people to contribute their novel thinking in pursuit of intellectual discovery. By contrast, in times of external threat national priorities tend toward the empowerment of centralized leadership. Rallying around the leader is a structurally intelligent response to the urgent challenge of rapid coordination. Not just for nations, but for political groups as well.

After the 2016 US presidential election, which saw the victory of Republican Donald Trump over Democrat Hillary Clinton, patterns of influence in online commentary networks exhibited radically different trajectories across the political parties. Among liberals, who felt under threat as a result of Trump's victory, centralization in online commentary groups increased dramatically, empowering a minority of voices to guide the majority opinion. Conservative online communities exhibited the opposite trend, with the distribution of online influence among conservative political commentators becoming significantly less centralized than it had been previously.

After the 2018 midterm elections, in which the Democrats won the majority of seats in the House of Representatives, liberals experienced a reduction in threat. The structural response was immediate: Liberal communities exhibited a dramatic decrease in centralization of influence among online political commentators, returning to a more egalitarian distribution of power. The opposite happened for conservatives. In response to the perceived political threat after the midterms, conservative communities rapidly self-organized into highly centralized information ecosystems. Influence quickly became concentrated among a small number of actors who took leadership of the party's online political commentary.

These diverging structural patterns are not essential features of either political party. Rather, they are strategic reorganizations of power within groups as a structurally intelligent response to the need for rapid coordination.

These patterns of self-organization are as old as civilization itself. Many have noted that the Roman legend of Lucius Quinctius Cincinnatus offers as an excellent example of this kind of structural adaptation. Like all legends, not everything in it lines up with fact, but as told, in 458 BCE, Rome was being threatened by the Aequi tribe of central Italy, who had besieged a Roman garrison in the foothills of Mount Algidus. The egalitarian weighing of sides and the careful, cooperative development of ideas is an intelligent approach to governing a large and complex state, but the collective intelligence of an egalitarian structure is not well-suited to the grand challenge of coordinating rapid military action. Debate in the senate would take time. Fearing a direct attack on the capital, the senate called upon the politician and nobleman Cincinnatus, who was asked to leave his farm, take control of the government, and quickly marshal troops to Rome's defense. Within a day, he was crowned dictator and empowered to lead Rome's armies against their foes.

This Roman policy was a brand of rapidly deployed structural intelligence. When communities must quickly organize under threat, the centralization of power is an effective means for solving a large and complex coordination problem. Under a single leader, a vast army can be mobilized without confusion or delay.

The story of Cincinnatus illustrates one remarkable path that human collective adaptation might take. After Cincinnatus swiftly won the war, he returned to Rome as the newly empowered magistrate extraordinaire. Much of Roman history (and recent US history) has taught us to anticipate the birth of a tyrant. But Cincinnatus honored his contract and gave up his rule. His work done, he relinquished his power in the same spirit of service in which he accepted it, and then returned home to his farm and resumed his quiet life.

Cincinnatus is remembered for how quickly he abdicated his role—within a mere fifteen days of receiving it. But his commitment to restoring egalitarian power was not the exception but the rule. In fact, between 501 BCE and 202 BCE, seventy different Roman dictators were empowered to solve state crises—many of them accepting the mantle of power more than once (including Cincinnatus, who was briefly retrieved for another short stint as dictator)—and each one of them gracefully relinquished their power shortly thereafter, just as Cincinnatus had.

Along this path of collective adaptation, the intelligence of centralization not only solves the rapid coordination problem but also comprehends its own limitations: This strategy works when the challenge is a simple coordination problem; once the challenge is solved and the enemy is bested, the structure realigns back to a more egalitarian form. That is a successful mode of collective adaptation.

Yet, there is an alternative trajectory that is more familiar, and far more concerning. Structures sometimes have their own inertia, and once a structural adaptation takes hold, it can then become a self-reinforcing trap. This is the story of the Caesars—the last guardians of Rome. After the Caesars took Rome, they rewrote its laws and rebuilt its institutions to support the perpetuation of their own monarchy. This is a failure mode of collective adaptation, in which the centralization of power cannot comprehend its own limitations. Centralization can thus endure long after its utility has been outlived, with tragic consequences for all.

When Success Courts Failure

A different kind of unintended consequence happens when an intelligent structural intervention unknowingly undermines the very solution it created. This problem is similar to the one that I showed you in Chicago's South Side, in which communities become the victims of their own success. It happens when groups adopt an intelligent structure that effectively solves a grand challenge, only to find that the result of their structural success is an almost Sisyphean reshaping of the social landscape in a way that reintroduces the original problem.

Take collectivist organizations.

When teams and departments are designed with an egalitarian division of power and rewards (such as money and credit) among coworkers, employees tend to display greater investments in training one another. They voluntarily help promote each other's accomplishments, and they invest selflessly in their team's success. Just like in neighborhoods with collective efficacy, egalitarian workplace structures inspire employees to feel a greater sense of individual accountability and take greater responsibility for their own performance, as well as for others'. These are the "free will" benefits of greater individual agency and moral accountability.

However, when these organizations achieve team success, every individual in the group becomes more desirable to other organizations (and even other parts of their own organization), making them attractive candidates for targeted offers. Poaching can quickly destroy a successful cooperative, as prominent employees (whose professional effectiveness and workplace autonomy were born from the cooperative investments of their peers) are strategically hired into high-status positions, with greater individual rewards, within more hierarchical organizations. These apparent individual successes undermine the very machinery of peer support and cooperative investment that powered the success of the collectivist organization and its members.

These changes are likely, but not inevitable. Understanding how collective adaptations are born from structural success creates the opportunity for intervention. Organizational managers who are attentive to these structural dynamics may adapt their teams to anticipate and stave off these problems, for instance by maintaining an attentive rotation of existing members through varied roles. This can prevent the centralization of networks around a small number of "expert" individuals and instead sustain a more egalitarian structure of interdependence, which is needed to support a cooperative enterprise. Not only that, but managers can also smartly continue to integrate more energetic junior staff into role rotations as a means of sustaining the benefits of peer learning and mutual investment.

THE EVOLUTION OF LIMITATIONS

Finally, there is another, somewhat peculiar kind of unintended consequence that can arise in successful organizations in which an intelligent structural adaptation invisibly undermines a group's capacity to solve future problems. For generations, cohesiveness of another kind—namely, the kind of team unity that arises from internet structures that foster accelerated information flow and seamless coordination—has been the watchword of successful teams. Military units, high-performance sports teams, and rapid-development engineering groups are often assembled from a roster of diverse individuals who must work together to achieve vital organizational goals. From the start, these goals are explicitly defined, with a short timetable, with the intent of using existing knowledge and systems to get from point A to point B, even if it may require some improvisation and inventive thinking to get there. The target is evident (for instance, build a barricade against a storm, win a critical game, snuff out an opposition's campaign), and the means are known; the challenge is to execute a win.

A team leader can build the structural intelligence required for this kind of effort by arranging a series of group meetings and regular one-on-one sessions with team members to integrate everyone into an effective network for rapid coordination—a densely connected internet structure. Once this structural adaptation takes form, the team's capacity for coordination increases exponentially. Team members can intuitively find ways to optimize their interdependence, trading off tasks to utilize one another's strengths while working around their weaknesses. Sharing a sense of loyalty, trust, and mutual respect, they become the guardians of one another's success and proud of the team's achievements.

But what happens when this highly unified team, strengthened by camaraderie and a strong esprit de corps, is faced with new kind of task—this time, one that involves the grand challenge of creativity? Complex problem-solving requires giving team members time and room to explore far-off reaches of the solution space. It requires a much slower pace of information flow—and an explicit reduction in team-wide coordination. Success demands building team structures that eliminate the social pressures for team members to conform to the approaches adopted by their colleagues.

A unified team is hard to break apart; the cohesiveness that comes as a reward for colleagues' investments of trust, time, and emotional energy is not easily abandoned. Recall Irving Janis's famous work on the unity and sense of camaraderie among President Kennedy's cabinet members. Those tight-knit relationships and emotional investments reduced independent explorations of alternatives and led to an unintentional and premature convergence in thinking, which was guided in part by their shared sense of conviction and mutual respect. This unification was a key handicap limiting the administration's ability to anticipate not only the fatal weaknesses of the invasion plan but also the much more sweeping tragedy of the Vietnam War. As Janis put it, "The more amiability there is among the members of a policy-making ingroup, the greater the danger that independent critical thinking will be replaced by groupthink."

Freedom and Intelligence

As should be clear by now, Sunstein and Thaler were right about one thing: There is no neutral structure; structural determinism is always already there, influencing us. What Sunstein and Thaler overlooked, however, is that structures are not simply tools to manipulate—they are also opportunities to liberate, to make people much freer and more capable than they could ever be as solitary individuals.

In Sunstein's Colorado experiment, he showed us that the only way to outsmart partisan bias is to keep people isolated from each other, letting them choose their answers independently from their cohorts' opinions. To achieve this outcome, Sunstein would likely need a way to nudge people into not talking to each other—a particularly challenging objective in the modern age. And, as we discussed earlier, when Democrats and Republicans made decisions as solitary individuals, there were no reductions in bias, nor any improvements in intelligence. Individuals stayed largely the same, though the groups became slightly more polarized. Alone, individuals are subject to a host of limitations, cognitive biases, personal histories, and failures of intelligence. These limitations cannot be overcome by introspection alone. In most cases, introspection cannot even reveal that these limitations exist.

But structural intelligence is much more than the aggregate opinion: its dynamics enable individuals to arrive at a new kind of collective understanding—one that can reverse a group's biases. As individual errors diminish, people learn from one another and come to see the world anew. This collective liberation from individual biases and misconceptions only emerges when people are woven together in a structure that is designed to free their general will from each of their particular wills.

Again and again, our experiments showed that even when everyone in a network suffers from the same bias—whether it was echo chambers filled with Democrats or Republicans or large groups of participants subjected to anchoring effects—egalitarian networks help populations move away from their collective biases. In the anchoring experiments, once participants started to exchange ideas with one another, they collectively started to undo their bias and move toward the correct answer, even when they had no idea whether the anchor was in the right direction or wrong direction. In fact, they had no idea that they were subject to anchoring bias at all. Without even realizing it, participants adjusted their responses to one another, rocking slowly back and forth, like a truck stuck in a muddy ditch, until they finally became unstuck—arriving individually and collectively at responses that were further from the harmful anchor and closer the truth. Every individual finished with a more accurate response, and so did the collective.

Individuals never figured out they had been nudged, but as an egalitarian collective, they figured out that something was amiss—and then they did something about it. This was an intellectual freedom that participants who remained isolated as solitary individuals never experienced.

POSSIBLE FUTURES

Where will these discoveries take us next? It's clear that the path of collective adaptation is not a walk in the park. Some structures—often the best ones—are delicate and hard to sustain. We find ourselves falling away from them without ever knowing why. Other structures are hard to escape.

The intelligence of any structural adaptation is ultimately determined by its alignment with the grand challenges that we face. Collective adaptations may at times be driven by evolutionary forces that help our cause, but they may also be driven by pressures that are hostile to our needs. Change can emerge both through the internal dynamics of structural evolution and also through the external pressures of organizational isomorphisms. Sometimes these changes bring welcome new capacities, like the formation of unified teams. Sometimes they can disrupt the structures that serve our collective intelligence, like undermining cooperative collectives.

What is the true potential for these various forms of collective adaptation to increase or decrease our collective intelligence? How can we take control of these evolutionary processes to become more than simply passive bystanders witnessing the tectonic forces of history? Our obligation as citizens living within these evolving structures is to steer these adaptations as best we can, so that we may secure forms of structural intelligence that increase our capacity for free thought and moral agency. We have already found some examples of how this can happen.

In Chicago's South Side, neighborhood networks that support cooperation and commitment have been able to enliven city blocks and improve the prospects of the children who are raised there. But these structures are fragile and can easily sow the seeds of their own demise. Vigilance is required to rejuvenate and renew these forms of structural intelligence. This is not only a matter of neighborhood success but a matter of life and death.

At the Hospital of the University of Pennsylvania, we successfully tested a system of structural intelligence that reduced medical errors and all but eliminated disparities in care by race and gender among thousands of physicians. Of course, once clinicians returned to their normal routines, the pathways of clinical influence resumed their classical hierarchical structures. Although the clinical networks we constructed offer hope for improving patient care, they are only a starting point. The real promise of structural intelligence may come from the opportunities to teach clinical trainees to look at their professional networks horizontally—across all ranks—to create new routines that deepen their own clinical acumen, and that of their peers, in unexpected ways.

We can also look to Alvin Roth's pioneering work on exchange networks, which cut the Gordian knot for kidney transplants, untangling a seemingly intractable quagmire of logistical and biological challenges and giving an unprecedentedly large number of patients renewed hope. This success story was made possible by a cultural web of reinforcing associations that create expectations for fairness. The fact that these assurances seem normal to us is a testimony to the structural intelligence that has already been established by the generations who came before and which is already hard at work in our lives today.

On social media, however, we see something different. There, the main attractor is power. The more centralized these networks become, the more highly rewarded are the vocal individuals who assume the leadership role of "influencer," both socially and financially. The challenge is that staying influential, particularly amid a changing climate of truth and sentiment, is often the art of leading by following, no matter the truth. In the evolutionary competition among firehose networks, the influencer who taps into group biases most effectively takes the top spot.

Even so, social media still has great promise. Earlier, I showed you that online communities are capable of remarkable intelligence and subtlety when they have the right structure. In particular, egalitarian networks offer enormous potential for digital collectives, particularly for online communities in which birds of a feather flock together. The right social structure places trust back into the hands of the people to collectively slough off their biases and decide anew which direction is right.

As individuals, the influences that control us are often invisible. The busy scientists walking the hallways of Building 20 rarely spent time thinking about the hallway affordances that invited casual conversations with some colleagues but not others. What potential for intellectual discovery was created by these hallways? What potential was lost? These hallway structures invisibly manipulated scientists' interactions, their ideas, and ultimately their capacity for innovation. So were these scientists free or not? Did the structural determinism of their physical setting liberate their thinking or oppress it? These questions are still germane for us today. From workplace transitions and residential neighborhoods, to internet platforms and classroom designs, they reveal the influences of the spaces in which we live and work.

Freedom comes from the fact that we see more together than alone. The challenge today is that a single voice that echoes the fears and uncertainties of a community can too easily lead collectives away from their greatest intelligence—too easily, in part, because the most subtle and interesting collective discoveries often require structures that deliberately slow things down and clear a space for many voices to be heard. These structures are an oasis, free from the tempting influences of status and power. They are a clearing amid the noise that invites each voice to make its own unique contribution and gives each one of us the rare opportunity to learn from it.

The promise of structural intelligence is that it creates a kind of freedom that individuals could never discover alone, nor could they ever come to enjoy without being embedded in a network of peers whose energies, demands, expectations, and influences help to liberate them from the hindering idiosyncrasies and biases that plague every solitary mind. These intelligent and liberating structures take time to cultivate. They require nuance and care to maintain. And while they can be fragile, they can also be sustained. Against all odds, Building 20 stood for nearly sixty years, and the Center for Advanced Study at Stanford has endured for seventy years and counting. We've seen how in impoverished neighborhoods, networks of collective efficacy have proven to be remarkably resilient for securing the well-being of urban communities. In these neighborhoods, social support for parents translates into a protective effect for children, who suffer significantly reduced levels of physical and psychological abuse, and neglect as a result of residential social networks that reduce parental stress. When we consider the lives of the children born into the South Side of Chicago, like Gakirah Barnes, and the fate that awaits them, it is clear that their potential for individual freedom cannot be detached from the structural reality of their surroundings. When communities are permeated by intelligent networks which support cooperation, and creativity, and intelligent choices, and smart cultural norms, children are afforded a moral and intellectual freedom that children in other neighborhoods will never know—but with the right structures, they could, helping these members of the next generation to become their most intelligent, capable, and civically engaged selves. This is the promise of freedom that comes from the intelligence of structure—a promise that should be kept for everyone.

13

Where We Stand

In the 1950s, the social psychologist Solomon Asch created an experiment in which eight people in a room were asked to answer a factual question—something along the lines of "Which line is longer, A or B?" The first person answered aloud "A." The second person said "A." Then the third, fourth, and fifth people each took their turns answering "A." By the time it was the eighth person's turn, the previous seven had all said "A."

The first trick in this study was that the correct answer was not "A" but "B." The second trick was that "A" was not just wrong but *obviously* wrong. The final trick was that these first seven respondents were actually laboratory staff pretending to be experimental subjects.

Across numerous trials, Asch found that a large fraction (about a third) of the participants who sat in the eighth chair would answer "A." In fact, some subjects became genuinely confused about the truth. As Asch puts it, "These subjects report that they came to perceive the majority estimates as correct." The main factor influencing people's compliance was not authority or bullying but rather the overwhelming force of the sequence of unwavering opinions that proceeded their response. As one compliant subject reported somewhat ruefully, "If I'd been the first, I probably would have responded differently."

That's exactly right.

Forty years after Asch's groundbreaking study, the economist Abhijit Banerjee published an influential model of crowd madness (also known as "herding behavior"), which showed more crisply how this happens. His model sets up a choice problem similar to Asch's famous experiment, in which a long line of investors must decide, one at a time, between two assets, A and B (with one being much better than the other). As in Asch's experiment, in Banerjee's model investors are lined up single file, so that the first person's choice can be seen by everyone. After the first person goes, the second person can reasonably assume that the first person must have based their decision on some useful information. Not wanting to be left behind, the second investor may lean toward choosing (and then choose) the same asset as the first. The third player can reasonably make a similar inference, and thus choose the same option as investors one and two. The fourth investor, who now has even more support for that option, makes the same choice, and so on, down the line. The accumulation of information from early "voters" drives subsequent voters to follow the first mover down an unwitting rabbit hole. Through no fault of their own, the first person exerts disproportionate influence over the decisions of all subsequent choosers, creating an unintentional or de facto form of centralization. Then Banerjee cleverly shows that this can happen even when the first mover has no more information than anyone else—and was in fact guessing randomly between A and B.

By this point in the book, you are likely to consider these findings predictable: They come from failing to account for the centralizing effects of "single-file" structures. But you can also see the way out. By attending to structure, and reducing centralization, we can catalyze learning dynamics that not only prevent the madness of crowds from happening but, much more importantly, elevate group intelligence significantly above the wisdom that's found within collections of solitary individuals. The real-life incarnation of this structural intelligence was famously found just a few steps away from the madness of Wall Street, along the unassuming neighborhood blocks of the West Village.

CREATIVITY'S RAINBOW

In 1960, Jane Jacobs was a simple New York City mom who set out to protect her West Village neighborhood from the encroaching highway plans of the dreaded New York City Park Commissioner's office—which, brimming with bureaucratic power, wanted to drive an expressway through lower Manhattan, and which was defeated, as the heroic legend goes, by this ordinary mom.

In Jacobs's famous ode to her city streets and neighborhood routines—and to everything that made them messy and imperfect and beautiful and sacred—she wrote:

> Under the seeming disorder of the old city, wherever the old city is working successfully, is a marvelous order for maintaining the safety of the streets and the freedom of the city. It is a complex order. Its essence is intricacy of sidewalk use, bringing with it a constant succession of eyes. The order is all composed of movement and change, and although it is life, not art, we may fancifully call it the art form of the city and liken it to . . . an intricate ballet in which the individual dancers and ensembles all have distinctive parts which miraculously reinforce each other and compose an orderly whole.

Jacobs's account of this intricate ballet led her to an enduring structural insight: The intelligence and vibrancy of city blocks depend upon the right balance of density and diversity among the residents. Jacobs recognized the dangers found in Asch's experiment and the potential it reveals for neighborhoods to blindly succumb to collective herding toward either the Scylla of decreasing engagement and increasing vacancy, or the Charybdis of economic growth and the pricing out of diverse residents. With too little density and diversity a neighborhood becomes empty, vacant, lacking sufficient texture and friction to ignite creative activity; with too much, the density of activity can drive up both desirability and rents, squeezing out artistic tenants and neighborhood shop owners, and inviting in large-revenue retailers and the bland horrors of gentrification. As we've seen, the trick is to chart a course that leads away from each of these extremes, toward the sweet spot in between.

Jacobs's observations pioneered a defense of "mixed-use neighborhoods," in which shops, studios, retailers, restaurants, and residents all live in harmonious interdependency. Every member of the sidewalk community feels a sense of membership, belonging, loyalty and responsibility. As Jacobs recounts, when a young girl was accosted by an older man, shop owners, neighbors, waiters and café readers were pulled from their daily routines to spontaneously intervene. These citizens living their varied and often non-intersecting lives were nevertheless all members of a neighborhood—bound together by an invisible community ethos that led everyone to act when action was needed. The structural insight that makes all of this work is the "just right" balance of independence and intersection that sustains a vibrant, interactive and creative neighborhood.

You saw a similar thing in MIT's Building 20, which gave rise to its own unprecedented, unplanned, and colorful forms of creativity. The vibrant "streets" of Building 20's corridors were alive with the intersecting yet distinctive activities of its community members. Building 20 owed its success to its structural "sweet spot" between too-little information exchange and too-much information flow. Building 20 had a just-right balance of independence and interaction, which supported thinkers' unusual and idiosyncratic explorations, while also stimulating productive collaborations and seamlessly fostering generations of creative thought. This balance is something that to this day defines the structural intelligence of organizational spaces—and urban spaces, too.

The key to success in such cases is finding the peak along *creativity's rainbow* (figure 13.1):

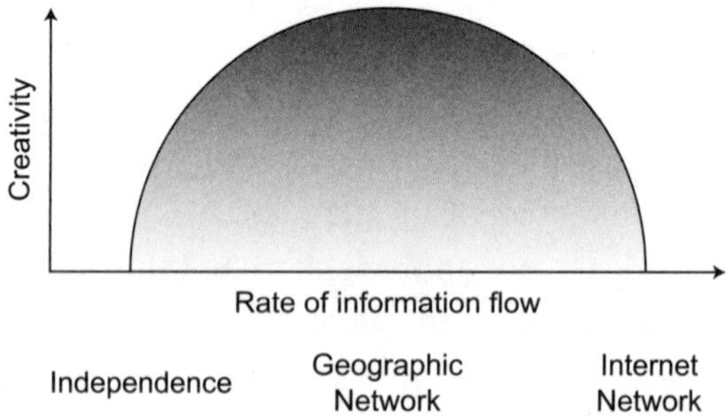

FIGURE 13.1
Creativity's rainbow: The parabolic effect of information on intelligence.

At one extreme of the rainbow (on the left), everyone is independent. The absence of information flow (equivalent to insufficient density) prevents creative synergies from forming, and eliminates the potential for the serendipitous exchanges that can trigger sparks of collaborative inspiration. At the other extreme (on the right), too much information flow (excessive density) creates strong interdependencies that limit individual freedom, leading to rapid convergence on conventional ideas. Between these two extremes (in the middle spot), lie the "goldilocks" spaces, which protect creative thinking among artistic and scientific mavericks, while also stimulating unlikely collaborations.

From a network-science point of view, the sweet spot between a completely solitary existence on the left, versus a forced synchronization on the right, is exemplified by a geographic network. This is the kind of neighborhood structure that catalyzed the romantic vibrancy of Jane Jacobs's West Village streets, and also stimulated the famous and unprecedented creativity along Noam Chomsky's dilapidated hallways. Without intentional design, these structures fostered excitement, involvement, discovery, and a sense of belonging.

HEROES AMONG US

It's true that intelligent structures can elevate individuals and collectives far above what they could achieve otherwise. But here's the kicker: None of this works without one or two brave and humble individuals who stand *against* the crowd.

Asch's experiment had in fact already come across this discovery, which turned out to be the same thing that I found seventy years later. He noticed that there was a small fraction of highly accurate people who stood their ground even when they went against a unanimous crowd. Asch reported that these independent thinkers nevertheless showed a surprising amount of respect for the incorrect majority view (in my studies, we found the same thing, which we referred to as *confidence in others*). One such participant in Asch's study commented, "I follow my own view, though my reason would tell me that I may be wrong." Asch reported that even after the study was over, this experimental subject—knowing he was right—still could not "commit himself [to saying] whether others were wrong."

There will be times when that person has to be you.

The greatest challenge we all face in achieving collective intelligence is to remember how important each one of us is. Without any fanfare or acknowledgment, your willingness to stand your ground can be decisive on a massive scale, and you—and everyone—will become smarter because of it.

The crucial insight from the grand challenge of choosing is that the extraordinarily powerful role of structure in shaping collective outcomes does not diminish your importance. In fact, it's just the opposite—it amplifies it. Contrary to the mythology of crowd wisdom, your individual choice—and your own self-weight—plays a decisive role in the fate of group intelligence. None of these findings work without you.

It's true for all of the grand challenges.

What makes the internet structure so effective for coordination is that when individuals are exposed to an overwhelming variety of different options, they stop trying to coordinate with everyone and just stick with the option that works for them. Ironically, this means that sometimes a little individual stubbornness is the key to collective harmony. For you, this means that sticking with an option that you know makes sense can be a crucial factor for successfully bringing your entire community into alignment on a shared norm.

Your individual role is even more important when quality is at stake. You might remember my colleague, Arnout van de Rijt, who uncovered important new findings about how cumulative advantage can increase the intelligence of crowds in cultural markets. His paper was first rejected from a leading scientific journal, then submitted to another journal, rejected again, submitted again, rejected again, and then finally—as a result of his perseverance—published. Less than a year later, Arnout's thrice-rejected study of cumulative advantage won one of most the prestigious awards in his field.

The thing that keeps cultural and scientific markets intelligent comes down to intrepid individuals who refuse to let their contributions be excluded from the cultural scene. They insist on their ideas, doing whatever it takes to keep them alive in the ecology of cultural options until they are eventually discovered—and the rest becomes history. Although the dynamics of cumulative advantage operate through a large-scale feedback process, the intelligence of those dynamics depends on individuals who refuse to let the ecology of options be artificially narrowed. Arnout's frustrations are nothing compared to J. K. Rowling getting the thumbs down twelve times, or Dr. Seuss's having to swallow twenty-seven rejections. But when it comes to ensuring the intelligence of cultural synchronization, one person really can—and often does—make a difference.

MIT's Building 20 created an ideal environment for innovation and discovery because it protected creative individuals from the forces of conformity. But here, too, individual decisions matter. Building 20 only worked because of the inherent energy and enthusiasm for discovery of the individuals who were housed there. The most successful scholars took advantage of their serendipitous encounters, seizing these opportunities to bravely explore unorthodox ideas and fortuitous collaborations. In this light, we might suggest that Noam Chomsky's revolutionary theory of language might never have happened without Building 20; but we would also hasten to add that it is unlikely to have happened without Noam Chomsky either. The uncompromising individual efforts of the researchers who inhabited the Magical Incubator were part and parcel of what made it an unrivaled site for intellectual discovery (for video games, gravitational wave detectors, theories of language, and so on). But here is why structure is vital: As much as any individual in history, Chomsky embodies Asch's notion of an "independent thinker"; yet he would be the first to say that the contributions that resulted from his individual genius did not come from his independence from the scholars in Building 20 but rather from their creative interdependence with one another. And, of course, the key to facilitating that is an intelligent structure.

Sometimes these structures emerge on their own, but sometimes they need to be built. For the past few years, I have been working with an enterprising group of organizers to design networks for eliciting citizens' opinions, developing key policy proposals, and growing consensus within citizen-led democratic assemblies. Building on lessons learned from around the country, I've worked to implement deliberation structures in towns across the Midwest—and, very soon hopefully, in your community too. The marriage of digital networking technologies with on-the-ground citizen advocacy has invigorated a new scientific model of "good old-fashioned democracy," premised on the idea that structural intelligence can be sustained and self-governed within every community and civic organization throughout the land. In every case, what these structures do—in Colorado and Ohio and Illinois and Pennsylvania and beyond—is hold centralization at bay to uncover the citizen voices within every community that can guide individuals and collectives to be their most intelligent selves.

As is surely clear by now, the advances I've discussed in this book should not be seen as simply academic in intent and impact. At a moment of social rupture, there could be few more important endeavors than attempting to rebuild and refashion our understanding of crowd wisdom, cultural synchronization, social cooperation, and team creativity. Today's networks might be more mechanically advanced than those of earlier ages, but they are still rooted in the science of interpersonal relationships. What this science has shown us is that there is reason for optimism: What we are now learning about how networks really work—and how the structures beneath our lives can function to inspire and liberate—illuminates a path forward, toward greater collaboration, greater intelligence, greater community and, as a result, even greater joy.

Epilogue: Useful Principles

Principle 1: Intelligent Uses of Space

Let's consider some settings in which networks are difficult to manipulate. What can we do then? What other features of a space may be calibrated to locate the "sweet spot" for cultivating collaboration and inspiring creativity?

There are several.

Take organizations. Within a firm, interaction, independence and the flow of information can be controlled by:

- moderating the size of team meetings (or the size of the rooms in which meetings take place),
- altering the frequency of team meetings (or the distance between the rooms in which team meetings take place), and
- altering the number of cross-team assignments that team members have (and also the distances between team members' offices).

These are just a few approaches for arranging physical spaces to calibrate density, diversity, and the flow of information among colleagues to stimulate both collaboration and creativity.

What about online?

What do the insights for intelligent spaces herald for the future of the virtual office? Must we be collocated in physical spaces to enjoy the benefits of serendipity? In all honesty, yes.

Virtual teams do indeed miss out on the opportunities for serendipity that emerge in well-designed physical spaces. Nevertheless, novel opportunities may still emerge from virtual collaboration tools. For instance, the ability to explicitly design (and adaptively redesign) virtual networks of team assignments and online working groups affords managers a new method for calibrating information flow and adjusting the density and diversity of activity on various projects. These networks may be carefully titrated to discover the "sweet spot" in the rate of cross-cutting ties between working groups. Such technological powers offer new opportunities for effectively steering organizational networks between the extremes of too little interaction across teams (on the left) and too much interaction (on the right); the middle passage between them may offer as yet unrealized possibilities for catalyzing creativity and innovation—even online.

- *Individual Principle*: Seek out new and unusual relationships; look for synergies that are unfamiliar and collaborations that seem heterodox.
- *Collective Principle*: Design collective spaces and routines (such as office hallways, neighborhood blocks and organizational meetings) to sustain extant relationships, while keeping a steady flow of new individuals and opportunities moving through the spaces where people meet. Serendipity can only happen in settings that foster new kinds of collaboration.
- *Cautionary Tale*: What are the implications of structural intelligence for redesigning physical workspaces, such as "open office" spaces? Open office spaces were designed to eliminate organizational silos and increase informal exchange among colleagues. However, one observation from recent experiments with open office spaces is that they can create so much continual exposure to peers that they inadvertently lead to a backfire effect of unintended behavioral adaptation that worsens the problem of independent silos. This can happen when employees compensate for overexposure to peers in the open office space by wearing headphones, which signal their desire not to be disturbed, thus reducing casual, or serendipitous, encounters with peers who may be standing or walking nearby. When this behavioral adaptation becomes widespread, it ironically reintroduces the problem of silos in a much more pervasive way. The cautionary lesson: When it comes to altering traditional office spaces to increase the potential for creative interaction, don't overcorrect.

PRINCIPLE 2: HOW TIME GOVERNS INTELLIGENCE

On Charles Darwin's voyage aboard the HMS *Beagle* (1831–1836), he experienced a lightning flash of scientific inspiration that would end up consuming his thoughts for the rest of his life. Although profound inspiration always begins with a "flash of genius," the hard work of transforming that ephemeral moment into a contribution of historical import requires years of patience, persistence, and painstaking work. By 1859, twenty-two years after he'd returned from sea, Darwin was still hard at work on his as yet unpublished manuscript, but competitive pressures forced him to submit *On the Origin of Species* to his publisher. Darwin's book changed the world. Yet, as brilliant as he was, without those long decades from 1837 to 1859, which enabled him to conduct his subtle and important investigations—allowing him to think slowly and linger over the details—his theory of evolution by natural selection is unlikely to have achieved the global and historical impact that it did.

Time matters in science, in the arts, and even in industry R&D. The ideas that circulate early and quickly within creative networks will, by definition, be those that hew most closely to familiar approaches and current-paradigm thinking. Breaking free of those established ways of thinking requires that innovators be sheltered from conventional influences. This is one reason why small scientific teams are more effective than larger scientific teams for thinking beyond the bounds of the current paradigm: on smaller teams, researchers enjoy longer stretches of time without exposure to the forces of convention. Protecting inchoate ideas from the sobering influence of popular opinion affords them the gestation time that is required for true originality to mature into world-changing breakthroughs. The more revolutionary the breakthrough, the greater the gestation time may be. When it comes to the grand challenge of creativity, structures that slow down the rate of convergence and preserve the diversity of ideas in a community significantly increase the possibility for the spark of serendipity to ignite, which may alter the path of human collective endeavor for generations to come.

- *Individual Principle*: Take time with your projects, work slowly, attend to your sense of integrity and purpose.

- *Collective Principle*: Provide teams, congresses, and committees with sufficient time to explore unlikely solutions and to uncover serendipitous overlaps that may lead to the spark of collaborative genius.

PRINCIPLE 3: THE HUMBLE HEROISM OF INTELLIGENT LEADERSHIP

In 1835, Alexis de Tocqueville observed, "in democracies men . . . are often obliged to do things which they have imperfectly learned, to say things they imperfectly understand, and to devote themselves to work for which they are unprepared by long apprenticeship."

In a free society, citizens need to be pliable and adaptive—"a thousand chances waft them to and fro, and their life is always the sport of unforeseen or extemporaneous circumstances." This tumult of opportunity and chance gives rise to a flexibility of mind, and a freedom of spirit, that is unique to a democratic context. As in the old parable of the fox and the hedgehog, this way of life cultivates a society of "foxes"—nimble thinkers able to draw from the wisdom of many fields, and to develop varied skills. These amalgamated democratic souls are masters of none. Instead, each person is located at their own unique intersection of many ways of thinking. Such is the American experience, which gives rise to a fractured and wild and distinctive quality of mind that engenders a heroic capacity.

More than once in our lives, each one of us will find ourselves thrust into the center of an important collective decision—perhaps at work, or on the school board, or in a civic assembly—and we will notice that through no conscious choice of our own, we are located at the unlikely intersection of ideas and experiences that enable us to see farther than anyone else. We are thrown into this heroic role, which requires that we accept the honor of securing our community's collective intelligence.

But we doubt ourselves, as do all sane people in such moments.

Without the trappings of expertise or rank, it is difficult to claim the right to authority. In fact, it is impossible to stand against the crowd without feeling cowed by the cognitive dissonance that sets in when your opinion disagrees so thoroughly with the majority around you. Nevertheless, in that moment, you are the person who must lead.

But how?

The champion of reluctant leadership is structural equality. An egalitarian setting enables an inspired voice to act as a clarion call, drawing everyone from near and far toward their unique contribution to the collective—not through status or prestige, but simply through the sheer gravity of one's conviction. Once the moment has passed, and a new challenge arises, an invisible reshaping of the contours of social gravity enables other leaders to emerge—primed by their own unlikely location at the intersection of ideas and experiences, which deliver them into their own moment of unexpected influence. Individuals need not bear the psychological burden of assuming a heroic posture. A deliberative structure that preserves equality among peers bears the weight of this role, enabling each person, when it is their time, to effortlessly embody the force of the better argument.

To be free is to be imperfect. This imperfection invites a humble form of heroism, which each of us may embody at one point or another, and which is made possible by egalitarian structures that instill in us the heroic character that is the beating heart of a democratic society.

- *Individual Principle*: The greatest moments of collective intelligence come from leaders who would not choose to have outsized influence—leaders who do not want power. As Plato said, "Only those who do not seek power are qualified to hold it." Humble leaders must nevertheless stand their ground—often against the crowd—to guide collective decisions toward better purpose.
- *Collective Principle*: Humble leadership requires bravery, but inspired leadership requires egalitarianism. Structurally, this means enforcing equality of connectivity in information-exchange networks. It also means removing the trappings of rank, wealth, and fame from deliberative spaces, thereby enabling the best ideas to percolate up and bring the population along with them.

Notes and Further Readings

Introduction

Page 3 **Judge Stuart Dalzell**: In a decision by the US District Court for Eastern Pennsylvania, Judge Stewart Dalzell ruled that the Communications Decency Act (CDA) (as part of the Telecommunications Act of 1996) was (in part) unconstitutional when it came to regulating free speech on the internet. This decision was upheld by the Supreme Court in Reno v. ACLU, 521 U.S. 844 (1997), which became the landmark case for Internet free speech.

Page 4 **not yet come to enjoy**: On the topics of public spirit and the tyranny of the majority, see Alexis de Tocqueville, *Democracy in America: Volume I* (D. Appleton, 1835); John Stuart Mill, *On Liberty* (Parker, 1859); and James Madison, "Federalist No. 10," in *The Federalist Papers*, ed. Clinton Rossiter (1787; New American Library, 1961), 77–84.

Page 4 **". . . an obnoxious individual"**: Madison, "Federalist No. 10."

Page 5 **quality of the collective decision**: An interesting technical note comes from Joshua Becker et al., who identify an exceptional case in which a dichotomization of the choice process leads to error. For individuals who become more accurate by moving their guesses from initially large underestimates toward more accurate estimates that slightly "overshoot" the true value, an arbitrary binary cutoff may cause a "majority rule" process to produce an incorrect binary choice. Joshua Becker et al., "The Crowd Classification Problem: Social Dynamics of Binary-Choice Accuracy," *Management Science* 68, no. 5 (2021): 3949–3965.

Page 5 **". . . put together from them"**: This famous passage is from the Preface Letter to Pope Paul III in Nicholas Copernicus, *On the Revolutions of the Celestial Spheres* (1543).

Page 5 **new solutions to them**: Readers familiar with George Orwell's *1984* will appreciate that this book's title, *Goodthink*, offers an ironic allusion to the Newspeak term "goodthink," which refers to thinking "in an orthodox manner."

Page 7 **social networks and grand challenges**: Excellent work by my colleague at the University of Pennsylvania, Daniel Levinthal, has begun to surface many of the distinctions between the grand challenges that I discuss in this book. His work also highlights the processes of collective adaptation that I explore in part IV of this book. See in particular: Özgecan Koçak, Daniel A. Levinthal, and Phanish Puranam, "Dual Challenge of Search and Coordination," *Organization Science* 34, no. 2 (2023): 851–869.

PART I: CHOOSING

CHAPTER 1: WHY WE'RE NOT AS SMART AS WE COULD BE—YET

Page 11 **protected by the First Amendment**: In 1787, Virginia delegate to the Constitutional Convention George Mason originally proposed adding the guarantee of liberties such as free speech to the Constitution. James Madison opposed this suggestion on the grounds that if only some liberties were included in the Constitution, it would imply that other liberties were not guaranteed (by virtue of their exclusion). After extended debate, Madison agreed to draft a set of constitutional amendments in 1789 guaranteeing certain liberties, which were later ratified in 1791, becoming the Bill of Rights.

Page 11 **"a *really* big house"** (emphasis added): Donald Burns's case was first heard in a Florida US District court, and then appealed to the US 11th Circuit Court of Appeals. The 11th Circuit Court's ruling (reported here) was then appealed by Burns's attorneys to the US Supreme Court, which declined to hear the case. This case is detailed in *Harvard Law Review* 135, no. 8 (June 2022), and has been widely commented on. See: 135 Harv. L. Rev. 2203. (2022) Burns v. Town of Palm Beach. Eleventh Circuit Rejects First Amendment Claim for Residential Architecture. Comment on: 999 F.3d 1317 (11th Cir. 2021). See also: "Editorial: Important Lessons Can Be Learned from Burns Case Against the Architectural Commission," *Palm Beach Daily News*, March 27, 2002.

Page 13 **thoughts on the matter**: While Condorcet was in hiding in 1794, he wrote his final work, *Sketch for a Historical Picture of the Progress of the Human Mind* (published posthumously, 1795). Condorcet identifies ten stages, or epochs, of human development. The tenth epoch promises the perfection of human society, which is characterized by: (1) the destruction of inequality between nations, (2) the destruction of inequality between classes, and (3) the indefinite perfectibility of human nature. Unlike Francis Galton's later attempt to establish a eugenic/biologistic agenda for human perfection (*Hereditary Genius*, 1869), Condorcet emphasized the importance of equality by race, religion, culture, and (quite ahead of his time) gender. While for Francis Galton, human perfection was putatively to be achieved through biology (i.e., breeding perfect people), for Condorcet—by stark contrast—perfection was to be pursued through education and social (structural) reform (i.e., liberating people from oppression). My sympathies clearly fall with Condorcet.

Page 13 **successful choice is almost guaranteed**: While a pure democracy requires 51 percent accuracy across the entire populace, a representative democracy, such as a republic, may succeed in satisfying this requirement for the electorate, even though it is not satisfied for the populace.

Page 13 **theory of democracy**: With regard to the importance of Condorcet's theorem (*Essay on the Application of Analysis to the Probability of Majority Decisions*, 1785) for democratic theory, I'm referring to the epistemic foundations of democracy, which pertain to the question: Why is democracy the preferred form of government for making intelligent decisions? I am not referring to philosophical arguments for why democracy is a more morally justified form of government than other forms of government (e.g., due to its representativeness, fairness, etc.). The latter are not epistemic questions but questions of justification, which have been expertly explored by contemporary scholars of deliberative democracy, such as Amy Gutmann, Dennis Thompson, and Joshua Cohen. See Amy Gutmann and Dennis Thompson, *Why Deliberative Democracy?* (Princeton University Press, 2004); Joshua Cohen, "Deliberative Democracy," in *Deliberation, Participation and Democracy*, ed. S. W. Rosenberg (Palgrave Macmillan, 2007); and Jon Elster (ed.), *Deliberative Democracy* (Cambridge University Press, 1998). These arguments fall into the broad category of "procedural democracy."

Related work on deliberative polling has explored the potential for using democratic deliberative forums for gathering more balanced and broadly representative accounts of public opinion. See James S. Fishkin, Robert C. Luskin, and Roger Jowell, "Deliberative Polling and Public Consultation," *Parliamentary Affairs* 53, no. 4 (2000): 657–666; Bruce Ackerman and James S. Fishkin, *Deliberation Day* (Yale University Press, 2008); and James S. Fishkin, Valentin Bolotnyy, Joshua Lerner, Alice Siu, and Norman Bradburn, "Can Deliberation Have Lasting Effects?," *American Political Science Review* 118, no. 4 (2024): 2000–2020.

In addition, Jürgen Habermas emphasizes the moral and rational justification of democratic deliberation (from the perspective of procedural democracy) while also broaching the epistemic question in terms of his idea of the "force of the better argument" (which is discussed in chapter 5 of this book). Jürgen Habermas, *Between Facts and Norms: Contributions to a Discourse Theory of Law and Democracy* (Polity Press, 2015). Many other scholars who discuss procedural democracy have also engaged the question of epistemic democracy, including, among many others: Joshua Cohen, "An Epistemic Conception of Democracy," *Ethics* 97, no. 1 (1986): 26–38; Jules Coleman and John Ferejohn, "Democracy and Social Choice," *Ethics* 97, no. 1 (1986): 6–25; James Fishkin and Robert Luskin, "Bringing Deliberation to the Democratic Dialogue," in *The Poll with a Human Face*, ed. Maxwell McCombs and Amy Reynolds, 3, 29–31 (Routledge, 1999); and Christian List and Robert Goodin, "Epistemic Democracy: Generalizing the Condorcet Jury Theorem," *Journal of Political Philosophy* 9 (2001): 277–306. Part I of this book explores an epistemic foundation for democracy based on the principles of structural intelligence.

Page 14 **question inevitably arises**: Some significant contemporary arguments for the importance of having an informed electorate in modern democratic societies include: Michael X. Delli Carpini and Scott Keeter, *What Americans Know About Politics and Why It Matters* (Yale University Press, 1996); Bryan Caplan, *The Myth of the Rational Voter: Why Democracies Choose Bad Policies* (Princeton University Press, 2007).

Page 14 **voters to vote**: An implication that emerges from the results presented in part I of this book (chapters 1–6) is that there may be measurable negative effects of voter suppression on national collective intelligence.

Page 15 **single person does not**: While Aristotle (*Politics*, 350 BCE) was among the earliest thinkers to argue for collective intelligence, ideas suggestive of Aristotle's optimistic vision of "intelligence from the multitude" had already been articulated (in a less definitive fashion) around 450 BCE by Protagoras, who is remembered for his influential theory of relativism: "Man is the measure of all things." According to Protagoras's relativism, which presages Aristotle's conception of collective intelligence, every individual has a valid point of view, and because each person's viewpoint is "equally valid," the combination of people's respective views (together) may offer a more complete picture of the whole than any individual can manage alone. The collective synthesis of many views (which are all of equal validity from a relativist point of view) can thus provide a kind of "intelligent group perspective" that offers greater insight (and potentially therefore greater validity) than any individual thinker's perspective. Thus, Protagoras's individual-level relativism creates the potential for a collective-level "objectivity" (or at least "intersubjectivity") that may outpace any individual's perspective. This interpretation of Protagoras closely resembles Aristotle's view of collective intelligence.

Somewhat more obliquely, this interpretation of Protagoras also bears a family resemblance to Edmund Husserl's phenomenology (*Ideas I*, 1913), in which, loosely stated, the intersection of a multitude of individual perspectives (on an idea or object) can reveal the essential nature of the "thing in itself." The connection between Husserl's notion of "intersubjectivity" (*Cartesian Meditations*, 1931) and the idea of collective intelligence as something that might offer a unique form of access to a "transcendental" (or perhaps "objective") understanding of experience is not formally developed by Husserl himself. However, it is brought out with impressive clarity in Maurice Merleau-Ponty's *The Phenomenology of Perception* (1945).

Looking further back than Protagoras, around 500 BCE Aeschylus's *Oresteia* (part III, *Eumenides*) uses the theatrical device of the Eumenides to demonstrate that citizens' collective evaluation of the innocence or guilt of the accused is superior to the judgment of the individuals who are aggrieved. Aeschylus's (poetic) conclusions suggest that the intelligence of a collective (such as a jury) is superior to that of an individual when it comes to the task of eliciting the truth of a situation, and therefore for determining justice.

Page 15 "**. . . can draw in concert**": John Rawls, *A Theory of Justice* (Harvard University Press, 1971), 358–359.

Page 16 **unprecedented skepticism**: In the millennia between Aristotle (*Politics*, 350 BCE) and Hobbes (*The Leviathan*, 1651), democracy largely fell into disrepute among the intelligentsia. Thinkers like Machiavelli (*The Prince*, 1532) and Hobbes and even, to an extent, Montaigne (*Essays*, 1580) criticized the notion of the rule of the masses. It was not until the Enlightenment that thinkers like Locke (*An Essay Concerning Human Understanding*, 1690), Hume (*An Enquiry Concerning Human Understanding*, 1748), and Rousseau (*On the Social Contract*, 1762) argued (as Aristotle had) for a naturalistic basis to the principles of democratic government.

It is a curiosity that in Machiavelli's *The Prince* (1532) there are contradictory quotes that celebrate the wisdom of the masses. However, these arguments in favor of popular democracy appear to be ironic in nature—in effect a reductio ad absurdum for collective intelligence. Machiavelli writes, "I say that a people is more prudent, more stable, and of better judgment than a prince. Not without cause may the voice of a people be likened to that of God." The ironic reading of this passage comes from its allusion to Alcuin (around 800 CE), whose advice to the French ruler Charlemagne was "those people should not be listened to who keep saying, 'The voice of the people [is] the voice of God' since the riotousness of the crowd is always very close to madness" (*Works*, Letter 164, 800 CE). On this reading, the "voice of the people" is equated with the "voice of God" because, as Gustav LeBon (*The Crowd: A Study of the Popular Mind*, 1895) would say centuries later, the people's voice will inevitably become a self-fulfilling prophesy, often to the detriment of all. For Montaigne (*Essays*, 1580), government was largely a matter of custom—or social norms—rather than political rights. From this point of view, people can become just as accustomed to monarchy as to democracy, and will be willing to defend whichever system is familiar to them; thus, democracy holds no special moral place among systems of government.

Page 17 **extract intelligence from ordinary collectives**: Condorcet's basic voting procedure (*Essay on the Application of Analysis to the Probability of Majority Decisions*, 1785), which later became known as Condorcet's jury theorem, had three simple steps: First, people must make a choice between options about which they are reasonably informed. Second, people need to reflect independently on their choices. Third, people needed to vote in good faith according to their sincere preferences. With these principles, Condorcet was able to lay out procedures that would yield an accurate and intelligent collective choice.

Another of Condorcet's famous contributions to democratic procedure is his voting paradox, which is not a matter of epistemic democracy (i.e., the correctness of a collective choice), but instead focuses on the problem of preference aggregation (i.e., how a multitude of opinions—in particular, discrete choices—can be aggregated in a way that accurately—and "rationally"—reflects the collective beliefs of the population). Although it is only obliquely related to his jury theorem, I will briefly summarize it because it has fascinated scholars for centuries. Condorcet shows that for any voting system with more than three candidates, at least one situation can be constructed in which it is impossible to choose a winner (e.g., because A defeats B and B defeats C, while C defeats A). Kenneth Arrow (*Social Choice and Individual Values*, Yale University Press, 1963) formally demonstrated and generalized this result, proving the "impossibility" theorem, showing that it is impossible to construct a "rational" democratic system of government that can definitively eliminate these intransitive cycles when there are more than two candidates in an election. Relatedly, see also Peyton Young's work on Condorcet and Borda (Jean-Charles de Borda, *Memoire sur les Elections au Scrutin*, Histoire de l'Academie Royale des Sciences, 1784), in which Young shows how the findings from Condorcet's "jury theorem" (originally stated for two candidates) may be generalized to situations in which there are more than two choices (i.e., a plurality rule rather than a majority rule). These results are found in: Peyton Young ("Condorcet's Theory of Voting," *American Political Science Review*, 1988; and "Optimal Voting Rules," *Journal of Economic Perspectives*, 1995). Other related work on this topic comes from Duncan Black, *The Theory of Committees and Elections* (Cambridge University Press, 1958); Bernard Grofman, Guillermo Owen, and Scott L. Feld, "Thirteen Theorems in Search of the Truth," *Theory & Decision* 15 (1983): 261–278; and Bernard Grofman and Guillermo Owen (eds.), *Information Pooling and Group Decision Making* (JAI Press, 1986).

Page 18 **collective truth that emerges from them**: Rousseau's famous passage (*On the Social Contract*, 1762) is: "The 'will of all' is very different from the 'general will'; the 'general will' looks only to the common interest, while the 'will of all' looks to private interest and is no more than a sum of 'particular wills.' But remove from these same 'particular wills' the pluses and minuses that cancel one another and what is left of the 'particular wills' adds up to the 'general will.'"

As a matter of clarification, it is useful to note that Rousseau is not referring to estimates—as Galton would many years later ("Vox Populi," *Nature*, 1907)—but rather to votes. Rousseau's logic of the "general will" is closer to Condorcet's counting system (and to the Miracle of Aggregation) than it is to Galton's emphasis on the central tendency of a continuous distribution. Galton's ("Vox Populi") averaging approach to crowd wisdom was based on the work of physicist-turned-social-theorist Adolphe Quetelet, *A Treatise on Man and the Development of His Faculties* (1835), and on the work of the great mathematician Carl Friedrich Gauss, *Theoria Motus Corporum Coelestium in Sectionibus Conicis Solem Ambientium* (1809), as discussed in chapter 11 of this book

Closer to Rousseau's approach, in the Miracle of Aggregation the basic idea (as in Rousseau's passage) is that errors cancel out until all that is left are the responses of those individuals who selected the best option. But Rousseau has one further idea in mind, which is that the general will is something that every individual comes to appreciate as "wise." This provision connects Rousseau's idea of collective intelligence with Aristotle's notion of the bountiful feast. Rousseau believes that the general will is a collective solution that can be widely appreciated by the individual members of the polity, who will all see it to be better for the collective than any of the individual suggestions that serve only their particular wills. For Rousseau, the general will is accepted as a superior solution because it effectively serves the needs of everyone rather than only serving the needs of some. An excellent discussion of the connection between Rousseau and Condorcet can be found in Bernard Grofman and Scott L. Feld, "Rosseau's General Will: A Condorcetian Perspective," *American Political Science Review* 82, no. 2 (1988): 567–576. Notably, a contrasting view of Rousseau comes from Gary Runcimen and Amartya Sen, "Games, Justice and the General Will," *Mind* 74 (1965): 554–562. Runcimen and Sen investigate the general will in light of a "prisoner's dilemma." While this is not my approach to understanding Rousseau's conception of the general will, the general problem of cooperation germane to the prisoner's dilemma will be addressed in chapter 9 of this book.

Page 19 **information, independence, and inclusiveness**: Textual interpretation of Rousseau (*On the Social Contract*, 1762) is famously thorny on the issue of group size. For Rousseau, the key issue is inclusiveness, not numbers. Rousseau wants as great a fraction of individuals as possible to participate (that is, direct democracy not representative democracy), but he acknowledges that the practical realities of a large state (of greater size) reduce the fraction of the populace who can participate in democratic deliberation and voting. In a large state, direct democracy becomes unwieldy—and representative democracy becomes necessary—thereby reducing the "generality" of the general will that results from democratic assemblies.

Rousseau's scientific commitment to inclusiveness motivates the suggestion that small states are necessary to ensure the generality of the general will. This group size restriction for Rousseau, which maintains the benefits of small states over large states, is not a philosophical principle but a practical limit on the functioning of a direct democracy in large states.

Consequently, while (1) large democratic groups are a philosophical requirement for Rousseau in terms of having greater numbers of opinions represented (i.e., fewer factions and more independent views) to increase the generality of the general will; simultaneously (2) the limit on the size of a state is a practical requirement that ensures inclusiveness, such that all members of a populace can participate in direct democracy. Thus, Rousseau requires that within a given state a large fraction of the population should participate, but warns, therefore, that a state that is too large will unintentionally reduce the number of independent participants engaged in the democratic process (e.g., because factions form, and citizens' diverse opinions coalesce into representative opinions), leading to, in effect, a less inclusive democracy. In which case, greater influence is given to the particular wills of each interest group, rather than to the general will. For similar reasons, Rousseau is wary of social influence, in which individuals are persuaded to share common beliefs, because it can lead to the homogenization of viewpoints, condensing many diverse opinions in a democratic assembly into a single particular will.

Thus, on the question of social influence, Rousseau and Condorcet agree that it is problematic. They also agree on the importance of an informed electorate. But when it comes to the ideal size of the state, they part company.

For Condorcet, a large state is better than a small state when individuals are on average correct 51 percent of the time; that is, when size benefits collective intelligence, a bigger democracy is better. Unlike Rousseau, Condorcet's meaning of "size" really does mean "numbers." Rousseau and Condorcet would agree on the benefits of inclusiveness (or greater size) for the voting population. However, they disagree on the desired size of the ideal state. For an informed populace, Rousseau advocates for smaller overall numbers of people (i.e., a small state), while Condorcet argues for a large state with greater numbers of people.

Page 20 **large-scale collective intelligence**: Bryan Caplan's well-known argument challenges the idea that the average voter has sufficient knowledge to make good decisions. This argument employs "the dark side" of Condorcet's theorem to question the merits of inclusive democracy with an uninformed populace. Caplan, *Myth of the Rational Voter.*

Page 23 **distrust of the multitude**: Criticisms of the untrustworthiness of the poorly educated and mercurial masses reach back to antiquity. Plato (390 BCE) was famously distrustful of the multitude (see *The Sophists*), as was the Roman historian Livy (20 BCE; see *History of Rome*), along with many (many) other scholars who set pen to paper between the age of Protagoras (450 BCE) and the Enlightenment (1700)—and ever since.

Page 23 **nevertheless a sticky one**: Contemporary economic scholars have nicely unearthed historical and scientific details germane to Mackay's journalistic accounts of "crowd hysteria" and "group madness," which challenge his long-standing narrative. See: R. B. Emmett (ed.), *Great Bubbles: Reactions to the South Sea Bubble, the Mississippi Scheme and the Tulip Mania Affair*, 3 vols. (Pickering and Chatto, 2000); P. M. Garber, *Famous First Bubbles: The Fundamentals of Early Manias* (MIT Press, 2000); J. Hoppit, "The Myths of the South Sea Bubble," *Transactions of the Royal Historical Society* 12 (2002): 141–165; P. M. Logan, "The Popularity of Popular Delusions: Charles Mackay and Victorian Popular Culture," *Cultural Critique* 54 (Spring 2003): 213–241; Anne Goldgar, *Tulipmania: Money, Honor, and Knowledge in the Dutch Golden Age* (University of Chicago Press, 2007).

Page 24 **". . . astonished at this"**: Gabriel Tarde, *Penal Philosophy*, trans. R. Howell (Little, Brown, 1912 [1890]).

Page 24 **". . . divine right of kings"**: The rest of Le Bon's well-known passage (*The Crowd*, 1895) reads as follows:

> Today the claims of the masses are becoming more and more sharply defined, and amount to nothing less than a determination to utterly destroy society as it now exists, with a view to making it hark back to that primitive communism which was the normal condition of all human groups before the dawn of civilisation. Limitations of the hours of labour, the

nationalisation of mines, railways, factories, and the soil, the equal distribution of all products, the elimination of all the upper classes for the benefit of the popular classes, etc., such are these claims.

Little adapted to reasoning, crowds, on the contrary, are quick to act. As the result of their present organisation their strength has become immense. The dogmas whose birth we are witnessing will soon have the force of the old dogmas; that is to say, the tyrannical and sovereign force of being above discussion. The divine right of the masses is about to replace the divine right of kings.

Page 25 **some scholars of the day deplored it**: *The Times'* review of Galton's 1869 book *Hereditary Genius* included the thoughtful retort, "universal knowledge of reading, writing and ciphering and the absence of pauperism would raise the national grade of ability far quicker and higher than any system of selected marriage." The same debate still occupies our attention today.

Page 25 **1 percent of the true answer**: In Galton's data ("Vox Populi," *Nature*, 1907), most individuals were not below the 51 percent threshold. The distribution of guesses regarding the ox's dressed weight approximates a normal distribution (the best fit comes from an asymmetric Student-*t* distribution), such that not only is the median guess close to the truth but the most popular guess (or modal guess) is also close to the truth. Thus, it wasn't just the central tendency of the population that was close to the true answer—lots of individual guesses were close, too. Among the many studies to reanalyze Galton's data (including the many volumes by Karl Pearson, *The Life, Labours and Letters of Francis Galton*, 1930), these data are reported, along with a helpful discussion of Galton's analysis, in Kenneth F. Wallis, "Revisiting Francis Galton's Forecasting Competition," *Statistical Science* 29, no. 3 (2014): 420–424.

Notwithstanding, Galton's basic insight generalizes to many settings in which all individuals may be far below the 51 percent threshold. For instance, in a bimodal distribution, the population may be polarized such that every individual is highly inaccurate (occupying one or the other extreme position), yet the mean of the population (i.e., the average of those extremes) is highly accurate—suggesting the curious potential for situations in which ideological polarization results in a population with very low individual accuracy and very high collective accuracy. (Cf. Cass Sunstein, Reid Hastie, and David Schkade, "What Happened on Deliberation Day," *95 California Law Review* 915 (2007), who suggest that ideological polarization is problematic in its own right, independent of an analysis of belief accuracy.)

Regarding the use of the median versus the mean to calculate the central tendency of a population, two weeks after Galton's paper was published, R. H. Hooker published a brief letter ("Letters to the Editor: Mean or Median," *Nature*, 1907) noting that the mean would have been even more accurate than the median. The correct answer was 1198. The median that Galton reported was 1207, while the mean that Hooker reported was 1197.

Page 27 **the grand challenge of choosing**: In her wonderful book *Democratic Reason*, Yale University political scientist Hélène Landemore provides a thoughtful history of the grand challenge of choosing, which she develops into an epistemic argument for deliberative democracy. I am clearly sympathetic to Landemore's objective; however, her formal arguments run afoul of a conflation of the grand challenge of choosing with the grand challenge of creativity, which ultimately undermines her conclusions. Lu Hong and Scott Page's formal model for the grand challenge of creativity makes assumptions about learning and about individuals' ability to receive feedback on the quality of their ideas, which are entirely appropriate for the grand challenge of creativity, but which extend beyond the boundaries of the grand challenge of choosing (as discussed in chapter 10 of this book). Nevertheless, the spirit of Landemore's attempt is very much appreciated. The present book offers a systematic framework that delineates and synthesizes the formal solutions for each of the grand challenges. From this synthesis, I am able to derive a novel epistemic argument for deliberative democracy in the grand challenge of choosing (which is developed in detail in chapters 2–4 of this book), which I then apply to the historically problematic cases of polarization and echo chambers in chapter 5. All of which owes much to Landemore's original efforts. See: Hélène Landemore, *Democratic Reason: Politics, Collective Intelligence, and the Rule of the Many* (Princeton University Press, 2013); Scott Page, *The Difference: How the Power of Diversity Creates Better Groups, Firms, Schools, and Societies* (Princeton University Press, 2008); Lu Hong and Scott Page, "Groups of Diverse Problem Solvers Can Outperform Groups of High-Ability Problem Solvers," *Proceedings of the National Academy of Sciences of the USA* 101, no. 46 (2004): 16385–16389; Lu Hong and Scott E. Page, "Some Microfoundations of Collective Wisdom," in *Collective Wisdom*, ed. Hélène Landemore and Jon Elster (Cambridge University Press, 2008).

Page 27 **collective error is 0**: A rudimentary clarification of nomenclature is as follows: An *estimate* is a calculation of an unknown value based on available data. Francis Galton's farmers were estimating the weight of the ox. A *prediction* is an expected outcome based on a model of how several independent factors may combine to affect a result. Determining the expected price of a house based on various factors such as size, location, etc. is a prediction. Finally, a *forecast* is a prediction about a future outcome, which typically relies on current or past data. Thus, predicting the future price of a stock is a forecast. In part I of this book, my experimental studies primarily focus on estimates (e.g., counting jellybeans) and predictions (e.g., identifying fake news), with some attention given to forecasts (e.g., patient prognosis).

Page 28 **most or all of its members**: The variety of methods for studying the wisdom of crowds generally conform to one of two types: either (i) Condorcet-style aggregation of discrete choices (in which the primary challenge is to strategically select subsets of voters to approximate the best collective choice for the entire population), or (ii) Galton-style aggregations of estimates, in which the challenge is to use the central tendency of the population to reveal an intelligent group estimate. Galton's tradition is rooted in the earlier work of Adolphe Quetelet, *A Treatise on Man and the Development of His Faculties* (1835), which in turn originates from the work of the great mathematician Carl Friedrich Gauss, *Theoria Motus Corporum Coelestium in Sectionibus Conicis Solem Ambientium* (1809), as discussed in chapter 11.

Some prominent recent work in Galton's tradition includes:

Albert Kao, Andrew M. Berdahl, Andrew T. Hartnett, Matthew J. Lutz, Joseph B. Bak-Coleman, Christos C. Ioannou, et al., "Counteracting Estimation Bias and Social Influence to Improve the Wisdom of Crowds," *Journal of the Royal Society Interface* 15, no. 141 (2018): 20180130.

Feng Shi, Misha Teplitskiy, Eamon Duede, and James A. Evans, "The Wisdom of Polarized Crowds," *Nature Human Behaviour* 3 (2019): 329–336.

Stefan M. Herzog, Aleksandra Litvinova, Kyanoush S. Yahosseini, Alan N. Tump, and Ralf H. J. M. Kurvers, "The Ecological Rationality of the Wisdom of Crowds," in *Taming Uncertainty*, ed. Ralph Hertwig, Timothy J. Pleskac, and Thorsten Pachur (MIT Press, 2019).

Mirta Galesic, W. Bruine de Bruin, M. Dumas, et al., "Asking About Social Circles Improves Election Predictions," *Nature Human Behaviour* 2 (2018): 187–193.

Thomas McAndrew, Nutcha Wattanachit, Graham C. Gibson, and Nicholas G. Reich, "Aggregating Predictions from Experts: A Review of Statistical Methods, Experiments, and Applications," *WIREs: Computational Statistics* 13, no. 2 (2021): e1514.

Abdullah Almaatouq, M. Amin Rahimian, Jason W. Burton, and Abdulla Alhajri, "The Distribution of Initial Estimates Moderates the Effect of Social Influence on the Wisdom of the Crowd," *Scientific Reports* 12 (2022): 16546.

And, specifically regarding the implications of AI: Jason Burton, Ezequiel Lopez-Lopez, Shahar Hechtlinger, Zoe Rahwan, Samuel Aeschbach, Michiel A. Bakker, et al., "How Large Language Models Can Reshape Collective Intelligence," *Nature Human Behaviour* 8 (2024): 1643–1655.

Some prominent recent work in Condorcet's tradition includes the following. (Unsurprisingly, many of these studies are in the field of medicine, which requires discrete choices, as discussed in chapter 6.)

Max Wolf, Jens Krause, Patricia A. Carney, Andy Bogart, and Ralf H. J. M. Kurvers, "Collective Intelligence Meets Medical Decision-Making: The Collective Outperforms the Best Radiologist," *PLOS One* 10 (2015): e0134269.

Juliane E. Kämmer, Wolf E. Hautz, Stefan M. Herzog, Olga Kunina-Habenicht, and Ralf H. J. M. Kurvers , "The Potential of Collective Intelligence in Emergency Medicine: Pooling Medical Students' Independent Decisions Improves Diagnostic Performance," *Medical Decision Making* 37, no. 6 (2017): 715–724.

Michael L. Barnett, Dhruv Boddupalli, Shantanu Nundy, and David W. Bates, "Comparative Accuracy of Diagnosis by Collective Intelligence of Multiple Physicians vs. Individual Physicians," *JAMA Network Open* 2, no. 3 (2019): e190096.

Claudia Winklmayr, Albert B. Kao, Joseph B. Bak-Coleman, and Pawel Romanczuk, "The Wisdom of Stalemates: Consensus and Clustering as Filtering Mechanisms for Improving Collective Accuracy," *Proceedings of the Royal Society B* 287, no. 1938 (2020): 20201802.

Ulrike Hahn, "Collectives and Epistemic Rationality," *Topics in Cognitive Science* 14, no. 3 (2022): 602–620.

Page 28 **wisdom of uneducated voters**: One of the strongest arguments in favor of the viewpoint that uneducated voters are collectively wise is the comprehensive study by Benjamin Page and Robert Shapiro, which uses Condorcet's approach to argue (contra Bryan Caplan, *The Myth of the Rational Voter*) that while the accuracy of voters' opinions may vary across individuals, collectively Condorcet's argument for intelligent democracy works, such that large democracies do in fact produce collectively intelligent policy opinions. See Benjamin Page and Robert Shapiro, *The Rational Public: Fifty Years of Trends in Americans' Policy Preferences* (University of Chicago Press, 1992).

Page 28 **the three positions**: The exact phrasing of each position in Sunstein et al., "What Happened on Deliberation Day," is:

1. The United States should sign an international agreement to reduce the greenhouse gases produced in this country that contribute to global warming.
2. When different applicants for the same job or educational opportunity are almost equal on relevant criteria, then the job or admission should be given to members of groups in society that have been discriminated against in the past.
3. Two adults of the same sex should be able to form a "civil union," which would entitle them to certain legal rights such as joint home ownership, or access to the other's retirement or medical benefits.

Page 29 **the crowd wisdom they started with**: Although Sunstein et al. ("What Happened on Deliberation Day") emphasize polarization in its own right as the problem, I tack on the (inferred) implication that increasing polarization leads crowds to become less accurate/less intelligent. Nevertheless, it is important to note that since Sunstein et al. examine questions of preference rather than fact, there is a potential for group intelligence that is untreated in his study—namely, that increasing polarization can result in a better mean approximation of the correct answer. Even though sub-groups become more polarized in Sunstein et al.'s ("What Happened on Deliberation Day") study, the central tendency of the entire collective (inclusive of all subgroups) may actually become more accurate. The problem with this technical observation is that even if the collective wisdom improves as a result of group polarization, individuals are nevertheless becoming more ideologically extreme, more affectively polarized, and individually less accurate. (See related work by Cass Sunstein and Reid Hastie, *Wiser: Getting Beyond Groupthink to Make Groups Smarter*, Harvard Business Review Press, 2015.) Ultimately, it is individuals who must make decisions about their daily routines, their household energy consumption, and their forms of political expression. All of which suggests, consistent with Sunstein et al.'s ("What Happened on Deliberation Day") reasoning, that creating an increasingly extreme and inaccurate populace raises legitimate worries for the quality of collective choice and civic engagement. Chapter 5 of this book elaborates these points with new findings from my recent experimental studies of political decision-making in polarized in echo chambers. For a very thoughtful and compelling alternative point of view, see my colleague Diana Mutz's work (*Hearing the Other Side: Deliberative Versus Participatory Democracy*, 2006) in which she emphasizes the importance of extremizing forces for reducing apathy and increasing popular engagement in productive forms of participatory democracy (e.g., civic activism, protest marches, sit-ins, etc.).

CHAPTER 2: CROWD MADNESS IN THE TWENTY-FIRST CENTURY

Page 32 **are actually influential**: Research on the network dynamics of social contagion shows that highly connected "influencers" can easily accelerate the spread of *simple contagions* (like information and disease) but are ineffective—often counterproductive—for the spread of *complex contagions* (behaviors that are costly, socially risky, or unfamiliar). Key studies of simple and complex contagions include: Damon Centola and Michael Macy, "Complex Contagions and the Weakness of Long Ties," *American Journal of Sociology* 113, no. 3 (2007): 702–734; Damon Centola, "The Spread of Behavior in an Online Network Experiment," *Science* 329, no. 5996 (2010): 1194–1197; Damon Centola, *How Behavior Spreads: The Science of Complex Contagions* (Princeton University Press, 2018); Damon Centola, *Change: How to Make Big Things Happen* (Little, Brown, 2021); Douglas Guilbeault and Damon Centola, "Topological Measures for Identifying and Predicting the Spread of Complex Contagions," *Nature Communications* 12 (2021): 4430.

Page 32 **relatively equal connectivity**: Self-organized network formation driven by homophily (without other constraints) typically leads to decentralized network patterns; see Damon Centola and Arnout van de Rijt. "Choosing Your Network: Social Preferences in an Online Health Community," *Social Science and Medicine* 125 (2015): 19–31; Damon Centola, "Social Origins of Networks and Diffusion," *American Journal of Sociology* 120, no. 5 (2015): 1295–1338; and Peter M. Blau and Joseph Schwartz, *Crosscutting Social Circles: Testing a Macrostructural Theory of Intergroup Relations* (Routledge, 1984). For a more general account of homophily in network formation, see also: Miller McPherson, Lynn Smith-Lovin, and James M. Cook, "Birds of a Feather," *American Sociological Review* 27 (2001): 415–444; and Sergio Currarini, Matthew O. Jackson, and Paolo Pin, "Identifying the Roles of Race-Based Choice and Chance in High School Friendship Network Formation," *PNAS* 107, no. 11 (2010): 4857–4861.

Page 34 **new online social circle**: In several review articles, Jingwen Zhang and I explore the relationship between social comparison, social network formation, and social influence; see: Jingwen Zhang and Damon Centola, "Social Networks and Health: New Developments in Diffusion, Online and Offline," *Annual Review of Sociology* 45 (2019): 91–109; and Jingwen Zhang and Damon Centola, "How Social Networks Shape Social Comparison," in *Social Comparison, Judgment, and Behavior*, ed. Jerry Suls (Oxford University Press, 2018). The latter addresses the effects of social comparison in social media networks on risk factors for adolescent health.

Page 34 **will think about you**: The key topological factor in the formation of firehose networks is the extremity of the degree distribution (in particular, inequity in degree centrality and eigenvector centrality). For elegant mathematical demonstrations of these effects, see: A. Barabasi and R. Albert, "Emergence of Scaling in Random Networks," *Science* 286 (1999): 509–512; Benjamin Golub and Matthew O. Jackson, "Naïve Learning in Social Networks and the Wisdom of Crowds," *American Economic Journal* 2, no. 1 (2010): 112–149; and Benjamin Golub and Matthew O. Jackson, "How Homophily Affects the Speed of Learning and Best-Response Dynamic," *Quarterly Journal of Economics* (2012): 1287–1338.

Page 34 **waiting to attack dissenters**: A phenomenon known as the majority illusion results from many people being connected to the same influencer. Since many people hear the same view (unknowingly from the same source), they all come to have the illusion that the influencer's view is widely held by a majority of people, when in fact it is simply held by a single person to whom many people are connected. This phenomenon can make an influencer's extreme views appear more normatively accepted, and therefore more legitimate among the community of followers than they actually are. See: Kristina Lerman, Xiaoran Yan, and Xin-Zeng Wu, "The Majority Illusion in Social Networks," *PLOS One* 11, no. 2 (2016): e0147617.

Page 35 **". . . ultimately 'you use what works'"**: K. Hagey and J. Horwitz, "Facebook Tried to Make Its Platform a Healthier Place. It Got Angrier Instead," *Wall Street Journal*, September 15, 2021.

Page 35 **keep running just to stay in the same place**: The "Red Queen Effect," in which competitive actors need to "keep running to stay in the same place," has implications for strategic behavior in the evolution of social networks, as discussed in Centola, *How Behavior Spreads*; and Damon Centola, "Cultural Tipping Points, Complex Contagion and the Ethics of Change," in *Nobel Symposium Volume* (Oxford University Press, forthcoming).

Page 36 **". . . viral branching process"**: S. Vosoughi, D. Roy, and S. Aral, "The Spread of True and False News Online," *Science* 359, no. 6380 (2018): 1146–1151.

Page 36 **". . . infectiousness of the information"**: There is a tendency for falsehoods to spread virally because they are often *simple contagions*, which can exploit the large number of weak ties connected to centralized hubs; by contrast, hard truths are more often *complex contagions*, which require social reinforcement to spread, and therefore cannot exploit the abundant weak ties flowing from firehose networks, but instead require overlapping networks of wide bridges to reach large numbers of people. These tendencies notwithstanding, the crux of the issue for determining the complexity of these belief contagions is not their truth or falsehood but rather their correspondence with group bias. If an idea accords with group bias, it will typically be accepted prima facie and therefore spread as a simple contagion. If it contradicts groups bias, it will require greater reinforcement to overcome countervailing influences and will typically be a complex contagion. While the examples in this chapter focus on cases in which group bias contradicts the truth of the matter, there may also be situations in which mobilizing extreme points of view in a population of moderates requires adopting the strategies of complex contagion to overcome countervailing influences from reasonable and respected neighbors (see, e.g., Damon Centola, Robb Willer, and Michael Macy, "The Emperor's Dilemma: A Computational Model of Self-Enforcing Norms," *American Journal of Sociology* 110, no. 4 (2005): 1009–1040).

The MIT study of viral spreading was: Soroush Vosoughi, Deb Roy, and Sinan Aral, "The Spread of True and False News Online," *Science* 359, no. 6380 (2018): 1146–1151; the excellent follow-up study was: Jonas Juul and Johan Ugander, "Comparing Information Diffusion Mechanisms by Matching on Cascade Size," *Proceedings of the National Academy of Sciences* 118, no. 46 (2021): e2100786118.

Page 37 **among reluctant conservatives**: A detailed discussion of why highly connected influencers are poorly positioned structurally to influence changes in social norms and behaviors that contravene existing expectations and entrenched beliefs (i.e., to spread *complex contagions*) can be found in Centola, *Change.*

Page 38 **unscrupulous media personalities**: For the details of these examples, see: Renee DiResta's fascinating discussion of her work with the Stanford Internet Observatory in *Invisible Rulers: The People Who Turn Lies into Reality* (Public Affairs, 2024).

Page 38 **almost irresistible falsehoods**: For an excellent analysis of the differences between the spread of anti-vaxxer disinformation versus the spread of accurate information about vaccines, see: Neil F. Johnson, Nicolas Velásquez, Nicolas J. Restrepo, et al., "The Online Competition Between Pro- and Anti-Vaccination Views," *Nature* 582 (2020): 230–233. See also: Victor Suarez-Lledo and Javier Alvarez-Galvez, "Prevalence of Health Misinformation on Social Media: Systematic Review," *Journal of Medical Internet Research* 23, no. 1 (2021): e17187.

Page 38 **from only a handful people**: See this helpful analysis: G. Nogara, P. S. Vishnuprasad, F. Cardoso, O. Ayoub, S. Giordano, and L. Luceri, "The Disinformation Dozen: An Exploratory Analysis of Covid-19 Disinformation Proliferation on Twitter," in *Proceedings of the 14th ACM Web Science Conference 2022* (ACM, 2022); and *The Disinformation Dozen* (Center for Countering Digital Hate, 2021), https://counterhate.com/research/the-disinformation-dozen/.

Page 38 **the bigger the lie, the faster this happens**: A discussion of why big lies are easier to spread than small lies can be found in Centola et al., "The Emperor's Dilemma."

Page 39 **curiouser and curiouser**: Although we know that Alice uses "curiouser and curiouser" to mean "stranger and stranger," my use here is meant to convey that I became increasingly curious, not that I became increasingly strange. Though, who's to say?

Page 43 **fanning the flames of doubt**: For a relevant discussion of the contagion dynamics of vaccine beliefs, see: Damon Centola, "The Complex Contagion of Doubt in the Anti-Vaccine Movement," in *2019 Annual Report of the Sabin-Aspen Vaccine Science & Policy Group* (2020); and Damon Centola, "The Contagion of Doubt: Vaccines and Social Media," *Psychology Today*, May 19, 2021, https://www.psychologytoday.com/us/blog/how-behavior-spreads/202105/the-contagion-doubt-vaccines-and-social-media.

Page 43 **of their social networks**: All participants were debriefed at the conclusion of the study, ensuring that all subjects had access to correct information and were provided with the most current resources and materials regarding vaccines and vaccine safety.

Page 43 **consistent and highly significant**: Reported findings are from Damon Centola, Jingwen Zhang, and Elaine Khoong, "Network Decentralization Disrupts the Spread of Online Disinformation in Vulnerable Populations," *ASC Working Paper* (2026).

Page 46 **network science of collective intelligence**: There are several landmark studies in this literature on networks and collective learning, starting with M. H. DeGroot, "Reaching a Consensus," *Journal of the American Statistical Association* 69, no. 345 (1974): 118–121. Key studies building upon DeGroot's seminal work include: Peter M. DeMarzo, Dimitri Vayanos, and Jeffrey Zwiebel, "Persuasion Bias, Social Influence, and Unidimensional Opinions," *Quarterly Journal of Economics* 118, no. 3 (2003): 909–968; Golub and Jackson, "Naïve Learning in Social Networks"; Jan Lorenz, Heiko Rauhut, Frank Schweitzer, and Dirk Helbing, "How Social Influence Can Undermine the Wisdom of Crowd Effect," *Proceedings of the National Academy of Sciences of the USA* 108, no. 22 (2011): 9020–9025; Cass R. Sunstein, "The Law of Group Polarization," *Journal of Political Philosophy* 10, no. 2 (2002): 175–195; Venkatesh Bala and Sanjeev Goyal, "Learning from Neighbours," *Review of Economic Studies* 65, no. 3 (1998): 595–621; Barbara Mellers et al., "Psychological Strategies for Winning a Geopolitical Forecasting Tournament," *Psychological Science* 25, no. 5 (2014): 1106–1115.

Key studies of networks and collective learning prior to DeGroot (1974) include: Morton Deutsch and Harold B. Gerard, "A Study of Normative and Informational Social Influences Upon Individual Judgement," *Journal of Abnormal Psychology* 51, no. 3 (1955): 629–636; J. R. P. French Jr., "A Formal Theory of Social Power," *Psychological Review* 63 (1956): 181–194; in Dorwin Cartwright and Alvin Zander (eds.), *Group Dynamics*, 3rd ed. (Harper, 1968), 557–568; J. R. P. French Jr. and R. B. Zajonc, "An Experimental Study of Cross-Cultural Norm Conflict," *Journal of Abnormal and*

Social Psychology 54 (1957): 218–224; Frank Harary, "A Criterion for Unanimity in French's Theory of Social Power," in *Studies in Social Power*, ed. Dorwin Cartwright (University of Michigan Press, 1959); Alex Bavelas, "Communication Patterns in Task-Oriented Groups," *Journal of the Acoustical Society of America* 22, no. 6 (1950): 725–730.

Page 46 **from the original group mean**: Daron Acemoglu and his colleagues found similar results: Daron Acemoglu, Munther Dahleh, Ilan Lobel, and Asuman Ozdaglar, "Bayesian Learning in Social Networks," *Review of Economic Studies* 78, no. 4 (2011): 1201–1236.

Page 46 **dynamics of persuasion bias**: In a fantastic set of papers, Jackson and Golub proved several key theorems regarding how DeGroot learning is affected by network structure. First they showed that convergence almost always happens, leading to group consensus, and that the process of convergence is governed by eigenvector centrality: The opinions of the individuals with the greatest eigenvector centrality become the opinions of the entire population. The greater the inequality of centrality, the greater the skew in the collective belief away from the group average (Golub and Jackson, "Naïve Learning in Social Networks"). They further show that the speed of convergence depends upon homophily within the social network (i.e., the clustering of people with similar opinions into the same network neighborhoods). With high levels of homophily, it takes much longer for the entire network to converge because each region of the network coalesces around its own beliefs, which slows down the overall balancing out of opinions across the network. The more integrated the network is, the faster that each neighborhood converges on the same average beliefs, leading to rapid network-wide consensus. Benjamin Golub and Matthew O. Jackson, "Network Structure and the Speed of Learning Measuring Homophily Based on Its Consequences," *Annals of Economics and Statistics*, nos. 107–108 (2012): 33–48.

Page 47 **findings among Colorado voters**: Vincenz Frey and Arnout van de Rijt show that sequential choice settings create order effects in which first movers have disproportionate influence over subsequent actors, creating de facto centralization. These sequential choice settings are shown to reduce collective intelligence in wisdom of the crowd settings (i.e., the grand challenge of choosing). Vincenz Frey and Arnout van de Rijt, "Social Influence Undermines the Wisdom of the Crowd in Sequential Decision Making," *Management Science* 67 (2021): 3985–4642. Similar effects of sequential choice (and de facto centralization) in the grand challenge of coordination are discussed in detail in chapter 13 and in the endnotes to chapter 8.

Page 48 **intelligence stayed the same**: Another group of researchers at the University of Pennsylvania also found that individual accuracy improves through social influence. Burcu Gürçay, Barbara A. Mellers, and Jonathan Baron, "The Power of Social Influence on Estimation Accuracy," *Journal of Behavioral Decision Making* 28, no. 3 (2015): 250–261; Bertrand Jayles et al., "How Social Information Can Improve Estimation Accuracy in Human Groups," *Proceedings of the National Academy of Sciences of the USA* 114 (2017): 12620–12625. Moreover, Gürçay et al. also found that upon reanalysis, the data from Lorenz et al. ("How Social Influence Can Undermine the Wisdom of Crowd Effect") showed improvements in accuracy among participants, consistent with the reanalysis by Simon Farrell: Simon Farrell, "Social Influence Benefits the Wisdom of Individuals in the Crowd," *Proceedings of the National Academy of Sciences of the USA* 108, no. 36 (2011): E625. These results were also consistent with earlier findings on the Delphi method: Gene Rowe and George Wright, "The Delphi Technique as a Forecasting Tool: Issues and Analysis," *International Journal of Forecasting* 15, no. 4 (1999): 353–375.

CHAPTER 3: DECIDING HOW TO DECIDE

Page 52 **just a few hours**: In 1987 dollars, total US losses on Black Monday were approximately $500 billion, and total worldwide losses were $1.71 trillion. See: Ulrike Schaede, "Black Monday in New York, Blue Tuesday in Tokyo: The October 1987 Crash in Japan," *California Management Review* 33, no. 2 (1991): 39–57.

Page 52 **". . . someone yells 'Fire!'"**: "The Market Plunge: Fall Stuns Corporate Leaders," *New York Times*, October 20, 1987, Business Section.

Page 53 ***Financial Analysts Journal***: Jack L. Treynor, "Market Efficiency and the Bean Jar Experiment," *Financial Analysts Journal* 43, no. 3 (1987): 50–53.

Page 53 **true value of the underlying assets**: For a novel evolutionary perspective on the efficient market hypothesis, see: Andrew Lo, "The Adaptive Markets Hypothesis: Market Efficiency from an Evolutionary Perspective," *Journal of Portfolio Management* 30, no. 5 (2004): 15–29.

Page 53 **". . . who err independently"**: Treynor, "Market Efficiency."

Page 55 **no reward for guessing poorly**: One methodological principle that has served both the ecological validity and scientific rigor of this approach to studying collective intelligence using internet-based network experiments is to always ensure that participants are incentivized to win rather than just to show up. In these studies, participants are not compensated for registering, participating, or completing the study. They are compensated solely based on the quality of their final response (which means that many earnest participants may receive no payment). This puts the burden entirely on the experimenter to create social environments with sufficient inherent interest to stimulate participants' engagement in these challenges and to encourage subjects to sign up for future studies (even when they have been unsuccessful in the present one). In chapter 6, I show how these strategies worked for the effective recruitment of thousands of physicians using the same strict compensation rules. The scientific principles, and practical guidelines, that underlie this experimental method are described in Centola, *How Behavior Spreads*.

Page 59 **the same statistical power**: "Because subjects in the control groups were independent from each other, fewer overall subjects were required for the control analyses. Nevertheless, for proper comparison with the experimental conditions, we still conducted our control trials with subjects in groups of 40 and conducted our analyses at the group level." Joshua Becker, Devon Brackbill, and Damon Centola, "Network Dynamics of Social Influence in the Wisdom of Crowds," *Proceedings of the National Academy of Sciences of the USA* 114, no. 26 (2017): 5070–5076.

Page 59 **And so on**: When it comes to calculating the central tendency of a population, Galton preferred the median, while others emphasize the value of the mean. These two measures may coincide if, for instance, a distribution is a perfectly symmetric normal distribution; however, the mean and the median will differ if the distribution is skewed, such as in a lognormal distribution, in which answers reflect a population bias. To identify how both the median and the mean may change under social influence, we examined both "count" questions, in which distributions tend to be skewed toward underestimation, and "percent" questions, in which distributions are symmetrically bounded above and below (i.e., 0 to 100) and thus tend to be symmetric.

Page 61 **increased collective intelligence**: In a fascinating recent study—Abdullah Almaatouq, Alejandro Noriega-Campero, Abdulrahman Alotaibi, P. M. Krafft, Mehdi Moussaid, and Alex Pentland, "Adaptive Social Networks Promote the Wisdom of Crowds," *Proceedings of the National Academy of Sciences of the USA* 117, no. 21 (2020): 11379–11386—Almaatouq et al. find results consistent with these findings; namely, that when the central actor is highly accurate, centralization can increase collective intelligence. However, they suggest that this finding may hold more generally (i.e., outside the conditions I describe). This conclusion unfortunately comes from stylistically bringing in features of the grand challenge of creativity that are outside the empirical and theoretical scope conditions of the challenge of choosing that guides their analysis (both in the theoretical model and the empirical experimental design of their study). In the grand challenge of choosing (such as predicting a stock price), there is no informational feedback about the quality of your guess until after the choice has been made. By contrast, in the grand challenge of creativity, individuals have real-time feedback on the quality of their guesses before their final solutions are chosen. Almaatouq et al. create a mathematical model, and experimental setting, in which individuals must try to solve an estimation challenge while they are able to gather information about the relative quality/accuracy of solutions, while also being given the opportunity to "rewire" their social networks. Naturally, actors quickly drop network ties to peers with low accuracy, and form new ties to peers with high accuracy. As expected, this process of network adaptation results in highly centralized networks in which the central actors are selected based on their accuracy. These findings are consistent with the Case 1 findings discussed in this chapter, which are also discussed in Becker et al., "Network Dynamics." However, a key empirical result from this chapter, elaborating Becker et al., is that individual accuracy varies quite broadly from question to question.

Thus, centralization around an individual who is accurate on a particular question can inevitably lead to a situation in which that individual would be perceived to be "generally" accurate on a range of questions on which they are not.

To preserve the intelligence of a centralized network across different substantive questions, the network would need to continually reorganize around accurate individuals, as in Almaatouq et al. For this to function effectively, individual accuracy on each question would need to be known prior to individuals' final decisions on each question. Thus, in such a design, the only way to preserve collective intelligence would be to assume that players can have a priori knowledge about each individual's accuracy on each question. While this assumption extends beyond the boundary of the grand challenge of choosing, it nevertheless raises interesting questions about how networks might be "guided" to adapt in intelligent ways. Expanding on these ideas, very interesting recent work on this problem has explored the potential for algorithmic approaches to dynamically rewiring networks without requiring information about the "ground truth" relating to individual accuracy; see, for instance: Jason Burton, Abdullah Almaatouq, M. Amin Rahimian, and Ulrike Hahn, "Algorithmically Mediating Communication to Enhance Collective Decision-Making in Online Social Networks," *Collective Intelligence* 3, no. 2 (2024).

The findings in this chapter show how egalitarian networks resolve this problem by enabling collectives to gravitate toward the most accurate responses without requiring any a priori knowledge about individuals' accuracy on any question. This chapter thus highlights a novel form of network adaptation in which the "center" (or most influential location) in the network changes as a function of the changing self-weights (i.e., changing accuracy) of the participants from question to question—even though the network topology itself remains fixed.

Recent, very helpful elaborations of the findings presented in Becker et al. show more precisely how the interaction between network structure and the underlying distribution of beliefs in the population can affect collective learning. These are reported in Almaatouq et al., "The Distribution of Initial Estimates."

Page 62 **far from their expertise**: Once a person occupies a position of influence, they typically remain influential even when the substantive topic ranges far outside their domain of expertise.

Page 62 **information was centralized**: Sequential choice can create de facto centralization of information by giving early movers disproportionate impact over the choices of subsequent movers. See: Frey and van de Rijt, "Social Influence Undermines the Wisdom of the Crowd"; see also Abhijit Banerjee, "A Simple Model of Herd Behavior," *Quarterly Journal of Economics* 107, no. 3 (1992): 797–817. Herding dynamics are those in which early movers can have outsized influence on the "informational" signal for all subsequent movers. See discussions of Banerjee in chapter 13, and in the endnotes to chapter 8.

Page 64 **networks they used were too small**: Interesting work has explored how multiple groups of small size may be used iteratively to increase population intelligence by repeatedly mixing members across modest groups of interacting individuals: Joaquin Navajas, Tamara Niella, Gerry Garbulsky, Bahador Bahrami, and Mariano Sigman, "Aggregated Knowledge from a Small Number of Debates Outperforms the Wisdom of Large Crowds," *Nature Human Behaviour* 2 (2018): 126–132. Related results (with a slightly different framing) are found in N. Pescetelli et al., "Modularity and Composite Diversity Affect the Collective Gathering of Information Online," *Nature Communications* 12 (2021): 3195.

Page 65 **population in new directions**: The key structural factor governing the grand challenge of choosing is network power. (See figure E12.1, *Network continua of speed and power.*) Egalitarian networks can be clustered geographic networks (e.g., lattices), uniform random graphs, or fully connected internet networks. Given the current state of knowledge, there is no reason to expect that collective accuracy would evolve differently in a uniform random graph as compared to a uniform clustered lattice.

Page 65 **to be a mover or a stayer**: In contrast to DeGroot's assumption that there may be heterogeneity of *influence* across neighbors (based on familiarity and tie strength), we discovered that there was heterogeneity in *self-weight*—which is the extent to which individuals listen to their neighbors versus to their own opinion—as a function of an individual's own accuracy. DeGroot, "Reaching a Consensus."

Page 67 **data from the 2011 Swiss study**: Another excellent reanalysis of the Swiss data (Lorenz et al., "How Social Influence Can Undermine the Wisdom of Crowd Effect") was conducted by Gabriel Madirolas and Gonzalo G. de Polavieja, "Improving Collective Estimations Using Resistance to Social Influence," *PLOS Computational Biology* 11, no. 11 (2015): e1004594.

Page 67 **self-reported confidence does not predict anything**: This result has been replicated many times, including Lorenz et al. ("How Social Influence Can Undermine the Wisdom of Crowd Effect"), Madirolas and de Polavieja ("Improving Collective Estimations"), and in our own studies. Doug Guilbeault and Damon Centola, "Networked Collective Intelligence Improves Dissemination of Scientific Information Regarding Smoking Risks," *PLOS One* 15, no. 2 (2020): e0227813; Calvin Isch and Damon Centola, "Experimental Evidence That Social Learning in Structured Information-Sharing Networks Corrects Anchoring Bias," *Journal of Social Computing* (2026).

Page 68 **put them into leadership positions**: This is a solution that has been suggested by Madirolas and de Polavieja ("Improving Collective Estimations"). The challenge, as discussed in the endnotes above, is that individual accuracy changes for each question, and thus raises the central problematic faced by Madirolas and de Polavieja (and others) of how to determine individual accuracy on a question before the question is answered. A clever solution to this problem was suggested by Sam Wooder, a student in my 2025 undergraduate seminar (notably, this is a solution that colleagues have already begun to explore). Mr. Wooder proposed asking each participant to make a wager (i.e., invest a sum of money) on each question, essentially choosing the stakes for their answer. This proposal was based on using the results reported in this chapter (on self-weight versus self-reported confidence) combined with the results reported in the next chapter (on confidence in others) to suggest that an individual's self-weight in their response to a question might be a measurable (detectable) quantity a priori based on the size of the wager that they would be willing to make on their response. A large wager (particularly if this information were private) might thus reveal, prior to answering the question, individuals with high self-weight (and thus high accuracy) on that question, despite their having low self-reported confidence in their answer. Chapter 13 explores how this tension between an individual's self-weight versus their self-reported confidence may illuminate the role of individual agency in the grand challenge of choosing.

Page 68 **following the more confident individual**: The most relevant studies for this discussion include: Bahador Bahrami, Karsten Olsen, Peter E. Latham, Andreas Roepstorff, Geraint Rees, and Chris D. Frith, "Optimally Interacting Minds," *Science* 329, no. 5995 (2010): 1081–1085; Asher Koriat, "The Self-Consistency Model of Subjective Confidence," *Psychological Review* 119, no. 1 (2012): 80–113; Asher Koriat, "When Are Two Heads Better Than One and Why?," *Science* 336, no. 6079 (2012): 360–362; Asher Koriat, "When Two Heads Are Better Than One and When They Can Be Worse: The Amplification Hypothesis," *Journal of Experimental Psychology: General* 144, no. 5 (2015): 934–950.

Page 68 **reflects popular consensus**: These results are consistent with the Dunning–Kruger effect, in which people overestimate their skill level, such that poor performers report high self-confidence. The reciprocal effect is also found, such that higher performers underestimate their quality and report low self-confidence. While the Dunning–Kruger effect is consistent with our findings, it does not offer an explanation for our findings, nor a mechanism for our main insight that persons who are more accurate (yet who correspondingly report lower self-confidence) nevertheless exhibit greater self-weight by sticking with their responses. Justin Kruger and David Dunning, "Unskilled and Unaware of It: How Difficulties in Recognizing One's Own Incompetence Lead to Inflated Self-Assessments," *Journal of Personality and Social Psychology* 77, no. 6 (1999): 1121–1134.

Page 69 **unmoved movers for the network**: The identification of these individuals in egalitarian networks bears an uncanny resemblance to the findings of my colleague at the University of Pennsylvania, Phil Tetlock, in his work on "superforecasters." Tetlock identified "unlikely" individuals who are surprisingly accurate yet do not claim to know more, nor do they seek attention as "experts." This humility found among superforecasters (low reported self-confidence) combined with their extraordinary self-belief (high self-weight) and their impressive performance (high accuracy) invites close comparison between Tetlock's findings and my own. See: Philip E. Tetlock and Dan Gardner, *Superforecasting: The Art and Science of Prediction* (Crown, 2015).

Page 69 **the majority view may be right:** In his experiments on conformity, Solomon Asch found that people could be forced into conformity with an obviously wrong "majority" opinion, as a result of peer influence in sequential choice settings. Notably, Asch found that a small fraction of "independent thinkers" did resist the effects of peer pressure. Asch reported that these independent thinkers nevertheless showed a surprising amount of respect for the incorrect majority (and were unwilling to criticize the incorrect majority opinion). As discussed in chapter 13, these findings are consistent with my own findings that highly accurate individuals exhibit high self-weight and yet low self-reported confidence in their answers. Chapter 13 shows that these observations have surprising implications for the role of individual agency in problems of collective intelligence. Solomon Asch, "Effects of Group Pressure upon the Modification and Distortion of Judgments," in *Groups, Leadership and Men; Research in Human Relations*, ed. Harold Guetzkow (Carnegie Press, 1951).

Page 69 **more extreme and less intelligent**: These observations may be particularly apposite for the study of opinion formation (and collective intelligence) in faculty meetings.

Page 69 **gallop over it with enthusiasm**: For a relevant discussion of how increasing information can increase confidence without increasing accuracy, see Claire I. Tsai, Joshua Klayman, and Reid Hastie, "Effects of Amount of Information on Judgment Accuracy and Confidence," *Organizational Behavior and Human Decision Processes* 107, no. 2 (2008): 97–105.

Page 70 **stand on Condorcet's shoulders**: Once again, we are reminded of Bryan Caplan's study, which uses Condorcet's account of "hard" problems as an argument against the merits of uninformed voters—and in favor of governance by elites. Caplan, *Myth of the Rational Voter.*

Page 70 **to endure under Stalin's rule**: *Groupthink* was coined by the sociologist William Whyte as an attack on growing American acceptance of "rationalized conformity" in corporate and social life (and in the modern science of "social physics"). William Whyte, "Groupthink," *Fortune,* March 1, 1952. Greg Lukianoff and Jonathan Haidt offer an extension and expansion of Whyte's central themes in their analysis of contemporary American undergraduate education. Greg Lukianoff and Jonathan Haidt, *The Coddling of the American Mind: How Good Intentions and Bad Ideas Are Setting Up a Generation for Failure* (Penguin, 2018).

Irving Janis adopted the term *groupthink* for his archival study of policy decision-making in Washington, DC: Irving L. Janis, "Groupthink," *Psychology Today* 5, no. 6 (1971): 43–46, 74–76; Irving L. Janis, *Victims of Groupthink: A Psychological Study of Foreign-Policy Decisions and Fiascoes* (Houghton Mifflin, 1972); Irving L. Janis, *Groupthink: Psychological Studies of Policy Decisions and Fiascoes* (Houghton Mifflin, 1982). Building on Whyte's critique of American culture, Janis used *groupthink* with explicit reference to the self-defeating (and absurd) obedience of the Stalinist crowd detailed in George Orwell's dystopian tale, *1984*.

Page 71 "**. . . Harvard Alumni Association**": The political commentator in this anecdote is Aaron Sorkin, who mouthed this clever line through his character, Ainsley Hayes, in *The West Wing*, season 3, episode 16, "The US Poet Laureate."

Page 71 **because elites are elites**: In academic settings, these concerns about groupthink among highly trained elites offer important reasons why new students are essential for successful scientific research labs. Their untrained eyes keep a steady flow of out-of-the-box ideas and diverse perspectives coming into otherwise top-heavy (and sometimes staid) academic research centers.

CHAPTER 4: HERD IMMUNITY FOR YOUR BRAIN

Page 74 **2002 Nobel Prize in Economics**: The Nobel Prize is not awarded posthumously, otherwise Amos Tversky would have shared the prize. In 2002, the Nobel Prize in Economics went to Daniel Kahneman and Vernon Smith.

Page 75 **questions from the jelly-bean experiment**: The results from this chapter are reported in Calvin Isch and Damon Centola, "Experimental Evidence That Social Learning in Structured Information-Sharing Networks Corrects Anchoring Bias," *Journal of Social Computing* (2026).

Page 75 **the anchor worked perfectly**: A key scientific study for the analysis of anchoring bias is Amos Tversky and Daniel Kahneman, "Judgment Under Uncertainty: Heuristics and Biases," *Science* 185, no. 4157 (1974): 1124–1131.

The "anchoring index" is the measure of the impact of an anchor on individual judgment in experimental settings. It is calculated as follows:

$$\text{Anchoring Index} = \frac{\Delta\ \text{Estimate}}{A_H - A_L}$$

where:

Δ Estimate—Difference in average estimates of those given higher anchor and lower anchor.

A_H—The high anchor.

A_L—The low anchor.

Page 78 **unlikely to be an influencer**: As discussed in the endnotes for chapter 3, our results showing greater "confidence in others" among individuals who have (i) the greatest self-weight; (ii) the greatest accuracy, and (iii) the lowest self-reported confidence in their own answer, resonate with Tetlock's characterization of the humility found among "superforecasters." These observations also align with Asch's findings that "independent thinkers," who exhibited steadfast adherence to the correct answer (standing against an incorrect majority), also exhibited low self-reported confidence in their own responses, and showed a great reluctance to criticize the incorrect majority. The practical implications of these findings for systems of collective decision-making are elaborated in chapter 13 and in the epilogue. Tetlock, *Superforecasters*; Asch, "Effects of Group Pressure."

Chapter 5: When Echo Chambers Are Smart

Page 83 **". . . legally or illegally"**: This fascinating tale of American woe was reported in *This American Life*, "Fear and Loathing in Homer and Rockville," episode 621, first aired on July 21, 2017. Unless otherwise noted, all quotes in this chapter are drawn from this report.

Page 85 **predictions about climate change**: These results were reported in Douglas Guilbeault, Joshua Becker, and Damon Centola, "Social Learning and Partisan Bias in the Interpretation of Climate Trends," *Proceedings of the National Academy of Sciences of the USA* 115, no. 39 (2018): 9714–9719.

Page 86 **into their ideological camps**: There is a long tradition of research on this phenomenon of "biased assimilation," including: Charles G. Lord, Lee Ross, and Mark R. Lepper, "Biased Assimilation and Attitude Polarization: The Effects of Prior Theories on Subsequently Considered Evidence," *Journal of Personality and Social Psychology* 37, no. 11 (1979): 2098–2109; Adam Corner, Lorraine Whitmarsh, and Dimitrios Xenias, "Uncertainty, Skepticism and Attitudes Toward Climate Change: Biased Assimilation and Attitude Polarization," *Climatic Change* 114 (2012): 463–478; and Geoffrey D. Munro and Peter H. Ditto, "Biased Assimilation, Attitude Polarization, and Affect in Reactions to Stereotype-Relevant Scientific Information," *Personality and Social Psychology Bulletin* 23, no. 6 (1997): 636–653. Also see more recent work on this topic by Chris Bail, Lisa P. Argyle, Taylor W. Brown, John P. Bumpus, Haohan Chen, M. B. Fallin Hunzaker, et al., "Exposure to Opposition Views on Social Media Can Increase Political Polarization," *Proceedings of the National Academy of Sciences of the USA* 115, no. 37 (2018): 9216–9221.

Page 86 **". . . controlling its *effects*"**: Madison, "Federalist No. 10."

Page 86 **four homogeneous groups**: These results were originally reported in Joshua Becker, Ethan Porter, and Damon Centola, "The Wisdom of Partisan Crowds," *Proceedings of the National Academy of Sciences of the USA* 116, no. 22 (2019): 10717–10722.

Page 87 **reconsider their responses**: The findings for control groups did not reach the threshold for statistical significance, but they were notable since they were consistently in the same direction across trials, as shown in figure E.5.1, adapted from Becker, Porter, and Centola, "The Wisdom of Partisan Crowds."

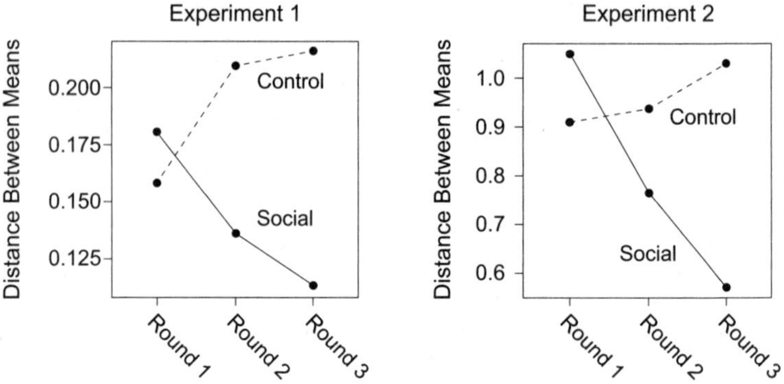

FIGURE E.5.1

Page 93 **two true and two false**: A fascinating study from the Annenberg Public Policy Center at the University of Pennsylvania shows how changing the identity of the source for new scientific information (e.g., NASA versus IPCC) significantly alters consumers' ability to understand and believe it. These "source effects" are detailed in: Kathleen Hall Jamieson and Bruce Hardy, "Leveraging Scientific Credibility About Arctic Sea Ice Trends in a Polarized Political Environment," *Proceedings of the National Academy of Sciences of the USA* 111, suppl. 4 (2014):13598–13605.

Page 93 **which are true and which are false**: The answers are: (1) false, (2) true, (3) false, (4) true.

Page 94 **true stories from false stories**: These findings were originally published in Douglas Guilbeault, Samuel Woolley, and Joshua Becker, "Probabilistic Social Learning Improves the Public's Judgments of News Veracity," *PLOS One* 16, no. 3 (2021): e0247487.

Page 95 **". . . possession of the multitude"**: This famous passage is from John Dewey, *The Public and Its Problems* (Allen & Unwin, 1927).

Page 96 **". . . developed countries in 2030?"**: The correct answer was based on available global population statistics when the experiments were conducted (in 2018). For more details, see: Doug Guilbeault and Damon Centola, "Networked Collective Intelligence Improves Dissemination of Scientific Information Regarding Smoking Risks," *PLOS One* 15 (2020): e0227813.

Page 97 **how people feel about one another**: The findings in this chapter raise an interesting theoretical and practical tension between the merits of *cross-group contact* and the merits of *group anonymity* for structural intelligence.

Earlier in this chapter, I showed you that partisan identity and partisan priming could undermine collective intelligence in bipartisan networks (Guilbeault et al., "Social Learning and Partisan Bias"; Bail et al., "Exposure to Opposition Views on

Social Media"). However, you also saw that those same factors could improve collective learning in politically homogeneous groups (i.e., "echo chambers"). The explanation for these opposing results is that within politically homogeneous groups, contextual features that amplify group identity can make partisans more willing to listen to members of their same group or "tribe." By contrast, in cross-party networks, political identifiers and party symbols may only serve to remind participants of the animus that they feel for the outgroup, thereby undermining the (very high) potential for collective learning that exists in bipartisan networks.

A puzzle arises from comparing these findings to the study of smokers and nonsmokers (Guilbeault and Centola, "Networked Collective Intelligence Improves Dissemination"), in which we found that, in cross-group networks, revealing people's group memberships (i.e., as smokers or nonsmokers) led to not only greater collective intelligence but also improved valuation of outgroup opinions. In these networks with group identity revealed, nonsmokers came to have higher regard for the opinions of smokers.

This result introduces a new element into the findings that is inconsistent with the results from the political networks. Our new puzzle is this: Do cross-group interactions in which "outgroup" identity is revealed increase collective learning, or undermine it?

One of the most debated yet long-standing hypotheses in contemporary sociology is Gordon Allport's contact hypothesis: that increasing intergroup contact would reduce cross-group hostility and increase cross-group understanding. The rub, of course, is that this hypothesis depends crucially on what intergroup contact consists of. Allport insists on four conditions: status equality, common goals, cooperation, and the support of law and custom. An enormous literature has arisen on this topic, most recently related to political polarization, exploring the benefits and pitfalls of increasing cross-group contact in bipartisan groups. Gordon Allport, *The Nature of Prejudice* (Perseus, 1954).

In the smoking study, we found that cross-group interactions in which group identities were revealed can improve collective intelligence and cross-group empathy. We might refer to this as an "Allport effect" in honor of the contact hypothesis, since our results showed that cross-group interactions generated increased understanding and empathy across those groups. Yet while our study of smokers and nonsmokers seems to support the Allport effect, this was certainly not what we found in the political networks.

The obvious difference is that tribal loyalties do not run as deep between smokers and nonsmokers as they do between political parties. This observation has face validity, but it lacks a scientific account: That is, it does not offer us mechanisms or parameters that help to anticipate the conditions under which revealing group identity will help improve collective intelligence versus those in which maintaining anonymity will best serve collective intelligence. This puzzle offers a new frontier for scientific work on structural intelligence.

Going further, there is another result that makes this question of anonymity even more complex (and more scientifically interesting). In chapter 6, you will see a series of studies in which anonymity among doctors participating in clinical information-exchange networks facilitates collective learning. Concealing the identity of clinicians is important because it eliminates factors such as status and rank, which can interfere with learning dynamics in egalitarian networks. In particular, although junior physicians are more inclined to defer to senior physicians in their clinical judgments, there may be some topics for which junior physicians have more accurate knowledge because (for instance) they have more recently been exposed to the latest clinical guidelines through their fellowship training, or because their expectations for cultural competency or their exposure to diverse patients are greater due to improved training modules in contemporary medical programs. For these and other reasons, preserving the egalitarianism in peer-learning networks in medicine may depend not only on having an egalitarian topological structure in the information-sharing networks but also on ensuring anonymity among the participants.

These effects of revealing identity versus maintaining anonymity among physicians are distinct from either the case of political adversaries or the case of diverse public health groups. The potential for factors such as status and rank to create unequal patterns of influence may also arise in other organizational settings, such as in financial investment centers or legal institutions where established hierarchies can create influence inequalities that can undermine collective intelligence; in these settings, anonymity would seem to improve the intelligence of network interactions. While these observations have face validity, there is as yet little scientific understanding of the actual parameters that define when anonymity amplifies the dynamics collective intelligence versus when it may hinder it. These observations offer important opportunities for new research on structural intelligence.

Page 97 **an intelligent consensus**: There is a large secondary literature on the use of the "ideal speech situation" as a philosophical tool (akin to Rawls's "original position"). Rawls, *A Theory of Justice*. The discussion here is based on Jürgen Habermas's articulation of the ideal speech situation in *Between Facts and Norms: Contributions to a Discourse Theory of Law and Democracy* (MIT Press, 1996).

CHAPTER 6: THE MYTH OF THE RATIONAL DOCTOR

Page 101 **". . . entire health care team"**: National Academies of Sciences, Engineering, and Medicine, *Improving Diagnosis in Health Care* (The National Academies Press, 2015).

Page 101 **reduce medical errors**: Many researchers have explored a range of "wisdom of the crowd" approaches to medical collective intelligence. Those using Galton-style estimation tasks include: Ralf H. J. M. Kurvers, Stefan M. Herzog, Ralph Hertwig, Jens Krause, Patricia A. Carney, Andy Bogart, Giuseppe Argenziano, et al., "Boosting Medical Diagnostics by Pooling Independent Judgments," *Proceedings of* *the National Academy of Sciences of the USA* 113, no. 31 (2016): 8777–8782; Juliane E. Kämmer, Wolf E. Hautz, Stefan M. Herzog, Olga Kunina-Habenicht, and Ralf H. J. M. Kurvers, "The Potential of Collective Intelligence in Emergency Medicine: Pooling Medical Students' Independent Decisions Improves Diagnostic Performance," *Medical Decision Making* 37, no. 6 (2017): 715–724; Michael W. Kattan, Colin O'Rourke, Changhong Yu, and Kevin Chagin, "The Wisdom of Crowds of Doctors: Their Average Predictions Outperform Their Individual Ones," *Medical Decision Making* 36, no. 4 (2016): 536–540. Those using Condorcet-style discrete choice include: Max Wolf, Jens Krause, Patricia A. Carney, Andy Bogart, and Ralf H. J. M. Kurvers, "Collective Intelligence Meets Medical Decision-Making: The Collective Outperforms the Best Radiologist," *PLOS One* 10, no. 8 (2015): e0134269. Several of the coauthors on my studies reported in this chapter have published an excellent review article on the state of research on "medical collective intelligence" (as of 2019, prior to the studies presented in this chapter): Kate Radcliffe, Helena C. Lyson, Jill Barr-Walker, and Urmimala Sarkar, "Collective Intelligence in Medical Decision-Making: A Systematic Scoping Review," *BMC Medical Informatics and Decision Making* 19, no. 1 (2019): 158.

In one particularly striking study, over the course of many months several researchers at Duke University recorded the decisions of 29 junior doctors (residents and fellows) and four senior doctors (attending physicians) as they estimated the survival rates of over 260 patients entering the local hospital for a variety of conditions. (See Robert L. Winkler and Roy M. Poses, "Evaluating and Combining Physicians' Probabilities of Survival in an Intensive Care Unit," *Management Science* 39, no. 12 (1993): 1526–1543.)

As you would expect, the senior clinicians were more accurate in their estimates than the junior clinicians. However, following Galton's lead, the researchers combined the predictions of the junior staff—so that individuals' overestimates and underestimates canceled each other out—leaving only the average prediction of the juniors. Even with everything you know, it's still a little surprising that the average prediction of the junior doctors was more accurate than the individual predictions of the senior physicians.

You've seen enough by now to believe this result.

So, let me ask you: Next time you go to the hospital, would you prefer to be seen by a group of novice doctors or an expert clinician?

The problem with the classic wisdom of the crowd in medicine is that in real life a single person needs to make a decision. So when it comes to real decisions, we all revert back to the good old fashioned logic of going with the expert. Although a crowd may be wise on average, its wisdom comes from the fact that its individual members are not. For Galton, crowds are only wise because individuals remain dumb—it takes many wrongs to make a right. Thus, while the Duke study showed that the crowd of novice doctors was wise on average, there was no mechanism for their collective wisdom to have any bearing on individual clinical decisions, to say nothing of improving the quality of patient care. The goal of the work reported in this chapter is to change that.

The findings presented in this chapter were first reported in Damon Centola, Douglas Guilbeault, Urmimala Sarkar, Elaine Khoong, and Jingwen Zhang, "The Reduction of Race and Gender Bias in Clinical Treatment Recommendations Using Clinician Peer Networks in an Experimental Setting," *Nature Communications* 12 (2021): 6585; and Damon Centola, Joshua Becker, Jingwen Zhang, Jaya Aysola, Douglas Guilbeault, and Elaine Khoong, "Experimental Evidence for Structured Information-Sharing Networks Reducing Medical Errors," *Proceedings of the National Academy of Sciences of the USA* 120, no. 31 (2023): e2108290120.

Page 101 **a patient checklist**: Background reading on the development of the patient checklist can be found in: Atul Gawande, *The Checklist Manifesto: How to Get Things Right* (Picador, 2010); Brigette Hales, Marius Terblanche, Robert Fowler, and William Sibbald, "Development of Medical Checklists for Improved Quality of Patient Care," *International Journal for Quality in Health Care* 20, no. 1 (2008): 22–30; Jaishankar Raman, Nancy Leveson, Aubrey Lynn Samost, Nikola Dobrilovic, Maggie Oldham, Sidney Dekker, and Stan Finkelstein, "When a Checklist Is Not Enough: How to Improve Them and What Else Is Needed," *Journal of Thoracic and Cardiovascular Surgery* 152, no. 2 (2016): 585–592.

Page 102 **by their network of peers**: For a more general discussion of how peer networks influence medical decision-making, see Centola, *Change*; see also Craig Pollack, Pamela R. Soulos, Jeph Herrin, Xiao Xu, Nicholas A. Christakis, Howard P. Forman, et al., "The Impact of Social Contagion on Physician Adoption of Advanced Imaging Tests in Breast Cancer," *Journal of the National Cancer Institute* 109, no. 8 (2017): djw330; Nancy Keating, A. James O'Malley, Jukka-Pekka Onnela, Stacy W. Gray, and Bruce E. Landon, "Association of Physician Peer Influence with Subsequent Physician Adoption and Use of Bevacizumab," *JAMA Network Open* 3, no. 1 (2020): e1918586; and Damon Centola, "Physician Networks and the Complex Contagion of Clinical Treatment," *JAMA Network Open* 3, no. 1 (2020): e1918585. Important work on this topic comes from the classic studies of the adoption of medical innovation by James Coleman, Elihu Katz, and Herbert Menzel, "The Diffusion of an Innovation Among Physicians," *Sociometry* 20 (1957): 253–270.

Page 104 **across the United States**: My coauthors on these studies were Jaya Aysola, Joshua Becker, Douglas Guilbeault, Elaine Khoong, Urmimala Sarkar, and Jingwen Zhang.

Page 105 **to independent control groups**: Independent reflection helped nominally in control groups—small (but not significant) improvements were found; however, improvements in egalitarian networks were significantly greater.

Page 106 **a woman's likelihood of being victimized in medicine**: This discussion is from Damon Centola, "Medical Bias Can Be Deadly. Our Research Found a Way to Curb It," *Los Angeles Times*, November 29, 2021.

Page 106 **nearly died from it**: There is a staggering volume of evidence for this problem. A few of the leading studies are: Kevin Schulman, Jesse A. Berlin, William Harless, Jon F. Kerner, Shyrl Sistrunk, Bernard J. Gersh, et al., "The Effect of Race and Sex on Physicians' Recommendations for Cardiac Catheterization," *New England Journal of Medicine* 340, no. 8 (1999): 618–626; William Hall, Mimi V. Chapman, Kent M. Lee, Yesenia M. Merino, Tainayah W. Thomas, B. Keith Payne, et al., "Implicit Racial/Ethnic Bias Among Health Care Professionals and Its Influence on Health Care Outcomes: A Systematic Review," *American Journal of Public Health* 105, no. 12 (2015): e60–e76; and Ashley N. Kyalwazi, Eméfah C. Loccoh, LaPrincess C. Brewer, Elizabeth O. Ofili, Jiaman Xu, Yang Song, et al., "Disparities in Cardiovascular Mortality Between Black and White Adults in the United States, 1999 to 2019," *Circulation* 146, no. 3 (2022): 211–228.

Page 107 **But the data show that it doesn't work**: Several excellent studies include Javeed Sukhera, Christopher Watling, and Cristina Gonzalez, "Implicit Bias in Health Professions: From Recognition to Transformation," *Academic Medicine* 95, no. 5 (2020): 717–723; Colin Zestcott, Iren Blair, and Jeff Stone, "Examining the Presence, Consequences, and Reduction of Implicit Bias in Health Care: A Narrative Review," *Group Processes & Intergroup Relations* 19, no. 4 (2016): 528–542; Elizabeth Chapman, Anna Kaatz, and Molly Carnes, "Physicians and Implicit Bias: How Doctors May Unwittingly Perpetuate Health Care Disparities," *Journal of General Internal Medicine* 28, no. 11 (2013): 1504–1510; Cayla Teal, Anne Gill, Alexander Green, and Sonia Crandall, "Helping Medical Learners Recognise and Manage Unconscious Bias Toward Certain Patient Groups," *Journal of Medical Education* 46, no. 1 (2012): 80–88.

Page 111 **problems have been identified**: See Paul Starr, *The Social Transformation of American Medicine* (Basic Books, 1982), for an illuminating history of the norms, incentives, influences, and entrenchment that shaped the American Medical Association and its associated professional practices.

Page 112 **on the use of e-consults**: All quotes in this discussion are from the helpful review of e-consults cases by C. Liddy, J. Joschko, S. Guglani, A. Afkham, and E. Keely, "Improving Equity of Access Through Electronic Consultation: A Case Study of an eConsult Service," *Frontiers in Public Health* 7 (2019) 7: 279; and from Dr. Atanda's address to the American Medical Association, which is reported in Tanya Albert Henry, "What e-Consults Can Do for Your Patients—and Your Practice," *AMA Digital Health*, July 25, 2023, https://www.ama-assn.org/practice-management/digital-health/what-e-consults-can-do-your-patients-and-your-practice.

Page 112 **". . . by the original physician"**: This quote is from Dr. Atanda's address to the American Medical Association, which is reported in Henry, "What e-Consults Can Do for Your Patients."

Page 114 **using digital technologies**: Several technologies that are already available for crowdsourced collective intelligence in medicine are: Crowdmed, https://www

.crowdmed.com (2023); HumanDx, https://www.humandx.org (2023); and Sermo, https://www.sermo.com (2023), among others. However, there are also notable challenges with technologies that do not adopt a structured network approach to medical collective intelligence. See: Elaine Khoong, Sarah S. Nouri, Delphine Tuot, Shantanu Nundy, Valy Fontil, and Urmimala Sarkar, "Comparison of Diagnostic Recommendations from Individual Physicians Versus the Collective Intelligence of Multiple Physicians in Ambulatory Cases Referred for Specialist Consultation," *Medical Decision Making* 42, no. 3 (2022): 293–302.

Page 114 **the advice they gave**: In Centola et al., "Reducing Medical Errors," we conclude:

> From a digital infrastructure perspective, the growing digitization of healthcare has resulted in a healthcare information technology infrastructure that could be adapted to include collaboration networks identical to the ones created for this study. Importantly, clinician acceptance of an intervention like this is greatly facilitated by the fact that many clinicians are accustomed to submitting and reviewing clinical cases on digital platforms. Digital case platforms are used not only for training purposes but also within current clinical care in the form of electronic consultations, or e-consults.
>
> E-consult technologies have been increasingly adopted within underresourced health systems, especially those with limited access to specialties. Within e-consult platforms, clinicians describe a clinical case and then submit it electronically for consultation with a specialist. Within a short timeframe (typically 24 to 48 h), the specialist then replies with their recommendations, and the referring clinician can then consider these recommendations when providing care for the patient. As more health systems adopt e-consults, we anticipate it will be feasible to harness medical collective intelligence from decentralized information-sharing networks within e-consult platforms. We anticipate, for instance, that instead of sending clinical cases to a single specialist, clinicians may instead submit cases to a network of specialists who participate in a structured information exchange process before providing a recommendation to the referring clinician. The clinician could then use the network feedback to inform their decision-making, consistent with current e-consults practices [as shown below in figure E.6.1].
>
> Our findings indicate that a proper implementation infrastructure, as described in our study, integrated within existing healthcare technologies may enable referring clinicians from any geographic location to benefit directly from the striking improvements in patient care that come from real-time engagement with medical collective intelligence, yet without requiring changes to the current e-consults experience or timeline.

Page 114 **whole lot smarter for everyone**: Structural sociologists such as Karl Marx famously argue that freedom comes from perceiving yourself in terms of social structure (e.g., "class consciousness"). My view of structure is different. The findings from the grand challenge of choosing show that social structure is not necessarily a prison from which we need to be liberated. To the contrary, egalitarian structures can be a mechanism for intellectual liberation—even when people are oblivious to the role of structure. Nevertheless, awareness of structure can be helpful for an interventionist who wants to alter existing structures—or design new ones—to increase the intelligence of their collectives.

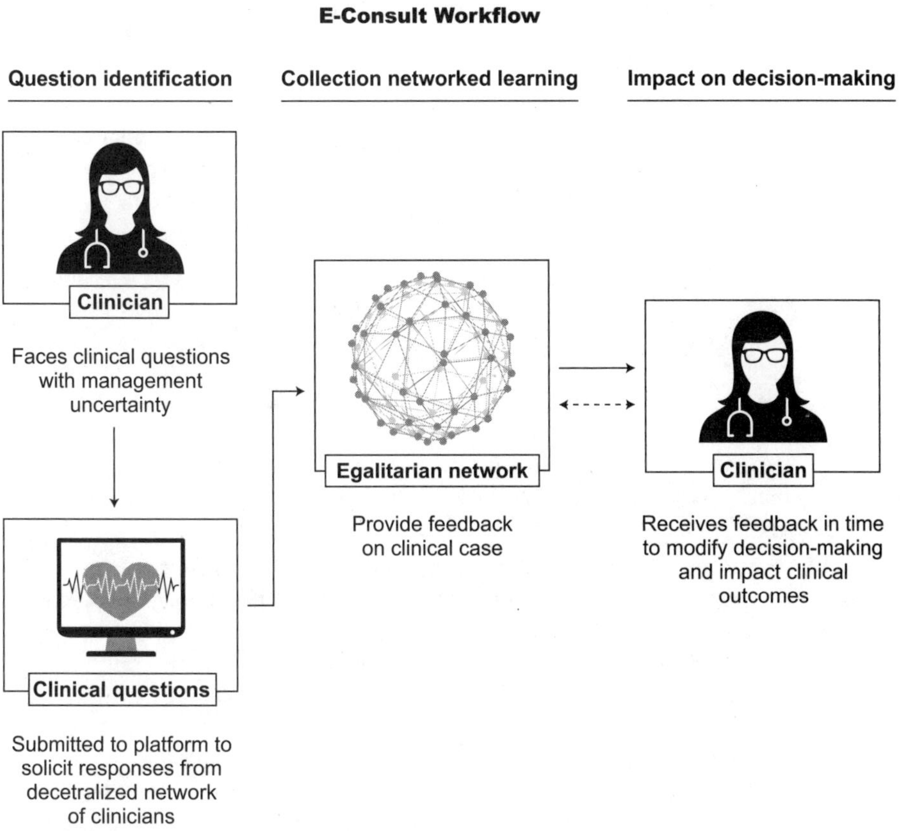

FIGURE E.6.1
E-consult workflow

PART II: COORDINATION: CONVENTION AND QUALITY

CHAPTER 7: SYNCING UP WITHOUT TRYING

Page 119 **smart in the first place**: The focus of this chapter is convention, as formalized by the philosopher David Lewis in *Convention: A Philosophical Study* (Harvard University Press, 1969). Conventions are coordination problems in which the actors are indifferent regarding which option they coordinate on—all that matters is that they coordinate. To illustrate this, the philosopher David Hume (*An Enquiry Concerning Human Understanding,* 1748) uses the example of two people sitting in a rowboat. It does not matter whether they row fast or slow, or forward or backward. All that matters is that they agree to row in the same way together. Once that coordination problem is solved, then they can both get to where they are going. The more rowers there are in the boat, the more important coordination is, and the more difficult the coordination challenge is. For this reason, Hume identifies the challenge of convention as a foundational challenge for civil society.

Beyond the problem of convention, there are several other strategic situations that have been broadly categorized as problems of coordination. Most of these challenges are not addressed in this chapter, but I will review them briefly to clarify what is (and what is not) addressed here and to provide a general overview of the variety of challenges of coordination, which are of interest for many readers:

(1) "Convention" or "pure coordination," discussed in this chapter, is a coordination challenge in which all coordination options have the same payoff; players receive the same reward for successful coordination regardless of the option they coordinate on, and they receive no payoff for failures to coordinate. See Peyton Young, "The Evolution of Conventions," *Econometrica* 61 (1993): 57–84; Damon Centola and Andrea Baronchelli, "The Spontaneous Emergence of Conventions: An Experimental Study of Cultural Evolution," *Proceedings of the National Academy of Sciences of the USA* 112 (2015): 1989–1994.

(2) A different kind of coordination problem involves "payoff dominance," in which one option has a higher payoff than the other(s); players receive greater rewards for coordinating on the better option rather than the inferior option, but they receive no reward for failing to coordinate. This can result in some instances in which entire populations coordinate on the inferior option. Classic economic work on equilibrium selection can be found in John Harsanyi and Reinhard Selten, *A General Theory of Equilibrium Selection in Games* (MIT Press, 1988); Brian Arthur, "Self-Reinforcing Mechanisms in Economics," in *The Economy as an Evolving Complex System,* ed. K. Arrow and P. Anderson (Addison-Wesley, 1988); and Peyton Young, "The Economics of Convention," *Journal of Economic Perspectives* 10, no. 2 (1996): 105–122.

(3) There are some coordination games known as "stag hunt" games, in which there is a high payoff ("payoff dominant") option and a lower payoff ("risk dominant") option. Players receive the greatest reward for coordinating on the payoff dominant option. However, if they fail to coordinate, the payoff dominant option offers zero rewards, but the risk dominant option yields a small reward. The risk dominant payoff is the same regardless of whether players coordinate on it, or if one player chooses it unilaterally. This makes the risk dominant option the safer play, since it does not require coordinating with the other player. There are several versions of stag hunt games, but they all have the same general tension between high payoff coordination versus the safer solitary option. The discovery of this particular coordination challenge is often attributed to Jean-Jacques Rousseau (*The Social Contract*, 1762). See also: Brian Skyrms, *Evolution of the Social Contract* (Cambridge University Press, 1996); Brian Skyrms, *The Stag Hunt and the Evolution of Social Structure*

(Cambridge University Press, 2003); and Harsanyi and Selten, *General Theory of Equilibrium Selection*.

(4) A somewhat more byzantine coordination game is anachronistically called "the battle of the sexes" (which today would more appropriately be called "the battle of the spouses"). In this game, each players prefers a different activity (e.g., one prefers surfing and the other kayaking); however, whichever activity they do, they both prefer to do it together than alone. If players fail to coordinate, they both receive no payoff, but to coordinate, one player must agree to choose an option that is not their first preference.

What all of these social situations—commonly referred to as "coordination games"—have in common is that people are attempting to align their choices with one another. The main reason for failure is fear. People don't know what others will do, and they are afraid to change their behavior to match the other player's choice without a guarantee that they will successfully match up with others. Because of the inherent risk of failing to coordinate, once players find an option that works (an option on which they have coordinated in the past or which allows them to achieve some reward), they are reluctant to switch to a new option without assurances that others will match their new choice. (This is why some coordination games are referred to as *assurance games*.)

There are many other kinds of social dilemmas that could conceivably fall into the domain of coordination challenges yet only have a peripheral relationship to the coordination problem discussed in this chapter; for instance, the "coloring problem" in computer science (Stephen Judd, Michael Kearns, and Yevgeniy Vorobeychik, "Behavioral Dynamics and Influence in Networked Coloring and Consensus," *Proceedings of the National Academy of Sciences of the USA* 107, no. 34 (2010): 14978–14982); and "matching markets," in which actors must find peers to match with who also want to match with them (e.g., marriage markets, kidney exchanges, etc.). The matching market challenge is discussed briefly in chapter 9, regarding the challenge of matching organ donors and recipients.

The present chapter focuses exclusively on the challenge of convention, in which all available options have equivalent value. Thus, it does not matter which option players choose, so long as they all choose the same one. The findings in this chapter show that increasing connectedness (reduced simple path length) accelerates network-wide convergence, offering a structural solution for the grand challenge of coordination.

Research focusing on payoff dominance, consistent with the studies of "quality" in cultural synchronization discussed in chapter 8, similarly show that increasing connectedness improves collective intelligence in the challenge of coordination by accelerating population convergence on the high payoff equilibrium. By contrast, research on "risk dominance" in Stag Hunt coordination games shows that global convergence on the risk dominant equilibrium is accelerated by reducing network connectivity in the population. Thus, the same geographic networks that slow down global coordination on conventions can in fact accelerate global coordination on a risk dominant equilibrium (Glenn Ellison, "Learning, Local Interaction, and Coordination," *Econometrica* 61 (1993): 1047–1071; Peyton Young, *Individual Strategy and Social Structure* (Princeton University Press, 1998); Gabriel Kreindler and Peyton Young, "Rapid Innovation Diffusion in Social Networks," *Proceedings of the National Academy of Sciences of the USA* 111, suppl. 3 (2014): 10881–10888; Andrea Montanari and Amin Saberi, "The Spread of Innovations in Social Networks," *Proceedings of the National Academy of Sciences of the USA* 107, no. 47 (2010): 20196–20201). These findings suggest that the best structure for solving the grand challenge of coordination depends on whether the challenge is a pure coordination game (i.e., convention), in which case the best structure is an informationally efficient internet structure, or a stag hunt (i.e., has a risk-dominant equilibrium), in which case the preferred structure is a clustered lattice network. However, there is a way to reconcile these findings.

Resolution comes from the fact that although structures with increased connectivity (like the internet structure) appear inefficient for the stag hunt because they slow down convergence on the risk dominant equilibrium, it is useful to note that the risk dominant equilibrium is not a collectively intelligent solution to the grand challenge of coordination. Rather, the collectively intelligent solution is for players *not* to be lured into the safety of the risk dominant solution (of coordinating on "hare") but instead to collectively coordinate on the payoff dominant solution (of coordinating on "stag").

From the viewpoint of collective intelligence, a highly connected internet network preserves populations' ability to achieve successful coordination on the high payoff option while it slows down their convergence on the risk dominant (lower payoff) equilibrium. Consistent with the findings on convention, informationally efficient internet structures improve collective intelligence in the grand challenge of coordination, while geographic structures slow down coordination on the collectively intelligent solution. Brian Skyrms discusses the nuances of these results, which depend on incidental features of the stag hunt game (as formalized in evolutionary game theory), such as varying individual decisions rules like "imitate the best" versus "best response." See Brian Skyrms, *Evolution of the Social Contract*, and *Stag Hunt* for details.

A provisional conclusion from these observations is that the internet structure is generally the best-performing structure for improving collective intelligence in a variety of coordination challenges. A notable exception is the battle of the spouses, which does not have a preferred ("intelligent") outcome in terms of which coordination equilibrium is selected; however, recent work shows that network structure can alter whether an entire population selects the same equilibrium, or whether there is diversity in the equilibria that emerge across a population. The key network feature governing these different outcomes is modularity—i.e., the "groupiness" of the network—which determines whether the population is segmented into distinct clusters (some choosing "kayaking" while others choose "surfing") or whether there is uniformity across the population, e.g., with all couples choosing "kayaking." See Joris Broere, Vincent Buskens, Henk Stoof, and Angel Sánchez, "An Experimental

Study of Network Effects on Coordination in Asymmetric Games," *Scientific Reports* 9, no. 6842 (2019).

Importantly, the grand challenge of coordination does not involve the strategic element of greed. Generally speaking, in coordination problems, players cannot win more by tricking their opponent into doing something that they themselves do not also do (there are variants of the stag hunt in which this form of trickery does arise; however, this strategic result still falls short of the best outcome, in which both players coordinate on "stag"). Rather, the mutual (and collectively intelligent) goal is to coordinate on the option that gives all players the greatest reward. Thus, the main obstacle to success is players' fear that the other player will fail to coordinate with them.

The problem of greed arises in the grand challenge of cooperation, discussed in chapter 9. In this challenge, individuals can exploit one another to gain greater rewards; however, they also run the risk of losing everything if they fail to reach an agreement. Collective intelligence requires overcoming the problem of greed to reach a mutually beneficial (i.e., "fair") outcome. The grand challenge of cooperation arises in classic bargaining dilemmas, in which actors must agree on a price that is mutually acceptable or else fail to make a deal at all. Greed also arises in the classic prisoner's dilemma problem. That particular social dilemma is made significantly more difficult because achieving collectively intelligent outcomes requires that players overcome not only their own greed, but also the fear that their partner will succumb to greed. Thus, the prisoner's dilemma is a challenge of cooperation that is famously difficult to solve because players must simultaneously overcome both fear and greed. Chapter 9 shows the role of structural intelligence in resolving the grand challenge of cooperation.

Page 120 **". . . 'spam mail' was born"**: "Why Is Junk Mail Called Spam? A Brief Inbox History," *Microsoft 365 Life Hacks*, May 12, 2023 (updated February 19, 2925), https://www.microsoft.com/en-us/microsoft-365-life-hacks/privacy-and-safety/what-is-email-spam.

Page 122 **before society has taken hold**: A more recent application of the state of nature comes from John Rawls's idea of the "original position" (*A Theory of Justice*). Rawls invents a thought experiment in which people evaluate the fairness of social and economic policies while they sit behind a "veil of ignorance," in which they have no information about their own identity. This is a social contract approach to the Kantian task of finding the "categorical imperative": a moral principle that each of us would agree to, such that it can be applied both to ourselves and to everyone else without any contradiction. For instance, without knowing your own race, gender, sexual orientation, intelligence, social status, income level, etc., how would you choose to structure society in order to ensure that it is fair? Rawls's argument is that in this "original position" each of us would reason our way to an identical conclusion—a set of moral and economic principles for society that are equally fair for everyone.

Prior to Rawls's late-twentieth-century incarnation of the state of nature, social contract theorists employed the state of nature as a tool to reveal what society must guarantee to humans to lure them away from the "freedom" of the wild and become "civilized." The solution to the social contract problem depends essentially on what kind of creatures humans are and what our existence is like in the state of nature. Is the state of nature an abundant garden of pleasures or a Dantean hellscape? Starting from these assumptions about the original position, social contract theorists asked: What kinds of benefits would a social contract need to guarantee each person (in terms of rights, liberties, protections, etc.) in order for them to rationally justify giving up the wild freedoms of the state of nature in exchange for becoming domesticated members of society? The answer to this question offers a philosophical justification for why a government can exercise power over its populace—the social contract tells us what a fair and moral government must offer its citizens in exchange for their obedience. Correspondingly, it also reminds us that a government that fails to provide these protections and assurances is no longer justified in exercising authority over us. This conception of natural rights played a significant role in the framing of the United States Declaration of Independence.

Page 122 **how is society even possible?** This question was also raised by the phenomenological sociologist Georg Simmel. In his attempt to answer a sociological version of the fundamental question asked by Immanuel Kant (*Critique of Pure Reason*, 1781), namely "How is nature possible?" Simmel asked, "How is society possible?" Georg Simmel, "How Is Society Possible?," *American Journal of Sociology* 16, no. 3 (1910): 372–391.

For the fundamental sociological inquiry undertaken in this book, my question is not "How is society possible?" but rather the more fundamental questions, "Why does society persist?"; "Is society an accident of history?"; and "If society is not accidental, then what is it?" Perhaps another way of phrasing this is: "How are *we* possible?" (See also Martin Buber, *I and Thou*, 1923.) Aristotle answers these questions by simply asserting (axiomatically) that social life is essential to human nature, in *Politics* (book I, ch. 2): "Hence it is evident that the state [i.e., the civic collective] is a creation of nature, and that man is by nature a political animal. And he who by nature and not by mere accident is without a state, is either above humanity, or below it." And in *Ethics* (book 9, ch. 9): "[M]an is meant for political association, and [it is his] nature to live with others." My answer to the above questions, which I present in part IV of this book, is that the necessity of society comes from its potential to be a vehicle for individual and collective intelligence. Consistent with social contract theorists, I view society (in its greatest potential) as a form of structural intelligence that serves the liberation of human consciousness, which would otherwise be bound to an existential plight defined by the inadequacies and eccentricities of solitary reasoning.

Page 123 **even up to six or ten people**: Exceptionally interesting and influential early work on this topic was done by Luc Steels, "A Self-Organizing Spatial Vocabulary,"

Artificial Life 2, no. 3 (1995): 319–332; Simon Garrod and Gwyneth Doherty, "Conversation, Co-Ordination and Convention: An Empirical Investigation of How Groups Establish Linguistic Conventions," *Cognition* 53, no. 3 (1994): 181–215; and Edna Ullmann-Margalit, *The Emergence of Norms* (Clarendon Press, 1977).

Page 123 **that was an impressive feat**: The majority of past game theoretic studies of social convention focused narrowly on situations in which all options were known in advance (e.g., people must choose option A or option B). In those models, the payoffs for every option were also known in advance (see: Harsanyi and Selten, *General Theory of Equilibrium Selection*). The coordination challenge then becomes a simple question of which option people will choose, and whether that choice will maximize their individual and collective payoffs. Evolutionary game theory relaxed many of the strict formal assumptions of classic economic models (such as "perfect information"; see Young, "Evolution of Conventions"; Skyrms, *Evolution of the Social Contract*), but still maintained the classical assumption that the number of options, and their payoffs, were known a priori by all players. My exploration (with Andrea Baronchelli) of the grand challenge of coordination in social convention prioritizes the ecological validity of the coordination problem. In our studies, we explore a state of nature in which new options can continually emerge at all times, from all participants, allowing an unbounded variety of social choices to emerge. This approach allows for individual creativity in the formation of new social options, engendering an evolving ecosystem of choices; moreover, we do not assume that there is any global information about population behavior, nor any a priori information about what options other people have been exposed to (or have knowledge of). This formal design was conceived for the purposes of studying ecologically valid and empirically relevant contexts (like cultural conventions and social norms) in which individuals exhibit creativity and real-time adaptation, and only have local knowledge of the behaviors of others, as defined by the set of individuals with whom they have interacted directly while attempting to synchronize their behavior (see Centola and Baronchelli, "Spontaneous Emergence of Conventions").

Page 124 **shared linguistic conventions**: Andrea Baronchelli worked with Luc Steels and Vittorio Loreto during his graduate research on the naming game. He is now a professor of complexity science at City St. George's, University of London.

Page 125 **baby names are boundless**: Here are a few examples of the unbounded variety of baby names: Frank Zappa famously named his daughter Moon Unit and his son Dweezil. A colleague of mine in the sociology department at Princeton University named his son Knuckles and his daughter E. There are many other fun examples that have sprung from the unorthodox minds of celebrities and intellectuals.

Page 125 **has created a cultural norm**: The term *norm* has many meanings in varied contexts. In this context, *norm* is used synonymously with *convention*—to refer to a mutually beneficial coordination equilibrium in a pure coordination game. See Centola, *Change*, for a detailed discussion of this conception of norms.

Page 128 **conformity with social conventions**: A long sociological tradition argues that conformity effects—such as persons adopting behaviors and fashions to "fit in" with their peers—are greatest among the middle-status individuals, for whom conformity is a means of asserting their membership in status-driven groups (such as residents in upper-middle-class neighborhoods). According to this argument, low-status individuals are not pressured to demonstrate conformity because they will not be accepted by the middle-status groups no matter what they do; conversely, high-status individuals are not burdened by conformity because their lack of conformity asserts their high status (i.e., flouting norms is used as a way of performing status, such as a celebrity arriving to a formal affair in a T-shirt, while a middle-status suburban professor or lawyer would arrive to the same event in a tie and jacket, conforming to normative expectations.) See Damon J. Phillips and Ezra W. Zuckerman, "Middle-Status Conformity: Theoretical Restatement and Empirical Demonstration in Two Markets," *American Journal of Sociology* 107, no. 2 (2001): 379–429; James Dittes and Harold Kelley, "Effects of Different Conditions of Acceptance Upon Conformity to Group Norms," *Journal of Abnormal and Social Psychology* 53, no. 1 (1956): 100–107; George Homans, *Social Behavior: Its Elementary Forms* (Harcourt, Brace, 1961).

Page 128 **they became oddly entrenched**: The findings in this chapter were first reported in Centola and Baronchelli, "Spontaneous Emergence of Conventions."

Page 131 **"soda" and "pop" have stuck around**: It is reasonable to ask whether this kind of "diversity" in cultural norms isn't a good thing. For instance, in the grand challenge of choosing, we saw that diversity helped to increase collective intelligence. We'll see that diversity once again increases collective intelligence in the grand challenge of creativity. However, it is different for the grand challenge of coordination. This is because for establishing social conventions the essential challenge is to figure out how to match your behavior with other people's behaviors and expectations. As discussed above, the philosopher David Hume (*An Enquiry Concerning Human Understanding,* 1748) effectively sums up the fundamental problem of convention with the example of two people sitting in a row boat. The key to this example is that the more people there are, the harder it is to establish a convention—diversity is not the solution, but the problem. The last thing you want in an octuple scull (a boat with eight rowers) is lots of diversity in people's rowing styles. When it comes to social conventions, the essence of collective intelligence is universal coordination on the same behavior.

These observations about the value of convention suggest a potential response to the philosophical arguments developed by Martin Heidegger (*Being and Time,* 1931), in which he critiques the inauthentic nature of "the They" (which is philosophical shorthand for broad patterns of unthinking social conformity). As Heidegger puts it, "[T]he 'they'-self [is distinct] from the authentic Self. . . . the 'they' [puts] itself in the right and makes itself respectable by tacitly regulating the way in which one has to comport oneself."

A useful response to Heidegger's philosophical critique of the sociological phenomenon of social convention is that there are many times when conformity (and vapid "idle talk")—both of which Heidegger regarded as "inauthentic" forms of Being—are in fact essential modes of social action for achieving intersubjectivity and mutual understanding (Edmund Husserl, *Cartesian Meditations, 1931*).

From this point of view, the philosophical and sociological importance of convention and idle talk is not grounded in the content of what people say, but rather in the basic fact that they're saying anything at all, and the manner in which they're saying it. Take greeting conventions. There is an enormous variety of such conventions across diverse cultures. These modes of communication may be regarded as idle talk, in the sense that the content of what is said is admittedly performative rather than substantive. Nevertheless, the form (rather than the content) of these communicative actions—for instance, in which dignitaries compliment one another's hairstyle and attire, or in which colleagues shake hands and inquire about each other's children—may be semantically vapid yet phenomenologically essential for authentically recognizing the value and agency of the Other. In these settings, conventional behavior—and idle talk—may enable independent persons to align their thinking "intersubjectively" through acts of social coordination, which enable them to see the world, and one another, anew and together. This kind of conventional behavior may thus provide a foundation for the empathy necessary to realize the Hegelian "phenomenological" principles of mutual understanding and mutual recognition. See: Alexandre Kojève, *Introduction à la Lecture de Hegel* (Gallimard, 1947).

Page 133 **the initial two dozen**: Results for internet networks with *N*=24, *N*=48, and *N*=96 participants all exhibit successful convergence within equivalent timescales are shown in figure E.7.1:

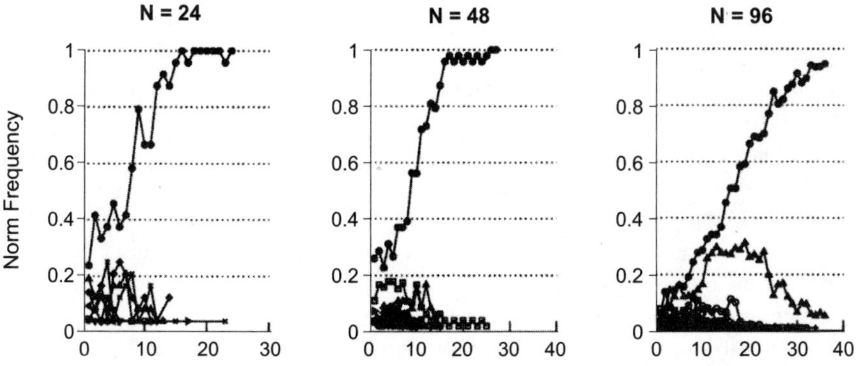

FIGURE E.7.1
Scaling of coordination

Page 133 **collective intelligence had been achieved**: One interesting implication of these results for cultural evolution concerns the accelerating rate at which neologisms arise and become widely understood. Within a few short decades of global connectedness via social media, many neologisms for novel online behaviors have rapidly reached consensus—just like "spam," but faster and more frequently. Within a year of the pandemic, the term "doom-scrolling" was universally adopted to describe the remarkably widespread behavior of perusing social media and compulsively following one catastrophic horror story after another. The term "Zoom fatigue" followed shortly thereafter. A few years earlier, the term "crowdsourcing" became widely adopted based on technologies designed to harness the wisdom of crowds. More recently, a host of novel social media tags have emerged, like "geo-bragging" and "ego surfer" (which mean exactly what they sound like). In essence, the emergence of globally distributed coordination dynamics across densely connected virtual networks has accelerated the evolution of language. From "frenemy" to "adorkable," consensus on new terms quickly arises, hastening the collective ability to articulate and communicate regarding the shifting nuances of modern life. One interesting upshot of these coordination dynamics is the unexpected degree of intergenerational alignment—from grandparents to grandchildren—on new concepts and terminology, like spam and Zoom fatigue. Mapping the evolutionary trajectory of these linguistic and cultural dynamics within and across populations is a fascinating new research frontier for structural intelligence, particularly for scholars working at the intersection of science, technology, and culture.

Page 133 **the grand challenge of coordination**: In his excellent book *Rational Ritual: Culture, Coordination, and Common Knowledge* (Princeton University Press, 2001), my colleague (and fellow CASBS cohort member) Michael Suk-Young Chwe gives examples of how cultural focal points, like the Super Bowl, enable large, nationwide coordination. Such phenomena are examples of informational centralization, much like the kind we observed with Treynor's description of markets (and the Saturday-afternoon announcement by the Treasury Secretary). It is important to observe that although Chwe provides an account of how this informational centralization becomes a mechanism for large-scale coordination, his analysis does not provide an explanation for how these centralized systems come into being in the first place. Why do we all agree to watch the Super Bowl?

To answer that question, we are forced to go back to the state of nature. The problem of how to get a large fraction of the US television audience to watch the Super Bowl is itself an instance of the grand challenge of coordination. How did so many people agree to watch that event (rather than, say, the Ryder Cup)? Prior to the formation of any cultural focal point, there must be a preceding cultural coordination process through which large swaths of the population come to coordinate on a ritual. This process of cultural synchronization invisibly sits behinds the rational rituals that Chwe describes—and is what makes such rituals possible in the first place. In this light, Chwe's book might have been entitled *Cultural Convention* rather than *Rational Ritual.*

Page 133 **". . . though it be in the woods"**: Ralph Waldo Emerson, *Journals of Ralph Waldo Emerson: With Annotations, vol. 8: 1849–1855*, edited by Edward Waldo Emerson and Waldo Emerson Forbes (Houghton Mifflin, 1912).

Page 134 **efficiency while typing**: See the discussion of Dvorak versus QWERTY keyboards in Centola, *Change*. Related studies of the QWERTY keyboard include: Paul David, "Clio and the Economics of QWERTY," *American Economic Review* 75 (1985): 332–337; and Paul David, "Understanding the Economics of QWERTY: The Necessity of History," in *Economic History and the Modern Economist*, ed. W. N. Parker (Blackwell, 1986). The grandfather of NetLogo, Seymour Papert, offers this classic analysis: *Mindstorms: Children, Computers, and Powerful Ideas* (Basic Books, 1980) notes:

> The top row of alphabetic keys of the standard typewriter reads QWERTY. For me this symbolizes the way in which technology can all too often serve not as a force for progress but for keeping things stuck. The QWERTY arrangement has no rational explanation, only a historical one. It was introduced in response to a problem in the early days of the typewriter: The keys used to jam. The idea was to minimize the collision problem by separating those keys that followed one another frequently. . . . Once adopted, it resulted in many millions of typewriters and . . . the social cost of change . . . mounted with the vested interest created by the fact that so many fingers now knew how to follow the QWERTY keyboard. QWERTY has stayed on despite the existence of other, more "rational" systems. (33)

Page 134 **clearly the better option**: In brief, Betamax had a higher quality picture, better sound, a quieter player, better navigation and "bookmarking" features, and a much more compact tape—about half the size of the VHS cassette.

Page 134 **decision-making networks**: See: Robin Cowan, "Nuclear Power Reactors: A Study in Technological Lock-in," *Journal of Economic History* 50, no. 3 (1990): 541–567, and the classic work by Brian Arthur, "Competing Technologies, Increasing Returns, and Lock-In by Historical Events," *Economic Journal* 99, no. 394 (1989): 116–131. See also my discussion of this phenomenon in terms of the familiar notion of "stickiness" in *Change*.

Page 134 **influence and coordination**: There is an interesting problem of power inequity in social coordination that is sometimes referred to as the "majority illusion" (Lerman et al., "The Majority Illusion"), which is discussed in the endnotes for chapter 2. In brief, by virtue of the central person's position of structural power in the network, they may convince many others that an inferior norm, or an unpopular bad idea, is in fact already popularly accepted by the majority of people. Once everyone coordinates on this idea, lock-in is hard to escape. The pressure to keep coordinating never goes away even if it is coordinating on something no one wants (see: Centola et al., "The Emperor's Dilemma").

CHAPTER 8: WHY BAD IDEAS SOMETIMES WIN

Page 135 **one of the most successful authors of all time**: My discussion of popular authors is not an endorsement of their political or social views, just as my discussion of the work Thomas Hobbes and Francis Galton is not an endorsement of their political or social views.

Page 136 **to take a chance on the book**: This and other stories are enjoyably recounted in Judith and Neil Morgan, *Dr. Seuss and Mr. Geisel: A Biography* (Random

House, 1995). In addition to his popular success, Dr. Seuss received three Caldecott Medals, a Legacy Award, and a Pulitzer Prize for his outstanding work in children's fiction. Recounting the famous anecdote about his fateful encounter with his friend at Vanguard Publishing (Mike McClintock), Dr. Seuss concluded: "That's one of the reasons I believe in luck. If I'd been going down the other side of Madison Avenue, I would be in the dry-cleaning business today!" Quoted in Philip Nel, *The Annotated Cat: Under the Hats of Seuss and His Cats* (Random House, 2007).

Page 137 **the contestants themselves**: See this classic analysis by the great economist John Maynard Keynes, *The General Theory of Employment, Interest and Money* (Harcourt Brace, 1936).

Page 137 **growing a mediocre product into a huge cultural success**: The well-known herding model of market behavior by Abhijit Banerjee ("A Simple Model of Herd Behavior," *Quarterly Journal of Economics* 107 (1992): 797–817) shows that in sequential decision processes, people use their peers' prior decisions as informational signals regarding the true underlying value of an asset or a behavior. (This model is discussed in greater detail in chapter 13.) Regardless of whether early movers in this decision process have any useful information (or are just choosing randomly), their choices are nevertheless treated as valuable informational signals. Each subsequent actor who follows the initial actors' choices reinforces the early mover's choice, further adding to the expected informational value of the initial signal. This sequential choice process creates a de facto form of centralization in the flow of information, in which the first player has disproportionate influence over subsequent movers and therefore has increasing influence on later movers down the line. The result is that everyone's choices are all unduly influenced by the perceived informational signal in first mover's choice.

As Banerjee puts it:

> paying heed to what everyone else is doing is rational because their decisions may reflect information that they have and we do not. It then turns out that a likely consequence of people trying to use this information is what we call herd behavior—everyone doing what everyone else is doing, even when their private information suggests doing something quite different.
>
> But this suggests that the very act of trying to use the information contained in the decisions made by others makes each person's decision less responsive to her own information and hence less informative to others. Indeed, we find that in equilibrium the reduction of informativeness may be so severe that in an ex ante welfare sense society may actually be better off by constraining some of the people to use only their own information. (798)

The conclusion from Banerjee's model is similar to (though stronger than) the authors' initial expectations for the Musiclab study—the essential idea being that enabling peers to pay attention to others' decisions in a sequential decision process (in which some choices are made before others) will create a flow of influence from early movers to later movers that can significantly reduce the collective intelligence of the popular choice.

I agree with Banerjee that sequential choice can lead to a feedback process in which the first player's move generates a perceived informational signal that can undermine the authentic/accurate private information held by subsequent individuals. In these cases, sequential choice dynamics can indeed create a de facto form of informational centralization that reduces collective intelligence by coordinating population choices on an inferior option.

In the Musiclab studies discussed in this chapter, the authors hypothesized that a similar herding dynamic would emerge in the Billboard worlds in their experiments. Matthew J. Salganik, Peter Sheridan Dodds, and Duncan J. Watts, "Experimental Study of Inequality and Unpredictability in an Artificial Cultural Market," *Science* 311, no. 5762 (2006): 854–856; Matthew J. Salganik and Duncan J. Watts, "Leading the Herd Astray: An Experimental Study of Self-Fulfilling Prophecies in an Artificial Cultural Market," *Social Psychology Quarterly* 71 (2008): 338–355. Why did they find the opposite of what they predicted empirically—and the opposite of what Banerjee observed in his model?

The difference is that Musiclab was studying preferences while the herding model was analyzing accuracy/performance. In the herding model, the decisions of prior actors in the sequential choice dynamics are perceived to carry informational value about the worth of an asset. Intuitively, the first mover's informational signal is given greater weight because that individual's signal has not been "corrupted" by social influence. Thus, in the herding model subsequent actors (who are eager to discern the truth of the asset's value) give greater weight to the initial "unadulterated" opinion than to their own. As the initial actor's choice gains further reinforcement from subsequent actors, the perceived accuracy of that choice increases, and it is given even more weight (attributed with even more informational value) than any subsequent actor's private information. The result is a herding dynamic in which everyone follows the choice of the first movers, independent of the actual quality of their choice.

In this herding model, the signals from prior players could overwhelm actors' private information because informational signals were used as evidence of objective accuracy/quality. In essence, Banerjee is identifying the effects of the sequential choice—i.e., informational centralization—in the grand challenge of choosing, in which everyone strives to be most accurate. Banerjee's theoretical results are thus consistent with the empirical findings presented in part I of this book. In particular, chapters 2 and 3 detail the hazards of centralization in the grand challenge of choosing. Additional empirical support for these effects of sequential choice—creating de facto centralization and undermining the wisdom of crowds—is found in Frey and van de Rijt ("Social Influence Undermines the Wisdom of the Crowd").

The reason why these herding dynamics do not dominate subjects' behavior in the Musiclab experiments (2006, 2008) is that unlike the herding model (which assumes the grand challenge of choosing), participants in Musiclab were not trying to optimize their accuracy or to make a "correct" decision. Rather, they were searching for music that they prefer. In these cultural markets, social influence becomes a search tool for discovering new and appealing options, rather than an optimization tool for selecting the correct choice. In such settings, peer information helps to reveal preference.

Because Musiclab participants were engaged in a search process to discover the music they liked the best, social information helped to surface options (and perhaps to shape preferences) in ways that accorded with the music that was generally perceived to be the most appealing. In such a setting, social information does not undermine the search process but rather accelerates it and improves the speed with which participants discover the most appealing songs. Social information thus enables a collective search that is much more efficient than individuals searching alone. We might even speculate that in some cultural markets with a larger number of songs (and thus a larger "space" of options to search), social information may be even more valuable for helping populations to quickly surface the songs with the greatest appeal, leading the collective to the rapid discovery of the best options.

What would be needed to "transform" the collectively intelligent dynamics of Musiclab into the "crowd madness" of Banerjee's herding process? To do so, one would only need to redesign the experience to reward participants for discovering a single correct choice. If these rewards are minimal and there is only mild social pressure, information cascades can still self-correct (see Jacob K. Goeree, Thomas R. Palfrey, Brian W. Rogers, and Richard D. McKelvey, "Self-Correcting Information Cascades," *Review of Economic Studies* 74, no. 3 (2007): 733–762). However, the key to Banerjee's herding dynamics is situations with high stakes and high uncertainty about the correct answer—what Condorcet would call a "hard problem." In such a setting—i.e., the grand challenge of choosing for a hard problem—the centralization of information via a sequential choice process can drive the population toward synchronizing on the behavior of the first mover, regardless of the quality of the first mover's choice. In such a setting, instead of exploring the space of options and coordinating on the most appealing choices, actors instead become fixated on following the aggregation of information, arbitrarily weighted by the influence of the first mover. This inevitably leads to the reduction of collective intelligence, via the "herding" dynamics predicted by Banerjee. A similar result follows from the discrete binary choice model developed by Sushil Bikhchandani, David Hirshleifer, and Ivo Welch, "Learning from the Behavior of Others: Conformity, Fads, and Informational Cascades," *Journal of Economic Perspectives* 12, no. 3 (1998): 151–170, which elaborates the conditions for the emergences of herding behavior.

By construction, the setting for Banerjee's model of herding (and Bikhchandani et al.'s model) assumes that there is no density dependence affecting the utility of the choice set. In other settings, such as Brian Arthur's "El Farol Problem" of choosing between two lively restaurants (Brian Arthur, "Inductive Reasoning and Bounded Rationality," *American Economic Review: Papers and Proceedings* 84 (1994): 406–411), there is a nonmonotonic utility function such that too many people choosing an option can make that option less attractive (as when a restaurant becomes overcrowded). We can also conceive of such density-dependent effects in the cyclical dynamics of popular culture (such as the overpopularity of baby names leading to their decline, and then their subsequent near-extinction leading to a resurgence, resulting in a historical sequence of cycles of popularity in baby names). See Stanley Lieberson, *A Matter of Taste: How Names, Fashions and Culture Change* (Yale University Press, 2000).

Page 137 **nothing more than a beauty contest**: In 1968, the renowned sociologist Robert Merton explored the implications of cumulative advantage for the culture of science and scientific rewards. Robert Merton, "The Matthew Effect in Science: The Reward and Communication Systems of Science Are Considered," *Science* 159, no. 3810 (1968): 56–63. Merton was less concerned with absolute rankings than with the tier distinctions that arise when cumulative advantage leads scientific careers to be dichotomized or categorized into ranks (or classes), which creates arbitrary discontinuities in the ranking of scientists. Merton's famous example concerns the small difference between the scholar considered to be the fortieth greatest living scientist in the UK. compared to the scholar that is ranked forty-first. The Royal Academy of Science only has forty chairs, or positions for membership. While the actual difference in skill and accomplishment between the fortieth ranked scientist and the forty-first ranked scientist may be small, the differences (and subsequent effects on career advancement) between being in the Royal Academy and not being in the Royal Academy are enormous. The scientist with the forty-first chair has a very different career than the scientist who is awarded the fortieth chair—due to an arbitrary dichotomization (or "cut-point") in the system of scientific rewards.

The resulting trajectory of scientific careers (and therefore of the history of ideas) may be indelibly altered by this simple dichotomization. Merton's observations extend to the notion of credit for ideas, suggesting that a more famous (higher-tier) scientist is likely to get credit for uttering the idea of a lower-tier (lesser-known) scientist—and as a result of this "misattribution by fame," the fame of the higher-tier scientist accumulates disproportionately, preventing lower-tier scientists from ever catching up, regardless of the quality of their scientific work. In 1980, the economist Stephen Stigler formalized this idea as Stigler's law of eponymy: "no scientific discovery is named after its original discoverer," of which Stigler's law is of course an example, given that Merton and others had already discovered this principle before Stigler named it. Luckily, Merton had achieved a significantly high tier of recognition within the field that his contribution is remembered nonetheless.

Page 138 **he could use in his study**: The final list of bands used for the study was sampled from an online clearinghouse for music industry resources (i.e., a website) to which Matt Salganik had access.

Page 140 **visible metrics of any kind**: The control condition had 1,441 participants; it was twice the size of each of the eight Billboard worlds. This was true for both experiment 1 and experiment 2.

Page 141 **different from the control condition**: This figure shows the rankings of songs in the first half vs. second half of experiments 1 and 2, adapted from Arnout van de Rijt, *Chance in Life* (forthcoming):

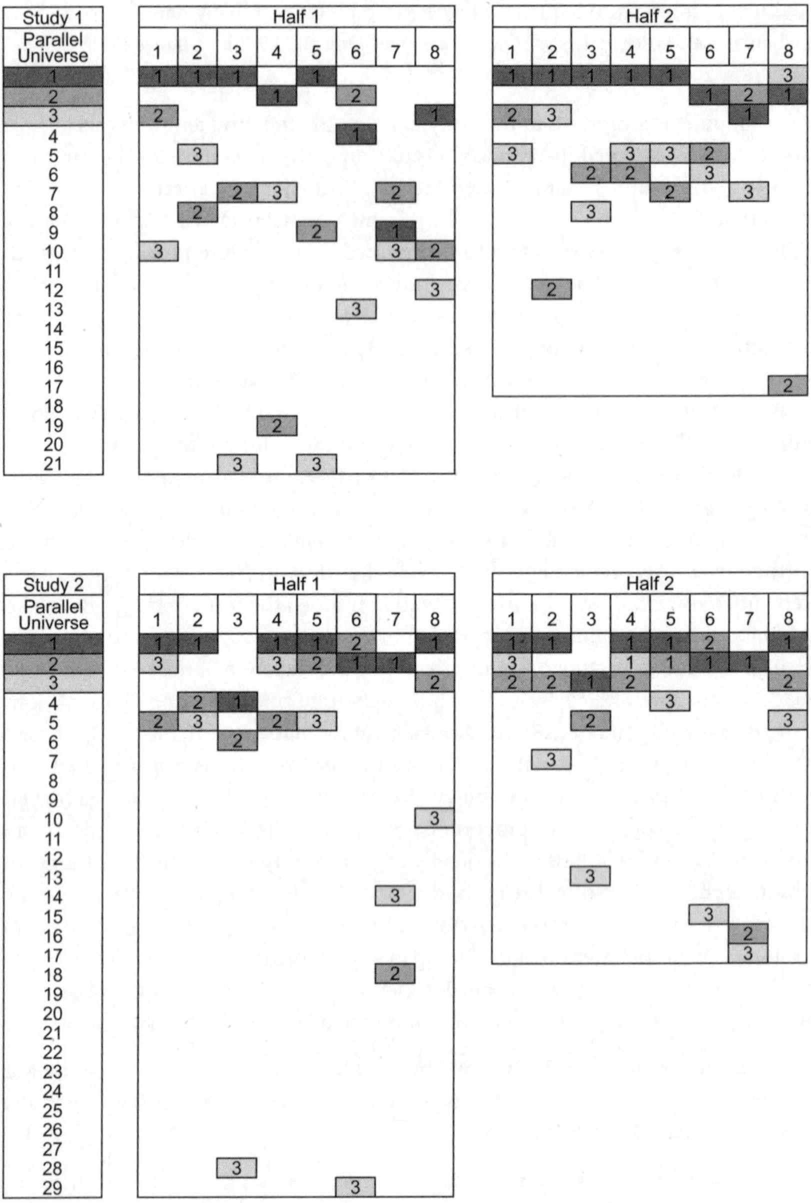

FIGURE E.8.1

Experiments 1 and 2. Adapted from Arnout van de Rijt, *Chance in Life* (forthcoming).

Page 141 **winners were actually the same songs**: In experiment 2, in the control (i.e., no social influence) condition, the top song, "She Said," was downloaded seventy-nine times, the second-ranked song seventy-six times, and the third-ranked song seventy times. These margins are minimal. However, in the final social influence worlds, the margins were dramatically amplified. For instance, in world 8, the download rates were 179 times for "She Said" (song 1 from the control condition), seventy-nine for song 2, and thirty-three times for song 3. Averaged over all eight social influence worlds, "She Said" was downloaded an average of 138 times per social world, while song 2 from the control condition was downloaded an average of seventy-seven times per social world, and song 3 from the control condition was downloaded an average of forty-three times per social world. The social worlds amplified the best songs, but they also introduced apparent tier distinctions. These tier distinctions facilitate the process of discovery—increasing collective intelligence in cultural synchronization on the highest "quality" choice; however, as per Merton's analysis of scientific careers (see earlier endnote in this chapter), the emergence of tiers can also conceal the fact that some options are more similar in quality than they may appear. See Merton, "The Matthew Effect in Science."

Page 142 **periods of disorder that would soon be corrected**: Many complex systems undergo transitory periods of temporary disorder before they settle down into a stable state. A useful description of transients in the dynamics of self-organized dynamical systems can be found in Steven Strogatz, *Nonlinear Dynamics and Chaos: With Applications to Physics, Biology, Chemistry, and Engineering* (CRC Press, 1994).

Page 142 **had practically disappeared**: In his analysis of the Musiclab results, Arnout van de Rijt ("Self-Correcting Dynamics in Social Influence Processes," *American Journal of Sociology* 124, no. 5 (2019): 1468–1495) states:

> These numbers show how strong correlations would be if subjects downloaded songs on the basis of quality only, as in the independent condition. The benchmark samples are constructed by randomly sampling downloads from the independent world. The size of each benchmark sample matches the average size of the social influence worlds. The benchmark correlations in both experiment 1 and experiment 2 decrease somewhat from half 1 to half 2. In the first half of each experiment, the rank correlations consistently lie well below the benchmark, showing that quality was an imperfect predictor of popularity. In the second half of each experiment, however, the correlations are nearly as high as the benchmark, showing that the self-correcting social influence dynamic was already close to completion. Initially popular songs of inferior quality had mostly lost their advantage. Together then these results suggest that under the social influence conditions created in the experiments, long run success rankings are largely insensitive to initial conditions and rather predictable from quality.

[TABLE E.1]
Changes in the Correlation Between Popularity and Quality in Experiments 1 and 2 reported in Salganik et al. (2006)

	Experiment 1			Experiment 2		
World	First half	Second half	Change	First half	Second half	Change
1	.58	.74	+.18	.56	.72	+.16
2	.65	.80	+.15	.66	.72	+.06
3	.61	.79	+.18	.52	.46	–.06
4	.57	.80	+.23	.53	.74	+.21
5	.62	.81	+.19	.61	.73	+.12
6	.69	.73	+.04	.57	.68	+.11
7	.68	.80	+.12	.59	.64	+.05
8	.62	.74	+.12	.51	.61	+.10
Benchmark . . .	.83	.79	–.04	.83	.75	–.8

Adapted from van de Rijt, "Self-Correcting Dynamics in Social Influence Processes," *American Journal of Sociology* 124, no. 5 (2019).

[Table E.1] shows for both experiments the rank correlation between the total number of downloads in the independent condition (quality) and download totals in benchmark samples.

Page 142 **remarkable feat of collective intelligence**: Path dependence is the idea that arbitrary events in the history of a population will determine its future trajectory. This would suggest that early accidents and anomalies in individual choices can have long-term consequences for the fate of collective intelligence. (This process is sometimes also referred to as *arbitrary lock in*, as a result of *non-ergodicity*.) If the music downloading experiment was path dependent, then slight differences between *Billboard* worlds in early downloading patterns would create arbitrarily large differences in their resulting song rankings. Such path dependence is one of the hypothesized implications of the theory of cumulative advantage that Salganik and his team were testing. The experimental results from Musiclab show that although cumulative advantage led some songs to become much more popular than they would have been in the independent control condition (without social feedback), the *Billboard* worlds in Matt's cultural marketplace were not path dependent. Once they passed through the initial transient, they became ordered systems, following the same ineluctable logic of appeal as the control condition (without social feedback). Because Matt's cultural marketplace experiment was structured so that all songs had a fair chance of being discovered, the appeal of the songs determined their ultimately popularity. Contrary to the expectation of path dependence, this cultural marketplace produced "self-organized sameness" across worlds, in which all eight *Billboard* worlds self-organized in the same way, suggesting that under these conditions—of equality of influence and equal access to all options—the trajectory of culture is not path dependent but is (in a sense) predictable.

Page 143 **all of the best songs were buoyant**: Arnout van de Rijt ("Self-Correcting Dynamics") reports:

> [The "inversion experiment"] showed that the inversion impacted download behavior in favor of the lower quality songs, which were initially downloaded more often than their quality would warrant. However, panel 2 in figure [E.8.2] shows that subjects nonetheless downloaded good songs over bad songs at a rate exceeding their relative popularity. As a result, later subjects were confronted with improved relative popularity scores for good songs, which in turn further increased their download rates.

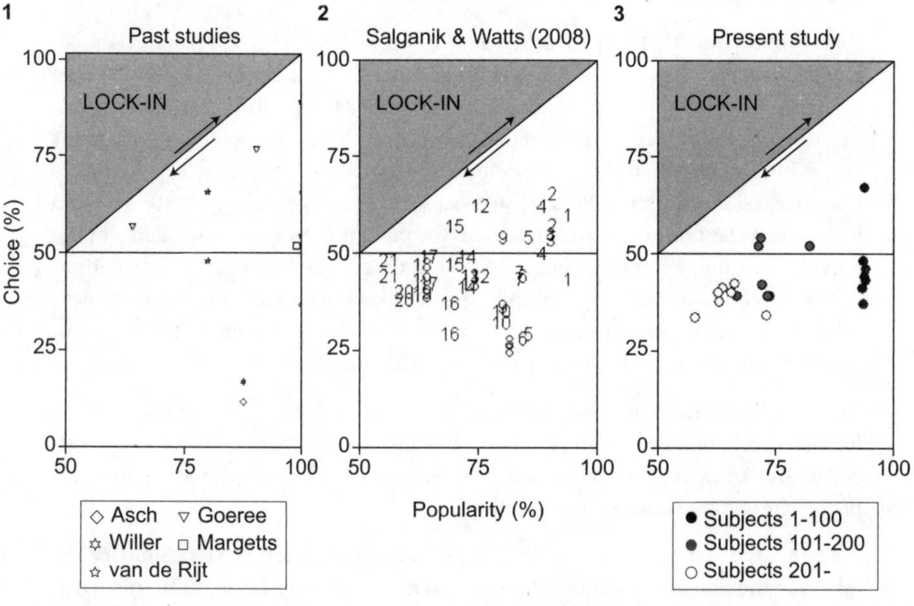

FIGURE E.8.2

Lock-in. Adapted from van de Rijt, "Self-Correcting Dynamics."

> The experiment was terminated while this corrective process was still ongoing, and we cannot definitively conclude from figure [E.8.2] that the process would not in some cases have entered the upper diagonal area. However, panel 2 shows that without exception, regardless of the magnitude of the advantage for the inferior option, the advantage always shrank during the experiment toward dominance of the superior alternative. Thus, regardless of whether uncertainty about relative quality was high or low, the better song consistently grew in relative popularity. Moreover, panel 2 shows that for most pairs the higher quality song was downloaded more often than the lower quality song after the inversion, despite the popularity information favoring the latter. In all these cases the natural popularity ordering had thus been restored.

Page 144 **the highest "quality" song**: Salganik and Watts came to a different conclusion than van de Rijt. They used linear projections, which suggested, "that it appears that in both inverted worlds song 1 will eventually return to the top spot, but that song 2 will not return to the second spot." Salganik and Watts, "Leading the Herd Astray," 347. Van de Rijt came to a different conclusion, suggesting that songs 2, 3, 4, etc. will continue to revert back toward their rankings found in the "unaltered" experimental worlds. Both conclusions rely upon statistical arguments and extrapolations. In personal communication, Salganik and van de Rijt both agree that the ultimate resolution of the issue comes down to an empirical question, which presents an excellent opportunity for new researchers interested in making important contributions to computational sociology and the study of structural intelligence in cultural markets.

Page 146 **downloaded just as easily as if it were at the top**: Screen position can amplify popularity effects; see Lev Muchnik, Sinan Aral, and Sean J. Taylor, "Social Influence Bias: A Randomized Experiment," *Science* 341, no. 6146 (2013): 647–651. In Musiclab, the top spot in the rankings was most likely to be clicked, regardless of the song. However, this screen position advantage did not accrue equally to the lower-ranked spots in the *Billboard* lists (e.g., song 20 compared to song 40). Interestingly, the second-most clicked location on the ranking list was not the middle of the rankings but the bottom. Because of scrolling effects that can jump to the bottom of the screen, the bottom spot enjoyed greater likelihood of attracting initial clicks than the higher-ranked songs in the middle. Eventually, however, these screen-position effects were dominated by the song quality effects.

Page 146 **attenuation of collective intelligence**: There are unexplored implications for the effects of cancel culture on the collective intelligence of cultural marketplaces, due to external forces eliminating options from the cultural scene irrespective of the options' inherent "appeal."

Page 147 **and which ones amplify them**: These observations surface similar concerns for the domain of cultural synchronization, similar to those once articulated by James Madison ("Federalist No. 10," 1787), Alexis de Tocqueville (*Democracy in America*, 1835), and John Dewey (*The Public and Its Problems*, 1927) for the grand challenge of choosing. Namely, a majority rule can quickly eliminate the best opinions and undermine the intelligence of a democratic process. The results for the grand challenge of choosing and the grand challenge of coordination on quality are aligned on the insight that the centralization of information (or reduction in the equality of access to options) can undermine collective intelligence.

Page 147 **signals for subsequent users**: Arnout van de Rijt ("Self-Correcting Dynamics," 14) says:

> early subjects, lacking social information, did not know what to sample, so many of them missed the best songs and could download only mediocre songs. Later subjects had good social information at their disposal so they mostly sampled popular songs, which tended to

be of high quality. Social information was increasingly correlated with song quality, leading later subjects to download better songs.

These remarks suggest that when cultural markets become flooded with many more options to choose from (and therefore much more noise), social information may become increasingly valuable for helping collectives to discover the best options—shepherding the collective through the transient stages to arrive at a collectively intelligent social order.

As discussed above, collective learning in cumulative advantage dynamics is distinct from Banerjee's model of herding, in which the disproportionate influence of early movers creates de facto centralization. Herding reduces collective intelligence by limiting the exploration of alternatives, as reported in Frey and van de Rijt ("Social Influence Undermines the Wisdom of the Crowd").

Page 147 **principle of fairness**: These observations offer an interpretation of the "conformity" experiments by Solomon Asch in "Effects of Group Pressure." In these studies, the ordered sequences of responses, beginning with a sequence of experimental "confederates" and ending with the lone experimental subject, were able to convince the experimental subject to conform to an obviously incorrect response given by the preceding majority of responses. This effect of sequential decision-making on negatively influencing outcomes in the grand challenge of choosing arises when (i) actors attempt to answer "factual" questions, with right and wrong answers, (ii) there are high stakes, and (iii) there are high levels of (actual or induced) uncertainty. When these conditions are met, centralization in the flow of information (or, in Asch's case, in the apparent flow of information) undermines collective intelligence. The behavioral tendency to "conform" to incorrect choices, which Asch observed, arises as a product of these structural features of the choice setting. Thus, what Asch labeled "conformity effects" may in large part be considered "structural effects." The implications of Asch's study for structural intelligence are discussed in chapter 13.

PART III: COOPERATION AND CREATIVITY

CHAPTER 9: WHY NICE GUYS FINISH FIRST

Page 151 **belly of a sixty-six-year-old man**: This narrative comes from the excellent retelling of this story by Kevin Sack, "60 Lives, 30 Kidneys, All Linked," *New York Times*, February 18, 2012.

Page 152 **economist Alvin Roth**: In my conversation with Alvin Roth, he emphasized that the success of a life-saving kidney exchange "isn't the work of a solitary economist but is the outcome of a lot of interaction among economists, surgeons, computer scientists, and operations researchers. One hero of the story is the transplant surgeon, Mike Rees, who organized the first nonsimultaneous nondirected donor chain (and founded the kidney exchange network, the Alliance for Paired Kidney Exchange)." Roth's important observations about the variety of people and skills necessary for successful innovation are discussed in chapter 10, where I will show you how diverse networks promote creativity in complex problem-solving.

Page 153 **intelligence to succeed**: Alvin Roth and Lloyd Shapley built upon the 1962 Gale–Shapley theorem, demonstrating its elaboration and application to real-world matching markets, such as kidney exchanges and physician placements (in the National Resident Matching Program, as refined by the Gale–Shapley algorithm). As with Tversky in 2002, David Gale did not share the 2012 Nobel Prize with Roth and Shapley because it is not awarded posthumously.

Page 153 **who can trade with each other**: Key papers for this result are Alvin E. Roth, Tayfun Sönmez, and M. Utku Ünver, "Pairwise Kidney Exchange," *Journal of Economic Theory* 125, no. 2 (2005): 151–188; Alvin E. Roth, Tayfun Sönmez, and M. Utku Ünver, "Kidney Exchange," *Quarterly Journal of Economics* 119, no. 2 (2004): 457–488. The results from these studies show that there are large welfare gains as the length of the chain of kidney donations increases. These studies also demonstrate how intelligent network structures can be engineered—i.e., designed and implemented—to solve practical social dilemmas with life-or-death consequences.

Page 156 **for fairness in exchange**: Regarding the prevalence of fairness, see Young ("Economics of Convention"): "There is nothing in classical bargaining theory—or for that matter in classical economic theory—that would predict these results." In his forthcoming book, Young relates a similar story about his boyhood farming community in Ohio, where landowners and tenant farmers commonly agreed to 50–50 splits—known as "farming on the halves"—despite the fact that classical game theory would predict inequity. Similarly, Nobel Laureate in Economics Joseph Stiglitz says, "The range of contract forms [in sharecropping] seems far more restricted than economic theory would suggest" ("Markets, Market Failures, and Development," *American Economic Review* 79, no. 2 (1989): 22. For "similarly situated" people, equitable distribution of resources is consistent with the moral principle of distributive justice in deontological normative ethics. See Jason Alexander and Brian Skyrms, "Bargaining with Neighbors: Is Justice Contagious?," *Journal of Philosophy* 96, no. 11 (1999): 588–598; Skyrms, *Evolution of the Social Contract*; Skyrms, *The Stag Hunt*. Fairness as a solution to the bargaining problem is consistent with utilitarian axiomatic solutions such as found in John Nash, "The Bargaining Problem," *Econometrica* 18, no. 2 (1950): 155–162; Ehud Kalai and Meir Smorodinsky, "Other Solutions to Nash's Bargaining Problem," *Econometrica* 43, no. 3 (1975): 513–518; and Kalai and Smorodinsky, "Other Solutions to Nash." It also aligns with expectations from field experiments on cooperation: M. E. Yaari and M. Bar-Hillel, "On Dividing Justly," *Social Choice and Welfare* 1, no. 1 (1984): 1–24.

Page 157 **stop trying to trade with them**: See Robert Axelrod's classic study of cooperation (*The Evolution of Cooperation* (Basic Books, 1984), 182). Important experimental extensions of this work explore situations in which participants have an option to "exit" the game.

Page 158 **identities in different interactions**: See stories of the 50c Party in Damon Centola, *Change*.

Page 158 **70–30 just appears to be the norm**: See discussions of these points in Young, "Evolution of Convention," and "Economics of Convention."

Page 160 **leading everyone toward fair dealing**: The illustration in figure 9.2 is taken from Alexander and Skyrms, "Bargaining with Neighbors," which relies upon a strategic learning model in which agents "imitate the best" actor in their neighborhood. This model parallels the evolutionary logic of the replicator dynamics model, in which the actors with the greatest payoff are given the greatest number of offspring in the next generation. In this illustration, the population dynamics of reproduction based on fitness are approximated by behavioral dynamics in which actors copy the behavior of their most successful peers. An alternative evolutionary implementation of the Nash bargaining game uses *myopic best response* dynamics, in which actors choose the strategy that yields the highest payoff against the strategies encountered in their history of recent interactions. The behavior of best-response models can be altered by (i) the memory length (*m*), which governs the number of past plays that are evaluated when calculating a best response; (ii) by the cardinality of the low and high payoffs (e.g., 3, 5, 7 versus 1, 5, 9); and (iii) by the granularity that is used to evaluate the payoff differences between strategies. A number of these topics are fruitfully explored in H. P. Young, "An Evolutionary Model of Bargaining," *Journal of Economic Theory* 59, no. 1 (1993): 145–168, and in Skyrms, *Evolution of the Social Contract* and *Stag Hunt*. Generally speaking, the results presented here on the effects of network structure on the evolution of fairness in the grand challenge of cooperation are consistent with the general dynamics corresponding to imitate-the-best models and best-response models of bargaining reported in these studies.

Page 160 **spreads to nearby neighborhoods**: Clustering in geographic networks and complex networks has been found to benefit cooperation in a variety of contexts, such as solving the start-up problem in large-scale collective action in Damon Centola, "Homophily, Networks, and Critical Mass: Solving the Start-Up Problem in Large Group Collective Action," *Rationality and Society* 25, no. 1 (2013): 3–40; and Centola, *How Behavior Spreads*; and in the biological and social evolution of cooperation, see Axelrod, *Evolution of Cooperation*, and Michael Cohen, Rick Riolo, and Robert Axelrod, "The Role of Social Structure in the Maintenance of Cooperative Regimes," *Rationality and Society* 13 (2001): 5–32.

The differences between clustered geographic networks (e.g., the Moore lattice) versus geographic networks without clustering (e.g., the von Neumann lattice) in the dynamics of the evolution of fairness in the Nash bargaining game can vary depending on the implementation rules of the learning model (e.g., "imitate the best" versus "best response"). As reported in this chapter, clustered geographic networks provide a reliable and robust architecture for the emergence and stability of cooperation across a wide variety of modeling implementations and empirical conditions. For more detail, see Jason Alexander, *The Structural Evolution of Morality*

(Cambridge University Press, 2007); Jason Alexander, "Social Deliberation: Nash, Bayes, and the Partial Vindication of Gabriele Tarde," *Episteme* 6, no. 2 (2009): 164–184; and Justin D'Arms, Robert Batterman, and Krzyzstof Gorny, "Game Theoretic Explanations and the Evolution of Justice," *Philosophy of Science* 65 (1998): 76–102.

Page 160 **to increase their numbers**: Assuming players' positions are equal such that a 50–50 split represents a fair division of resources.

Page 161 **50–50, just like everyone else**: Fair dealing can successfully spread and take over even when exploitation is exceedingly profitable for "greedy" players. Figure E.9.1 shows a compelling example from Alexander and Skyrms, "Bargaining with Neighbors."

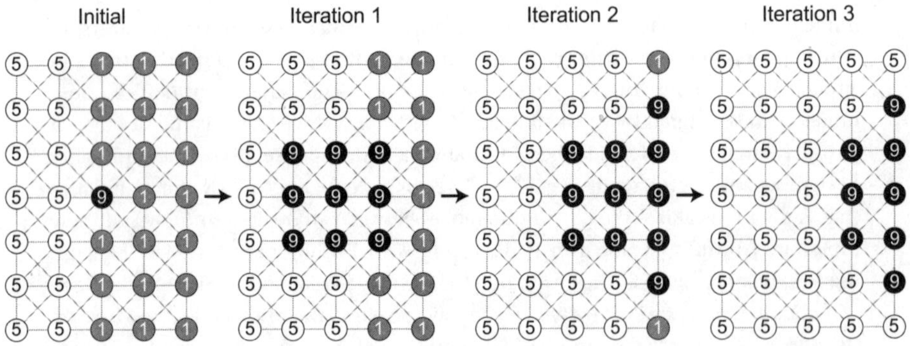

FIGURE E.9.1
The spread of fairness. Adapted from Alexander and Skyrms, "Bargaining with Neighbors."

In the figure, the initial exploiters demand 90 percent (demanding 9), while the exploited individuals accept only 10 percent (asking for 1). As always, fair dealers ask for a 50–50 split (requesting 5). In the first round, the very high payoff received by the exploiter (demanding 9) causes a few of the fair dealers, and a few of the exploited players' neighboring exploiters, to copy the exploitation strategy (demanding 9 in the next round). Exploited players (who asked for 1 in the first round) who were not directly connected to the exploiter choose to adopt the fair-dealing strategy from their cooperative neighbors (asking for 5 in the next round). In the second round, the new crop of exploiters are all forced to trade with one another. The poor payoff (of 0) that they all receive from their failed attempts to trade with fellow exploiters leads many of them to switch back to fair dealing. By round three, even the initial exploiter is frustrated by the low payoffs from trying to exploit fair dealers, and they, too, choose to become fair dealers—as do many of the initially exploited players. By round four, only a few exploiters remain. Since they are once again forced to interact with one another, on the next round, they, too, choose to abandon exploitation and become fair dealers, just like the rest of their neighbors.

Page 161 **expectations of fairness between them**: The same principle of fairness can also be applied to the household dynamics of marriage. In a strange yet convincing series of studies, sociologists have found that the best explanation for who dates whom and who marries to whom is a matching process that is surprisingly similar to the kidney exchange.

To study this, researchers quantify things like attractiveness, wealth, and professional status, and then try to determine the factors that explain who ends up with whom. Many of the early results were exactly what you would expect. It was the clichéd logic of mid-twentieth-century economic theory in which more attractive persons "exchange" their attractiveness for the status and wealth of their spouse. This distasteful calculus becomes even less palatable when you discover that the earliest studies on this topic argued that the world was rationally organized along precisely the kinds of gendered trade-offs that serve as a cultural basis for the subjugation of women (see John Stuart Mill, *On the Subjugation of Women*, 1869). Everything became much more interesting once women's role in the workforce increased. Financial contributions to a marriage were no longer as gendered and the balance of domestic roles in the household began to change. What did marital exchange look like then?

With an increasing number of social factors to consider, classical economic exchange theory gave way to an interesting new sociological approach, which revealed that coupling patterns emerge based on likes choosing likes. Instead of people choosing spouses based on trade-offs—like trading money for attractiveness—they instead began to look for peers who matched them in factors like status and attractiveness but also complemented them in other respects, such as social values and emotional investment in the partnership.

Even more interestingly, in contemporary marriages the trade-offs among partners are increasingly based less on people's individual properties, such as wealth and attractiveness, and more on their ability to negotiate fair bargaining in their shared domestic responsibilities. The new economy for marital success is based on fairness in the balance of household duties, such as parenting, managing finances, cleaning, and cooking. While these chores seem mundane, contributing more on these fronts can effectively alter the entire landscape of your life at home.

The most successful marriages thrive on an impressively fair balance in partners' contributions. This balance can take many forms, and it often changes with the age of the couple. Younger couples tend to evaluate their current relationship trade-offs against the trade-offs that they might receive from another relationship. A curious but intuitive result is that the more potential partners someone has, the less they need to invest in their current relationship in order to maintain it. Having lots of options for other partners, and forgoing those options by staying faithful to one person, is felt by both partners to be a contribution that the more desirable partner makes to the relationship. In short, in young couples the more attractive partner often does fewer chores. Correspondingly, the more chores that the less attractive partner does, the more balanced the relationship becomes. Up to the point where fairness in the exchange is achieved, at which point the more attractive partner no longer enjoys any advantage in bargaining power in the relationship.

The most interesting part of how this intimate exchange economy works is that it changes with time. Once both partners are committed, the balance between them takes on more practical dimensions. Attractiveness depreciates in value. Household chores become the coin of the realm for determining the balance of fairness in a marriage.

But the most striking findings are for marital intimacy. A partner's investment in their spouse's enjoyment of sex can be directly changed by their spouse doing more chores around the house. Cooking, in particular, proved to have significant effects on a partner's investment in their spouse's sexual satisfaction. Strikingly, the exchange principle works the same way, with equal strength, for both men and women. A better sex life for both partners hinges on this basic principle of fairness in the kitchen. The more that one spouse was willing to do in the kitchen, the more the other one was willing to do in the bedroom. As one study concluded, "Apparently, the way to a lover's heart is through his or her stomach." Arnout van de Rijt and Michael W. Macy, "Power and Dependence in Intimate Exchange," *Social Forces* 84, no. 3 (2006): 1455–1470.

Page 161 **"When should a person cooperate?"**: The renowned political scientist Robert Axelrod (*Evolution of Cooperation*) studied a prisoner's dilemma game in which individual decisions were guided by both fear and greed, as discussed in the endnotes to chapter 7. His results are similar to the ones I report here, namely, that clustered geographic networks facilitate the spread of cooperation, and protect cooperative populations from being invaded by defectors. See also: Cohen et al., "Role of Social Structure"; Martin Nowak and Robert May (*Nature*, 1992), Bernardo Huberman (*PNAS*, 1993); Cristina Bicchierri, *The Grammar of Society: The Nature and Dynamics of Social Norms* (Cambridge University Press, 2006); and the seminal work by 2009 Nobel Laureate in Economics, Eleanor Ostrom, *Governing the Commons: The Evolution of Institutions for Collective Action* (Cambridge University Press, 2015).

Page 161 **". . . cooperation with each other"**: Axelrod, *Evolution of Cooperation*, 181.

Page 161 **vulnerable to exploitation from strangers**: See Arol Eckay's fascinating analysis of how changing network structure affects cooperation: "Collapse and Rescue of Cooperation in Evolving Dynamic Networks," *Nature Communications* 9, no. 1 (2018): 2692.

Page 161 **splits that persist indefinitely**: Noise (random error) can eventually disrupt inequity, leading populations to find the Nash bargaining solution of fairness (50–50 split). The fair (50–50) solution is also the stochastically stable equilibrium (Peyton Young, *Individual Strategy and Social Structure* (Princeton University Press, 1998)), which means that fairness has (statistically speaking) a certain inevitability to it. However, despite the long-term ineluctability of fairness, the "transitory" state of inequity can endure for generations, making cultural and normative entrenchment a genuine concern for citizens trapped in norms of inequity.

CHAPTER 10: COURTING SERENDIPITY

Page 164 "**. . . where radar was invented**": Contrary to this physicist's recollection, radar was not actually invented at MIT. Early on, Great Britain and other nations developed radar prototypes, which were then refined for military application during World War II by the scientists in Building 20.

Page 164 "**. . . it was extremely interactive**": This quote by Chomsky comes from Peter Dizikes, "The Office Next Door," *MIT Technology Review*, October 25, 2011, https://www.technologyreview.com/2011/10/25/21338/the-office-next-door/.

Page 165 **Nobel Prize in Physics**: Building 20 was also home to a homeless phantom botanist, who turned down a position at the Field Museum in Chicago in favor of sleeping in a Building 20 storeroom and wandering the dilapidated hallways for nearly twenty years.

Page 166 **MIT's Magical Incubator**: Other interesting examples of intelligent organizational structures include Pixar headquarters, in Emeryville, California; Apple headquarters, in Cupertino, California; and CIA headquarters in Langley, Virginia.

Page 168 **regardless of their individual accolades**: In Anita Williams Woolley, Christopher F. Chabris, Alex Pentland, Nada Hashmi, and Thomas W. Malone, "Evidence for a Collective Intelligence Factor in the Performance of Human Groups" *Science* 330 (2010): 686–688, Woolley et al. argue for a collective intelligence "c" factor that is putatively an intrinsic property of certain types of people (roughly equivalent to the capacity to "work well with others"). Simply put, their argument suggests that biologically gendered persons (i.e., women by birth) increase teams' capacity for solving complex problems. (See also Anita Woolley and Tom Malone, "Defend Your Research: What Makes a Team Smarter? More Women," *Harvard Business Review*, June 2011.) For many reasons—both scientific and ethical—I resist the proposition that collective intelligence boils down to demographic characteristics (such as gender or race), and that such traits could circumscribe and define a community's potential for complex problem solving. While there are many distributions of traits, I would argue that the structures and contexts in which group members interact (rather than any essentialist attributions associated with the group members' demographic characteristics) are the preeminent factors governing a group's capacity for creativity, innovation, and successful collaboration.

Page 168 **simply the best thinkers**: Lu Hong and Scott Page ("Groups of Diverse Problem Solvers") distinguish their technical concept of diversity from common uses of the term in social science research and in popular culture. Hong and Page are referring to neither demographic diversity nor social or cultural diversity (in a general sense) but rather specific differences in how people solve problems—which they refer to as "cognitive diversity." Cognitive diversity includes the kinds of solutions people look for, the types of models they employ, and their strategies for problem-solving. This terminological clarification suggests several relevant caveats for the "diversity trumps ability" result. The first is that in any successful model of team collaboration, team members must have some level of similarity, such as speaking the same language; understanding the nature of the problem to be solved; and having the raw ability to model ideas and concepts effectively—even if their particular approaches to problem-solving may vary widely. In addition, there is an expectation that the diverse people who join a successful team will all be technically competent enough to understand the problem to be solved and sufficiently invested in solving the problem that they will work hard with others to solve it.

Hong and Page's "diversity trumps ability" result assumes that the pool of problem-solvers consists of high-ability individuals with the interest and background to work on the problem together. Their central finding is that selecting the very best people within a specific domain expertise runs the risk of selecting a group of people who all think the same way (like a group of Nobel Laureates in Economics who all believe that the theory of rational choice is an excellent model for predicting human behavior). By contrast, selecting individuals who are talented in different domains but not necessarily ranked among the best in a common problem domain (like inviting psychologists and sociologists to the economists' party) can invite alternative approaches that increase a team's problem-solving ability.

These insights bear a family resemblance to Robert Merton's argument about the discontinuous nature of scientific rewards (Merton, "The Matthew Effect in Science"), as recounted in greater detail in the endnotes for chapter 8. Building on that discussion, we might infer that the difference between the fortieth chair and the forty-first chair may simply be differences in styles of thinking. A scientist who conforms to the preferred style of thinking may be afforded a higher rank in the scientific community (and thus make the cutoff for the Royal Academy). In this light, Hong and Page might suggest that when bringing several members of the Royal Academy onto a problem-solving team, this effort should be complemented by also (explicitly) bringing on others who were not members of the Royal Academy (because their ideas and approaches may fall too far outside the mainstream). These nontraditional thinkers, perhaps at lower-tier universities, may provide exactly the kind cognitive diversity that Hong and Page have in mind for improving collective intelligence for the grand challenge of creativity.

There is also an intuitive connection between these ideas and the insights of the philosopher of science Thomas Kuhn in *The Structure of Scientific Revolutions* (University of Chicago Press, 1962). Kuhn won great renown for identifying the existence of "paradigm shifts" in science, which are discontinuities in problem-solving strategies. Historically, younger scientists from the new paradigm were kept out of power at elite institutions until the old guard (defending the old paradigm) retired or died off. Hong and Page's findings suggest that the ostensible incommensurability across different scientific paradigms might offer unexpected potential for innovative discoveries if junior or lower-tier members (of the new paradigm) are brought onto otherwise elite scientific teams with members of the old paradigm.

There is one caveat, however, that remains an interesting outstanding question for Hong and Page's point of view, which concerns the implication of Kuhn's claim about paradigm shifts: If scientific paradigms truly are incommensurable, as Kuhn maintains, then how would these cognitively diverse scientists, who are committed to different scientific paradigms—and thus have different definitions of what a scientific problem is and what constitutes a valid solution—effectively work together to produce coherent discoveries? The answer for Hong and Page is, I suspect, that there exists a multidimensional representation of cognitively diverse approaches (which may perhaps be simplified along the lines of a Venn diagram) that can reveal whether there is sufficient overlap between diverse thinkers' paradigms to determine whether they can effectively work together. Defining the parameters that determine how much overlap is needed between thinkers for productive collaboration is an interesting direction for future research on the "diversity trumps ability" findings in the grand challenge of creativity.

Page 168 **"satisficing" rather than optimizing**: As Alan Greenspan, the chairman of the US Federal Reserve Bank, famously remarked, the economic theory that he had relied upon while overseeing the US economy for nearly two decades suffered from "a flaw in the model that defines how the world works." After this flaw led to the near-collapse of the US economy in 2008, Greenspan testified to Congress that he and his peers in Washington were collectively "in a state of shocked disbelief." Gary Stix, "The Science of Economic Bubbles and Busts," *Scientific American Magazine* 301, no. 1 (July 2009). One useful corrective to this viewpoint was published by the psychologist Herb Simon, who identified the differences between "satisficing" behavior versus "optimizing" behavior in organizational decision-making (for which he was awarded the 1978 Nobel Prize in Economics): Herbert Simon, "Rational Choice and the Structure of the Environment," *Psychological Review* 63, no. 2 (1956): 129–138; Herbert A. Simon, *Administrative Behavior: A Study of Decision-Making Processes in Administrative Organization* (Macmillan, 1947); Herbert A. Simon, "Rational Decision Making in Business Organizations," *American Economic Review* 69, no. 4 (1979): 493–513.

Page 170 **"hallway effects" on scientific collaborations**: See the classic work by Tom Allen, *Managing the Flow of Technology* (MIT Press, 1977).

Page 171 **main factor driving communication and collaboration**: With respect to the effects of novel digital communication technologies on the formation of collaboration networks, Thomas Allen and Gunter Henn maintain that the importance of classic hallway effects remains largely unchanged:

> For example, rather than finding that the probability of telephone communication increases with distance, as face-to-face probability decays, our data show a decay in the use of all communication media with distance (following a "near-field" rise). . . . We do not keep separate sets of people, some of whom we communicate with by one medium and some by another. The more often we see someone face-to-face, the more likely it is that we will also telephone that person or communicate by another medium. (58)

See: Thomas J. Allen and Gunter W. Henn, *The Organization and Architecture of Innovation: Managing the Flow of Technology* (Butterworth-Heinemann, 2006).

Page 171 **not just better—it is *different***: Nobel Prize–winning physicist Philip W. Anderson ("More Is Different," *Science* 177 (1972): 393–396) identified crucial scaling dynamics in the emergence of complex (and unanticipated) system properties at larger scales. In the network dynamics of creativity, the lesson goes the other way, too—reducing the scale of connectivity in scientific research networks can qualitatively change their capacity for innovation.

Page 172 **architect Frank Gehry**: There are many "classic MIT" anecdotes about the Stata Center, such as metal water pails placed around the massive foyer to catch rainwater drip-dropping through the Stata Center's hundred-million-dollar roof. Later anecdotes about the Stata Center focused on the lawsuit in which MIT sued Frank Gehry (Frank O. Gehry & Associates) and the construction firm that built the Stata Center (Beacon Skanska, USA Building, Inc.), for design and construction defects, such as leaks, mold, cracking walls, poor drainage, and ice falling off the angled roofs. There was also one memorable tale about a lecture hall on the first floor of the Stata Center that had diagonal wooden slats on the front wall, which created a vertigo effect when a rectangular projection screen was placed in front of the wall. One colleague recalled teaching an introductory programming class at 8am on Monday morning, and having several first-year students run out of the classroom with severe nausea due to these vertigo effects.

Page 173 **monkeys in the treetops**: From the Hunter Douglas Architectural website:

> Characteristically, Frank Gehry's design for the MIT Stata Center matches visually engaging exteriors with carefully considered interior spaces. Inspired in part by an "orangutan village," the design segregated "tree house" offices above and below communal laboratory spaces. From that starting point, Gehry and his team constructed dozens of configurations using physical models. After a long process of perfecting the models, CATIA software generated digital models for building specifications. Nysan shading systems from Hunter Douglas were a particularly distinctive feature of Gehry's final design. Nearly 1,200 custom roller shades were created to fit openings that ranged from rhombuses to trapezoids and various other parallelograms.

Page 173 **optimize their creativity**: There are several relevant theoretical and empirical studies of optimizing team networks for creative problem solving, including: David Lazer and Allan Friedman, "The Network Structure of Exploration and Exploitation," *Administrative Science Quarterly* 52 (2007): 667–694; Devon Brackbill and Damon Centola, "Impact of Network Structure on Collective Learning: An Experimental Study in a Data Science Competition," *PLOS One* 15 (2020): e0237978; Centola, *Change*; Roger Guimerà, Brian Uzzi, Jarrett Spiro, and Luís A. Nunes Amaral, "Team Assembly Mechanisms Determine Collaboration Network Structure and Team Performance," *Science* 308, no. 5722 (2005): 697–702; and Charles J. Gomez and David M. J. Lazer, "Clustering Knowledge and Dispersing Abilities Enhances Collective Problem Solving in a Network," *Nature Communications* 10 (2019): 5146. Related findings by Abdullah Almaatouq, Mohammed Alsobay, Ming Yin, and Duncan J. Watts ("Task Complexity Moderates Group Synergy," *Proceedings of the National Academy of Sciences of the USA* 118, no. 36 (2021): e2101062118) are consistent with these findings, suggesting that simple problems may be more efficiently solved by autonomous individuals, while more complex problems are more efficiently solved by interconnected teams of researchers. Other related work (W. Mason and D. J. Watts, "Collaborative Learning in Networks," *Proceedings of the National Academy of Sciences of the USA* 109, no. 3 (2012): 764–769), suffers from complications due to the confounding of learning dynamics with popularity dynamics, as discussed in D. Barkoczi and M. Galesic, "Social Learning Strategies Modify the Effect of Network Structure on Group Performance," *Nature Communications* 7 (2016): 13109; and Damon Centola, "The Network Science of Collective Intelligence," *Trends in Cognitive Sciences 26, no. 11* (2022): 923–941.

Page 174 **winning teams bragging rights**: The results from these experiments were first reported in Brackbill and Centola, "Impact of Network Structure," and subsequently discussed in Centola, *Change*.

Page 175 **records of Fortune 500 firms**: This formalization of complex problems using a "rugged fitness landscape" is based on Stuart Kaufmann's evolutionary optimization model (*The Origins of Order: Self-Organization and Selection in Evolution*, Oxford University Press, 1993) by David Lazer and Allan Friedman ("Network Structure"), which is a cognate of the well-known one-armed bandit problem: Dinah Rosenberg, Eilon Solan, and Nicolas Vieille, "Social Learning in One-Arm Bandit Problems," *Econometrica* 75, no. 6 (2007): 1591–1611; Susan Athey, Undral Byambadalai, Vitor Hadad, Sanath Kumar Krishnamurthy, Weiwen Leung, and Joseph Jay Williams, "Contextual Bandits in a Survey Experiment on Charitable Giving: Within-Experiment Outcomes Versus Policy Learning," arXiv preprint (2002), arXiv:2211.12004.

As shown in figure E.10.1, a simple problem has a single peak and can be solved by iterative hill-climbing; by contrast, a complex problem has a rugged landscape with multiple peaks, such that there is no way for hill-climbers to know whether their immediate hill is a local maximum or a global maximum, since the space of peaks can be indefinitely large.

In the grand challenge of choosing, I showed you that there are "easy" problems and "hard" problems. Easy problems are those for which the vast majority of people can approximate the right answer, and hard problems are those for which most people get it wrong. For most populations, guessing the weight of a cow is an easy problem, while estimating the amount of federal spending on foreign is a hard one.

The basic finding from part I of this book is that for easy problems any structure will do. Since the vast majority of people know the right answer, a simple majority-rule procedure will suffice for making a good collective choice. But as Condorcet observed, things are different when it comes to hard problems. When most people are wrong, majority rule will also be wrong, as will the conclusions that typically emerge from centralized information networks. When it comes to hard problems, egalitarian networks offer a way out of Condorcet's bind. Egalitarian networks create gravity wells around accurate individuals, which help to pull the population past

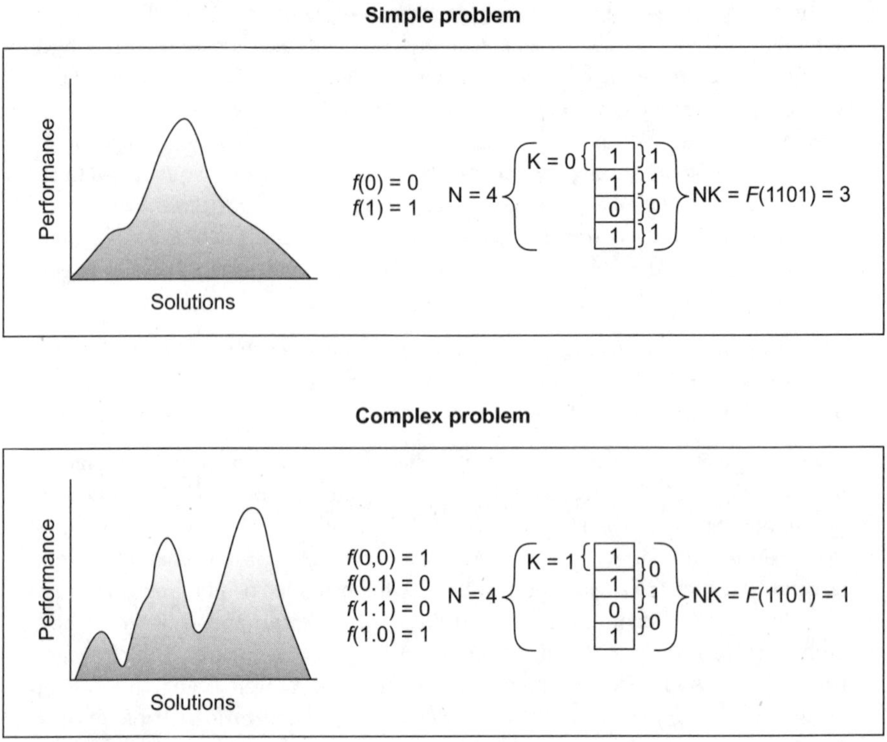

FIGURE E.10.1
Simple and complex problems. Adapted from Centola, "Network Science."

their collective biases. As populations converge, collective bias dissipates and individual judgment improves—often without anyone noticing.

But things are different for the grand challenge of creativity, in which problems are not divided between easy and hard, but between "simple" and "complex" (figure E.10.2). This is because both easy problems and hard problems for the grand challenge of choosing are considered to be simple problems for the grand challenge of creativity. A simple problem has a single, continuous dimension along which incremental progress can approach the optimal answer—such as approximating the weight of a cow, the rate of US foreign aid spending, or the number of jelly beans in a jar. In every case, repeated revisions can lead populations toward an increasingly accurate approximation. This holds true for all simple problems, regardless of whether they are easy or hard. This is because the line between easy and hard is cultural and contextual. It changes with the group and with the times. For instance, a simple problem that may be easy for one group (like farmers guessing the weight of a cow) may be hard for another group (like professional political scientists, for whom guessing the rate of federal funding on foreign aid would be "easy," but—except for part-time cowboy Scott Page—guessing the weight of a cow might be "hard"). In this sense, calling a simple problem easy or hard is more like a description of a population, rather than a problem.

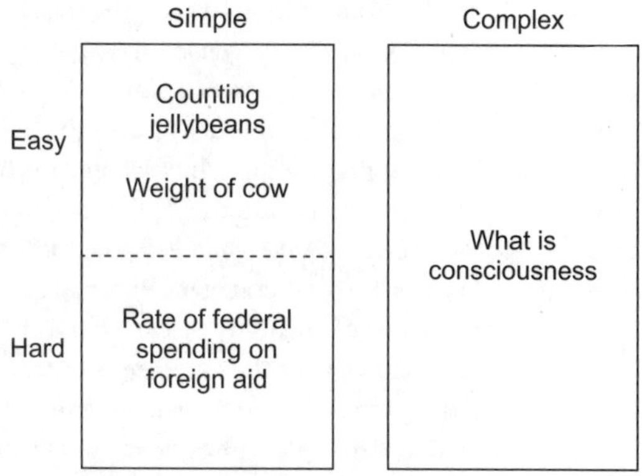

FIGURE E.10.2
Distinction between simple and complex problems.

Complex problems are a different beast. Regardless of the culture or the context, complex problems are challenging because they have multiple interacting dimensions. Improving along one dimension without attending to the others may yield quick, incremental improvements that may also undermine the potential for further improvement, or may even obscure which features of the problem are essential to reach an optimal solution. Complex problems require multiple points of view, and thus benefit from diverse teams of people exploring different approaches to problem-solving. The solution to a complex problem may come from an unusual and unfamiliar combination of ideas, which may be so unorthodox as to birth an entirely new field of discovery—for instance, research into the problems of "language, thought, and consciousness" cultivated exploratory collaborations between philosophers, linguists, psychologists, and neuroscientists, giving birth to the new field of "cognitive science."

Unlike simple problems, for which the goal of collective intelligence is to reach an accurate consensus to optimize a single choice, for complex problems, the goal is to create a space for serendipity and collaboration, which can cultivate the unbounded potential for creativity and innovation.

Page 179 **capacity for innovation**: This discussion on the size and structure of scientific teams (and the associated quotations) come from several important articles by James Evans and his collaborators: Lingfei Wu, Dashun Wang, and James A. Evans, "Large Teams Develop and Small Teams Disrupt Science and Technology," *Nature* 566 (2019): 378–382; Fengli Xu, Lingfei Wu, and James A. Evans, "Flat Teams

Drive Scientific Innovation," *Proceedings of the National Academy of Sciences of the USA* 119, no. 23 (2022): e2200927119; and Santo Fortunato, Carl T. Bergstrom, Katy Börner, James A. Evans, Dirk Helbing, Staša Milojević, et al., "Science of Science," *Science* 359, no. 6379 (2018): eaao0185.

Page 181 **large teams still have their place**: In the 1940s, the social theorist Michael Polanyi ("The Growth of Thought in Society." *Economica* 8 (1941): 428–456; "Planning and Spontaneous Order," *The Manchester School of Economic and Social Studies* 16 (1948): 237–268) used the idea of spontaneous order to describe the principal force that underlies all scientific and social practices in which people freely and creatively produce stable norms and productive communities. These insights bear a striking resemblance to those of Friedrich Hayek (*Studies in Philosophy, Politics and Economics*, Routledge, 1978). Polanyi's account of social emergence resonates with the dynamics of discovery in the grand challenge of creativity discussed in this chapter.

In the 1950s, Polanyi's bottom-up view of the emergence of creativity and innovation in science stood in stark contrast to the Soviet program of science, which fiercely advocated for centralized leadership as the best way to ensure that scientific efforts would serve the interests of society. According to the Soviets, centralization would guarantee that science was steered in the service of solving real-world problems of national importance, rather than simply exploring ideas for the sake of discovery. Polanyi argued, in opposition, that the freedom of decentralized research to explore new topics and directions—especially the impractical ones—was the lifeblood of science. Polanyi's "Building 20" account of scientific innovation suggests that the most productive scientific work comes from the "spontaneous order" that emerges from serendipitous encounters and unexpected scientific collaborations.

There are still scientists today who suggest that social science should be structured in a top-down "solution-oriented" way (rather than encouraging scientists to pursue discovery for discovery's sake). (See Duncan Watts, "Should Social Science Be More Solution-Oriented?," *Nature Human Behaviour* 1 (2017): 0015.) The findings in this chapter offer a response to this position. I agree that a centralized or "directed" system for governing the trajectory of scientific efforts may be very effective for solving well-defined engineering problems (as discussed in this chapter). However, as Polanyi argued, such a system of directed research would inevitably limit the potential for serendipitous discoveries and heterodox collaborations, which may give rise to entirely new fields of scientific endeavor (as was the case for the recent innovations of "cognitive science" and "network science"). Even if a centralized authority has the best of intentions, it would inevitably hem in the horizons of scientific research. See also Philip Kitcher (*The Advancement of Science: Science Without Legend, Objectivity Without Illusions*, Oxford University Press, 1993) on the value of independent exploration for creating useful intellectual redundancies, which enable independent confirmation of scientific discoveries.

Page 181 **J. Robert Oppenheimer**: Robert Oppenheimer is typically considered to have been the hub of the Manhattan project research network, although that distinction may have in fact been granted to a key military official.

Page 182 **". . . that's the secret"**: This quote is from Dr. Nelson Y. S. Kiang (founding director of the Eaton-Peabody Laboratories) during a retrospective event for Building 20 (at the time of its razing), "MIT's Building 20: The Magical Incubator." The video recording of the event includes enjoyable speeches and anecdotes from many Building 20 residents; see more at https://infinite.mit.edu/video/mits-building-20-magical-incubator/.

PART IV: COLLECTIVE ADAPTATION

CHAPTER 11: UPENDING SOCIAL ENGINEERING

Page 188 **". . . before its eyes"**: P. Laplace, *A Philosophical Essay on Probabilities* (Dover, [1814] 1951).

Page 188 **is already determined**: Theological and philosophical debates about free will date back to at least 450 BCE.

Page 188 **free will is an absolute necessity**: See the transformative free-will argument by Peter F. Strawson, "Freedom and Resentment," *Proceedings of the British Academy* 48 (1962): 1–25.

Page 188 **arbiter of moral accountability**: The necessity for free will notwithstanding, the forward march of science has irrevocably altered its parameters. Take crime. At one time, a person's moral failings were viewed as evidence of evil, which demanded swift, often grotesque punishment. As science has progressed, some behaviors once viewed as immoral have come to be seen as the causal result of neurological or psychological deficiencies. If these arbitrary deviations from normality impair a person's ability to act morally or drive a person to act immorally, a jury may conclude that the person didn't have the necessary moral agency required to be responsible for their crime. In such a case, punishment is not a just dessert.

Page 188 **he called "social physics"**: Adolphe Quetelet (*Essay on Social Physics: Treatise on Man and the Development of His Faculties*, 1835) borrowed the phrase *social physics* from the sociologist Auguste Comte, who first coined the term in 1825 and then abandoned it once Quetelet's use became popular. Comte defined social physics as "that science which occupies itself with social phenomena, considered in the same light as astronomical, physical, chemical, and physiological phenomena, that is to say as being subject to natural and invariable laws, the discovery of which is the special object of its researches."

Page 189 **". . . great, good or beautiful"**: Adolphe Jacques Quetelet, *Sur l'homme et le développement de ses facultés, ou essai de physique sociale* (1835); English translation: *A Treatise on Man and the Development of His Faculties*, trans. R. Knox, ed. T. Smibert (1842).

Page 189 **ideal of the perfect person**: At the beginning of this book, I showed you how Francis Galton followed in Quetelet's footsteps by applying the mathematics of averages to human populations. In 1907, Galton used this method to uncover the wisdom of the crowd among farmers at a county fair. It was not just Galton who followed Quetelet's lead. Quetelet's social physics helped to guide John Snow's approach to uncovering the source of English cholera (*On the Mode of Communication of Cholera*, 1849), a discovery that effectively founded the field of social epidemiology. Quetelet's thinking also inspired the emerging scientific field of experimental psychology, which was premised upon the ability to distinguish between normal and abnormal minds. These rapidly growing fields were a testament to the exploding intellectual enthusiasm for the applied sciences of society and the promise of Quetelet's social physics to deliver an optimal model for public policy based on a statistical model of "normal" human behavior. These innovations were galvanized by Quetelet's central philosophical conceit that at the heart of humanity lies a perfect, ideal protype of human agency. For an expanded discussion of these topics, see Todd Rose, *The End of Average: How We Succeed in a World That Values Sameness* (HarperCollins, 2016).

Page 189 **anchoring bias and availability bias**: Daniel Kahneman, in *Thinking, Fast and Slow* (Farrar, Straus and Giroux, 2011), provides a useful catalogue of cognitive biases that highlight the primary insights of prospect theory.

Page 189 **model of human perfection**: During the 1977–1978 fellowship year, Kahneman was a fellow at the Center for Advanced Study at Stanford, Tversky was on the faculty at Stanford, and Thaler was visiting at the NBER offices at Stanford (which were located on Alta Road, halfway down the hill from the Center for Advanced Study).

Page 190 **not, in the everyday sense, normal**: The best performers on economics problems are sometimes referred to sardonically as *Homo economicus*. See Cass Sunstein and Richard Thaler, *Nudge: Improving Decisions About Health, Wealth, and Happiness* (Yale University Press, 2008).

Page 190 **referred to as "nudging"**: See the excellent and highly engaging book by Sunstein and Thaler, *Nudge*.

Page 191 **enlightened public policy**: Opt-in strategies have also been deployed in clinical settings. These interventions use electronic forms that auto-select generic medications over brand-label medication, resulting in an increase in the prescription of generics from 40 percent to 96 percent. As in earlier examples, most nudges focus on individual behaviors, such as exploiting the effort tax of thinking through alternatives. Nevertheless, some nudges have tried to explicitly harness social norms, such as providing information about peers' household energy consumption to encourage neighboring households to lower their energy consumption (and conform to neighborhood norms). Many useful discussions of nudging strategies—their success and failures—can be found in the journal *Behavioural Public Policy*, including: Shai Davidai and Eldar Shafir, "Are 'Nudges' Getting a Fair Shot? Joint Versus Separate Evaluation," *Behavioural Public Policy* 4, no. 3 (2020): 273–291; Alejandro Hortal, "Nudging and Educating: Bounded Axiological Rationality in Behavioral Insights," *Behavioural Public Policy* 4, no. 3 (2020): 292–315; Cass R. Sunstein, "Nudges That Fail," *Behavioural Public Policy* 1, no. 1 (2017): 4–25; Nara Rela, "On Nudges That Fail," *Behavioural Public Policy* 7, no. 3 (2023): 758–772; Sander Van Der Linden,

"The Future of Behavioral Insights: On the Importance of Socially Situated Nudges," *Behavioural Public Policy* 2, no. 2 (2018): 207–217.

Page 191 **even backfiring**: "Boomerang effects" have been found to arise when nudging strategies provide social information that informs high performing individuals that they are "overperforming" (e.g., students with higher than average attendance rates, or households with excellent energy consumption rates). The result can be to subsequently lower high performers' performance (e.g., increase absenteeism among students, and increased energy consumption among households). See: Avishalom Tor, "Nudges That Should Fail?," *Behavioural Public Policy* 4, no. 3 (2020): 316–342; and Thomas Schramme, "Why Health-Enhancing Nudges Fail," *Health Care Analysis* 32, no. 1 (2024): 33–46.

Page 192 **saving us from ourselves**: Some argue that the moral justification for nudges is that they enable people to do what they would have done without situational influences—again referring back to their private, solitary selves as the reference point for moral agency (as many philosophers do). I advocate, in the spirit of Barnard Williams (*Ethics and the Limits of Philosophy*, Harvard University Press, 1985), a contextualized conception of ethical and moral reasoning—in which the "nudge situation" cannot make reference to preserving or recovering some original "solitary/reflective" intelligence of the individual without also taking into account the social and contextual expectations surrounding them. In particular, in our experimental and theoretical studies in the grand challenge of choosing, we consistently found that both individuals and collectives underperform in the placebo control groups, and excel in the structured information-exchange networks. The solitary condition did not provide a reference point for "free thought," but rather for unchallenged and often biased thought. Thus, the reasoning of solitary individuals may be qualitatively different (but not freer) than that of socially embedded actors. For a helpful analysis of the problems and consequences associated with applying individual-focused public policies to socially embedded populations, see Nick Chater and George Loewenstein, "The i-Frame and the s-Frame: How Focusing on Individual-Level Solutions Has Led Behavioral Public Policy Astray," *Behavioral and Brain Sciences* 46 (2023). See also: Robert Sugden, "Do People Really Want to Be Nudged Towards Healthy Lifestyles?," *International Review of Economics* 64 (2017): 113–123.

Page 192 **the best of all possible worlds**: Compare this to Voltaire's foil in *Candide* (1759), Dr. Pangloss, who is used to mock the philosopher Gottfried Wilhelm Leibniz via his conception of the "best of all possible worlds."

Page 192 **nudging us in the right direction?** See: Gerd Gigerenzer, "On the Supposed Evidence for Libertarian Paternalism," *Review of Philosophy and Psychology* 6, no. 3 (2015): 361–383.

Page 193 **torrent of conspiracy theories**: See Dolores Albarracin, Julia Albarracin, Man-pui Sally Chan, and Kathleen Hall Jamieson, *Creating Conspiracy Beliefs: How Our Thoughts Are Shaped* (Cambridge University Press, 2021).

Page 193 **African American community**: See Rebecca Kluchin, *Fit to Be Tied: Sterilization and Reproductive Rights in America, 1950–1980* (Rutgers University Press, 2009). Useful research on the downstream effects of the history of medical mistreatment on the uptake of preventive health measures among vulnerable populations can be found in Bernice Roberts Kennedy, Christopher Clomus Mathis, and Angela K. Woods, "African Americans and Their Distrust of the Health Care System: Healthcare for Diverse Populations," *Journal of Cultural Diversity* 14, no. 2 (2007): 56–60; and Elizabeth B. Blankenship et al., "Sentiment, Contents, and Retweets: A Study of Two Vaccine-Related Twitter Datasets," *Permanente Journal* 22 (2018): 17–138.

Page 193 **less clinical care for pain management**: The referenced study is: Kelly M. Hoffman, Sophie Trawalter, Jordan R. Axt, and M. Norman Oliver, "Racial Bias in Pain Assessment and Treatment Recommendations, and False Beliefs About Biological Differences Between Blacks and Whites," *Proceedings of the National Academy of Sciences of the USA* 113, no. 16 (2015): 4296–4301.

Page 194 **"You haven't addressed the harm from years ago!"**: The quote comes from: Sayuri Sekimitsu, Jessica Simon, Mika Matsuuchi Lindsley, et al., "Exploring COVID-19 Vaccine Hesitancy Amongst Black Americans: Contributing Factors and Motivators," *American Journal of Health Promotion* 36, no. 8 (2022): 1304–1315.

Page 194 **more suspicious they are of mainstream public health services**: Sekimitsu et al., "Exploring COVID-19 Vaccine Hesitancy Amongst Black Americans." Related work at the intersection of race and mistrust of American public health can be found in: Mohsen Bazargan, Sharon Cobb, and Shervin Assari, "Discrimination and Medical Mistrust in a Racially and Ethnically Diverse Sample of California Adults," *Annals of Family Medicine* 19, no. 1 (2021): 4–15; Martha Hostetter and Sarah Klein, "Understanding and Ameliorating Medical Mistrust Among Black Americans," *Transforming Care* (newsletter), Commonwealth Fund, January 14, 2021.

Page 195 **the risk of skin cancer**: Readings related to past "U-turns" in American public health include, on the topic of breast milk: Aifric O'Sullivan, Xuan He, Elizabeth M. S. McNiven, Neill W. Haggarty, Bo Lönnerdal, and Carolyn M. Slupsky, "Early Diet Impacts Infant Rhesus Gut Microbiome, Immunity, and Metabolism," *Journal of Proteome Research* 12, no. 6 (2013): 2833–2845; Lauren M. Rossen, Alan E. Simon, and Kirsten A. Herrick, "Types of Infant Formulas Consumed in the United States," *Clinical Pediatrics* 55 (2016): 278–285. On the topic of topical tanning solutions: Robert Stern, "Prevalence of a History of Skin Cancer in 2007: Results of an Incidence-Based Model," *Archives of Dermatological Research* 146, no. 3 (2010): 279–282. And on the topic of radiation therapy: M. D. Lichter, M. R. Karagas, L. A. Mott, et al., "Therapeutic Ionizing Radiation and the Incidence of Basal Cell Carcinoma and Squamous Cell Carcinoma," *Archives of Dermatology* 136, no. 8 (2000):1007–1011.

Page 195 **with a vaccination drive**: In recent work, Douglas Guilbeault and I define new network measures underlying the successful dynamics of mobilization for behavior change via social reinforcement in wide bridges (Centola, *Change*, and Guilbeault and Centola, "Topological Measures"). To see how these networks operate in the mobilization of vaccination drives by faith-based organizations, see: Uzma Syed, Olive Kapera, Aparajita Chandrasekhar, Barbara T. Baylor, Adebola Hassan, Marina Magalhães, et al., "The Role of Faith-Based Organizations in Improving Vaccination Confidence & Addressing Vaccination Disparities to Help Improve Vaccine Uptake: A Systematic Review," *Vaccines* 11, no. 2 (2023): 449.

Page 196 **"teen queen of Chicago's gangland"**: This descriptive phrase is used in Desmond Patton, Jeffrey Lane, Patrick Leonard, and Jamie C. Macbeth, "Gang Violence on the Digital Street: Case Study of a South Side Chicago Gang Member's Twitter Communication," *New Media & Society* 19, no. 7 (2017): 1000–1018. An earlier article discussing Gakirah Barnes but not using this phrase is J. Swaine, "Chicago Gang Shootings Go on as Mayor Emanuel Boasts Crime at 'Record Low,'" *The Guardian*, April 19, 2014, https://www.theguardian.com/world/2014/apr/19/chicago-deadly-shooting-guns-rahm-emanuel-2014.

Page 197 **the horrors of teen infamy**: Gakirah Barnes's story has been thoughtfully explored by my colleague in the Annenberg School for Communication at the University of Pennsylvania, Desmond Patton: Desmond Patton, Jamie MacBeth, Sarita Schoenebeck, Katherine Shear, and Kathleen McKeown, "Accommodating Grief on Twitter: An Analysis of Expressions of Grief Among Gang Involved Youth on Twitter Using Qualitative Analysis and Natural Language Processing," *Biomedical Informatics Insights* 10 (2018): 1178222618763155.

Page 197 **Where is free will now?** These pictures of Gakirah Barnes (figure E.11.1) draw out the moral question: Was she an assassin by nature, or were her life chances bound to the neighborhood networks in which she was embedded?

Figure E.11.1
Gakirah Barnes at thirteen (left) and fifteen (right). Images adapted from Frank Main, "'She Called Herself a Hitta'—a 17-Year-Old Female Assassin Operated on the South Side," *Chicago Sun Times*, July 23, 2015.

CHAPTER 12: THINGS FALL APART—AND THAT'S PROGRESS

Page 200 **ineluctably drawn into it**: See these groundbreaking studies by Andrew Papachristos on networks, contagion, and gun violence:

Geoffrey Wood and Andrew V. Papachristos, "Reducing Gunshot Victimization in High-Risk Social Networks Through Direct and Spillover Effects," *Nature Human Behaviour* 3 (2019): 1164–1170.

Andrew V. Papachristos, "Murder by Structure: Dominance Relations and the Social Structure of Gang Homicide," *American Journal of Sociology* 115, no. 1 (2009): 74–128.

Andrew V. Papachristos, David M. Hureau, and Anthony A. Braga, "The Corner and the Crew: The Influence of Geography and Social Networks on Gang Violence," *American Sociological Review* 78, no. 3 (2013): 417–447.

Andrew V. Papachristos, Christopher Wildeman, and Elizabeth Roberto, "Tragic, but Not Random: The Social Contagion of Nonfatal Gunshot Injuries," *Social Science & Medicine* 125 (2015): 139–150.

Andrew V. Papachristos, Anthony A. Braga, and David M. Hureau, "Social Networks and the Risk of Gunshot Injury," *Journal of Urban Health* 89, no. 6 (2012): 992–1003.

Matthew Tracy, Anthony A. Braga, and Andrew V. Papachristos, "The Transmission of Gun and Other Weapon-Involved Violence Within Social Networks," *Epidemiologic Reviews* 38, no. 1 (2016): 70–86.

Page 200 **pattern of shootings within each community**: See Northwestern Neighborhood & Network Initiative (N3), *A Network Analysis of Three Weekends of Shootings in Chicago, June 18–July 5* (Institute for Policy Research, January 8, 2021).

Page 200 **housing projects and multifamily dwellings**: Because most people don't end up as dots on the map, how is it possible to figure out who (of the tens of thousands of people in each neighborhood) are at the greatest risk for violence? This is the question for which Andrew Papachristos's work on networks was able to provide a new answer. See also: Papachristos and Braga, "Social Networks."

Page 201 **nodes do not tell a story**: The network displayed in this figure is an ego network subgraph extracted from a much larger network of gun violence in Chicago; see N3, *Network Analysis of Three Weekends.*

Page 203 **in person or via Wi-Fi**: For an account of the "digital street," and how face to face conflict manifests online, see: D. U. Patton, J. Lane, P. Leonard, J. Macbeth, and J. R. Smith Lee, "Gang Violence on the Digital Street: Case Study of a South Side Chicago Gang Member's Twitter Communication," *New Media & Society* 19, no. 7 (2017): 1000–1018.

Page 203 **called "collective efficacy"**: See the groundbreaking work on this topic by fellow sociologist Robert J. Sampson: "Neighborhoods and Violent Crime: A

Multilevel Study of Collective Efficacy," *Science* 277 (1997): 918–924; *The Great American City: Chicago and the Enduring Neighborhood Effect* (University of Chicago Press, 2011). See also related work on neighborhood-based organizational ties in Mario Luis Small, "Neighborhood Institutions as Resource Brokers: Childcare Centers, Interorganizational Ties, and Resource Access among the Poor," *Social Problems* 53, no. 2 (2006): 274–292; and Robert Putnam, *Bowling Alone* (Simon & Schuster, 2000), in particular 307–310. The implications of these findings for the effects of geographic space on collective intelligence bear a family resemblance to the findings discussed in chapter 10 of this book regarding the creativity and productivity of MIT's Building 20. See, for instance, Jane Jacobs's discussions of "mixed-use" buildings and neighborhoods (*The Death and Life of Great American Cities*, Random House, 1961), which draw out a strong analogy between Building 20 and successful urban planning, as discussed in chapter 13.

Page 205 **bonds from which moral sentiments are born**: See the influential philosophical work of Bernard Williams, *Ethics and the Limits of Philosophy* (Harvard University Press, 1985).

Page 205 **invitation for poor performance**: Hierarchical organizations have been argued to place a lower cognitive burden on individuals attempting to understand organizational structure (see: Emily M. Zitek and Larissa Z. Tiedens, "The Fluency of Social Hierarchy: The Ease with Which Hierarchical Relationships Are Seen, Remembered, Learned, and Liked," *Journal of Personality and Social Psychology* 102, no. 1 (2012): 98–115). This view offers a psychological reason why egalitarian organizations suffer pressures to conform to more familiar hierarchical structures. However, there is an important sociological response, which is that the greater cognitive burden experienced by individuals attempting to understand the structure of relations within collectivist organizations may also be due to the familiarity of hierarchical organizations with modern industrial economies. See, for instance, the discussion below on the ecological pressures for "organizational isomorphism" in Paul DiMaggio and Water Powell ("The Iron Cage Revisited: Institutional Isomorphism and Collective Rationality in Organizational Fields," *American Sociological Review* 48, no. 2 (1983): 147–160); see also Michel de Montaigne (*Essays*, 1580) for the effects of custom (i.e., familiarity) on normative views and preferences.

Page 205 **". . . worth of the individual to the organization"**: Joyce Rothschild-Whitt, "The Collectivist Organization: An Alternative to Rational-Bureaucratic Models," *American Sociological Review* 44, no. 4 (1979): 509–527.

Page 205 **commitment to one another's success**: We might also consider cases where communities attempt to catalyze collective efficacy (e.g., by organizing protest marches), but fail to achieve any of the structural or long-term benefits (such as buy-in from clergy, greater investment from city hall, and sustained engagement among neighbors) because their community does not have a sufficiently cohesive structure to support sustained collective action. See a related discussion of the changes in collective efficacy that supported the Black Lives Matter movement (prior to 2014 versus after 2020), which were a direct result of the changing structure of online community networks (see Centola, *Change*). See also related structural insights regarding Minnesota residents' mobilized responses to ICE attacks on US citizens, which are discussed in Adam Serwer, "The Pushback Against ICE Exposed a Series of Mistaken Assumptions," *The Atlantic*, January 26, 2026.

Page 206 **"The basic thesis is . . ."**: William Julius Wilson, *The Truly Disadvantaged: The Inner City, the Underclass, and Public Policy* (1987; University of Chicago Press, 2012), 144.

Page 207 **structural principles of collective intelligence that ensure success**: Two primary features of network structure govern the grand challenges discussed in this book: *speed* and *power*.

The speed of information flow is measured in terms of simple path length, which is the typical number of steps (i.e., narrow bridges) required to travel across the shortest path from any person to any other person. An internet structure (complete graph) is the limiting condition, which has a minimal simple path length of 1. Regardless of population size, in an internet structure everyone is one step away from everyone else. Centralized "star" networks, such as the firehose structure, have the next lowest simple path length of slightly less than 2. Everyone is at most two steps away from everyone else, while the central node is only one step away from everyone. Again, this is regardless of population size. In some instances, like the grand challenge of coordination, firehose networks may converge faster than internet networks even though they have a larger simple path length. This is because the central actor can force coordination on their own idea.

Power is determined by the distribution of ties in the social network. The more skewed the connectivity in a network, the greater the inequality in power. Firehose networks have the greatest inequality in power—i.e., they give the smallest fraction of the population (a single person) the greatest control over the flow of information—and therefore these structures can have the greatest negative impact on the dynamics of collective intelligence (for instance, in the grand challenge of choosing). Egalitarian structures, by contrast, give equal control over the flow of information to everyone in the population.

In the uncontrolled empirical world, there are vast topological differences across social networks. None conform to the ideal types discussed here. However, every network, empirical or theoretical, is bound to the governing parameters of speed and power (shown in figure E.12.1). The main contribution of a theoretical analysis of network structure is that it enables us to identity how these governing topological features of social networks (which are measurable for every network, across every setting) can predict the trajectory of collective intelligence for each of the grand challenges. Thus, given any empirical or theoretical network structure, the network's location along the continua of speed and power indicates how that topology will affect the population's collective intelligence for each grand challenge.

Take the familiar example of a small world network. There are many empirical settings in which the introduction of weak ties into an otherwise clustered geographic structure will accelerate the flow of information. Although the small world network topology was not discussed in these chapters, the results nevertheless encompass the small world structure (and the unbounded number of other network topologies that may arise in uncontrolled empirical settings, or exploratory theoretical settings). The analyses in the foregoing chapters reveal how a small world network would affect collective intelligence in each of the grand challenges.

Figure E.12.1 explains how.

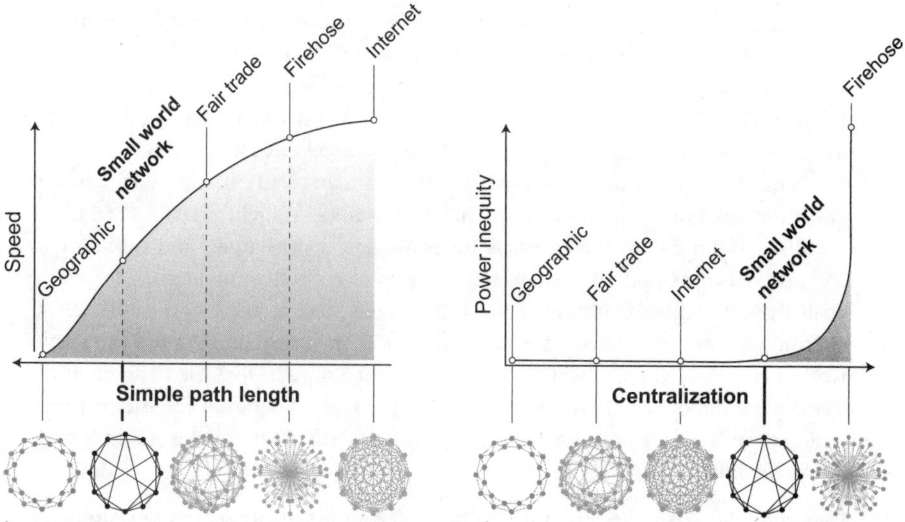

FIGURE E.12.1
Network continua of speed and power.

First, consider the grand challenges in which informational speed (i.e., simple path length) governs collective intelligence. In a small world network, simple path length is typically smaller than it would be for an equivalently sized geographic network, but larger than it would be for the limiting case of an internet network. Thus, in the grand challenge of coordination, successfully reaching consensus on social convention in a small world network would be more difficult than it would be in an internet network, but easier than it would be in a clustered geographic network.

The speed of information flow affects collective intelligence in the opposite way for the grand challenge of creativity. In that grand challenge, a small world network would be less effective than a geographic structure for creating innovative teams, but slightly more effective than an internet structure or a firehose network.

When it comes to the grand challenges that are governed by power rather than speed, a small world network is less equitable than any of the egalitarian networks—i.e., a geographic network, a fair-trade network, or an internet network—since they each have an equal distribution of ties among all members of the community. (N.B.: This observation about equity assumes that the small world topology is created via the Watts–Strogatz rewiring, or via the Newman–Watts tie-addition method—both of which create small inequities in the distribution of ties. By contrast, the Maslov–Sneppen rewiring method creates the small-world structure while keeping the degree distribution constant. In the case of Maslov–Sneppen rewiring, the small world network would be an egalitarian network and would perform the same as the other egalitarian networks with regard to power.)

See Duncan Watts, "Networks, Dynamics, and the Small-World Phenomenon," *American Journal of Sociology* 105 (1999): 493–527; Mark Newman and Duncan Watts, "Scaling and Percolation in the Small-World Network Model," *Physical Review E* 60 (1999): 7332–7342; Sergei Maslov and Kim Sneppen, "Specificity and Stability in Topology of Protein Networks," *Science* 296, no. 5569 (2022): 910–913.

Using the Watt–Strogatz rewiring, or the Newman–Watts tie-addition network alteration methods, the small world network would be slightly less equitable in the distribution of ties than any of the egalitarian architectures, and thus would be expected to exhibit slightly degraded levels of collective intelligence in grand challenges for which equity increases intelligence, such as the grand challenge of choosing. However, the small degree of inequity in the distribution of ties in a small world network is still significantly less than the inequity in firehose network, thus a small-world architecture would be expected to exhibit far greater robustness in its performance in the grand challenge of choosing than a firehose network, in which power inequity it maximized.

Page 208 **less centralized than it had been**: For an excellent analysis of centralization as a structural adaptation in responses to threat, see N. Gizem Bacaksizlar Turbic and Mirta Galesic, "Group Threat, Political Extremity, and Collective Dynamics in Online Discussions," *Scientific Reports* 13 (2023): 2206.

Page 209 **rapid military action**: For a general discussion of the many forms of collective adaptation, see this excellent review article: Mirta Galesic, Daniel Barkoczi, Andrew M. Berdahl, Dora Biro, Giuseppe Carbone, Ilaria Giannoccaro, et al., "Beyond Collective Intelligence: Collective Adaptation," *Journal of the Royal Society Interface* 20, no. 200 (2023): 2020220736. See also early insights about these collective dynamics in the classic work by James March and Herb Simon, *Organizations* (Wiley, 1958).

Page 209 **just as Cincinnatus had**: For a thoughtful historical discussion of Rome's policy of appointing dictators during a crisis, see Andrew Lintott, *The Constitution of Rome* (Oxford University Press, 1999). From this history, it is clear that Cincinnatus was neither the first nor the last citizen to take on this mantle. In addition to military action, dictators could also be appointed to address internal matters of state, such as convening the Senate or quelling sedition. The later incarnations of this state policy, leading up the rule of the Caesars, gave much broader powers to the dictator, including the ability to rewrite Roman law and change the constitution—which inevitably led to structural adaptations that made centralization self-reinforcing; which in turn undermined the adaptive capacity (and therefore the structural intelligence) of the Roman Empire.

Page 211 **watchword of successful teams**: The evolution of network terminology across fields has led to an unfortunate confounding of the nomenclature. *Cohesiveness* is used in urban sociology to refer to clustered geographic networks (as in Chicago neighborhoods), while in organizational studies and management science it corresponds to teams that have an internet structure (such as highly unified teams). This conflation of meanings can lead to obvious challenges for collective intelligence research, given the important differences between clustered geographic networks and internet networks. My preferred solution is to reserve the term *cohesiveness* for clustered geographic networks, as in urban sociology, and to use *unifying* to capture the desirable effects of internet networks for team camaraderie, rapid coordination, and overall esprit de corps in team settings.

Page 212 **approaches adopted by their colleagues**: This analysis of collective adaptation across grand challenges offers a resolution to the paradox of why cohesive teams (in the organizational sense of *unified teams*) have been found to be both more successful *and* less successful in organizational settings (Brian Mullen and Caroline Copper, "The Relation Between Group Cohesiveness and Performance: An Integration," *Psychological Bulletin* 115, no. 2 (1994): 210–227). Resolution comes from the observation in internet networks highly unified teams achieve high performance in the grand challenge of coordination, corresponding to well-defined, rapidly deployed engineering projects. However, when organizational needs shift to the grand challenge of creativity, then these same unifying team structures fail to produce innovation. The rapid information flow and effective team coordination that comes from internet structures is counterproductive for creativity. Thus, while highly unified teams perform exceptionally well in the grand challenge of coordination, they perform poorly in the grand challenge of creativity.

Page 212 **always already there, influencing us**: Martin Heidegger offers a compelling account of the "always already" nature of social and material facts in framing human experience, in *Being and Time* (1931):

> This characteristic of Dasein's Being—this 'that it is'-is veiled in its "whence" and "whither," yet disclosed in itself all the more unveiledly; we call it the "thrownness" of this entity into its "there"; indeed, it is thrown in such a way that, as Being-in-the-world, it is the "there." The expression "thrownness" is meant to suggest the facticity of its being delivered over. The 'that it is and has to be' which is disclosed in Dasein's state-of-mind is not the same 'that-it-is' which expresses ontologico-categorially the factuality belonging to presence-at-hand. This factuality becomes accessible only if we ascertain it by looking at it. The "that-it-is" which is disclosed in Dasein's state-of-mind must rather be conceived as an existential attribute of the entity which has Being-in-the-world as its way of Being. (174)

From this passage, a loose interpretation of the "always already there" nature of structural determinism is that as soon as we are conscious of ourselves and our environment, our possible ways of Being are already hemmed in by the shared world of norms and conventions and facts (facticity) that defines our place in the world, and thereby our historical (ontologico-categorial) possibilities for self-understanding. This facticity *is* the world into which we are thrown and through which an understanding of ourselves and our freedom must be discovered. Because this "thrownness" can never be escaped, the goal of freedom is not to step outside of the "hermeneutic circle," but to get into it "in the right way" (*Being and Time*, 195), which for our purposes means approaching our understanding of the world through the right intersubjective structures—i.e., networks.

Page 214 **pressures of organizational isomorphisms**: Another unintended consequence that can emerge from collective adaptation comes from the external pressures for conformity experienced by successful firms, such as those faced by innovative organizations forced to match the appearance of more familiar organizational models in an industrial ecology. For years, sociologists have observed that competitive organizations often become increasingly similar to one another in their organizational structure—what sociologists Paul DiMaggio and Woody Powell ("Iron Cage Revisited") call "isomorphisms." The process of organizational isomorphism is a primary reason why collectivist organizations and egalitarian structures are hard to sustain in competitive market ecologies. It isn't because egalitarian firms are less efficient or inferior in their capacity to compete within the ecology of the market. Rather, the driving factor is dependence relations: the extended set of outside people and organizations that firms rely upon for support as they pursue their goals and aspirations. Established individuals and organizations have to believe in the legitimacy and capacity of a newcomer firm, or else they won't partner when necessary. Unfortunately, the most compelling evidence for an organization's legitimacy is its structural resemblance to other successful firms in the market.

And therein lies the rub.

Once collectivist organizations begin to accommodate their partners' demands, they often fail, as did many of the free schools, free clinics, and alternative media founded on the principles of egalitarianism in the late 1960s and 1970s. Once they bent (sometimes because of pressure to conform and sometimes because of an inability to sustain internal coherence), they broke, abandoning the structural intelligence of egalitarianism altogether. Traditional forms of authority and social control became necessary to manage cooperation within these now increasingly hierarchical organizational structures.

It appears as though there are only two possible trajectories—fail or conform. But the story of organizational isomorphism is not Manichean. Indeed, sometimes organizational isomorphism can take everyone *toward* structures that support cooperation, forcing older, more hierarchical organizational forms to catch up with the new patterns of cooperative business—or else go extinct. One such movement arose in Silicon Valley in the 1980s. In the San Francisco Bay Area, newly emerging

American tech firms began to emulate the innovative cooperative industrial model of their Japanese cohorts. In the Japanese model, sharing of ideas and technologies across organizational boundaries was part of a collective strategic initiative designed to improve the overall success of the national industry.

Start-ups in Silicon Valley adopted a similar model of cooperative technology sharing and mutual investment in the creation of new consumer markets. One firm's software innovations would complement another firm's hardware improvements, which could in turn catalyze another firm's investments in telecommunication networks. Competitors' software teams were invited to visit other firms' research facilities, enabling them to coordinate efforts to grow consumer demand. This kind of creative cooperation was an anathema to the old model of organizational competition championed by blue-chip firms like IBM who would be left behind and ultimately remain only as a shell of their once colossal selves. See a discussion of these organizational isomorphisms that took place in Silicon Valley in Centola, *Change*.

Foundational work in this area of research is DiMaggio and Powell, "Iron Cage Revisited," which builds on Max Weber's analysis of bureaucracy and progress in American industry in *The Protestant Ethic and the Spirit of Capitalism* (Scribner, 1930).

Page 215 **already hard at work in our lives today**: This reinforcing web of associations is obviously not the same in every culture or nation. There are many settings in which cooperation is less normative, and expectations for fairness are less robust. Related work on loose versus tight cultures help to illuminate some of the circumstances under which background expectations of fairness are held in place by reinforcing networks of social cooperation (Michele J. Gelfand, Jana L. Raver, Lisa Nishii, Lisa M. Leslie, Janetta Lun, Beng Chong Lim, et al., "Differences Between Tight and Loose Cultures: A 33-Nation Study," *Science* 332 (2011): 1100–1104).

Page 216 **spaces in which we live and work**: For scholars interested in pursuing new research on the topics discussed in this book, there are several exciting and unexplored frontiers for novel work on structural intelligence:

Artificial Intelligence. Perhaps the most obvious question for the field of structural intelligence is how the rapidly evolving domain of Artificial Intelligence (i.e., Large Language Models) will inform (and improve) our understand of human decision making. Exciting work at this frontier has begun to explore how embedding AI actors into human social networks can influence the dynamics of collective judgment. So far this nascent field has begun with one-on-one dialogues between humans and AI agents. (See Ethan Goh, Bryan Bunning, Elaine C. Khoong, Robert J. Gallo, Arnold Milstein, Damon Centola, and Jonathan H. Chen, "Physician Clinical Decision Modification and Bias Assessment in a Randomized Controlled Trial of AI Assistance," *Nature Communications Medicine* 5 (2025): 59; and Michael Henry Tessler, Michiel A. Bakker, Daniel Jarrett, Hannah Sheahan, Martin J. Chadwick, Raphael Koster, et al., "AI Can Help Humans Find Common Ground in Democratic Deliberation," *Science* 386 (2024): eadq2852.) The natural next step will be to explore the dynamics of multiple AI agents interacting with human collectives, and to determine whether these "hybrid" populations may offer new opportunities (or pitfalls) across each of the grand challenges of collective intelligence. The immediate obstacle is that AI bots can quickly converge on the same view of the world—turning "many" bots into a "single" interlocutor (see Ariel Flint Ashery, Luca Maria Aiello, and Andrea Baronchelli, "Emergent Social Conventions and Collective Bias in LLM Populations," *Science Advances* 11, no. 20 (2025)). A first priority for "structural intelligence and AI" is to consider how to maintain diversity among AI agents interacting with human populations; the second priority is, of course, to ensure the intelligence of whatever is produced by this diversity.

Anonymity. Within the grand challenge of choosing, there is as yet no clear scope condition that defines when or why revealing participants' group identities in cross-group interactions will improve or impede collective learning. The results thus far suggest that there is some kind of qualitative difference in the dynamics of politics versus health. But other than the "commonsense" difference between these domains (e.g., political loyalty in a polarized age), there is no theoretically understood scientific distinction between the cases of health versus politics. There is more much more work to do to identify the boundary conditions that govern the "switch in sign" in social learning dynamics that occurs when group identifiers are revealed (as discussed in greater detail in the endnotes for chapter 5).

Simultaneity. Another interesting set of questions emerges at the boundaries between grand challenges during the process of collective adaptation. In chapter 12, I discussed the unintended consequences that can arise from well-intentioned (and sometime highly effective) structural interventions. However, another kind of unintended consequence may emerge, which happens when communities are confronted by multiple grand challenges at the same time. In these situations, an enormous variety of factors—such as personal and group histories, differing technological capacities, individual and group emotions, and the changing dynamics of exclusion—may all come into play for determining how individuals and groups manage simultaneous grand challenges with conflicting implications for structural intelligence (see Galesic et al., "Beyond Collective Intelligence").

Strategy. A related topic of inquiry that emerges at the boundary between grand challenges is how to resolve the tension that arises when actors have different perceptions about which grand challenge they are facing. Suppose one person views an imminent challenge as the grand challenge of coordination while another views it as the grand challenge of creativity—how do they resolve this conflict and its differing implications for the most effective structural adaptations? For instance, recall from chapter 2, Irving Janis's ("Groupthink") critique of the level of camaraderie and mutual respect among the members of the Kennedy administration.

Consider this hypothetical scenario: Perhaps Janis perceived the grand challenge for Kennedy's "groupthinkers" to be the grand challenge of creativity—namely, to discover a new and effective solution to the Communist threat in Cuba. This explains why Janis criticized the Kennedy administration's highly interconnected internet network with its high level of camaraderie and mutual agreement. However, (again hypothetically) suppose that for President Kennedy, his initial efforts to form a coherent military plan were continually being stifled by enmity and discord within the ranks of his administration. Perhaps the challenge that he perceived to be most urgent was the grand challenge of coordination, and thus his strategic interest was to design a structure that would strengthen solidarity and successfully build a robust foundation for mutual respect among his cohort of advisers. In this hypothetical scenario, the camaraderie and confidence that emerged within the Kennedy administration would be an important and necessary form of structural intelligence to eliminate petty infighting and to prevent members of the cabinet from undermining one another. By these lights, the design of Kennedy's administration was a success for solving the grand challenge of coordination. Though, in the end, it was not a structure well-suited to creative problem-solving.

The kind of disagreement that I'm proposing—in this hypothetical conflict between Janis's view and Kennedy's view—may also arise in the form of a strategic conflict. While individuals may sometimes have legitimately different ways of perceiving a grand challenge, at other times these differences in perception may be based on differing strategic agendas. For instance, an organizational actor may frame his team's goals in terms of the grand challenge of coordination. The resulting team design (using an internet structure) ensures that the proposed solutions that emerge from the team will not be too "outside the box." An organizational actor who prioritizes the grand challenge of coordination may thus implement forms of structural intelligence that place constraints (from the viewpoint of creativity) on the collective intelligence of a team. These constraints may serve the interests of organizational actors who want their teams to produce results that fall narrowly within existing models and standard ways of thinking. By contrast, another organizational actor may object to placing these constraints on their team's thinking, and thus may perceive the challenge facing their team in terms of the grand challenge of creativity, rather than the grand challenge of coordination. This organizational actor may thus argue for an alternative form of structural intelligence for team design (a decentralized geographic structure) that prioritizes creativity and innovation, rather than conformity. When such a conflict arises, how are actors to decide which grand challenge is actually the proper grand challenge to address? And thus how do they decide which structural adaptation is most intelligent for organizational success?

Leadership. In the grand challenge of choosing, another open topic for research concerns the identification of which individuals will be the "unmoved movers" for a given task. After a collective task is complete, we know who those individuals are because we can observe their positive influence on the intelligence of the collective via their self-weight. As discussed in the endnotes for chapter 3, there is considerable interest in determining who those accurate individuals are prior to the initiation of a choice task. (See Kao et al., "Counteracting Estimation Bias.")

Categorization. Another fascinating form of collective intelligence that is not discussed in this book concerns the social dynamics of categorization, in which human groups organize vast amounts of data—from markets, to scientific findings, to social and demographic descriptors—into structured "chunks of meaning." Although the world is presented us to as an undifferentiated stream of continuous stimuli, we nevertheless experience it through the "categories of apperception" (Immanuel Kant, *Critique of Pure Reason*, 1781). Kant emphasized the structuring of the noumenal world to create phenomenal experiences such as "causality." However, we can start a bit more simply by considering the basic idea of categorizing continuous visual stimuli into discrete visual phenomena. Take color. The various colors of light are composed of wavelengths that exist on a smooth continuum. There are no natural partitions between one wavelength and another. Nevertheless, human communities seem to agree on the seemingly arbitrary classification of these continuous stimuli into discrete groupings, such as "red," "green," "blue," etc. (A. Baronchelli, T. Gong, A. Puglisi, and V. Loreto, "Modeling the Emergence of Universality in Color Naming Patterns," *Proceedings of the National Academy of Sciences of the USA* 107, no. 6 (2006): 2403–2407.)

If we take a step back, we can appreciate that this process is happening almost everywhere we look. Scientists divide "messy" research topics into well-defined categories (like the grand challenges). Organizations and market analysts partition a vast universe of products into discrete market categories, which enable products (and companies) to be compared, and valued, based on their "peer" competition (see the cleverly titled and very insightful article by my former MIT colleague, Ezra Zuckerman, "The Categorical Imperative: Securities Analysts and the Illegitimacy Discount," *American Journal of Sociology* 104, no. 5 (1999): 1398–1438). This imperative to identify things as "recognizable" members of established (i.e., familiar) categories governs not just products. It governs us, too. When scientists go on the job market, it does not matter how clever or innovative their work is unless they can identify themselves as a "member" of an organizational field—that is, a member of a "legitimate" discipline (with hiring lines) within the ecology of academic institutions; otherwise, they will need to look elsewhere to find a job. And, it's not just job markets that depend on these categories, but our home lives, too. Marketing firms and advertisers segment complex and highly varied human populations into tightly binned consumer categories (i.e., "target demographics"), which enable commercial firms and political campaigns to efficiently design and deploy advertising material in an attempt to systematically influence collective outcomes.

It's not just being done to us, we are doing it, too. Every member of society regularly engages in the categorization of the unbounded space of complex and evolving social behaviors, binning them into discrete social and moral categories, such as "praiseworthy," "acceptable," "transgressive," and "shameful." We evaluate everyone we meet in terms of these social and moral categories. How do these systems of categorization emerge—and what makes them stable?

The famous Building 20 alumnus Noam Chomsky offered an answer that came from the "poverty of stimulus" faced by all newborns when they try to learn language (see Noam Chomsky, *Language and the Problems of Knowledge*, MIT Press, 1988). Chomsky noted that when researchers assess the quantity of meaningful linguistic information to which an infant is exposed (amid the unbounded volume and variety of auditory input that is present in any environment), it is impossible to explain how complex language learning ever happens. Children appear to "intuit" linguistic rules without ever having been given sufficient data from which to make those intuitive leaps. Chomsky concluded that language is not actually "learned." Instead, he reasoned that language acquisition would be impossible unless there was a cognitive structure already at work in the brain, effectively categorizing all the sounds into meaningful groupings that could be used for the function of language. From Chomsky's point of view, infants don't learn language at all. Rather, the language function simply matures. The same way that children mature into puberty, they also mature into language speakers. In both cases, the machinery is already inside. At some point, language just sort of happens to us.

Is that also true of our other cognitive processes for classification and sense-making? Not just for language, but for our ability to organize economic markets, and even our ability to form moral judgments? Are all of these things already in the heads of every infant? Or are they completely arbitrary? Are they universal properties of human brains, or do they self-organize communally in a different way in each society, inevitably shaped by the social structure of those communities? If the logic of categorization does evolve culturally, how might social structure affect the collective dynamics by which human groups create new categories in business, art, science, culture, and religion? How does the structure of our society shape our potential for perceiving and engaging new objects in the world in terms of basic categories such as size, color and shape? It remains an open question to determine the features of society that may govern the failure or success of these important, and underexplored, forms of collective intelligence—which may ultimately lead us to the "grand challenge of categorization" (see D. Guilbeault, A. Baronchelli, and D. Centola, "Experimental Evidence for Scale-Induced Category Convergence Across Populations," *Nature Communications* 12, no. 327 (2021); and D. Guilbeault and D. Centola, Structural Synchronization in Classification of Controversial Content," *Journal of Social Computing* 6, no. 4 (2025): 287–299).

Page 217 **social networks that reduce parental stress**: This vital demonstration of how community network structure directly affects patterns of parental behavior (and thus child well-being) comes from Dan Wang and Ami Mariko Hood Frost, "Neighborhood Collective Efficacy Reduces Child Maltreatment through Decreasing Parenting Stress: A Longitudinal Path Model," *Child Abuse and Neglect* 161 (2025): 107247.

CHAPTER 13: WHERE WE STAND

Page 219 **staff pretending to be experimental subjects**: Asch ("Effects of Group Pressure") experimented with many variations of this design, in which the position of the experimental subject changed (typically in the seventh chair out of eight). He also varied the number of participants in the room (from one to sixteen) and the fraction of participants who were instructed to give the wrong answer, even including the presence of comrades for the experimental subject who also gave the correct answer (B), defying the incorrect majority. For a detailed account of his fascinating results, see also Solomon Asch, "Opinions and Social Pressure," *Scientific American* 193 (1955): 31–35. All quotes are from Asch, "Effects of Group Pressure."

In Asch's experiments, returns for conformity appear to be monotonically increasing, such that more people choosing the same answer increases the perceived value of the popular choice. However, Asch's analyses suggest that these effects are not strictly monotonic, such that once a critical threshold of individuals confidently giving the wrong answer is reached (approximately three in Asch's studies), the main conformity effects were achieved and did not increase as the number of individuals providing the wrong answer increased. These findings are reminiscent of the threshold effects for complex contagions discussed in Centola, *How Behavior Spreads*, and *Change*.

Page 220 **and so on, down the line**: See a detailed discussion of Banerjee's ("Simple Model of Herd Behavior") model of rational herding, as compared to the self-correcting dynamics of Musiclab, discussed in the endnotes for chapter 8; see also the related work by Goeree et al. ("Self-Correcting Information Cascades"); and Frey and van de Rijt ("Social Influence Undermines the Wisdom of the Crowd"). For a discussion of the fragility of information cascades see: Sushil Bikhchandani et al., "A Theory of Fads, Fashion, Custom, and Cultural Change as Informational Cascades," *Journal of Political Economy* 100, no. 5 (1992): 992–1026.

Page 220 **de facto form of centralization**: Although Banerjee's model of rational herding was highly influential within the field of economics, it was not the primary work for which he was awarded the Nobel Prize. In 2019, Banerjee and his wife Esther Duflo (both at MIT), along with their Harvard colleague Michael Kremer, received the Nobel Prize in Economics "for their experimental approach to alleviating global poverty."

Page 220 **collections of solitary individuals**: An illuminating account of how "structural determinism" (and emergent centralization) unintentionally arises in face-to-face settings such as town meetings comes from a recent New England citizen assembly:

A couple of years ago in northern New Hampshire, a citizen assembly gathered to do democracy the "old-fashioned" way. Citizens were recruited from across the state for a three-day event to discuss key issues. Dedicated volunteers and NGO experts carefully designed the convening to elicit diverse opinions from the delegates.

The New Hampshire voters were gathered in a large conference room near the center of town. The walls of the assembly hall were replete with state flags, American flags and posters of great New England political leaders. The parking lot was a sea of New Hampshire license plates, all reading "Live Free or Die." This was not a crowd that would be easily pushed around.

The convening closed with a town-meeting-style vote, in which each delegate had the opportunity to stand and register their final vote (yea or nay) on the proposed initiatives. The organizers were thrilled to find that the citizen representatives (composed of roughly equivalent numbers of Democrats, Republicans, and Independents) reached over 80 percent consensus in their recommendations. It sounds like a great victory for democracy.

The organizers of the New Hampshire citizens' assembly were serious people with a serious goal. They wanted to restore citizen-led democracy and sound, representative decision-making to the state responsible for the nation's first primary election in every presidential cycle. The organizers' diligent preparations ensured that citizens were not mocked nor pressured by their peers, nor were they shouted down for voicing unpopular views. The assembly was a safe, open space for free expression and rational argument. But even such a temple of democratic assembly, with its earnest and rational populace, has an invisible structure that can be decisive for the outcome. And unfortunately, in this case it was a highly centralized one.

In the foregoing chapters, my goal has been to show you that structure is a real, manipulable, and consequential feature of social life. It is not abstract. Sometimes structure is clearly visible, as in the arrangement of the hallways where we work. Other times it is more invisible, as in the geometry of network connections that shape our online groups. Either way, it is always there and it is influencing our collective intelligence, sometimes despite our best intentions.

The sequential pattern of public votes in the New Hampshire town assembly—as informed by Asch and Banerjee and many scholars since—is predicted to lead to a high level of consensus. Which is exactly what they found in New Hampshire. But it is also a structure that is highly prone to error—and can easily lead populations toward choices that are profoundly mistaken.

Page 220 **by this ordinary mom**: See the excellent profile piece by Adam Gopnik, "Jane Jacobs's Street Smarts," *New Yorker*, September 19, 2016.

Page 221 **". . . compose an orderly whole"**: This passage is from Jane Jacobs's classic work, *The Death and Life of Great American Cities*.

Page 223 **against a unanimous crowd**: One implication of my findings is that Asch's "independent thinkers" may not be most productively conceived of as referring to specific types of people (even if that is what Asch intended). Perhaps independent thinkers are best understood as individuals who take up the mantle of intelligence for that specific task. Suppose, for instance, that Asch had run a similar study with very different kinds of cognitive tasks—say, using memory rather than perception; I suspect that different people would have emerged as the independent thinkers. This view is consistent with my overall resistance to the essentialist conception of intelligence as a property that is intrinsic to "types" of persons. Rather, I have endeavored to show that intelligence is an aspect of cognition that emerges in concert with features of problem-solving structures (such as team networks, neighborhood blocks and collaborative hallways) and features of problem-solving tasks (i.e., the grand challenges).

Page 224 **alignment on a shared norm**: The role of individual agency arises somewhat differently for the grand challenge of cooperation, in which clustered geographic networks engender fair dealing. In the bargaining game, individuals seek out the best possible deal without any moral investment in fair behavior. Individuals adopt whichever strategy wins them the greatest rewards. Under these conditions, inequity can easily arise. However, as soon as players are embedded in a clustered geographic network, cooperation quickly takes hold and spreads. Individual and collective behavior shifts toward fair dealing not due to a change in beliefs, or moral attitudes, but because fair dealing is the most advantageous strategy when the individuals in each neighborhood are forced to play with one another.

The story of how individuals respond to structure is different in the modern neighborhood context, in which cohesive networks can catalyze moral sentiments that strengthen individual agency. In these neighborhoods, network clustering creates a social reward and expectation system that supports social responsibility. The answers to the questions "Will individuals intervene to stop vandalism?" or "Will they prevent truancy among the neighborhood children?" depend upon the presence of network structures that encourage the formation of affective social bonds and shared commitments. Once the barriers to action are lowered, the responsibility still rests with each individual to meet the moment. One way of formalizing the phenomenology of individual agency in these settings would be to say that effective structures create social rewards that shift individual motivations away from the fear and greed that are found in a prisoner's dilemma setting toward the increasing returns for participation that are found in a privileged game (see Ostrom, *Governing the Commons*, and Centola, "Homophily, Networks, and Critical Mass," *Rationality and Society*).

Page 225 **an intelligent structure**: It's easy to forget that the structures around us are always evolving, and that even the most effective structures may require attention and improvement from time to time. All the while, life goes on—in firms, in universities, and in nations. So how do we fix and improve what is always in use?

The great sociologist Otto Neurath made a lasting impression in the philosophy of science by suggesting that science, like society, is a ship that must constantly rebuild itself while remaining perpetually at sea.

When it comes to society, short of outright revolution, a civilization cannot be put into dry dock for repairs. We are always at sea, always balancing improvement with stability. The only way we are able to stay afloat and never founder is if improvements are carefully put into place plank by plank, using the rest of the boat for support as we repair and restore each broken or rotten piece. Once all of the pieces have been rebuilt, nothing may remain of the original vessel—and thus a society may evolve.

Science is in the same boat. (See Otto Neurath, "Anti-Spengler," in *Empiricism and Sociology*, Vienna Circle Collection, vol. 1 (1921; D. Reidel, 1973); and Willard Van Orman Quine, *Word and Object* (MIT Press, 2013)). Science never goes into dry dock. The advances in this book have endeavored to rebuild and refashion our understanding of crowd wisdom, of cultural synchronization, of social cooperation, and of team creativity. With these planks firmly in place, our attention may now turn to adjacent boards which cry out not simply for mending but improvement.

Page 225 **citizen-led democratic assemblies**: There is a long and impressive history of organizations working on many sides of this civic process to facilitate deliberative democracy—including citizen juries, participatory budgeting, deliberative polling, and citizen initiative reviews. These programs help to improve everything from polling procedures to citizen-led government-oversight initiatives. Amid this large number of inspiring programs, the role of structural intelligence is to shape the networks within civic assemblies to improve the capacity for collective decision-making and to grow collective efficacy across communities (see Centola, *Change*).

EPILOGUE: USEFUL PRINCIPLES

Page 227 **stimulate both collaboration and creativity**: Related non-network tactics for managing the flow of information are discussed in Brackbill and Centola, "Impact of Network Structure"; and Ethan Bernstein, Jesse Shore, and David Lazer, "How Intermittent Breaks in Interaction Improve Collective Intelligence," *Proceedings of the National Academy of Sciences of the USA* 115, no. 35 (2018): 8734–8739.

Page 227 **benefits of serendipity**: Tom Allen's argument for the persistence of hallway effects even after the digital revolution of the twenty-first century can be found in: Thomas J. Allen and G. Henn, *The Organization and Architecture of Innovation: Managing the Flow of Technology* (Butterworth-Heinemann, 2006).

Page 229 **patience, persistence, and painstaking work**: Analogous effects concerning the benefits of longer "gestation periods" have been observed in the long-term performance prospects of the world's greatest athletes and intellectuals—i.e., comparing optimal performance among early prodigies versus the best long-term performers. The latter (greatest performers) exhibit a longer maturation period than early prodigies, but reach greater heights of achievement. Strong support is found across both intellectual and athletic domains. See: Arne Güllich, Michael Barth, David Z. Hambrick, and Brooke N. Macnamara, "Recent Discoveries on the Acquisition of the Highest Levels of Human Performance," *Science* 390, no. 6779 (2025).

Page 229 **even in industry R&D**: The principle "Move Slowly, Explore Things" is a counterpoint to the Silicon Valley motto "Move Fast, Break Things," which works well for commercial engineering, but assumes that the metric for success is salability rather than the social or scientific significance of what is produced.

Page 230 **". . . by long apprenticeship"**: These passages are from Alexis de Tocqueville, *Democracy in America: Volume I.*

Page 230 **the fox and the hedgehog**: See the classic work by Isaiah Berlin, *The Hedgehog and the Fox: An Essay on Tolstoy's View of History* (Weidenfeld & Nicolson, 1953); and the recent application of these ideas to intelligence in prediction by Phil Tetlock and Dan Gardner, *Superforecasting: The Art and Science of Prediction* (Crown, 2015).

Acknowledgments

It is only fitting that a book dedicated to exploring the intelligence of collectives is itself a product of collective intelligence. In spring 2025, I taught an advanced graduate seminar in the Annenberg School for Communication at the University of Pennsylvania, in which my students engaged in a close reading and discussion of each chapter. These thoughtful students brought me many levels deeper into my own work, unveiling important problems but also revealing significant insights that I had not fully appreciated. I had never before taught the pages of a book while I was writing them. It was a thrilling adventure, resulting in a far better manuscript than I could have imagined. This book owes much of its clarity and insight to the collective intelligence of these brave students who ventured inside this project while it was still under scaffolding: Vrinda Agarwal, Luca Garzino Demo, Sandhya Jha, Collin Kather, Xiaoyang Liu, Steven Mapes, Billy Pierce, Lillian Steinhauser, and Anlan Wang. My thanks to each of you.

I must also extend a (somewhat heavy) heartfelt and deeply grateful acknowledgement to mentors recently passed, Daniel Dennett and George Smith, whose maxim—"at Tufts, we *do* Philosophy," rather than simply appreciating it—has guided my study of society ever since. It is in this spirit that I also want to acknowledge and thank my colleagues, and my dean, at the Annenberg School for Communication for providing a near-perfect environment in which to *do* Sociology. I am grateful for all of you.

The network of intelligence supporting this book also extends beyond 3620 Walnut Street. My deepest gratitude goes to all of my collaborators (including my current graduate students and former graduate students) many of whom took the time to review these materials and offer thoughtful comments and suggestions: Jaya Aysola, Andrea Baronchelli, Joshua Becker, Devon Brackbill, Douglas Guilbeault, Calvin Isch, Elaine Khoong, Urmimala Sarkar, and Jingwen Zhang. I am also incredibly grateful for my decades-long collaboration with my technical lead, Alan Wagner, and to the many designers and engineers with whom I have worked on these projects, who have dedicated countless hours to discussing strategies for practical applications.

Many generous friends and colleagues have taken the time to read and/or discuss various parts of this book, offering essential advice for this project. These heroic citizens of the scientific community include: Anita Allen, Cristina Bicchieri, Joshua Cohen, Paul DiMaggio, Emily Erickson, James Evans, Mike Gaetani, Mark Granovetter, Amy Gutmann, Matt Jackson, Asher Koriat, Simon Levin, Dan Levinthal, George Lowenstein, Diana Mutz, Scott Page, Andrew Papachristos, Desmond Patton, Alvin Roth, Matt Salganik, Rob Sampson, Sally Schroeder, Oliver Sheldon, Brian Skyrms, Mario Small, Paul Starr, Cass Sunstein, Richard Swedberg, Phil Tetlock, Lara Tienders, Arnout van de Rijt, and Peyton Young.

I am also deeply indebted to my editor, Catherine Woods, and the entire MIT Press team, including Caroline Helms and Judy Feldmann, for shepherding this project through to its conclusion. And, to Deborah Douglas of the MIT Museum for providing wonderfully detailed accounts of the scientific biographies and institutional history of Building 20. I also want to thank my illustrator, Valentina Monaco, who deftly rendered many quite complex ideas into elegant visions, and to acknowledge the superb editorial contributions of Geoffrey Shandler. This book would never have come into existence in the first place if not for the guidance of my exceptional agent, Margo Beth Fleming, and the entire Brockman team, who saw potential in this book even when it was only a glimmer of an idea.

Over the last two years, I have presented the material in this book at various research centers and university departments in which participants offered wonderful and insightful comments, questions, and suggestions that propelled this project forward. They include, chronologically: UCLA, Cornell University, Perelman School of Medicine at Penn, USC, MIT, NYU Abu Dhabi, Penn Sociology, Aspen Institute, Northwestern University,

Carnegie Mellon University, University of Virginia, University of Lyon Institute for Cognitive Science, the University of Amsterdam and UCSF.

I also want to acknowledge several generous funders who supported this work: James S. McDonnell Foundation, MIT Faculty Prize for Research in Computers and Communications, National Institutes of Health, National Science Foundation, Perbak Capital Partners, Robert Wood Johnson Foundation, John Templeton Foundation, Hewlett Foundation, Spencer Foundation, SICSS (Princeton University), and the John Simon Guggenheim Memorial Foundation for a 2026 Fellowship.

As Edmund Husserl noted, science always takes place amid the shared practical reality of the Lebenswelt. This book, like all work, emerges from a context that is immediate and lived, and as such I also want to acknowledge the extended network of family and friends whose care and intelligence sustained our family during a time of great loss over the last two years, and in doing so made this work possible. Thank you to all of my dear friends, and to the wonderful community of teachers, parents, and neighbors at SRV. My heartfelt gratitude to all of you.

Index

Page locators in italics indicate figures.